THE ILLUSTRATED ENCYCLOPEDIA OF
WINE

A DEFINITIVE TOUR THROUGH THE WORLD OF WINE,
WITH OVER 450 PHOTOGRAPHS, MAPS AND WINE LABELS

STUART WALTON

HERMES
HOUSE

For my parents

This edition is published by Hermes House
an imprint of Anness Publishing Ltd
Blaby Road, Wigston
Leicestershire LE18 4SE
Email: info@anness.com
Web: www.hermeshouse.com;
www.annesspublishing.com

Anness Publishing has a new picture agency
outlet for images for publishing, promotions
or advertising. Please visit our website
www.practicalpictures.com for more information.

Publisher: Joanna Lorenz
Senior Editor: Felicity Forster
Designers: Sheila Volpe and Ian Sandom
Jacket design: Nigel Partridge
Picture Researcher: Lynda Marshall
Special photography and styling: Steve Baxter
    with Roisin Neild
Illustrator: Madeleine David
Maps: Steven Sweet
Production Controller: Mai-Ling Collyer

Photographs: All photographic material supplied by
Cephas Picture Library, with the following exceptions.
Bridgeman Art Library: 8 (courtesy Pushkin Museum,
Moscow), 9 (courtesy British Library, London). Eddie Parker:
220. German Wine Information Service: 184. Jane Hughes:
41 (right), 96, 102, 177 (bottom), 205 (bottom), 207, 209,
210 (bottom). Morris & Verdin/Robert Wheatcroft: 210 (top).
Patrick Eager: 50–1, 231 (bottom). Sopexa (UK) Ltd: 130.
South American Pictures: 223. SuperStock: 42, 43 (right),
61 (top) 228. Wines of Chile: 217.

ETHICAL TRADING POLICY

At Anness Publishing we believe that business should be
conducted in an ethical and ecologically sustainable way,
with respect for the environment and a proper regard to the
replacement of the natural resources we employ.

As a publisher, we use a lot of wood pulp in high-quality
paper for printing, and that wood commonly comes from
spruce trees. We are therefore currently growing more than
750,000 trees in three Scottish forest plantations: Berrymoss
(130 hectares/320 acres), West Touxhill (125 hectares/
305 acres) and Deveron Forest (75 hectares/185 acres).
The forests we manage contain more than 3.5 times the
number of trees employed each year in making paper for
the books we manufacture.

Because of this ongoing ecological investment programme,
you, as our customer, can have the pleasure and reassurance
of knowing that a tree is being cultivated on your behalf
to naturally replace the materials used to make the book
you are holding.

Our forestry programme is run in accordance with the
UK Woodland Assurance Scheme (UKWAS) and will be
certified by the internationally recognized Forest Stewardship
Council (FSC). The FSC is a non-government organization
dedicated to promoting responsible management of the
world's forests. Certification ensures forests are managed
in an environmentally sustainable and socially responsible
way. For further information about this scheme, go to
www.annesspublishing.com/trees.

© Anness Publishing Ltd 2011

A CIP catalogue record for this book
is available from the British Library.

PUBLISHER'S NOTE

Although the advice and information in this book
are believed to be accurate and true at the time of going to
press, neither the authors nor the publisher can accept any
legal responsibility or liability for any errors or omissions
that may have been made nor for any inaccuracies nor for
any loss, harm or injury that comes about from following
instructions or advice in this book.

CONTENTS

INTRODUCTION

Van Gogh's depiction of grape-harvesting at Arles in the 1880s (above) would still be recognizable today in parts of southern France.

The past century has seen more revolutionary change in the world than any other before it, and the world of wine has been swept right up along with it. At the dawn of the 20th century, wine was just a simple agricultural product, mostly made by the rural populations of a few countries in western Europe, in pretty much the same way they had made it since medieval times. There may have been famous estates, such as the great châteaux of Bordeaux, and there may have been illustrious celebration wines like champagne and vintage port, but what most people drank most of the time was plain old uncomplicated wine – red or white.

By the time the new millennium broke upon us, the global wine industry was a complex edifice of many mansions. Within its walls, different schools of thought contended with each other in sometimes courteous, sometimes embittered battle, as those outside – the loyal consumers of wine – struggled to keep track of it all, while being assailed on all sides by a combination of aggressive marketing and anti-alcohol campaigns. Wine is a hot political issue as never before, as witness the enormous, heartening spread of wine blogging all over the world. We all have opinions about wine, and we're all entitled to express them.

One of the most vigorous debates has been about how wine is made. Nobody can pretend that it isn't nowadays a highly technological process, involving critical decisions at every level, from the budding grapes on the summer vines to the question of what treatments the wine should or shouldn't receive before bottling, that can make or break the reputations of producers. But has it become over-technologized? Is there just too much science involved in what should be a simple product?

The most extraordinary revolution in winemaking of recent times is the biodynamic movement. Not to be confused with straightforward organic production, which does away with chemical herbicide and pesticide sprays, biodynamic vineyard management is a quasi-mystical observance that involves consulting astrological star-charts, and such practices as the burying of a cow's horn full of dung in the middle of the vineyard over the winter to encourage the earth to regenerate for the coming growing season.

Now, I'm not one of those who believes in astrology, and there is an awful lot of undiluted gibberish uttered by biodynamic practitioners, which they can barely begin to justify rationally when pressed. On the other hand, taste the results in the glass, whether from Nicolas Joly in Savennières on the Loire, or from Millton Vineyards in New Zealand's Gisborne region, to name just two, and only a sceptic without tastebuds would deny that these are fabulous wines. Biodynamism will sweep the world in the coming generation, and if the wines continue to benefit as they have so far, we can only give thanks, however sceptically.

What else is new? Screwtops, once reserved only for the cheapest slosh, are now widespread. One can only regret that they didn't quite arrive in time to protect us all from synthetic corks, but now that they are here, they have eliminated the risk of taint from real cork. The incidence of corked wine was always blithely exaggerated by those who were against cork, but it is undeniable that a corked wine puts a major crimp in an evening. That said, there still isn't any better closure for a bottle that you're intending to age for several years, so reports of the death of cork have proved to be premature. They're replanting cork oak in the regions of Portugal where it was traditionally grown, and I for one wish them well in finding customers. It is, after all, a renewable resource.

A growing lament about the international standardization of wine styles addresses the most urgent issue of all. Too much wine tastes the same, overripe, full of fruit perhaps, but disappointingly one-dimensional, and with far, far too much alcohol – the last a result of the warming of the climate in many of the traditional wine regions. It can sometimes seem as though there are basically only three types of wine available now. At opposite ends of the spectrum are the sweet-tasting plonk of the big brands and the hyper-expensive prestige wines from global superstars old and new, with a huge, undifferentiated swathe of perfectly drinkable but soulless identikit stuff for the rest of us in the middle.

That's too pessimistic a picture, perhaps, but to look at what's on offer these days in the high-street retailers of the UK and North America doesn't do a great deal to convince you otherwise. The ranges are narrow, the flavours on offer monotonously similar, and the trade is geared to special offers of branded wines that virtually sell themselves anyway. More than ever, it makes sense to shop at the independent wine merchants. Browse their lists online (with this book to hand, of course), and let the experts tell you something you *don't* know once in a while.

Before too long, there will be more wine-producing countries in the world than can be fitted into a book of this size. I await developments in China with particular interest, having recently tasted some thoroughly exciting Xinjiang Province reds in Beijing. There are great wines being made in all styles, albeit on a small scale, on Malta, and Georgia and Ukraine are teeming with stirring, hearty reds. Exciting times lie ahead for the adventurous.

The first part of this book deals with the practicalities of keeping and serving wine, how to taste it, what to drink it with, and what to serve it in. The second section looks at 12 of the most important grape varieties used in international winemaking. I've tried to give an indication of the different regional styles each grape can take on, how the wines typically taste, and also an overview of the current debates surrounding each one, so you can make up your own mind where you stand.

Finally, we fasten our seatbelts for a global tour of the world's vineyards, exploring what grows where and why, and also shedding some light on the often arcane wine classification systems in use in Europe and beyond.

Summaries of the comparative qualities of recent vintages, where appropriate, should enable you to buy with confidence in the wine shop and the restaurant.

Armed with this knowledge, I hope you will continue to taste and try as broad a range of different wines as possible. That remains the best way that all of us can both celebrate and sustain the copious diversity that wine was always intended to be about. Happy drinking.

Stuart Walton

The vintage has traditionally been one of the ceremonial high points of the year in Europe's wine-growing regions, as this illustration from the medieval Book of Hours, c.1520 (above) vividly demonstrates.

PRINCIPLES *of* TASTING

All that sniffing, swirling and spitting that the professional winetasters engage in is more than just a way of showing off; it really can immeasurably enhance the appreciation of any wine.

WATCHING A PROFESSIONAL winetaster at work, you could be forgiven for wondering whether they really like wine at all. The ritual of peering into the glass, swirling it around and then sniffing suspiciously at it, before taking a mouthful only to spit it out again, doesn't look much like the behaviour of someone who loves the stuff. It is, however, a sequence of perfectly logical steps that, quite apart from helping you evaluate a wine's quality, can also immeasurably enhance the enjoyment of good wine. Here's how.

When pouring a tasting sample, be sure to leave enough room in the glass for giving it a good swirl (below).

Don't pour a full glass for tasting, because you're going to need room for swirling. About a third full is the optimum amount.

Firstly, have a good look at the wine by holding it up to the daylight or other light source. Is it nice and clear? Does it contain sediment or any other solid matter? In the case of red wines, tilt the glass away from you against a white surface, and look at the colour of the liquid at the far edge. Older wines start to fade at the rim, the deep purplish-red taking on lighter crimson tones, and later an autumnal brownish hue with dignified old age.

Now swirl the glass gently. The point of this is to activate the aromatic compounds in the wine, so that when you stick your nose in, you can fully appreciate the bouquet. The aim is to get a fairly vigorous wave circulating in the glass. Some people swirl the glass while it's still resting on a surface, before bringing it to their nose, but make sure the surface isn't likely to damage any good glassware.

When sniffing, tilt the glass towards your face and get your nose slightly inside it, keeping it within the lower half of the opening of the glass. The head should be bent forward a little. Inhale gently (as if you were sniffing a flower, not filling your lungs on a blustery clifftop) and for a good two or three seconds. Nosing a wine can reveal a lot about its origins and the way it was made, but don't overdo it. The sense of smell is quickly neutralized. Two or three sniffs should tell you as much as you need to know.

Now for the tricky part. The reason that wine experts pull those ridiculous faces when they take a mouthful is that they are trying to spread the wine all around the different taste-sensitive parts of the tongue. At its very tip, the receptors for sweetness are most densely concentrated. Just a little back from those, saltiness is registered. Acidity or sourness is tasted on the edges of the tongue, while bitterness is sensed at the very back. So roll the wine around your mouth as thoroughly as you can.

It helps to maximize the flavour of a wine if you take in air while it's in your mouth. Using gentle suction with the lips pursed, draw in some breath. Allow only the tiniest opening (less than the width of a pencil), and suck in immediately. Close your lips again, and breathe downwards through your nose. In this way, the flavour of the wine is transmitted past the taste receptors in your nasal cavity, as well as via your tongue, intensifying the whole sensation.

In polite company, swallow it. If you are tasting a number of wines at a time of day when you wouldn't normally be drinking, say at a market or fair, spit it out into whatever receptacle is provided (the ground will do). Spit confidently, with the tongue behind the ejected liquid, and spit downwards.

There are five principal elements to look for in the taste of a wine. Learn to concentrate on each one individually, and you will start to assemble a set of analytical tools that will stand you in good stead for evaluating any wine.

Dryness/Sweetness From a bone-dry Sancerre at one end of the spectrum to the most unctuous Liqueur Muscats at the other, the amount of natural sugar a wine contains is its most easily noted attribute.

Acidity There are many different types of acid in wine, the most important of which is tartaric, which is present in unfermented grape juice. How sharp does it feel on the edges of the tongue? Good acidity is necessary to contribute a feeling of freshness to a young wine, and to help the best wines to age. Don't confuse dryness with acidity. A very dry wine like fino sherry can actually be quite low in acid, while the sweetest Sauternes will contain sufficient acidity to offset its sugar.

Tannin Tannin is present in the stalks, seeds and skins of grapes. Since the colour in red wine comes from the skins (the juice being colourless), some tannin is extracted along with it. In the mouth, it's what gives young red wines that furry, sandy or abrasive feel, but it disappears with age.

Oak Many wines are matured (and sometimes even fermented too) in oak barrels. An aroma or taste of vanilla, nutmeg or cinnamon is an indicator of oak in white wines, and an overall feeling of creamy smoothness in richer reds. A pronounced smokiness like slightly burned toast indicates that the barrels were heavily charred (or 'toasted') on the insides.

Fruit We're all familiar with wine writers' flights of fancy ('I'm getting raspberries, passion-fruit, melon...'), but there are sound biochemical reasons for the resemblance of wines to the flavours of fruits, vegetables, herbs and spices. We'll come across these in the Grape Varieties section, but let your imagination off the leash when tasting. Bright fruit flavours are among the great charms of wine.

Faults Not everything in the garden is lovely, and sometimes wines can display problems. Cork taint, leading to corked wine, bestows a nasty, stale aroma of old dishcloth or bread mould, but is much less widespread now that screwcaps have begun to replace real cork. Older wines can sometimes show oxidation, which deepens the colour of white wines alarmingly, and makes all wines taste flat and dead. Take back any wine that shows either of these faults. Sometimes tartrate crystals can be present in an imperfectly stabilized wine, but these don't affect its drinking quality.

Wait for the mousse to subside in a sparkling wine before tasting it (above).
The different shades of colour in wine can convey a lot of information to the taster (below).

A gentle swirling action of the hand is sufficient to produce quite a vigorous wave in the glass (above).

Sniff lightly and long, with the nose slightly below the rim of the glass (above).

Take a good mouthful of the wine, in order to coat all surfaces of the mouth with it (above).

STORING *and* SERVING

Where is the best place to keep wine for maturation? Should it be allowed to breathe before being served? What does decanting an old wine involve? None of these questions is as technical as it seems.

NONE OF THE TECHNICALITIES involved in the storage and serving of wine needs to be too complicated. The following guidelines are aimed at keeping things simple.
Creating a cellar Starting a wine collection requires a certain amount of ingenuity now that most of us live in flats or houses without cellars. If you have bought a large parcel of wine that you don't want to touch for years, you can pay a nominal fee to a wine merchant to cellar it for you, but the chances are that you may only have a couple of dozen bottles at any one time. Where to keep it?

The two main points to bear in mind are that bottles should be stored horizontally and away from sources of heat. You can pile them on top of each other if they are all the same shape, but it's safer and more convenient to invest in a simple wooden or plastic wine rack. Keeping the bottles on their sides means the wine is in constant contact with the corks, preventing them from drying out and imparting off-flavours to the wine.

Don't put your bottles in the cupboard next to the storage heater or near the cooker because heat is a menace to wine. Equally, don't leave it in the garden shed in sub-zero temperatures.

A simple wine rack is much the best way of storing bottles (right). This one allows enough space to see the labels too, so that they don't have to be pulled out to identify them.

Choose a cool cupboard that's not too high up (remember that heat rises) and where it can rest in peace in the dark.

Serving temperatures The conventional wisdom that white wine should be served chilled and red wine at room temperature is essentially correct, but it isn't the whole story.

Don't over-chill white wine or its flavours will be muted. Light, acidic whites, sparkling wines and very sweet wines (and rosés too for that matter) should be served at no higher than about 10°C (50°F) but the best Chardonnays, dry Semillons and Alsace wines can afford to be a little less cool than that.

Reds, on the other hand, generally benefit from being slightly cooler than the ambient temperature in a well-heated home. Never warm the bottle by a radiator as that will make the wine taste muddy. Some lighter, fruity reds such as young Beaujolais, Dolcetto or the lighter

Loire or New Zealand reds are best served lightly chilled – about an hour in the refrigerator.

Breathing Should red wine be allowed to breathe? In the case of matured reds that are intended to be drunk on release, like Rioja Reservas or the softer, barrel-aged Cabernet Sauvignons of Australia, the answer is that there is probably no point. Young reds with some tannin, or immature hard acidity, do round out with a bit of air contact, though. Either pour the wine into a decanter or jug (pitcher) half an hour or so before serving or, if you haven't anything suitable for the table, pour it into another container and then funnel it back into the bottle. Simply drawing the cork won't in itself make any difference because only the wine in the neck is in contact with the air. And remember the wine will develop in any case in the glass as you keep swirling and slowly sipping it.

Here is an ingeniously designed wine rack that ensures that the undersides of the corks are kept constantly in contact with the wine, thus preventing them from drying out.

Corkscrews With the increasing use of the Stelvin closure (aka the screwcap) for all quality levels of wine – pioneered in the southern hemisphere, but now widely in use in Europe too – you can leave the corkscrew in the drawer. The great advantage is that any leftover wine can be easily resealed, and of course there is no risk of cork taint.

For corks, the spin-handled corkscrew is the easiest to use, because it involves one continuous motion, and very little effort. The type with side-levers is less good, because it often needs two or three attempts with longer corks, and can break a fragile cork in two, especially if it's the type with a solid shaft as opposed to a hollow spiral. The simplest model, the Wine Waiter's Friend, is good for those who like displaying their brute strength, but an obstinate cork can reduce you to a study in red-faced futility.

The Spin-handled Screwpull (above) was the corkscrew that revolutionized the business of bottle opening. Not only does it require very little in the way of brute force, but it virtually never breaks a cork in two. That is because the screw itself (or thread) is so long.

The most basic type of corkscrew (above left) involves simply tugging. The levered model (above right) can sometimes break a long or old cork. A bottle with a screwcap (right) avoids the need for any sort of special implement at all. There are now three kinds of bottle closure (far right): natural cork, synthetic cork and the Stelvin or screwcap.

Avoid if you can any wines sealed with synthetic cork. When they get stuck, they stay stuck. They are the only closure that won't go back in the bottle, and they can break a plastic corkscrew. Briefly seen as the alternative to real cork some years ago, they have now thankfully begun to be widely superseded as a technology by more efficient screwcaps.

Opening fizz Many people are still intimidated about opening sparkling wines. Remember that the longer a bottle of fizz has been able to rest before opening, the less lively it will be. If it has been very badly shaken up, it may need a week or more to settle. Also, the colder it is, the less likely it will be to go off like a firecracker.

Once the foil has been removed and the wire cage untwisted and taken off too, grasp the cork firmly and take hold of the lower half of the bottle. The advice generally given is to turn the bottle rather than the cork, but in practice most people probably do both (twisting in opposite directions, of course). Work very gently and, when you feel or see the cork beginning to rise, control it every millimetre of the way with your thumb over the top. It should be possible then to ease it out without it popping. If the wine does spurt, put a finger in the neck, but don't completely stopper it again.

When pouring, fill each glass to just under half-full, and then go round again to top them up once the initial fizz has subsided. Pour fairly slowly so that the wine doesn't foam over the sides. Pouring into tilted glasses does preserve more of the fizz, though some see it as vulgarly reminiscent of pouring lager.

Decanting Decanting can help to make a tough young wine a bit more supple, but it is only absolutely necessary if the wine being served is heavily sedimented. In that case, stand the bottle upright for the best part of the day you intend to serve it (from the night before is even better) so that the deposits settle to the bottom. After uncorking, pour the wine in a slow but continuous stream into the decanter, looking into the neck of the bottle. When the sediment starts working its way into the neck as you reach the end, stop pouring. The amount of wine you are left with should be negligible enough to throw away, but if there's more than half a glass, then strain the remainder through a clean muslin cloth. Do *not* use coffee filter-papers or tissue as they will alter the flavour of the wine. Decanting is particularly essential for old bottles of vintage port.

When opening sparkling wines, it is important to restrain the release of the cork (left). Control it every millimetre of the way once it begins to push out.

The quicker you pour, the more vigorous will be the foaming of the wine in the glass (left). Pour carefully to avoid any wastage through overflowing.

The Champagne Saver is a good way of preserving the fizz in any unfinished bottles of sparkling wine (left). Some swear, quite unscientifically, by inserting a spoon-handle in the neck.

GLASSES

Wine doesn't have to be served in the most expensive glassware to show it to advantage, but there are a few basic principles to bear in mind when choosing glasses that will help you get the best from your bottle.

Glasses these days come in all shapes and sizes (below). From left to right in the foreground are: a good red or white wine glass; a technically correct champagne flute; the famous 'Paris goblet' much beloved of wine-bars, not a bad shape but too small; an elegant-looking but inefficient sparkling wine glass with flared opening, causing greater dispersal of bubbles; a sherry copita, also useful for other fortified wines.

ALTHOUGH I CAN scarcely remember any champagne that tasted better than the stuff we poured into polystyrene cups huddled in my student quarters after the examination results went up, the truth is that, certainly when you're in the mood to concentrate, it does make a difference what you drink wine from. Not only the appearance but the scent and even the taste of wine can be substantially enhanced by using appropriate glasses.

They don't have to be prohibitively costly, although – as with everything else – the best doesn't come cheap. The celebrated Austrian glassmaker Georg Riedel has taken the science of wine glasses to its ultimate degree, working out what design features will emphasize the specific aromatic and flavour compounds in dozens of different types of wine. Some of

them are very peculiar shapes and they're expensive, but they undeniably do the trick.

There are some broad guidelines we can all follow, however, when choosing glasses. Firstly, always choose a plain glass to set off your best wines. Coloured ones, or even those with just the stems and bases tinted, can distort the appearance of white wines particularly. And, although cut crystal can look very beautiful, it has now fallen from fashion. I tend to avoid it for wines because it doesn't make for the clearest view of the liquid in the glass.

Look for a deep, wide bowl that tapers significantly towards the mouth. With such glasses, the aromas of the wine can be released more generously, both because the deeper bowl allows for more vigorous swirling, and because the narrower opening channels the scents of the

wine to your nostrils more efficiently. Also, the thinner the glass it's made from, the less it will interfere with tasting.

Traditionally, red wine is served in bigger glasses than white. If you are serving both colours at a grand gastronomic evening, it helps to allot different wines their individual glasses, but the assumption is that reds, especially mature wines, need more space in which to breathe. More development of the wine will take place in the glass than in any decanter or jug you may have poured it into. If you are only buying one size, though, think big. A wine glass can never be too large.

Sparkling wines should be served in flutes, tall thin glasses with straight sides, so that the mousse or fizz is preserved. The champagne saucers familiar from old movies (and originally modelled, as legend has it, on the breast of Marie Antoinette) are less efficient because the larger surface area of the wine causes faster dispersal of the bubbles. That said, they have defiantly come back into fashion in some quarters, and I have to own up to a guilty fondness for their elegance myself.

Fortified wines should be served in smaller, narrower versions of the ordinary wine glass, in recognition of their higher alcoholic strength. The *copita*, traditional glass of the sherry region, is a particularly handsome receptacle, and will do quite well for the other fortifieds too. Don't use your tiniest liqueur glasses: apart from looking spectacularly mean, they allow no room for enjoying the wine's aromas.

These three glasses (left) are all perfectly shaped for tasting. The one on the right is the official international tasting-glass.

DRINKING WINE *with* FOOD

Matching the right wine to its appropriate dish may seem like a gastronomic assault course but there are broad principles that can be easily learned. And very few mistakes are complete failures.

AT ONE TIME, the rules on choosing wines to accompany food seemed hearteningly simple. It was just a matter of remembering: white wine with fish and poultry, red wine with red meats and cheese, with sherry to start and port to finish. Recent thinking has hugely complicated that basic picture, although its essential principles remain sound.

What is clear is that this is one of those areas in which there are no fixed rules. Even though a particular dish may be a firm favourite, why drink the same wine with it every time? Whenever I go to tastings of wine with food, there are always at least a couple of matches that are completely surprising successes.

The following are rough guidelines that are intended to send you off in some new directions. On the whole, you can afford to be bold: very few combinations actually clash.

Pre-dinner nibbles with strong flavours such as prawns (shrimp), tomato, hollandaise sauce, watercress, avocado, salmon and coriander (cilantro) (below) are best served with either a chilled fino or manzanilla sherry or a fresh, young dry white wine, such as an unoaked Chardonnay.

APERITIFS

The two classic (and best) appetite-whetters are sparkling wine and dry sherry. Choose a light, non-vintage champagne (blanc de blancs has the requisite delicacy), or one of the lighter California or New Zealand sparklers. If you are serving highly seasoned canapés, olives or nuts before the meal, dry sherry is better. Always serve a freshly opened bottle of good fino or manzanilla. Kir has become quite trendy again: add a dash of cassis (blackcurrant liqueur) to a glass of crisp dry white – classically Bourgogne Aligoté – or to bone-dry fizz for a Kir Royale.

FIRST COURSES

Soups In general, liquidized soups are happier without wine, although thickly textured versions containing cream or truffle oil work with richer styles of fizz, such as blanc de noirs

Chicken and pistachio pâté with crusty bread (above) is best with a white wine that has some aromatic personality, perhaps a Torrontes.

champagne. A small glass of one of the nuttier-tasting fortified wines such as amontillado sherry or Sercial madeira is a good friend to a meaty consommé. Bulky chowders and minestrones may benefit from a medium-textured red – perhaps a Montepulciano d'Abruzzo – to kick off a winter dinner.

Fish pâtés Light dry whites without overt fruit are best: Chablis, Alsace Pinot Blanc, Muscadet *sur lie*, Spanish Viura, South African Chenin Blanc, shading to something a little richer, such as Spain's Rias Baixas, with the oilier fish like smoked mackerel.

Chicken, duck or pork liver pâtés Go for a big, pungently flavoured white – Alsace Gewurztraminer, dry Bordeaux from Pessac-Léognan, Hunter Valley Semillon. The traditional partner for foie gras is Sauternes (which I find much too sickly a combination).

Smoked salmon Needs a hefty white such as Gewurztraminer or Pinot Gris from Alsace, or an oak-fermented Chardonnay from the Côte de Beaune or California. Beware: champagne will wither under the onslaught of salt, smoke and fat, however traditional it seems.

Melon The sweeter-fleshed aromatic varieties require a wine with its own gentle sweetness. Try late-picked Muscat or Riesling from Washington or California, or even young Canadian Ice Wine.

Prawns, shrimp, langoustines, etc Almost any crisp dry white will work – Sauvignon Blanc is a good grape to choose – but avoid heavily oaked wines. Go for high acidity if you are serving mayonnaise or garlic butter.

Deep-fried mushrooms Best with a midweight simple red such as Côtes du Rhône, Valdepeñas or Valpolicella.

Asparagus Richer styles of Sauvignon, such as those from New Zealand, are perfect.

Pasta dishes and risottos These really are best with Italian wines. Choose a concentrated white such as Vernaccia, Arneis, Falanghina or good Soave for cream sauces, or dishes involving seafood. Light- to medium-bodied reds from Italian grapes (Barbera, Montepulciano) work best with tomato-based sauces. A wild mushroom risotto with Parmesan is great with one of the richer styles of Chianti.

FISH AND SHELLFISH

Oysters Classic partners are champagne, Muscadet or Chablis. Most unoaked Sauvignon also makes a suitably bracing match.

Scallops Simply poached or seared, this most delicate of shellfish needs a soft light white – Côte Chalonnaise burgundy, medium-dry German or New Zealand Riesling, Italian Pinot Grigio – becoming correspondingly richer, the creamier the sauce.

Salt-cured salmon (above) needs a white wine with plenty of weight, such as an Alsace Gewurztraminer or a Pinot Gris.

Salmon Goes well with elegant, midweight whites with some acidity, such as *premier cru* Chablis, Chilean Chardonnay, dry Rieslings from Alsace or Germany. Equally, it is capable of taking a lightish red such as Côte de Beaune Pinot Noir.

Tuna Go for a fairly assertive red in preference to white: well-built Pinot Noir (California or New Zealand), mature Loire red (Chinon or Bourgueil), Chilean Merlot.

Sushi and sashimi What else but sake?

MEAT AND POULTRY

Chicken If roasted, go for a soft-edged quality red, such as mature burgundy, Rioja Crianza or California Merlot. Lighter treatments such as poaching may need one of the richer whites, depending on any sauce.

Turkey The Christmas or Thanksgiving turkey deserves a show-stopping red with a little more power than you would serve with roast chicken: St-Emilion claret, Châteauneuf-du-Pape, California Cabernet.

Rabbit As for roast chicken.

Pork Roast pork or grilled chops are happiest with fairly full reds with a touch of spice: southern Rhône blends, Australian Shiraz, Chianti Classico.

Lamb The two best mates are Cabernet Sauvignon (Médoc, Napa, Chile, etc) and Rioja Reserva.

Lobster Thermidor (above) is best with a rich, ideally oak-aged white. Best white burgundy or hot-climate Chardonnay are ideal.

Lobster Cold in a salad, it needs a pungent white with some acidity, such as Pouilly-Fumé, dry Vouvray, Chablis *premier cru*, South African Chenin Blanc, Australian Riesling. Served hot as a main course (e.g. Thermidor), it requires an opulent and heavier wine – Meursault, California or South Australian Chardonnay, Alsace Pinot Gris.

Light-textured white fish Sole, lemon sole, plaice and the like go well with any light, unoaked or very lightly oaked white from almost anywhere.

Firm-fleshed fish Fish like sea bass, brill, turbot, tilapia or cod need full-bodied whites to match their texture. *Cru classé* white Bordeaux, Australian Semillon, and most of the richer Chardonnays of the southern hemisphere will fit the bill.

Rabbit dishes (right) will take either red or white wines, depending on the treatment. A rich white would be good with mustard sauce, while Pinot Noir would work well alongside rabbit with red wine and prunes.

Monkfish Either a weighty white such as Hermitage or top burgundy, or – if cooked in red wine or wrapped in ham – something quite beefy such as Moulin-à-Vent or Rioja Crianza.

Beef Rump or sirloin can cope with the burliest reds from anywhere: Hermitage, the sturdiest Zinfandels, Barolo, Coonawarra Shiraz. A little lighter for fillet: South African Merlot, Bordeaux. Peppered steaks, mustard sauces and horseradish all demand a wine with bite, perhaps Crozes-Hermitage.

Duck A midweight red with youthful acidity to cut the fat is best: Chianti Classico, Zinfandel, New Zealand Pinot.

Game birds Best with fully mature Pinot Noir.

Venison Highly concentrated reds with some bottle-age are good. Cabernet, Shiraz or Zinfandel from hotter climates work well.

Offal Liver and kidneys are good with vigorous young reds such as Chinon, Barbera or *cru* Beaujolais. Sweetbreads are better with a high-powered white such as a mature Alsace.

Indian Fruity whites with a cutting-edge of acidity (Chenin, Riesling) are best with highly spiced dishes, but go red (Cabernet, Merlot) for lamb dishes like rogan josh.

Thai The chilli heat and abundance of lime and ginger make Sauvignon Blanc the surefire choice, whether from Sancerre, South Africa or New Zealand.

Chinese Perfumed whites such as Gewurztraminer, Viognier, Argentinian Torrontés and most Riesling are good cover-all wines for the huge diversity of Chinese food.

DESSERTS

Fresh fruit salads are best served on their own, on account of their natural acidity. Similarly, frozen desserts like ice-creams and sorbets tend to numb the palate's sensitivity to wine. Anything based on eggs and cream, such as mousses, crème brûlée and pannacotta, deserves a noble-rotted wine such as Sauternes, Coteaux du Layon, or equivalent wines from outside Europe. Chocolate, often thought to present problems, doesn't do much damage to botrytized wines, but think maximum richness and high alcohol. Fruit tarts are better with a late-picked rather than fully rotted wine, such as Auslese German or Austrian Riesling, Alsace Vendange Tardive, or late-harvest South African Muscat. Meringues and creamy gâteaux are good with the sweeter styles of sparkling wine, while Asti or Moscato d'Asti make refreshing counter-balances to Christmas pudding. Sweet oloroso sherry, Bual or Malmsey madeira and Australian Liqueur Muscat are all superb with rich, dark fruitcake or anything nutty such as pecan pie.

The classic partner for boeuf bourguinonne (left) is a soft, mature burgundy – the region from which the dish originated.

Mince pies with orange whisky butter (below) could be paired either with sparkling Italian Asti, or with a marmaladey Australian Liqueur Muscat.

LABELLING

Champagne labels are rarely complicated. The house name will always dominate, since it is a form of brand, in this case Billecart-Salmon at Mareuil-sur-Ay. Below is the style, Brut being virtually the driest, and this one is pink. Champagne is the only AC wine that doesn't require the words *appellation contrôlée* to appear. Along the bottom, the reference number of this house denotes that it is an NM (*négociant-manipulant*), a producer that buys in grapes and makes its own wine.

The most prominent detail on a Bordeaux label is the property at which the wine was made. A classed growth always announces itself with the formula "*cru classé* en 1855". Lower down, the sub-region from which the wine hails is stated, in this case St-Julien, which also forms the name of the appellation.

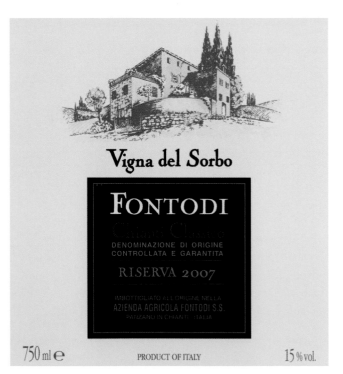

Burgundy labelling can be a minefield. The merchant's name (Drouhin) is followed by the appellation. This label tells you this is a *grand cru* wine, but doesn't have to state which village it belongs to (Morey-St-Denis, in fact). Note that *mis en bouteille* is not followed by *au domaine*, because it has not been bottled on an individual estate, but by a négociant based elsewhere.

Reading down this Italian label, we have the name of the vineyard (Vigna del Sorbo), then the producer (Fontodi) and then the appellation or denominazione (Chianti Classico). Then comes the quality level – Italy's highest, DOCG. Riserva denotes a wine aged for at least three years before release. Below is the information that the wine was bottled at the estate by its producer.

The practised eye begins to discern similarities among the labels of different European countries. On this Spanish label, we see the name of the producer (La Rioja Alta SA), then the appellation or denominación (Rioja), and the standard formula that announces its quality level – DOCa, Spain's highest. Under the vintage comes the wine name. Gran Reserva denotes a wine that has been kept for five years before release, of which at least two must be spent in oak, 904 being a kind of brand name for this producer's top wines. *Embotellado en la propiedad* means 'bottled on the estate'.

German labels can look even more fiendishly complicated than the French. Underneath the proprietor's name here (Dr Pauly-Bergweiler), we have what amounts to the designated appellation. This one comes specifically from the Alte Badstube am Doctorberg vineyard in the village of Bernkastel on the Mosel, which happens to be solely owned by this producer, and is so called because it adjoins the famous Bernkasteler Doctor vineyard. This is roughly comparable within the classification structure – and also in size – to a tiny *grand cru* within one of the village appellations of Burgundy (say, the Romanée-Conti vineyard of Vosne-Romanée). Next to the vintage date, we are told the grape variety is Riesling, and the style of this wine is Spätlese (late-picked). In the absence of any other qualifier, we can therefore take it to be very delicately sweet in style. A dry version would be labelled Spätlese Trocken.

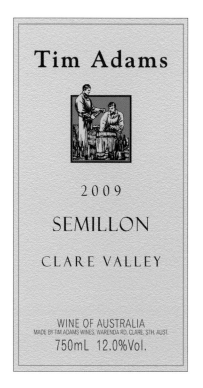

In the sometimes complex world of bottle labelling, what could be simpler than the information on this varietal wine from an acclaimed South Australia producer? The proprietor has given his own name to the estate, which appears prominently at the top (Tim Adams), with the vintage (2009), grape variety (Semillon) and region (Clare Valley) following on below it. In essence, this is pretty much what that German label is also telling you, but notice how much more straightforward the Australian label looks.

This label simply tells us the name of the estate (Thelema), the vintage year (2007), the grape variety (Merlot) and the region of the country in which it was grown and produced (Stellenbosch). Even though there is a regional denomination system in South Africa, the label itself still manages to be crystal-clear.

GRAPE VARIETIES

Soil is furrowed the ancient way to catch winter rain (above), in the sweltering south of Spain.

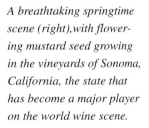

A breathtaking springtime scene (right),with flowering mustard seed growing in the vineyards of Sonoma, California, the state that has become a major player on the world wine scene.

Such is the mystique and reverence attached to the appreciation of wine that it is easy to forget just what a simple product it is.

Visiting a modern winery today, with its acres of carefully trained vines, the giant tanks of shining stainless steel, the automated bottling line, and perhaps the rows of oak barrels resting on top of one another in deep cavernous cellars, you might think this was the end product of centuries of human ingenuity.

To the extent that the techniques for making good wine have been steadily refined through succeeding generations, indeed it is. Unlike beer, though, which had to await the discovery of malting grains before it could be produced, the rudiments of wine have always been there, for it is nothing other than spoiled grape juice.

Any substance that is high in natural sugars – whether it be the sticky sap of palm trees, or honey, or the juice of ripened fruit – will sooner or later start to ferment if it comes into contact with yeast. Wild yeasts, transported on the bodies of insects and falling on to the fruit that they hover around, feed on the fruit sugar and initiate fermentation, creating two principal by-products in the process.

One is carbon dioxide gas, which is why anything that has accidentally started fermenting tastes slightly fizzy, and the other is alcohol. And we know what that does to us.

Long before the earliest human societies had begun to live settled rather than nomadic existences, and begun to cultivate the land, a basic type of alcoholic drink could be derived from the controlled fermentation of fresh fruit or honey. This was the prototype of wine.

One particular species of wild vine, which originated in the area around the Black Sea that today takes in Georgia, Armenia and eastern Turkey, proved especially well suited to quick fermentation, owing to the naturally sweet berries it produced. It is in fact the only vine species native to Europe and the Near East and, because it came to play such a pre-eminent role in the development of winemaking all over the world, it was later given the botanical classification *Vitis vinifera* – 'the wine-bearing grape'.

Within that one species, however, there are as many as 10,000 different sub-types, known as varieties. Some of these developed by natural mutation; many have been created by deliberate cross-fertilization. Only a small percentage of those 10,000 are important in the commercial production of wine today (the French wine authorities recognize around 200), and many of those are fairly obscure and consequently hardly ever used. A mere handful, overwhelmingly French in origin, now constitutes the international language of wine, and it is these that this section deals with.

Not all of the 12 varieties we'll look at are grown throughout the world, and the last of them – Gamay – is mostly concentrated in its own little corner of France (Beaujolais). But these are the 12 varieties – seven white and five red – whose flavours it is most useful to become familiar with. They are responsible between them for producing all the most famous French wine styles, from champagne in the north to the richly heady reds of the sweltering south, and they therefore provided the original models when serious winemaking first began to be pioneered beyond the shores of Europe.

All the European countries have indigenous grapes of their own, some of which have made it on to the international wine scene. There are plantings of some of the best Spanish, Italian and Portuguese grapes in North and South America, and in the enterprising wine cultures of Australia and New Zealand. We begin in this section, though, with the French grapes (plus Germany's Riesling), because those have been the earliest and most widely travelled ones.

All sorts of factors influence the taste of wine. The climate in which the grapes are grown; the type of soil in the vineyards; the way the vines are trained and managed during the growing season; the temperature at which the juice is fermented; what it ferments in (stainless steel or wood); how much contact red

wines have with the grape-skins; the duration and type of any cask-ageing. But nothing affects the style more importantly than the grape or grapes the wine is made from.

There are as many styles of wine as there are winemakers, an equation augmented by the number of different vintages each practitioner will oversee during his or her career. But the identity of the grapes in the fermenting vat is the first and foremost determinant of taste.

If you want to drink a delicately crisp, simple white, it doesn't make sense to go for Gewürztraminer. Similarly, if you're after a featherlight, fruity red for a summer's day, you may get more than you bargained for from Cabernet Sauvignon. The most widely met grape varieties have innate common characteristics.

As we are introduced to each of these 12 VIPs of the wine world, we shall also take a look at the different regions in which they feature, both at home and abroad, and explore the typical styles and flavours to be found in each of them.

The impressive vaulted cellars of Ch. de Meursault, in Burgundy's Côte de Beaune (above), filled with wine ageing in oak barrels.

CHARDONNAY

From its homeland in Burgundy, Chardonnay has travelled the world to become the most fashionable and sought-after of white varieties. This chameleon of grapes bows to the whim of the winemaker, offering a diversity of styles to appeal to all palates.

Chardonnay matures in the warm vineyards of California (right). A vigorous vine, relatively unfussed by climate or soil, this golden grape is neutral in character and has a natural affinity with oak. It is as suited to classic white burgundies as to Australian sparkling wines.

AS SOMEBODY once (nearly) said, if Chardonnay didn't exist, it would be necessary to invent it. No other grape, white or red, has even now achieved quite the degree of international recognition that Chardonnay has. In many consumers' minds, it stands as a synonym for dry white wine in general, and the reason is not hard to find. It is grown is some proportion in virtually every wine-producing country on the planet.

Its adaptablity in the vineyard and its almost limitless mutability in the winery are what made Chardonnay the first big success story among grape varieties. Compared with most other major grapes, it is relatively easy to grow. It can take a wide spectrum of climatic conditions in its stride, from the pinched summers of northern France to the broiling sun-traps of South Australia, and it isn't especially fussy about the kinds of soils it grows in. It ripens well, and it yields plentifully in most vintages. While it's true that great wines are for the most part produced from low-yielding vines, the truth is that the vast bulk of worldwide Chardonnay is destined for straightforward, everyday wines that are intended to be drunk young.

Just as Chardonnay has been everybody's flexible friend in the vineyard, so it proves similarly malleable in the winery. It isn't in itself an especially characterful variety (although there are certain sub-types of it that do have some intriguingly musky perfume), hence its suitability for everyday drinking. On the other hand, it is precisely that innate neutrality that fits it so well – perhaps more obviously than any other white variety – for responding to oak treatments.

Given even a short period of maturation in oak barrels, whether new or used once or twice already, it begins to take on some of those buttery or vanilla scents we classically associate with premium Chardonnay. Ferment it in barrel to begin with, with a further period of ageing in the cask, and those buttery notes are backed up by savoury, toasty aromas. If the insides of the barrels have been given a thorough charring, we may end up with something that is, in effect, smoked wine.

Various economic shortcuts to impart the taste of oak to a wine can be used by producers keen to avoid the outlay of putting their Chardonnays through an expensive finishing-school. A 'chipped' Chardonnay has had a bag of oak chippings (something like a giant teabag) macerated in the wine. One that has been 'staved' has been held in specially designed steel vats that incorporate vertical strips of oak on their inner surfaces. All of which is far cheaper than investing in a consignment of new barrels every year.

With the asset of huge popularity comes the liability of changing fashion. In the years since the 1990s, Chardonnay has undergone something of a rocky period in consumers' affections. The international palate eventually grew fatigued with wines that tasted as though the oak had been laid on with a trowel. Australia's Chardonnays (a little unfairly) were suddenly seen as the prime culprits, leading to the wholesale abandonment there of oak-ageing at the simpler end of the spectrum. Suddenly, labels proudly proclaimed their Chardonnays to be 'unoaked', as though they were being declared free of some adulterating substance.

While that welcome development certainly led to a generation of more finely balanced wines, it also contained within it a paradoxical drawback. As we learned above, Chardonnay is an extremely simple wine when it doesn't have anything beyond basic vinification done to it. And the sudden worldwide preponderance of what were essentially rather prosaic, lightly lemony dry whites of no great personality is what led to Chardonnay fatigue, best expressed by the emergence of a movement among dissenting drinkers in the United States known as ABC – Anything But Chardonnay.

The search was on for a white grape that could replicate some of the reliability of Chardonnay, while providing drinkers with something a little more idiosyncratic, a little more varied from one wine to the next, than Chardonnay is capable of. Viognier (see page 84) was where a lot of the smart money went, although the answer has turned out for the time being to lie more readily to hand in the shape of another already established variety, Sauvignon Blanc (see page 50).

As well as making one of the most famous styles of white table wine, Chardonnay is also indispensable to the production of quality sparkling wines the world over. It forms one of the triumvirate of grapes used in champagne, and nearly all producers of classic sparklers elsewhere have plantings of Chardonnay. Once again, it is the grape's inherent neutrality that bestows elegance and finesse on the best fizz.

FRENCH ORIGINS
Almost all of the white wines of Burgundy, from Chablis down to Beaujolais. Champagne (where it makes up 100 per cent of wines labelled blanc de blancs). May appear as varietally labelled *vin de pays* across the south, especially Languedoc, and also in the Loire.

WHERE ELSE IS IT GROWN?
Wherever the vine will grow.

TASTING NOTES
Light and unoaked (e.g. Chablis) – tart apple, lemon, sometimes pear. Lightly oaked (e.g. Rully, St-Véran) – melting butter, baked apple, nutmeg, oatmeal. Heavily oaked (e.g. Meursault, classic Australian Chardonnay) – vanilla, lemon curd, butterscotch, praline, bacon fat, woodsmoke.

Burgundy

If Chardonnay represents the monarch among white wine grapes, then the Burgundy region in eastern France is its official residence. From the isolated enclave of Chablis in the *département* of the Yonne down to the wide swathes of vineyard known as the Mâconnais to the west of the river Saône, Chardonnay is the overwhelmingly predominant white grape variety.

The entire gamut of styles is produced. There are easy-drinking, everyday whites of honest simplicity, as well as powerfully complex wines intended to be aged in the bottle. There are wines that rely on youthful acidity and freshness alone for their appeal, while others mobilize the fat buttery opulence imparted by oak.

Cooperatives and négociants (merchants who buy in grapes from growers under contract and bottle the resulting blend under their own name) tend to be the sources for much of the commercial white burgundy seen in high-street drinks outlets, while the many individual producers who operate entirely self-sufficiently

The rich, golden colours of a Burgundian autumn (below) spread through the sloping grand cru *vineyards of Vaudésir (nearest) and Grenouilles, in Chablis.*

are responsible for some of the world's most extravagantly rich – and extravagantly expensive – dry white wine.

Chablis in some ways deserves to be considered as a region in itself, because it is not geographically part of Burgundy proper, lying as it does slightly nearer to the most southerly part of the Champagne vineyards than to the northernmost tip of the Côte d'Or. Its climate is cool and fairly wet, its winters often severe, and late frosts in spring are a regular occurrence. Those conditions mean Chardonnay ripens quite late, tending to produce a high-acid wine, often described as steely.

At their best, these are squeaky-clean, bone-dry wines that can be crisp to the point of brittleness in their youth. As they age, they lose some of that sharp edge and become mellower. That said, there is a general tendency to make softer wine these days, which runs the risk that they lack bite when young, and don't mature with quite the same complexity as the traditional style.

The great majority of the wines are made without oak, Chablis being the original reference for the world's unwooded Chardonnays. Some producers, however, do use a certain amount of oak on their best *cuvées*, particularly those with land in one or more of the seven *grand cru* vineyards that sit at the top of the quality tree. Even without oak, Chablis from a good producer in a fine vintage (such as 2007 or 2009) can develop its own inherent richness, often tantalizingly hinting at some phantom oak presence, with a few years in the bottle.

Southeast of Chablis, white wines from the Côte d'Or – and in particular the Côte de Beaune, its southern stretch – represent the pinnacle of Burgundian Chardonnay. It is here, in the exalted appellations of Corton-Charlemagne, Puligny-Montrachet, Meursault and others, that oaked Chardonnay really began.

The top wines, often produced in tiny quantities selling at dizzyingly elevated prices, are sumptuously rich and concentrated, often deep golden in colour from months of ageing in oak barrels, and generally high in alcohol (13–13.5 per cent is the norm). Many possess an intriguingly vegetal flavour, like green beans, leeks or even cabbage, that can be something of a shock to

those used to fruitier-tasting Chardonnays. The Burgundians argue that this is their famous *goût de terroir* – the unique taste of the limestone soils in which the vines are grown.

It is still fair to say that many winemakers aiming to produce premium-quality oaked Chardonnay began by looking to the top wines of the Côte d'Or for their original inspiration, however much they may since have diverged from that earliest model.

The Côte d'Or is connected to the Mâconnais by a strip of land called the Côte Chalonnaise, so called because it lies just to the west of the town of Chalon-sur-Saône. Its Chardonnays, from appellations such as Montagny, Rully and Mercurey, are considerably lighter in style than those from further north, but can possess their own lean elegance. They tend to have correspondingly less oak (if any) than the Côte d'Or wines, but as so often, certain individual producers can provide the exception to the rule.

In the south of Burgundy, the Mâconnais is the largest of the sub-regions. Here is where most of the everyday quaffing wine is made, much of it of rather humdrum quality, often vinified without oak. The best appellation, Pouilly-Fuissé, can have something of the depth

and ageability of lesser Côte de Beaune wines, while St-Véran is often as good as anything from the Chalonnaise.

Certain villages within the overall appellation of Mâcon Blanc-Villages are considered to produce wines of sufficiently distinct quality for their names to be added to the label (hence Mâcon-Lugny, Mâcon-Verzé, and so forth).

In recent years, some quality producers have taken to selling wine under the simplest appellation of all, Bourgogne Chardonnay, the result sufficiently full and rich (and perhaps oaky) as to belie the apparently humble designation – and also to allow them to compete on the shelves with Chardonnays from elsewhere.

The rare white wine of Beaujolais, Burgundy's southernmost sector, is Chardonnay too, a chalky-dry, usually unoaked style a little like a less graceful Chablis.

Burgundy's sparkling wine, Crémant de Bourgogne, made by the same method as champagne, relies principally on Chardonnay. The grapes can theoretically come from anywhere in the region, and the bottle maturation varies between producers, so styles run the range from overly delicate to something approximating the complex, yeasty fullness of champagne itself.

Hand-picked Chardonnay grapes are loaded on to a trailer at Fuissé (above) in the Mâconnais, the largest sub-region of Burgundy.

United States

Wineries in New York State, especially those on Long Island (above), are increasingly producing elegant, complex Chardonnays.

Undoubtedly, the most dynamic Chardonnay developments outside Europe have taken place in the United States. Indeed, by the end of the 1980s, the state of California alone had more extensive plantings of the grape than the whole of France, where its growth has not exactly been stagnant. No group of winemakers beyond the ancestral heartland of Burgundy has taken greater pains with the variety than the Californians, and the transformations that the wines have undergone in the last two decades have been a fascinating barometer of changing Chardonnay trends.

In the 1970s and 80s, the fashion was for a massively overblown style of rich golden wine, with dollops of sweet new oak all over it, not dissimilar to what was then the southern hemisphere mode. When the backlash came, it sent the pendulum hurtling in the other direction, so that it suddenly seemed as if everybody was competing to produce West Coast Chablis, so lean and green and biting were many of the wines.

By the late 1980s, the picture was beginning to even out, and there is now a much greater diversity of styles, each representing a more relaxed expression of its microclimate and the intentions of the individual winemaker.

The very best Stateside Chardonnays – such as those from the cooler areas of California like Carneros and Sonoma Valley, from Oregon and New York State – can sometimes achieve an almost eerie similarity to certain top burgundies, partly because of the comparable levels of acidity, and partly because of the sensitive use of new French oak.

A lot of work has been done in researching types of oak, and the different levels of flame treatment the cooper can give the barrels, to find out what best suits American Chardonnay. Some producers, veterans of field trips to Burgundy, put their faith in the flavours of French oak, but others have looked again at native American woods and have disproved the theory that you can't make a subtle Chardonnay in US oak.

Another French habit that has taken root among many of the premium producers is avoidance of the filtration procedure, in which microscopic solid residues of the fermentation are cleaned out of the wine. While filtering a wine certainly results in a crystal-clear, stable

Madonna Vineyards in the cool Carneros region of northern California (right), a region that produces some of the state's finest Chardonnays, eerily similar in style to certain top burgundies.

product, many feel that it also strips it of some of its flavour complexity and richness of texture. The anti-filtration brigade has often proudly inscribed the word 'Unfiltered' on the labels.

It is no more possible to generalize about a typical California style of Chardonnay than it is to talk about a French style. The state contains a multitude of different microclimates, reflected in the various AVAs (American Viticultural Areas, the equivalent of appellations): Calistoga, at the northern end of Napa Valley, is one of the hotter areas, as are the inland districts of San Joaquin, while Santa Ynez, to the south, is relatively cool.

Most of California's coastal regions are affected each day by Pacific fog drifts, which can take until mid-morning to clear. Those, and cool night-time conditions, help to ensure that the ripening grapes don't become heat-stressed, so that acidity levels at harvest-time are not too low.

Good California Chardonnays have the same sort of weight in the mouth as wines like Puligny-Montrachet, with a carefully defined balance of oak and fruit. Acidity is usually fresh, though with perhaps not quite the same tang as young burgundy. Owing to the specific clonal types of the grape favoured, the fruit flavours are altogether more overt, California wines often having a riper citrus character

(mandarin orange), even a tropical element like fresh pineapple. By and large, despite what some producers intend, they are not particularly susceptible to improvement in the bottle, other than an allowance for the softening of youthful acids. Most will never be better than they are at one or two years old, and may already be beginning to taste a little tired at not much more than three. Drink young and fresh.

In the Pacific Northwest, Oregon Chardonnay tends to be crisper and slightly more austere on the palate than the wines of California, and the characteristic style is leaner, and less ostentatious as to fruit. Washington State has some fine Chardonnays, their erstwhile tendency to flabbiness having been overcome by some attractively balanced wines, though again with somewhat less fruit than California examples. Idaho has a more extreme climate, and tends to produce wines with high acidity, though they can be rounded out with gentle oak treatment.

Back east, New York State has a much cooler climate than the West Coast, and the Chardonnays it produces are in a correspondingly more bracing style, but the best wineries – notably on Long Island – are capitalizing on that to turn out some elegant and complex wines with ageing potential.

Chardonnay is also gaining in importance in Texas, where it makes a broad, immediately approachable style with plenty of ripe fruit.

Chardonnay ageing in new oak barrels (above). A lot of research has been carried out in the US to find out which oak best suits American Chardonnay, leading to a trend among certain producers away from French oak to native American oak.

Australia

Carpets of purple flowers surround Mountadam Estate (below) on the High Eden Ridge, in South Australia. Eden Valley, part of the Barossa Range, shares the soils and climate of the Barossa Valley, source of richly concentrated Chardonnays.

Such was the soaring popularity of Australia's Chardonnays on external markets by the late 20th century that, at one stage, it began to look as if the country might not be able to produce enough to cope with the worldwide demand for them. One consequence is that there is now more Chardonnay planted across the country's vineyards than any other grape variety, white or red.

With the advent in the 1990s of the so-called flying winemakers – travelling wine consultants who flit between the hemispheres working as many vintages as they can fit into their schedules – the success of Australian wine had received the global endorsement that it was due.

Although it often involved a great swallowing of cultural pride on the part of the natives, the Australian itinerant winemakers were instrumental in revolutionizing winemaking practices in the viticultural backwaters of southern Europe. It was their skill with Chardonnay that, more than anything, served to create the demand for their services.

Australia taught the wine world that Chardonnay could be as unashamedly big and ripe and rich as you wanted it to be. Since the climate in most of the vineyard regions, the majority of which lie in the southeast of the country, is uniformly hot and dry, the fruit grown there regularly attains sky-high levels of natural sugar. Winemakers thus generally have to sharpen their wines up by controlled additions of tartaric acid to prevent them from tasting too sweet.

Nonetheless, the benchmark style of Aussie Chardonnay for years was a sunshine-yellow, extraordinarily luscious wine that, married with the vanilla and butterscotch flavours of new oak, was quite a way off being fully dry. High sugar means high alcohol (up to 14.5 per cent in some wines) so that, at the end of a generous glass, you certainly knew you'd had a drink.

As British and American wine consumers discovered an almost insatiable thirst for Australian Chardonnay, it became the habit in some critical quarters (myself included) to start calling into question whether these wines possessed true balance.

In latter years, trends in Chardonnay have begun to diversify in Australia, just as they have in California. There is a desire on the part of many winemakers, notably in the state of Western Australia, in South Australia's Coonawarra region, and in the Yarra Valley in Victoria, to make a subtler, more ageworthy (dare one say, more European?) style of Chardonnay, with better complexity.

At the top end of the quality ladder, there are some world-class wines. The problem, as so often, arises lower down the scale, where the unoaked Chardonnays in particular often seem to fighting to attain an elusive balance. Acidification is not always as finely judged as it might be, and where it isn't, a feeling of conflict with the obviously ripe fruit can be the result. Residual sugar levels are still often uncomfortably high, leading to wines that taste cloying after a glass, and are not best suited for accompanying food.

Much of Australia's wine is made from grapes sourced from different areas, blended to get the best balance of attributes in the final wine, so regional characteristics are proportionally less significant. However, an

increasing number do bottle wines that are the produce of particular vineyard areas (the system of Geographical Indications, or GIs, is loosely and much less restrictively based on the European appellation approach), vinified separately so as to give a true expression of what the French would call their *terroir*.

In the state of South Australia, the Barossa Valley GI is one of the most important regions, producing broad-beamed, richly concentrated Chardonnays that make a dramatic impact on the palate. The McLaren Vale and Padthaway GIs are responsible for wines with perhaps a touch more finesse. Clare Valley is distinctly cooler, and its wines are correspondingly lighter and less upfront in style.

Chardonnays from the Goulburn Valley GI, Victoria, often possess hauntingly tropical fruit characters, while the cooler-climate Yarra Valley wines can resemble those of the less torrid parts of California. In Western Australia, the Margaret River GI is producing some unabashedly Burgundian wines that sometimes have that pungent whiff of green vegetable found on the Côte d'Or. For me, these are some of the most refined and attractive wines Australia has yet produced.

On the island of Tasmania, which constitutes its own GI, Chardonnay can be more austerely European still in its orientation, owing to the cool and fairly wet climate. Levels of grape acidity comparable to Chablis are not unheard of.

Stormy skies at first light (above) over the high ridges of the Barossa Range, South Australia.

New Zealand

(Above) Montana Estate, Marlborough, South Island. New Zealand Chardonnay is light, with juicily ripe fruit.

Chardonnay is New Zealand's second most widely planted white grape, behind Sauvignon Blanc. Grown in what is a considerably cooler and damper climate than Australia, the wines it produces tend, on the whole, to be noticeably lighter and more acidic.

That doesn't mean to say that Chardonnay lacks anything in terms of character because, in common with the even more fashionable Sauvignon, it nearly always possesses a positively unearthly degree of juicily ripe fruit. It is quite the norm to find pineapple and mango, grapefruit and apple, chasing each other around the glass, almost as though the grower had set out to confound the notion that Chardonnay isn't an aromatic variety.

About the richest styles come from the Gisborne and Poverty Bay regions on the eastern tip of the North Island, and these are the ones that respond best to oak-ageing. A little to the south, the wines of Hawkes Bay have more of a tang to them, and require a correspondingly more delicate touch with the wood.

Hopping over to the South Island, the climate becomes distinctly cooler still, and the typical Chardonnay style is snappier and more citric in Marlborough, and then quite taut and austere from Waipara and Central Otago.

South Africa

The lush green vineyards of Stellenbosch wineries Warwick Estate (above), and Thelema Vineyards (right), producers of rounded, golden Chardonnays. Coastal Stellenbosch is home to many of South Africa's finest producers.

When South Africa began to play a full part on the international wine scene in the early 1990s, many consumers were surprised to discover that Chardonnay was not the major force that it is elsewhere in the southern hemisphere. It played second fiddle to the much more widely planted Chenin Blanc. It still accounts for only a small percentage of vineyard land planted with white grapes, and what there is has been losing ground to Sauvignon Blanc.

Although South Africa remained largely isolated from world trade while the wine boom of the 1970s and 1980s was gathering momentum, it did profit in one respect. It was able to observe the trend for the heavily oaked, blockbuster style of Chardonnay (then inextricably associated with so-called New World winemaking) as it fell from favour among forward-looking winemakers, and simply sit it out.

How today's Chardonnays taste depends crucially on how far the vineyards lie from the southern coast. Those from further inland are grown in hotter conditions. So the Breede River Valley – over 96km (60 miles) from the cooling maritime influence of the Indian Ocean – is home to some of the Cape's biggest, burliest Chardonnays, while those from coastal Walker Bay are subtler, with the emphasis on fruit and more sharply defined acidity.

Rest of the World

SOUTH AMERICA

Chile's Chardonnays, as with its Cabernet Sauvignon wines, are made in two broad style categories. Some are made in a recognizably French vein, with pronounced acidity, light appley fruit and restrained oak maturation. Others go the whole hog, with full-blown charred oak flavours and a high-extract, alcoholic feel. It depends on the producer as much as the region. Argentina's wines, made largely in Mendoza in the foothills of the Andes, occupy a midway point between those two styles, with impressive balance and class.

EUROPE

Increasing concentrations of Chardonnay are cropping up across Italy now, from Aosta in the northwest all the way down to Puglia and Sicily, so that the variety is now the fourth most widely planted white grape. Although some rugged individualists are aiming for top-flight, barrel-fermented wines (and charging energetically for them), the basic style – best typified by the wines of the Alto Adige DOC on the Austrian border – are delicate, very lightly creamy wines made without recourse to wood.

Northern Spain is getting in on the act too, with plantings of Chardonnay vines in Penedés, Lérida, Somontano and Navarra, where it is often blended with local varieties such as Macabeo and Viura to make clean-cut, nutty, dry modern whites. It has achieved some significance in the production of the sparkling

wine, cava, although many quality-conscious producers feel they can do without the reflected glory a non-Spanish variety appears to confer on the wines.

Chardonnay is of some modest importance in central Europe, particularly in Hungary, where the flying winemakers have been regular visitors. The wines tend to be made in the straightforward neutral style, clean and sharp for everyday drinking. When they do have some oak on them, it is only to add a gentler, rounder feel to them.

Further east, Bulgaria has been making Chardonnays since its heavily state-subsidised entry into western markets in the 1980s. A little on the clumsy side, they often didn't taste especially fresh, although the odd wine from Khan Krum in the east of the country could display a sort of sour-cream palatability.

There are also limited plantings in Slovenia and Romania but, among the other big western players, only Germany and Portugal managed largely to bypass the Chardonnay craze of the late 20th century.

Chardonnay is taking root in northern Italy, especially in Piedmont (above), in the foothills of the Alps, where it produces delicate, lightly creamy wines.

Harvesting Chardonnay grapes (left) in Blatetz, Bulgaria. The quality of Chardonnay, one of many wines produced for the export market, varies, some of the best coming from Khan Krum.

CABERNET SAUVIGNON

Its pedigree is firmly founded in the gravelly soils of the Médoc, in the heart of Bordeaux. The king of red grapes, Cabernet Sauvignon has conquered vineyards across the world without losing the classic character that brought it such renown.

The small, dusty-blue Cabernet Sauvignon grape (right) produces wines of good tannin, body and aroma. It adapts easily to differing soils and climates, and in its finest form, with warm, late summer sun to ripen it fully, Cabernet creates complex, deeply coloured reds, packed with juicy blackcurrant fruit.

THE RED HALF of that hugely successful partnership that came to dominate international winemaking in the most recent generation is Cabernet Sauvignon. Alongside Chardonnay, it strode imperiously through the world's vineyards in the 1980s, often insisting that native varieties get out of its way wherever serious red wine was to be made. Although the example set before Cabernet growers – the classed-growth clarets of the Médoc in Bordeaux – is an illustrious one, it wasn't immediately easy to see why Cabernet came to be perceived as the pre-eminent red counterpart to the crowd-pleasing Chardonnay.

Its adaptablity to a variety of soils and climates is quite as impressive as that of Chardonnay, but its crop yield is more grudging, meaning that, even in the warmest climates, it has a heavy responsibility to earn its keep. Producers in regions with high climatic variation can often find that their higher-volume wines are basically subsidising the Cabernet.

As against that, Cabernet Sauvignon has suffered far less from the contempt induced by over-familiarity that has been Chardonnay's fate, for all that, among educated American consumers, ABC implicitly represents Anything but Cabernet as much as it stands for Anything but Chardonnay. There are three principal reasons for this.

Firstly, Cabernet comes in a much broader and more nuanced range of styles than Chardonnay. It isn't simply a question of deciding whether you want to make an unoaked, lightly oaked or very oaky wine. There are much finer gradations of style, and the grape is much less led by the nose when treated with oak than Chardonnay is.

Secondly, being a red wine, it is more often than not capable of developing with age. Just as the basic styles can be vastly different, so too the reactions of the wine to bottle maturation are excitingly divergent.

And thirdly, while it certainly conquered the known wine world quite as extensively as Chardonnay did, it somehow never became quite as axiomatically synonymous with red wine as Chardonnay did with white. Nobody ordering in a wine bar was ever heard asking for 'a glass of Cabernet' in the way that the fabled 'glass of Chardonnay' became the *lingua franca* of everyday white wine.

When on song, Cabernet Sauvignon wines deliver a heady rush of pure blackcurrant fruit, bolstered by density of texture and substantial ageing capacity, the sum of which seems to many wine-lovers the essence of all that is noble in a red wine. The greatest productions of the Médoc – Châteaux Lafite, Latour, Margaux, Mouton-Rothschild – are among the most famous names in wine, and if some of the class of those wines could be seen, however distantly, in a Cabernet Sauvignon from Chile, California or Australia, then the winemaker behind it might stand a fair chance of making the big time. (And so they have.)

Cabernet responds supremely well to oak-ageing, when the vanillin in new wood helps to soothe some of the natural acerbity of the young wine. That acerbity is basically tannin, that substance in youthful red wine that furs up the drinker's mouth, and which can obscure the fruit flavours. Cabernet is a thick-skinned variety, so its vinification results in naturally high tannin. Furthermore, its berries are relatively small compared to other red varieties, meaning that the proportion of tannin-bearing pip to flesh is higher.

What this means is that Cabernet producers need to make some finely detailed decisions in the winery about how to treat their wine. If you're selling to an audience that will kill for your next vintage, and expect to cellar the wine for upwards of a decade, you can spread your wings. If, on the other hand, your market positioning is about quick turnover from the winery to the retail industry, a great unwieldy slew of indigestible tannin is going to be box-office poison. And how much youthful fruit is too much for today's palates?

FRENCH ORIGINS
Bordeaux, specifically the left bank of the river Gironde, from the north of the Médoc down to the Graves. (On the right bank, it tends to play second fiddle to Merlot.)

WHERE ELSE IS IT GROWN?
Just about everywhere, although it has not made significant inroads into the cooler climates of northern Europe.

TASTING NOTES
In warm climates, almost any of the purple-skinned fruits – classically blackcurrants (perhaps most startlingly so in the best wines of Chile), but also black plums, brambles, damsons, etc. Often has a distinct note of fresh mint or even eucalyptus, especially in parts of Australia and Chile. Cooler climates can create a whiff of bitterness in it, often uncannily like chopped green pepper. Oak treatments generally emphasize a mineral austerity in the wine, likened in Bordeaux to the smell of cigar-boxes, cedarwood or – most recognizably – pencil shavings. With several years' bottle-age, it can take on aromas such as well-hung game, plum tomatoes, warm leather, dark chocolate, even soft Indian spices like cardamom, while the primary fruit begins to taste more like preserved fruit.

It's partly those considerations that have led to the realization that Cabernet Sauvignon is often much better-behaved in company. The original Bordeaux model is about blending in any case, and even a modest admixture of one or two other grapes can negotiate the toughness and brutality out of young Cabernet. Enter Merlot, Cabernet Franc and others in Bordeaux. Hello Shiraz in Australia.

Whatever the blend, the holy grail is a wine capable of acquiring complexity through long cellaring. Cabernets and Cabernet-based blends evolve in fascinatingly various ways as they age, depending on the quality of the primary fruit, the type of wood used for maturation, duration in the cask, and the length of time the wine spends in the bottle before you open it. Even in quite advanced old age, the telltale mineral purity of Cabernet Sauvignon still shines invitingly through.

Lighter styles of Cabernet are made in regions such as northern Italy and New Zealand, and many of these rub along quite well without oak. Indeed, when the wine is fully ripe and made from low-yielding vines, it can often be quite difficult to tell whether it has any oak on it or not. It can also, in common with others of the more assertive red varieties, make an attractive, full-flavoured rosé.

It is this potential for gathering complexity, though, that explains the high prices consistently paid for top Cabernets around the world. And that in turn is why so many winemakers take such enormous pains with it, when they may well be able to turn a faster buck growing something more mundane.

Bordeaux

A landmark in the Pauillac vineyards of first growth Château Latour (above), one of the five great premier cru châteaux of the Médoc.

The chai at Château Mouton-Rothschild, Pauillac (below). The four famous communes of the Médoc – St-Estèphe, St-Julien, Margaux and Pauillac – are where the reputation of red Bordeaux is founded.

Although Cabernet Sauvignon occupies far less vineyard land in Bordeaux than its traditional blending partner Merlot, it is nonetheless widely considered the pre-eminent grape variety in the region. This is because it plays a major part in the wines on which the reputation of Bordeaux is primarily founded – the *crus classés*, or classed growths, of the Médoc and Graves. When the region's classification system was drawn up in 1855, it was not that the judges ignored the Merlot-based wines of Pomerol and St-Emilion on the right bank; they simply didn't think they were in the same class.

That classification (outlined in detail in the chapter on Bordeaux) is now considered seriously outdated by many commentators, but the general perception that the majority of Bordeaux's most illustrious wines derive the greater part of their authority from the presence of Cabernet Sauvignon has never really changed, Pomerol notwithstanding.

Cabernet equips the young wine with those austere tannins that give it the structure it needs to age well, its pigment-rich skins endowing the wine with full-blooded depth of colour too. When claret-lovers refer to their favourite wine as having a profoundly serious quality that appeals as much to the intellect as it does to the senses, it is essentially Cabernet Sauvignon they have to thank for it.

If Cabernet enjoys such an exalted status, you may ask why more châteaux don't simply produce an unblended Cabernet wine, instead of making it share the bottle with Merlot and other varieties. The answer is partly that the grape works better in a team. Solo Cabernet, as some winemakers in California have found, is not necessarily an unalloyed blessing. In hot years, it can be just too much of a good thing, the resulting wines having colossal density and concentration, but not really seeming as though they are going to be ready to drink this side of the next appearance of Halley's comet.

The other reason for blending in Bordeaux is that, even though its southerly position makes this one of the warmest of France's classic regions, the summers are still highly variable. In problem vintages (such as the region endured through most of the 1970s, in 1980, 1984, during much of the early 1990s, and in 2002), Cabernet Sauvignon is the grape that suffers most. If the late summer is cool – and, what's worse, wet – it simply doesn't ripen properly, resulting in those vegetal, green-pepper tastes that make for harsh, depressing wine.

Since Merlot has much better tolerance for less-than-perfect vintage conditions, it makes sense for the growers to have the option of blending in some of the lighter Merlot to soften an overly astringent or green-tasting Cabernet.

In the great vintages, however, such as 2000, 2005 and 2009, the richness and power of Cabernet are worth celebrating, and the Merlot will only play a discreet supporting role, just smoothing the edges a little, so that the full glory of ripe Cabernet can be shown to maximum advantage.

Most of the wines that occupy the five ranks of the 1855 hierarchy come from four vineyard areas to the west of the river Gironde: St-Estèphe, Pauillac, St-Julien and Margaux. From top to bottom, collectively, they extend over not much more than 40km (25 miles), but there are subtle differences in the styles of Cabernet-based wine they produce.

St-Estèphe generally makes the fiercest wine, with typically tough tannins that take years to fall away, and a very austere aroma that is often compared to fresh tobacco. Pauillac – the commune that boasts three of the five first growths in Lafite, Latour and Mouton-Rothschild – is a little less severe, even when young. Its wines have more emphatic blackcurrant fruit than those of St-Estèphe, and a seemingly more complicated pot-pourri of spice and wood notes as they age.

St-Julien, which adjoins Pauillac, exhibits many of the characteristics of its neighbour, although its wines somehow display a softer fruit – more like dark plums and blackberries than blackcurrants – as they begin to mature. The best wines of Margaux are noted for their extravagant perfume, although in general the

underlying wine is lighter than anything from further north, the exception being first-growth Château Margaux itself.

South of the city of Bordeaux, the large area of the Graves makes wines that vary in character. These range from relative featherweights that constitute some of the region's lightest reds, to those that have a mineral earthiness to them, thought to derive from the gravelly soils that give this part of Bordeaux its name. Elsewhere, the quality becomes gradually more prosaic until, at the lowest level of AC Bordeaux, the bulk of the produce is hard red jug-wine of no obvious appeal.

In Bordeaux, it is the name of the property rather than the producer that goes on the label. Much time and attention is devoted to studying the relative form and fitness of the most famous estates as each new vintage appears on the market. Those planning to buy even a single bottle of top-flight Bordeaux would do well to consider the present reputation of a château as well as the quality of the vintage.

Cabernet Sauvignon vines (above) planted in the poor, gravelly soils of St-Estèphe, in the Médoc, on the right bank of the Gironde river.

United States

Cabernet Sauvignon was introduced to California in the 19th century in the form of cuttings from Bordeaux. The readiness with which it took to the fertile soils in which it was planted is evidenced by the fact that it already had something of a reputation among the American wine cognoscenti before that century was out. The best was held to come from the Napa Valley, north of San Francisco, where the late hot summers resulted in strapping great wines of swarthy hue, thickly textured, and capable of delivering a hefty alcoholic blow to the unsuspecting drinker.

Some might facetiously say that not much has changed. Certainly, in many consumers' minds, the benchmark style of California Cabernet has been fiercely tannic, often virtually black wines that potentially took a decade or two to unravel into a state of anything like drinkability. It would be grossly simplistic to characterize all California Cabernets in that way today, but it was undeniably the predominant style of the wine in the 1970s and 1980s, and there are certainly some wineries that still nail their colours to that particular mast.

The tower in the vineyard at Silver Oak Cellars, Napa Valley (below).

Moreover, it is not as though there aren't perfectly good antecedents for it. Most classed-growth Bordeaux in the hot years like 2003 and 2005 would answer that description – or something very like it – when first released. The wines are not intended to be drunk straight away in any case. Château Latour is after all still black as sin and guarded by snarling tannins at ten years old. It's almost as though a dose of old-world condescension were at work here: it's fine for the Bordelais, but really doesn't suit you.

The problem lay in the fact that not many consumers are attuned to drinking wine that tastes so forbidding, even if they can readily afford the prices commanded by it. Producers realized a middle way had to be found between budding West Coast Latours and insipid commercial jug-wine.

What happened from the 1970s on was a huge upsurge in experimental plantings of Cabernet Sauvignon across the state of California, as growers set out to find the optimum microclimates for the variety. Experiments, by their nature, can produce failures, and where the

Picking Cabernet Sauvignon grapes in vineyards south of Prosser, Washington State (left). Despite the fairly cool climate, some fine Cabernets have been made in the Pacific Northwest.

A vineyard worker harvesting Cabernet Sauvignon grapes in Calistoga, California (above).

grape was grown in cooler areas, the outcome was wines that had more than a touch of the familiar green bell pepper/asparagus vegetal quality that Cabernet is prone to when it lacks sufficient ripening time. Oak maturation was sometimes excessive too, giving wines with an exaggeratedly woody taste.

Without a doubt, however, California – the Napa Valley in particular – has also turned out some wonderfully sleek, opulently fruit-filled Cabernets of world-class status, many of them blended with others of the Bordeaux varieties (these blends sometimes given the label Meritage).

In the Pacific Northwest, the climate is generally a little too cool for producing great Cabernets, although Washington State has come up with some fine examples. The tendency is to compensate for less than generous fruit flavours by applying fairly heavy oak maturation, which runs the risk of creating top-heavy wines. Oregon indeed is a much safer bet for cool-ripening Pinot Noir than sun-seeking Cabernet.

Texas, on the other hand, is proving to be highly Cabernet-friendly, and the grape is now the most widely planted red variety there, having expanded rapidly over the last 20 years. The state style is one of big, rich, upfront fruit, some savoury herb characters and good weight, but with tannins kept in check. In time, this could emerge as the best American Cabernet territory outside the Napa Valley. Virginia too is producing some distinguished Cabernets.

Australia

Australia's approach to Cabernet Sauvignon, its second most planted red grape after Shiraz, has been much less conflicted than than of California. The aim among its growers is all about emphasizing the kind of ripe juicy drinkability that wins friends even among those who don't consider themselves fans of rich red wine. In the ultra-reliable climates enjoyed by most of Australia's wine-growing regions, Cabernet more often than not attains levels of ripeness Bordeaux's producers would give their eye-teeth for.

Oak barrel ageing is used enthusiastically by the great majority of Cabernet growers. When your wine is as rich and dense and blackcurranty as much Australian Cabernet is, you can afford to be generous with the oak treatment. At the same time, however, the classic style aims to maximize fruit characters without extracting too much tannin from the grapeskins. Thus, although it is an intensely concentrated wine, it doesn't necessarily scour your mouth with harsh astringency when it's young.

The chances are that, even if you are unfamiliar with the producer, a Cabernet from practically anywhere in Australia will deliver plump, soft, cassis-scented wine with an enagaging creamy texture and no hard edges. That is not to say that there aren't wineries intent on producing more austere Cabernets in a style built to age, but even these tend to come round far sooner than most California Cabernets, or Cabernet-based clarets, made in the same idiom. Even tasted in their infancy, the tannins on Australian wines such as these are nowhere near as severe as the colour may lead you to expect.

Blending is widely practised for Cabernet here too, with Shiraz having been its best bottle-friend since the 1960s, a recipe that Australia taught the world.

Australia's Cabernet pioneer was one John Riddoch (honoured in the name of one of the country's best classic Cabernets), who first planted the variety in the last decade of the 19th century in a part of South Australia called Coonawarra. Coonawarra's chief distinguishing characteristic is a narrow strip of red soil the colour of paprika, known as *terra rossa*. And it is here that Cabernet Sauvignon still produces its most gorgeously distinctive performances in Australia, and some of the world's best.

Endless rows of Cabernet Sauvignon vines under an endless Australian sky (below), in Clare Valley, South Australia. The hotter, drier climate encourages rich, dense Cabernets.

Coonawarra wines often have a chocolatey richness to them, tinged with hints of mocha coffee beans. Some, noting the relatively cooler climate the region enjoys, have compared it to a southern-hemisphere Bordeaux, but Coonawarra stands in no need of such vicarious honour. Its wines are nothing like claret; they have their own uniquely spicy style.

South Australia is the most important state overall for Cabernet wines. In the heat of the Barossa Valley GI, they tend to be richly coloured and thickly textured, with an intensity like preserved fruits. From McLaren Vale, the wines are often more delicately proportioned, with slightly higher acid levels. In the Eden Valley, Cabernets of almost European profile are being produced, with aromatic spice notes in them, and often a dash of mint.

Coonawarra takes that spice component a little further, and there is sometimes a fugitive hint of something exotically pungent, like Worcester sauce. Riverland is a much less distinguished bulk-producing region, where the wines are made in an easy-drinking, uncomplicated style.

Victoria makes Cabernet in the leaner, mintier manner. The vineyards are mainly located in the centre of the state, especially in the fashionable region of Bendigo. Despite its notably cool climate, Yarra Valley has been responsible for some of Australia's most extraordinarily intense Cabernets, with astonishing depth.

Cabernets from the Margaret River GI in Western Australia tend to the hauntingly scented end of the spectrum, with particularly defined acidity and consequently good ageing potential.

Tasmania's cool, damp climate is better suited to other varieties, but there have been successes with lighter, more sharply angled Cabernets than are found on the mainland.

The famous terra rossa soil of Coonawarra, South Australia (above). Vineyard land here is highly prized for the quality of grapes it yields.

Other Non-European

SOUTH AFRICA

Cabernet Sauvignon became, in the early 1990s, the most widely planted red grape variety in South Africa. Early efforts were often discouraging, partly as a result of Cabernet being grown in sites that were either too cool or too hot for it, and partly because the specific variant of the grape widely grown in Cape vineyards wasn't of the best quality. The results were often wines that lacked convincing fruit definition.

All that has changed in recent years, with new clones of the grape yielding riper, richer fruit flavours, and growers allowing them full ripening time on the vine. Coastal Stellenbosch, Franschhoek, and inland Paarl have turned out to be the most promising regions, with many convincingly classy, ageworthy wines emerging. Wines made according to the Bordeaux recipe, using Cabernet Franc and Merlot to soften some

of Cabernet Sauvignon's severity, have been the best, but blends with Shiraz can be juicily appealing too in their way.

CHILE

During the course of the 1980s, Chile was the southern-hemisphere epicentre for European wine consultants, and no variety was more consulted on than Cabernet Sauvignon. When no less an eminence than Gilbert Rokvam of Château Lafite arrived at the Los Vascos winery in Colchagua, it seemed pretty clear that Chile had made its entrance on the world wine map with due fanfare, at least as far as Cabernet was concerned. Early results were amazing.

What has happened since is that Chilean Cabernet has diverged into two broadly identifiable styles. One is what Europeans tend to think of as the benchmark New World idiom, ripely blackcurranty Cabernet of sumptuous, velvety texture, with low tannins and plenty of oak. There are numerous examples of this style and, while they all benefit from a couple of years' ageing, they can be enjoyed relatively young, at barely more than a year old.

The other style is much more austere, cedary wine of high acidity and more pronounced tannins, vinified in a way that is intended to help it to age in the bottle, and owing much to the taste of classic Médoc claret. Wines from the Maipo, Rapel and Casablanca regions have registered some stunning successes in this style.

At its best, Chilean Cabernet Sauvignon can display scents of the most intensely pure essence of blackcurrant to be found in any Cabernet produced anywhere. They may taste a little one-dimensional at first, but they broaden and deepen with age into something altogether thrilling. The wines made in the French style are the longest-lived, with older vintages taking on the savoury complexity of fine mature Médoc.

ARGENTINA

On the other side of the Andes, the Mendoza province of Argentina is now showing its own potential as a major runner in the Cabernet stakes. Strangely enough, the grape has had to play understudy in the vineyards to Malbec, one of the bit-part players in red Bordeaux (blending the two is widely practised), but plantings are steadily on the increase.

The towering Drakensteinberg mountains form a stunning backdrop to the higher and cooler district of Franschhoek in coastal Stellenbosch, South Africa (below), source of classy Cabernets capable of ageing.

Initially, varietal Cabernets were rather sternly tannic, and dominated by wood flavours rather than fruit, on account of their having been aged too long in old oak casks. Outside investment was slower to arrive in Argentina than it was in Chile, and so the wines, Cabernet in particular, took a little longer to settle into their best style.

Cabernet is now being made in a generally French-oriented manner, from plantings in high-altitude vineyards to mitigate some of the formidable heat of the growing season. Expect rich plum and cassis fruit, backed by savoury herb flavours and a judicious amount of tannin.

High-altitude sites in Argentina's second biggest region, San Juan, look equally promising for Cabernet.

NEW ZEALAND

Most of New Zealand's vineyard land has proved to be too cool and damp for Cabernet, which is notoriously bad-tempered if it doesn't get enough sun. Some varietal Cabernet has that telltale green pepper flavour, with high acidity, though low tannin. Painstaking site selection has, however, produced some encouraging successes on the North Island, particularly in the Hawkes Bay area, and from Waiheke Island near Auckland.

As elsewhere, blending is the key, and the Cabernet-Merlot partnership has emerged as a surefire winner for many growers. There are now some very attractive wines of real complexity and depth, in a midweight style not a million miles from the softer wines of Bordeaux, though quicker to mature.

Harvesting Cabernet Sauvignon at Los Vascos (above) in the hot Colchagua Valley, Rapel, Chile. Los Vascos produces Cabernets moulded in the classic Médoc style.

Old Cabernet Sauvignon vines owned by the grand 19th-century bodega, Cousiño Macul (left), in Maipo, Chile. The vines date back to the 1930s.

Other European

Pickers on the Marqués de Griñón's estate near Toledo, in the hot centre of Spain (above). The estate has drawn attention for its structured, long-ageing Cabernets.

The Torres Mas la Plana vineyard in Penedés, planted solely with Cabernet vines (below). Torres and Jean León set a precedent for Cabernet in Spain in the '60s.

FRANCE

Just outside Bordeaux, in appellations such as Bergerac and Buzet, the permitted grape varieties are the same as in Bordeaux itself, and from certain producers, the wines can rival everyday claret. Cabernet Sauvignon has made major inroads into the Languedoc-Roussillon, in France's warm southern zone, where it most often appears as varietal Vin de Pays d'Oc. A small amount is also grown in the Loire as blending material with Gamay, or as a minor component in sparkling rosés.

SPAIN AND PORTUGAL

Cabernet Sauvignon established a bridgehead on the Iberian peninsula when it was planted in Penedés by the Torres family and Jean León in the 1960s. Varietal Cabernets from that region, from Castile and the Montes de Toledo are often made in the opaquely concentrated, monumental style for long keeping.

Many producers, in regions such as Ribera del Duero and Costers del Segre, have developed blends of Cabernet Sauvignon with Spain's indigenous superstar grape Tempranillo, often with exciting results.

The same inclination towards blended wines has tended to be followed by those Portuguese growers who have planted Cabernet, although there are some accomplished varietal wines produced on the Setúbal peninsula south of Lisbon. Otherwise, the grape has become an important blending ingredient for many growers in the Douro and Alentejo regions.

ITALY

Italy's growers have always been a little cavalier, particularly in the northern regions, in distinguishing Cabernet Sauvignon from its Bordeaux sibling Cabernet Franc. Thus a Trentino wine labelled Cabernet may be one or the other, or both. Yet the two grapes are in reality quite distinct, and produce different styles of wine.

Less confusion arises in Tuscany, where Cabernet Sauvignon is allowed to make up a minor part of the blend in Chianti, and in lesser-known reds such as Carmignano. A revolution in Italian wine was effected in the 1970s by a group of Tuscan innovators, led by the highly respected family house of Antinori. They began working outside the Italian DOC regulations to produce towering reds that made free use of Cabernet Sauvignon, either blended with the Chianti grape Sangiovese, or the other Bordeaux varieties. Eventually, these wines were brought into either the Bolgheri DOC or the wider regional IGT designation for Tuscany.

Cabernet has also gained a foothold in Piedmont in the northwest, where it is often bottled either wholly or almost unblended in the Langhe DOC.

CENTRAL AND EASTERN EUROPE

The cheap red wine boom in the 1970s and 1980s was sustained almost single-handedly by the state-subsidised exports of Bulgaria. For a supposedly marginal winemaking climate, Bulgarian Cabernets generally offered the sorts of easily lovable, softly plummy fruit flavours that producers of less expensive Bordeaux could only dream about. The wines were smoothed with plenty of oak, and were often released as Reserve bottlings after several years' ageing in the state cellars.

At their best, these wines managed to combine enough depth of character to grace a serious dinner table with the kind of instant drinkability that made them surefire party wines. Sadly, the breakup of the old communist state monopoly immediately resulted in wild inconsistencies in quality but, with gathering private investment, Bulgaria is gradually coming back into contention.

Hungary, Moldova and Romania are all capable of producing good Cabernet at a price the wine-drinker wants to pay. Hungary's Villany and Romania's Dealul Mare are among the most propitious regions.

Other Cabernet-based one-offs include the legendary Château Musar of Lebanon, a blend of Cabernet with Cinsault and Carignan made in the Bekaa Valley by the indefatigable Serge Hochar. Where other growers worry about problems like spring frost, the Bekaa has been more prone to war, invasion and rocket attacks. That the fruit of Hochar's labours is a magnificently long-lived and powerful wine is a due tribute to his indomitability.

Greek Cabernet Sauvignon may one day be a force to be reckoned with, if varietal and blended bottlings from areas such as the Atalanti Valley in central Greece, and the Côtes de Meliton in Sithonia in the north, are anything to go by.

Bulgaria's vineyards, like these overlooking the village of Ustina, near Plovdiv (above), were the source of much commercially successful Cabernet in the 1980s.

France

Early-morning mist (above) over Sauvignon vines in the Loire's famous Pouilly-Fumé appellation.

LOIRE

In the vineyards around the upper reaches of the river Loire, in the centre of France, unblended Sauvignon Blanc reigns supreme. It wasn't that long ago that these crisp, scented dry white wines, designed to be drunk within a couple of years of harvest, were not especially highly regarded even within France itself. As fashion has shifted away from richer and oakier styles of white, Loire Sauvignon – Sancerre in particular – has found itself catapulted to the height of popularity.

Pouilly-Fumé and Sancerre are the two most famous appellations for Sauvignon. They are situated on opposite sides of the river, on the east and west banks respectively. It is a very accomplished taster indeed who can spot one from the other when, at their best, they both capture the combination of refreshing green fruit flavours, snappy acids and distant smoky aromas that typify the grape in these parts.

The fashionability of the wines has elevated their prices, which – at the generic supermarket own-brand end of the quality spectrum – have become all but unpalatable, given the fact that there is nothing particularly expensive about their production. As well as that, there is the uncomfortable fact that, in Pouilly-Fumé particularly, there are too many indifferent producers making unfocused wines from the product of overcropping vines.

To the west of Sancerre are three less well-known Sauvignon appellations. They offer most of the flavour of the wines of their more exalted neighbours at generally kinder prices. The best, and closest to Sancerre, is Menetou-Salon. Further west, across the river Cher, Quincy and Reuilly produce brisk, assertive Sauvignons in a clean but slightly less concentrated style than the others.

In the heartland of the Loire region, the Touraine district – more famous for its Chenin Blanc wines – also has a lot of Sauvignon. A fair amount of it gets used as blending fodder, but some varietal wines are bottled under the label Touraine Sauvignon. In good years, they too can offer a glass of cheerfully fruity white, increasingly showing something of the intensity of the wines of the upper Loire.

The village of Sancerre (right) that gives the appellation its name stands on a hilltop close to the river Loire, overlooking the vineyards.

BORDEAUX

The dry white wines of Bordeaux were taken by the scruff of the neck and marched into the modern world during the 1980s. Too often stale and dispiriting creations based on over-produced Sémillon prior to that, they have benefited hugely from the trend towards cooler fermentations in temperature-controlled stainless steel.

As Sauvignon wines from further north gained in modishness and therefore retail value, it dawned on the Bordelais that perhaps they could play a part in the Sauvignon craze by vinifying more of what was after all one of their own main grapes. The percentage of Sauvignon in many of the blends has accordingly sharply increased, bringing in its train a greater freshness and zip to the wines.

Top of the quality tree is the region of Pessac-Léognan at the northern end of the Graves, where a healthy scattering of wines from properties such as Domaine de Chevalier, and Châteaux Haut-Brion and Laville-Haut-Brion, have always shown true class. Some producers, such as Couhins-Lurton, use only Sauvignon in their whites. The smart operators have also employed barrel-ageing (and even fermentation in oak too) in order to achieve a rich, tropical-fruit style that is far more opulent than the unoaked Sauvignons of the Loire.

The large production of the Entre-Deux-Mers region is generally more humble stuff, although the best of even these are beginning to shine, and there are producers turning out oaked, unblended Sauvignon to rival the best of Pessac-Léognan. Sauvignon also plays a supporting role in the great sweet wines of Bordeaux, to lend a flash of balancing acid to the noble-rotted Sémillon.

ELSEWHERE

The Bergerac appellation on the river Dordogne has the same grape varieties as Bordeaux, and can turn out some light, refreshing Sauvignon-based blends, as can the Côtes de Duras to the south. White wines labelled Vin de Pays des Côtes de Gascogne, from further down in southwest France, may be made from any of a number of grapes, and there is a smattering of varietal Sauvignon among them.

Although it may seem inauspiciously hot, the increased plantings of Sauvignon in the Languedoc are yielding some attractively crisp, fruity Vins de Pays d'Oc that owe their super-fresh quality to cold fermentation in stainless steel. Choice of the right harvest-time is all. That, and controlling the vigour of the vines so they don't over-produce.

Finally, there is a lone outpost of Sauvignon in the far north of what is technically the Burgundy region, near Chablis. Sauvignon de St-Bris is an historical oddity, best described as tasting like Sauvignon made in the style of Chardonnay, with the recognizable green fruit but with smoother contours than are found in the Loire versions. (Some Chablis growers also possess vineyard land here.) The wines were promoted to the full AOC designation in 2003.

In the Sauternes region, as here at Château Suduiraut (below), Sauvignon Blanc brings a streak of fresh acidity to balance the sweetness of noble-rotted Sémillon.

New Zealand

The Cloudy Bay winery in New Zealand's Marlborough district (below), one of the country's greatest success stories with the Sauvignon grape.

Sauvignon Blanc devotees weaned on the exhilarating flavours of New Zealand's finest efforts won't be surprised to learn that it is now the country's most extensively planted white variety, recently overtaking Chardonnay in acres of vineyard. The grape shot to prominence here in the 1980s on the back of the wine made by the bulk-producing Montana winery in Marlborough on the South Island. The commercial success of its Sauvignon – never less than a harvest festival of pure raw-fruit ripeness – was founded on its sheer exuberance of flavour, and shored up for many years by the fact that its export price hardly moved. And that despite the fact that few wines have further to travel to the international marketplace than those of southern New Zealand.

Having sparked a trend, Montana's example was quickly followed by a host of other wineries. That surge of abundant fruit is present in nearly all the wines of the Marlborough region, although occasionally the acidity can be out of focus, or – as in the troubled vintages of 2003 and 2008 – just a little too aggressive. There has been a distinct tendency among some producers to aim for more Loire-like levels of acidity, which has resulted in wines that have some of the flintiness of their French counterparts, and correspondingly less obvious fruit. Blending with Semillon can achieve a textural depth and lushness in certain wines.

Adjacent to Marlborough, the South Island region of Nelson makes some sharply defined, cool-climate Sauvignons in the nettly, herbaceous style.

The slightly softer style of Sauvignon really comes into its own in the North Island region of Hawkes Bay. The fruit here seems less green and more peachy, and there is a concomitantly greater readiness to use a little oak in the vinification, though by no means universally. These can be very attractive wines.

Other Regions

SOUTH AFRICA

As elsewhere, it's the cooler areas that do best with Sauvignon Blanc in South Africa, and there are now some brilliantly aromatic, concentrated wines being produced. Most of the premium examples are made in the acerbically dry, smoky style of the Loire, with some even recalling the flintiness of good Pouilly-Fumé. The fruit characters of the wines tend to the green, sappy end of the scale, but there is the odd one with something like the fruit-basket juiciness of the textbook New Zealand style. Walker Bay, Elgin, Durbanville and the cooler parts of Stellenbosch have been the best regions for Sauvignon.

SOUTH AMERICA

There was a large, and for some time intractable, problem with Sauvignon Blanc in Chile, which was that a lot of it wasn't. Quite a few growers had a grape called Sauvignonasse, thinking it was the Loire variety, whereas it was in fact the dull, neutral-tasting relative of a grape native to northeast Italy. Chilean Sauvignon, however, can now be bought with confidence, with most wines representing a gentler version of the crisp Loire style. Wines from the cooler Casablanca region are a good bet.

Astonishingly well-defined Sauvignons with tropical fruit, sharply etched acids and a touch of smoke are being made in Argentina's high-volume Mendoza province.

AUSTRALIA

The hotter the wine region, the less likely it is to be capable of producing the appetizing fruit and natural crispness that Sauvignon wines need. Many of Australia's efforts have traditionally been hampered by a lack of sharp definition. Not unexpectedly, the cooler Margaret River GI in Western Australia has proved the most propitious, with some refreshing, sappy wines.

UNITED STATES

The Mondavi winery's attempt to elevate the status of California Sauvignon by renaming it Fumé Blanc didn't manage to persuade many other growers to take the variety to their hearts. If they have Sauvignon at all, they often try to disguise what they see as a troubling pungency in the flavour of the grape by ageing in oak, or

else leaving a distracting quantity of residual sugar in the wine. Washington State is very often a better source of fruit-driven, tangy Sauvignon for drinking young.

The Cullens winery in the Margaret River area of Western Australia (above) has consistently produced one of the country's more sharply defined Sauvignons.

Chile's cooler Casablanca Valley (left) is proving a good spot to grow characterful, fruity Sauvignon Blanc.

PINOT NOIR

Difficult to grow, difficult to vinify, but still producers across the globe are attracted to this temperamental grape variety, tempted to try matching the classic style of Burgundy's greatest red wines.

OF ALL THE French grape varieties that have migrated around the viticultural world, this is the one that excites the greatest passions. More tears are shed, greater energy expended, more hand-wringing despair engendered over it than over any other variety. It is not, by and large, an endeavour for those who relish a quiet life.

Pinot Noir is the only grape permitted in the great majority of red burgundies (the only exceptions being at or near the bottom end of the quality ladder). At the summit sit the *grand cru* wines of the region's most illustrious estates, wines of positively exotic complexity that offer a once-in-a-lifetime experience of dazzling opulence at a once-in-a-lifetime price. All the red-wine appellations of the Côte d'Or, however, are capable of producing great Pinot at one time or another – they don't call it the Slope of Gold for nothing.

So why all the heartbreak?

First off, it emphatically doesn't like being heat-stressed. Burgundy is cool and wet, prone to spring frosts and hail, to an extent that, even here in its ancestral home, it is profoundly vintage-dependent. It has been estimated that, on average, two years out of every three are inadequate for producing great wine (although climate change may gradually be lending its producers a helping hand for the time being).

In off-vintages, the result is a thin, bitter wine with no fruit to speak of, and a streak of hard, spiteful acid that acts as a powerful repellent in its youth. Pinots produced in these conditions are among the feeblest red wines in the fine wine sector, and the labour of love that has to be lavished on them accounts for that part of the sky-high asking prices that isn't accounted for by the region's reputation.

Early experiments with Pinot outside Europe too often fell into this trap. Plantings in the cooler areas of the United States and in New Zealand often combined scything acidity with chaotically high alcohol, while Australian

efforts grown in sweltering conditions were muddy, unfocused and clumsily smothered with extraneous oak.

So should we just draw a veil over Pinot Noir and move on to the next grape? Ah, no.

Grow it in the right climate, preferably in soils with some limestone in them (as in Burgundy), and protect it against the rash of diseases that its flesh is heir to, including rot if there is any rain at harvest-time, and the potential payoff is wine of uniquely haunting beauty, and extraordinary longevity.

Ripe, healthy bunches of Pinot Noir grapes (right). A thin-skinned grape that is highly sensitive to climate and soil, and notoriously difficult to nurture, Pinot Noir can make ripely fruity reds of great class. It is also invaluable in the production of sparkling wine.

It is a thin-skinned variety – physically as well as temperamentally – which means that it generally produces lighter, less forbiddingly tannic wines than Cabernet Sauvignon does. They are correspondingly approachable earlier in their development, although their naturally high acidity does need time to settle. Keep the most concentrated ones for a few years more, and their maturation is astonishing for such a comparatively light wine. An intense gaminess comes over them, something between well-hung meat and black truffle, and their initial red fruit deepens into the savoury scents of herbs and grilling meat.

Increasingly, since the 1990s, growers outside France have got the hang of Pinot Noir. In California (particularly Carneros) and Oregon, and in selected sites across New Zealand, fantastic results are being achieved. The wines often possess brighter, more resonant red fruit in their first flush than burgundy does (think raspberries and red cherries), but the savouriness is there too, and the acid profiles are such that they age majestically. They aren't necessarily much more affordable than mid-range burgundy, but you are appreciably getting your money's worth.

Additionally, Pinot Noir plays an important role in the production of champagne and other sparkling wines, where it adds depth and potential longevity to the Chardonnay, as well as colour to the rosés. Red Pinot wine adds scented charm to much pink champagne. It has enjoyed a highly successful entrée on to the Spanish cava scene, for example, where its delicacy compared to the traditional Spanish red grapes has made for some more graceful pink sparklers than was usually the norm.

FRENCH ORIGINS
Burgundy and Champagne. Also used in some of the light reds and rosés of the Loire, and the red wine of Alsace.

WHERE ELSE IS IT GROWN?
California, Oregon, Australia, New Zealand, Chile and South Africa. Quite important in central Europe – southern Germany, Switzerland, and points east – but still fairly rare along the Mediterranean. Anybody making sparkling wine by the traditional champagne method is likely to use some Pinot.

TASTING NOTES
In youth, it can possess light aromas of red fruits, typically raspberry, strawberry, redcurrant, cherry. In parts of California and Australia, it also has a faint note of coffee bean or mocha. Nearly always has an element of meatiness – beef stock in young wines, shading to well-hung game as it ages, overlaid in the very best with the other-worldly pungency of black truffle. Classically (or notoriously, depending on your tastes) mature wines can also display a distinctly rank smell, politely described as 'barnyardy', but really referring to what you might accidentally put your foot in as you walk through the barnyard.

France

Levelling Pinot Noir grapes in the traditional wooden press at Champagne Bollinger (above).

Harvested Pinot Noir grapes resting in traditional wicker baskets (below) at Louis Latour, in Aloxe-Corton on the Côte d'Or, the home of most of Burgundy's famous names.

Betting on vintage conditions in Burgundy as harvest-time approaches makes for slightly more peace of mind than playing Russian roulette – but only just. In most years, the region's white grape variety, Chardonnay, fares reasonably well: only torrential rain during the picking can really ruin it at the eleventh hour. Pinot Noir, the only runner in the red wine stakes, is a horse of another colour altogether.

At least until the late 1990s, it was possible to say that, more often than not, Pinot Noir yielded disappointing results. Precisely because out-and-out successes were so hard-won, great red burgundy came to be valued by many as the most precious of all France's classic wines, consort to Bordeaux's monarch perhaps, but held in special esteem just because of its relative scarcity. (As well as being less reliable from one vintage to the next, the produce of the Burgundy region is a tiny fraction of that of Bordeaux.)

The Pinot grape reaches the apex of its potential on the Côte d'Or, the narrow escarpment running southwest of the city of Dijon, and home to most of Burgundy's famous names. Its narrower northern strip, the Côte de Nuits, which includes such appellations as Gevrey-Chambertin, Nuits-St-Georges and Morey-St-Denis, tends to produce the weightiest style of Burgundian Pinot, with all sorts of meaty notes ranging from the singed skin of roasting poultry to gravy bubbling in the

dish. Further south, the Côte de Beaune, which takes in Aloxe-Corton, Pommard and Volnay among others, specializes in a lighter, gentler Pinot, scented with soft summer fruits and sometimes flowers as well.

The further south of the Côte d'Or you travel, into the Côte Chalonnaise and then the workhorse region of the Mâconnais, the more ordinary the Pinot Noir wines become. At the bottom of the scale, wine labelled Bourgogne Rouge may be a blend of grapes from different sources in the region. It once covered a multitude of sins, but is now increasingly a useful varietal designation for some simple but conscientiously crafted wines.

If the growing season has been relatively chilly or, worse, plagued with intermittent rainfall (as in 2008), the resulting wines can be extremely light, both in colour as well as texture. When a red wine is full of hard acids and bitterly unripe fruit, and feels no richer on the palate than a heavyish rosé, then it's hard to get consumers to see why they should pay the inflated prices.

On the other hand, if burgundy is noted for one thing, it is a resistance to generalizations. Some producers can manage to make densely concentrated wines in even the less auspicious vintages, even while their near neighbours may be wringing their hands. It pays to know who the high fliers are.

Because Pinot often lacks adequate natural sugar to ferment into a full-bodied red that will stay the distance, producers may be permitted to add ordinary cane sugar to the freshly pressed juice. The process is known as chaptalization after its inventor, Jean-Antoine Chaptal. By giving the yeast more sugar to work on, the potential alcohol content of the finished product is raised in the direction of the regional average of 13 per cent. Sometimes, especially when young, it can give off a telltale whiff of burnt sugar, a probable indicator that the winemaker has resorted to fairly heavy chaptalization.

In the best vintages, however, such as 2002, 2005 and 2009, when the Pinot Noir has attained full ripeness, it turns out richly perfumed, exquisitely elegant wines that go at least some way to explaining the heart-stopping prices they sell for. These are the wines that are most worth stashing away for a rainy day.

Autumnal Pinot Noir vines (left) running down towards the town of Aÿ, in Champagne. The inclusion of Pinot in champagne lends it a nuttier, darker hue, and gives the wine depth and good ageing potential.

The beginnings of a red burgundy – Pinot Noir gently fermenting in an open wooden vat (above).

Although it is a red grape, Pinot is hugely important in the making of champagne. The colourless juice is vinified without its skins so that the resulting wine remains white, although if you compare a blended champagne with one that has been made entirely from Chardonnay, you will notice a deeper, nuttier hue in the one that contains Pinot Noir.

Champagne producers consider that Pinot gives their wines depth and the ability to age well. Some champagne, labelled Blanc de Noirs, is made entirely from Pinot Noir and/or the region's other red grape, Pinot Meunier, but is still a white wine. A small amount of still red wine, vaguely Burgundian in style though even more crisply acidic, is made, and may be added to white wine to make rosé champagne. Tiny

quantities of pink champagne are made by the painstaking method of infusing the red grape skins briefly in the white juice to tint it to the desired shade.

In the eastern Loire, Pinot Noir is used to make the red (and rosé) versions of Sancerre and Menetou-Salon. These are much lighter in style than burgundy, often with a slightly vegetal hint. They aren't intended for ageing but, served lightly chilled, can make good summer drinking.

Pinot Noir also makes the only red wine of Alsace, again in a typically featherlight and not overly fruity style. Increasingly, though, a handful of producers are starting to take it more seriously, and making wines with the muscle to take some well-judged oak-ageing in their stride.

United States

CALIFORNIA

California has undoubtedly been the most successful region across the board for Pinot Noir outside Burgundy itself. Although they are extremely unlikely to admit it, Burgundy's growers could profitably learn a fair bit from the approach of the more conscientious producers of Pinot Noir in America.

The most successful area to date has been the Carneros AVA, a cool district straddling Napa and Sonoma Counties and benefiting from the coastal fogs that waft in from San Francisco Bay. The afternoons and early evenings in Carneros are sufficiently warm to endow the developing grapes with the exciting flavours of ripe red fruits that are characteristic of the best Pinot wines. At the same time, the cooling influence of those thick mists, which often hang around until mid-morning, ensures adequate levels of fresh acidity, so the wines are impeccably balanced and capable of ageing.

Its ripe fruit intensity means that California Pinot is generally ready for drinking earlier than traditional burgundy, although it does benefit from keeping for a couple of years after release just to allow the nervy edge on those acids to calm down. If the top wines have any noticeable problem, it is that alcohol levels are frequently uncomfortably high. That can result in wines that are very attractive until you swallow them, whereupon they leave a definite smoulder at the back of the throat. There are more balanced wines around now, though, than there were, say, 20 years ago, and the truth is that a lot of them do have the stuffing to carry a weighty alcohol load. Get to know your producers.

In addition to Carneros, parts of Santa Barbara County south of the Bay have proved successful for Pinot Noir, as has the mountainous inland AVA of San Benito, and the AVAs of Russian River Valley and the Santa Cruz Mountains to the north and south of San Francisco respectively.

OREGON

Because of its cooler, damper climate, this Pacific Northwestern state was seen as ideal Pinot territory when the search for appropriate vineyard sites began to gather momentum. Climatically, it is indubitably much closer to Burgundy than most of California, and there are indeed now some stunning wines. The trailblazer was David Lett of Eyrie Vineyards, who first planted Pinot in the 1960s.

It wasn't all plain sailing for many growers. High yields, lack of true physiological ripeness in the grapes and uncertain site selection hampered many early efforts, but Oregon's has been a true tale of dedication to a cause. A succession of good to great vintages since the late 1990s has helped, and some wineries are now showing just what thrilling Pinots the state is capable of making.

Oregon's *premier cru* region is the Willamette Valley AVA, which lies to the west of the Cascade Mountains. A series of smaller AVAs has been demarcated within the overall valley region, with the Dundee Hills and McMinnville looking especially enthralling. The style is generally lighter than in most of California, less meaty but with more accentuated strawberry fruit, and generally approachable sooner.

Terracing a new Pinot Noir vineyard in Oregon (below). The grape of Burgundy is making itself at home in the Pacific Northwest.

Other Regions

NEW ZEALAND

The coolest wine climate in the southern hemisphere has proved perfectly hospitable for Pinot Noir, which is now its most widely planted red grape. Although initial efforts often lacked for enough flesh to cover their bare bones, there are now dozens of world-class producers of top-flight Pinot, and prices have climbed accordingly. The very best display that elusive savoury intensity that adds complexity to the ripe raspberry fruit.

So far, the most exciting wines have come from the Wairarapa region, around the town of Martinborough in the south of the North Island. Most of the cooler South Island is turning out quality Pinot Noir too, from Marlborough and Nelson at the northern end, down through Canterbury and – perhaps most electrifyingly of all – Central Otago. If there is a flaw, it is that some wines are made in a more highly extracted, densely coloured, even tannic style than they need to be (some lighter Beaune-like showings would be nice to see), but these are without question among the world's most attractive versions of this most demanding grape.

AUSTRALIA

As with other cool-climate grapes, it is crucial to find the right site for Pinot Noir in Australia, in order to avoid the gloppy or jammy characters

that can so easily spoil it. The Yarra Valley GI in Victoria fits the bill because of its altitude. Western Australia's Margaret River GI has made great strides, while on Tasmania, the cool conditions are responsible for some of the most Burgundian Pinot Noir produced outside France.

SOUTH AFRICA

As in Australia, much of the country is simply too hot to achieve great elegance in wines made from Pinot Noir, and the grape is not that important in South Africa, except for fine sparkling wines. The best varietal red Pinots have so far come from the coastal Walker Bay region.

SOUTH AMERICA

Chile now has some convincing Pinots, grown in the cooler, high-altitude regions such as Casablanca, and even from the hotter environs of the Rapel in Colchagua. The style can be a little overripe and heady, but the fruit is there.

GERMANY

In Germany, they call it Spätburgunder, and it has long been a traditional grape in some of the tiny production of red wines. Typically, they are light as a feather, not much further on from rosé. The southerly region of Baden makes wines with decent fruit, while the northerly Ahr has somehow built a reputation for reds. The odd one, made at the northern limits of world wine-growing, shows true complexity.

A vineyard in the Bannockburn district of Central Otago (above), one of New Zealand's premier regions for growing Pinot Noir.

Hand-plunging the grape skin cap on a tank of Pinot Noir (left) at the Yarra Yering winery in Victoria.

SEMILLON

To many producers, Sémillon suffers a lack of individuality that has destined it to be blended with more fashionable varieties. Yet as the source of rich, golden, honeyed Sauternes, and the unique, aged dry white of Australia, Sémillon is second to none.

WHILE IT IS undoubtedly one of the world's foremost grape varieties, Sémillon has a surprisingly low profile. In the northern hemisphere, it was traditionally not seen very much as an unblended varietal wine. This is largely because, in its native Bordeaux, it is always mixed with Sauvignon Blanc.

However, its highly prized susceptibility in the right conditions to botrytis, the so-called noble rot that concentrates the sugars of overripe grapes by shrivelling them on the vine, makes Sémillon a surefire bet as a dessert-wine producer. The lofty reputation enjoyed by sweet Sauternes and Barsac – in which Sémillon typically represents around four-fifths or more of the blend – has been such that the grape's role in the production of dry white wine has been largely eclipsed.

In Bordeaux today, producers of dry white wine are in the business of pulling out a lot of their Sémillon vines and replacing them with further plantings of its partner Sauvignon. (As we saw when we looked at Sauvignon Blanc, some of the trendiest dry whites of Bordeaux use no Sémillon at all.) That said, it still accounts for far more acreage in the vineyards than Sauvignon, so if it is in decline, the process will be a lengthy one. Many producers frankly consider it to have far less character than its brasher stablemate, being short of aromatic appeal and general *joie-de-vivre*.

To which one can only reply, tell that to the Australians. Semillon (as it is commonly spelt outside France) has been used to produce a varietal dry wine in southern Australia since the 19th century. Its homeland Down Under is the Hunter Valley in New South Wales. True, many growers weren't sure what the variety was, and its traditional (and misleading) name was Hunter Riesling. It does share some of the aromatic characteristics of real Riesling, most notably a minerally aroma of lime-zest, but it almost always gives a fatter, oilier wine than Riesling.

The most peculiar trait a dry Sémillon wine can have is to smell and taste as if it has been wood-matured when it hasn't. Often, there is a distinctly toasty quality to the wine that becomes steadily more pronounced as it ages. Its colour darkens rapidly too, making old Hunter Semillon one of the strangest but most memorable experiences in the world of white wine.

In areas where a lot of cheap bulk wine is produced, Sémillon's easy-going temperament in the vineyard has made it the grape of choice for those who haven't yet caught the Chardonnay bug. Much of South America's vineland, especially in Chile, is carpeted with the variety. An indication of the status in which it is held here is that these are not the wines Chile chooses to boast about on the export markets.

For many, Sémillon provides a relatively trouble-free source of blending material for more fashionable varieties. Although the Bordeaux precedent is to blend it with Sauvignon, Sauvignon is too much in vogue currently to be thought by many producers to need a partner in the bottle. That is why many winemakers, in Australia particularly, have taken to blending Semillon with Chardonnay.

The resulting wines have become bargain-basement alternatives to neat Chardonnay. The lowish prices of these wines indicate how seriously we are being asked to take them. In a hot vintage, where both grapes have yielded similarly rich, fat, silky-textured wines, it is difficult to see what they are supposed to be doing for each other in a blend.

On the other hand, the Sémillon-Sauvignon partnership is nearly always a happy one. The acidity of the latter gives definition to the textural opulence of the former.

The blend makes particular sense in the production of sweet wines. What makes great Sauternes, Barsac and Monbazillac so sought-after, and so extremely long-lived in the bottle, is that a good balance of sugar and acid is present in the wines to start with. Compared to lesser dessert wines from other wine regions, they are hardly ever cloying, despite their massive, syrupy concentration.

Sémillon, a golden-coloured grape with markedly deep green leaves (right) is often used to blend with Sauvignon or Chardonnay. When affected by botrytis (noble rot), it creates the world's finest dessert wines.

FRENCH ORIGINS
Bordeaux.

WHERE ELSE IS IT GROWN?
Australia, South America, a little in South Africa, the USA and New Zealand, and isolated pockets of southern France.

TASTING NOTES
When dry, lime-peel, exotic honey, sometimes has a little of Sauvignon's gooseberry too. Often has a hard mineral purity, even slightly metallic. In the Hunter Valley, deceptive woodiness even when unoaked, turning to burnt toast with age. Blended with Chardonnay, lemon-and-lime squash seems to be the main flavour. When subjected to botrytis for sweet wines, can take on a whole range of exotic fruit characters, but classically has overripe peach or apricot flavour, barley-sugar, honey, allied to a vanilla-custard, *crème brûlée* richness from oak ageing. Australian sweet Semillon can have an emphatically medicinal tinge to it as well.

Bordeaux

Sémillon grapes left on the vine that have been affected by botrytis (right). The shrivelled, blackened grapes will yield a lusciously sweet, concentrated juice.

The elegant Château La Louvière in Pessac-Léognan, Graves (below), owned by the Lurton family. Dry white Bordeaux from the Graves is often the best of its style.

Sémillon's most glorious display in its home region is in the wines of Sauternes and Barsac. At the top of the tree, with a classification all to itself, is the legendary Château d'Yquem, the most expensive sweet wine in the world. The late-summer and autumn climate in Bordeaux provides perfect conditions in many years for the development on Sémillon of the noble rot, botrytis, which causes the berries to moulder and dry out on the vines. As the liquid proportion of the grapes drops, so the sugar in them comes to represent an ever higher percentage, and the result is lusciously sweet, alcoholic, viscous wines of enormous longevity.

If the top wines are so expensive, it is in large part because the more conscientious châteaux take great pains over the harvest. They will hand-select only those berries that are fully rotted, so labour costs are accordingly very high. Most of the wines are aged in at least a proportion of new oak, adding further

dimensions of richness to them. Such wines have long been the inspiration for the production of botrytized Sémillon the world over, and deservedly so.

Elsewhere in Bordeaux, in the making of dry wines, Sémillon rather hangs its head these days. The finger of blame for the notoriously flabby, fruitless dry whites the region once turned out by the vatload came to be pointed its way. But this style has waned as fresh young Sauvignon Blanc, with its tangier fruit, began to show it the door in the late 1980s. As a result, consumers may get the idea that Sémillon is incapable of making great dry wine in Bordeaux, but it ain't necessarily so.

In the northern Graves region of Pessac-Léognan, some of Bordeaux's most illustrious names in dry white wine production still use a greater percentage of Sémillon than Sauvignon in their wines. These include Châteaux Laville-Haut-Brion, Olivier and Latour-Martillac. The results can be breathtaking, the wines having more solidity and savoury concentration than the solo Sauvignon.

Australia

Dry Semillon is one of a handful of unique styles of wine that Australia has contributed to the world. Nor is it a product of some antipodean search for novelty, conceived in a struggle to find ways of doing things that escape the eternal French archetypes. Australia was making Semillons like this in the late 19th century, even though it may have been calling them Hunter Riesling or – even less convincingly – White Burgundy.

The classic Hunter Valley style can be quite austere, as typified by the wines of Tyrrells. Crisp and acerbic in youth, they age to a wonderful roasted-nuts complexity, all achieved without recourse to the expense of oak barrels. Some producers do actually use a modicum of oak to emphasize that natural toastiness. With the tendency now for consumers to drink most wines young, greater stress is being laid on primary fruit flavours – sharp green fruits, usually lime, being the main reference point. Other good Hunter producers are Rothbury, Brokenwood and Lindeman's.

The grape pops up in most Australian regions, though, and fares equally well in areas that are considerably cooler than the Hunter. In the Clare Valley, for instance, Semillon produces a less oily version. As a rough guide, producers who make good Riesling are likely to be reliable for Semillon too: in a cool part of the Clare called Lenswood, Tim Knappstein makes fine, bracingly tart but certainly ageworthy wines.

Western Australia's Margaret River region makes some generously fruity, distinctly smoky Semillons in a style hugely reminiscent of Sauvignon. Evans & Tate is a prime example here.

Although unblended Sauvignon can too often be a disappointment from many parts of Australia, when it is blended with Semillon in the Bordeaux fashion it can produce impressively ripe-fruited wines capable of gaining real complexity with ageing. Cape Mentelle in Margaret River and even St Hallett, in the broiling Barossa Valley region of South Australia, make good blends.

Botrytized, or noble-rotted, Semillon has a long and distinguished tradition here, too. The style may be big and obvious when compared with the top wines of Sauternes, but then there is no particular reason to compare them to Sauternes. De Bortoli in New South Wales was among those who blazed this particular trail, while Peter Lehmann makes a textbook orange-barley-sugar version in the Barossa.

The de Bortoli winery in New South Wales, Australia (below), complete with irrigation canal.

The verdant landscape of South Australia's Clare Valley (below), with Lenswood Vineyard in the foreground. A cool upland district, it can produce bracingly tart but ageworthy Semillons.

SYRAH

Whether recognized as the French grape of the northern Rhône, Syrah, or in its popular guise as Shiraz, in Australia, this grape remains one of the noblest red varieties, fabled for its ability to age majestically for decades.

SUCH IS the success of this grape in Australia that many may know it only by its southern hemisphere name of Shiraz. More of it is grown in Australia than of any other red wine grape, and it appears varietally, as well as in blends with Cabernet Sauvignon and Merlot.

At the pinnacle of its achievements, it shows why it thoroughly deserves its place among the first division of international grape varieties. Australia's most feted red wine, Penfold's Grange, is overwhelmingly composed of Shiraz, usually with only the merest dash of Cabernet as seasoning. In France, it produces some of the most highly prized single-vineyard wines in Europe, wines made in tiny quantities that are sold on allocation to a lucky few favoured customers.

Shiraz produces some of the world's deepest, darkest, most intense red wines, full of black-fruit richness, hot spice and alcoholic power. Then again, it can be used to make the kind of sweetly jammy, oak-smoothed nursery wine that can lure confirmed white wine drinkers on to a bottle of red once in a while.

Syrah, as we should call it when in France, blends well with a number of other grapes, and hangs out with a whole crowd of assorted pals in the wines of the southern Rhône and Languedoc-Roussillon.

The Rhône valley is the ancestral home of Syrah. In viticultural terms, the valley divides into two zones – northern and southern – and represents two very different approaches to the grape. In the south, it makes its way among a large coterie of mostly minor varieties, from the everyday wines of the Côtes du Rhône and Côtes du Ventoux up to the giddy heights of Châteauneuf-du-Pape and its understudy Gigondas. Up to thirteen varieties are permitted in Châteauneuf, of which Syrah generally plays second or third fiddle alongside Mourvèdre, with Grenache playing lead.

It's in the northern Rhône that Syrah really comes into its own. Here, it is the sole red grape, appearing in wines from Hermitage and Côte-Rôtie at the top of the scale to Crozes-Hermitage at the affordable (but still highly reliable) end. The former two can be monumental classic reds that age for at least as long as the very greatest Bordeaux, on account of their precise and complex balance of hugely concentrated fruit, acidity and massive tannic extract. Clenched and surly in youth, they gradually uncoil into the exotically seductive beauties they can be. A topnote of violets frequently adds to the charm.

One of the most commonly encountered descriptions of Rhône Syrah is 'peppery', and even a simple Crozes-Hermitage from a cooperative can display something of that characteristic, although it may vary in intensity from a mild suggestion of spiciness at the back of the throat to the exact and inescapable scent of freshly milled black peppercorns, quite as though the grower had given the wine a few twists of the grinder before sealing the bottle.

Some debate has been occasioned as to whether the famous pepperiness is a varietal property, or whether it isn't at least partly caused by Syrah that hasn't quite attained full ripeness. It is a late-ripening variety, and invariably needs time to show its paces, even in one of the hotter environs of southern France. Compare Australian Shiraz, where the pepperiness is distinctly more muted, if indeed it's really there at all.

In Aussie Shiraz, the fruit is sweetly ripe and right upfront, and the wines rarely have that sharp edge of tannin that northern Rhône examples do. In youth, the softer contours of Shiraz are often derived from the overt influence of creamy oak flavours, so the wine can be drunk sooner. It can be surprisingly delicate aromatically from certain regions, offering a refreshing waft of eucalyptus, rather than the leather and tar and blackberry it traditionally rejoices in. That said, the most concentrated wines are black as sin, and need plenty of time to unwind.

The vibrant blue of the Syrah grape variety (right). Syrah has a unique character most often described as 'peppery', and responds well to oak. In its classic form as the grape of northern Rhône's finest reds, and in Australia as Shiraz, it can make wines that will age for decades.

FRENCH ORIGINS
Northern Rhône.

WHERE ELSE IS IT GROWN?
Australia. Becoming important in the US, South America and South Africa. Traditional in parts of Switzerland.

TASTING NOTES
Can smell of almost any dark purple fruit – blackberries, blackcurrants, black cherries, damsons, plums. Freshly ground black pepper in the northern Rhône. Exotic flavours can include liquorice, ginger, dark chocolate, often a distinct floral note, too, like violets. Cool topnote of mint characteristic in parts of South Australia. Aged wines can take on something of the gaminess of old Pinot Noir.

Given that there is so much Shiraz in Australia, it isn't surprising that a lot of it finds its way into very basic wines. A cloyingly sweet, jammy, offputting style is depressingly widespread. On the other hand, its use in thoroughly innovative red sparkling wines in both sweetish and powerfully dry, tannic styles, has been a head-turner. Relinquish any memories of wafer-thin fizzy red Lambrusco. Sparkling Shiraz is a muscled-up blockbuster. I tend to prefer those wines with a little residual sugar, rather than heavy tannic fizz.

France

The greatest producers in Rhône Syrah are now ranked up with Bordeaux's and Burgundy's finest. This is still, however, a fairly recent phenomenon. While the burly red wines of Hermitage had always had a lofty reputation among British wine enthusiasts, the production of the region as a whole was not held in particularly high regard. When the influential American wine critic Robert Parker began, in the 1980s, to rate some of the best wines of Marcel Guigal (now one of the northern Rhône's superstars) as the equals of the great vintages of Mouton-Rothschild, the international wine trade was persuaded to take notice.

That development inevitably prompted the producers to put up their prices, but it has to be said that the best had certainly been undervalued in the past. These are wines with the same sort of structure and ageing capacity as Cabernet-based clarets (often even more muscularly built, in fact) and their flavours resemble no other red wines in France.

Of the northern Rhône appellations for varietal Syrah, Hermitage is traditionally the biggest and beefiest. Although solidly constructed, the wines are not without grace and elegance, and the fruit flavour can be surprisingly lighter than the reputation – more raspberries than blackberries. At their most immense, though, these are densely textured, ferociously dark stunners, but retaining their primary fruit well into their maturity.

Côte-Rôtie is the appellation that has created all the excitement in recent years, the most frenetic buzz being around Guigal's three single-vineyard wines – La Mouline, La Landonne and La Turque. These are mind-blowingly concentrated expressions of fine Syrah that sell for sky-high prices. Up to 20 per cent of the white grape, Viognier, is permitted in Côte-Rôtie under the appellation regulations, and can add a bewitching note of apricot to Syrah's blackberry.

St-Joseph makes slightly lighter wines, piercingly blackcurrant in the good years, while the bottom-line appellation of Crozes-Hermitage is well worth trying as an introduction to the flavours of Rhône Syrah. I say 'bottom-line', but there are growers now making Crozes as opaque and intense and long-lived as some Hermitage.

The final appellation of the northern Rhône, Cornas, is an odd one, in that its Syrah is the least immediately recognizable. The wines are often rather tough, and lacking the benefit of youthful fruit, or they can simply taste like blended wines from appellations further south such as Châteauneuf-du-Pape. Some growers are working with the grain of Cornas Syrah to make some excitingly individual, if austere, wines. Long bottle-ageing is mandatory.

In the southern Rhône, and down into the Languedoc, Syrah is blended with many other red grapes, among them Grenache, Mourvèdre, Cinsault and Carignan. Unless a producer has used a particularly high percentage of Syrah, the grape may not be individually perceptible in these wines, though it does beef up the structure.

The chapel and vines on the famous hill of Hermitage (below), overlooking the river Rhône and the towns of Tournon and Tain l'Hermitage.

Australia

Shiraz has been the pre-eminent red grape variety in Australia for as long as anyone can remember, but it is only since the 1970s that there has been a significant impetus towards producing world-class wine from it. At its most humdrum, Shiraz is a rather gloopy plum-jam sort of wine with too much heavy oak influence in it, so that the toffeeish sweetness of its aftertaste can be quite sickly. Thankfully, there are more than enough accomplished Shiraz producers to make for a brighter picture overall.

It's all a question, as so often, of microclimate. In the hotter GIs, such as the Hunter and Barossa Valleys, Shiraz is responsible for the thickest, most opulently fruity of all Australia's reds. In the warmer central sector of Victoria, the Goulburn Valley GI is home to some especially concentrated Shirazes of great aromatic intensity.

The red soil of Coonawarra is as distinguished a hotbed of Shiraz as it is of Cabernet Sauvignon, producing subtly spiced wines, as well as accessibly fruit-filled offerings, not all of which use oak.

From old vines in parts of the Barossa Valley, Shiraz results in small amounts of extraordinarily deep, resonant and complex wines that can stand next to top Côte-Rôtie.

The Hill of Grace vineyard, owned by Henschke (above), in the Barossa Valley, South Australia. The Shiraz vines planted here are over 100 years old.

Other Regions

SOUTH AFRICA

As in Australia, it took a while for Shiraz to persuade its growers that it was worth taking seriously as a variety. Inspired by success elsewhere, some impressive Shiraz is now emerging. It should work after all, given the sultry climatic conditions the grape loves. Stellenbosch and Paarl are among the premier growing regions.

CALIFORNIA

Despite the West Coast fashion for Rhône grape varieties, Syrah (as it tends to be known here) has been slow to establish itself as an important grape. The trend so far has been to make wines with French levels of acidity and memorably aromatic fruit, but not quite the degree of concentration of the most well-bred Côte-Rôtie. San Luis Obispo has the most extensive plantings, but Santa Barbara and Napa may well be the best regions for it.

CHILE

Chile started to flex its muscles with Syrah only in the 1990s, with results that are already beginning to intrigue. Rhône comparisons are plentiful, with wines from various sub-zones of Colchagua, together with San Antonio and coastal Casablanca, beginning to look very tasty. The best will age well.

Orderly rows of Shiraz vines at Franschhoek's Bellingham Vineyards, Paarl, South Africa (above).

Vineyards of Joseph Phelps, (left), a trend-setter for quality Syrah in California, in springtime Napa Valley.

RIESLING

Germany's noble white grape variety, Riesling, is a versatile performer. It is prized in northern Europe and the southern hemisphere for its ability to produce classic sweet whites as well as impeccable dry wines.

THE ONLY FINE wine grape of international importance not to have originated in France, Riesling is the great speciality of German winemaking. Its only base in France is in the Alsace region, a sheltered northeastern enclave between the Vosges mountains and the Rhine valley that has intermittently, usually by force, been a geopolitical part of Germany. Like Sémillon, Riesling is capable of making impeccably dry wines of surprising longevity, as well as lusciously sweet dessert wines affected by the noble rot, botrytis, but unlike Sémillon it also runs the whole gamut of styles in between.

In recent years, Riesling has come to be considered the most underrated of all the top grapes. Why this should be so when it is such a versatile performer might seem a mystery, but is at least partly explicable by the wholly irrational association in many consumers' minds of Riesling with cheap, extraneously sweetened German wine such as Liebfraumilch – the low-alcohol, low-acid introduction to the world of wine that drinkers of my own generation cut our teeth on.

Although Liebfraumilch may not have quite the same purchase on the tastes of young consumers that it once had, it remains infuriatingly confusable with quality German wine. The bottles look the same as top-quality Rhine Rieslings and, even though it's always worth looking for the name of this grape on a German wine label, the good wines turn out to share the same basic characteristics – lightness and often a delicate sweetness (albeit from natural grape sugars) – as the slosh.

How to persuade people that these are in fact much better wines? Only time and tasting practice will tell. For one thing, the clear varietal characters of the grape can be breathtakingly beautiful, a whoosh of citric freshness like squeezing a lime, together with mineral notes and often something like the

The Riesling (right) is a hardy, frost-resistant vine, which makes it ideal for the cool vineyards of northern Europe. Riesling can produce long-lived wines of intense aroma and character, ranging in style from bone-dry to lusciously sweet.

flesh of a juicy-ripe peach, all suspended in a wine that then belies its apparent fragility by surviving intact in the bottle over many years. There is far more joy in a ten-year-old Riesling of perhaps 7 per cent alcohol than there is in a ten-year-old, 13 per cent Sauvignon.

Because Germany's vineyards are at the northern extremity of where vines can be grown, the country's quality classification system developed along the lines of assessing just how ripe the grapes were when harvested, and therefore how potentially sweet the resulting wines would be. Severely low winter-time temperatures might then arrest the fermentation of the wines, leaving them low in alcohol and retaining a degree of unfermented grape sugar. These were precisely the attributes that aficionados came to treasure in them.

International tastes in wine provoked an experimental movement in Germany in the 1980s and 90s to ferment some of the wines – Rieslings and others – to dryness. Initially, many of these wines were disastrously unbalanced, and the technique appeared to work better with other varieties than Riesling, but more rounded wines have since emerged.

Riesling always gives a high-acid wine, which is perhaps best offset in Germany by some level of natural sweetness, so that even those at the drier end of the spectrum (the styles known as Kabinett and Spätlese) have a softening edge on them. In warmer climes, there is generally enough ripeness and alcohol to balance the high acidity, making for appetizing dry wines that can age well.

This has traditionally been the case in Alsace and the cooler parts of Australia, the world's two best sources of dry Riesling. Other countries have appeared to struggle with the grape. In time, cool-climate New Zealand will doubtless become a reliable producer of outstanding dry Rieslings, but for the time being, there are too many unfocused wines that taste vaguely of boiled sweets. It will not go down well in the Rhine and Mosel valleys to say so, but it may well be that the more success producers outside Europe have with Riesling,

ORIGINS
Germany.

WHERE ELSE IS IT GROWN?
Alsace. Australia and
New Zealand. Austria and
northern Italy. Some in the
United States and Canada.

TASTING NOTES
Nearly always has the scent of
lime, whether bitter zests or
freshly pressed juice. Riper
German ones can have softer
fruit like ripe peach or apricot, as
well as a gentle floral aroma. In
Alsace, there is a very austere
mineral quality in the wines and
a texture on the palate like
sharpened steel. A whiff of petrol
(or gasoline) flowing from the
pump generally comes with age,
although some Australian wines
can display it quite young.

the greater the chance that people may come back to an enjoyment of German wines, freed of the inaccurate preconceptions that still stand in their way.

At the sweetest and richest end of the spectrum, Riesling makes some of the most enticing, and beautifully balanced, botrytized wines in the world. The Beerenauslese and Trockenbeerenauslese offerings of Germany and Austria, as well as the most carefully tended Noble Rieslings of Australia, South Africa and the United States, all combine fresh acidity with layers of honey-soaked, citrus-spiked lusciousness.

Germany

Riesling is grown in nearly all of the wine regions of Germany, and has since the 1990s been the country's most widely planted variety. It is in many ways particularly well suited to the cold climates it encounters there, because the tough stems of its vines enable them to cope with the worst the winters can throw at them.

The drawback comes at the other end of the annual cycle, when ripening the grapes is something of a gamble against the elements. Picked too early, Riesling can be full of hard, unripe acidity. Waiting for the right levels of ripeness can often mean leaving the bunches hanging into November, when French growers have long since picked, pressed and fermented, and when the weather is so bitter that it can be hard to get a natural fermentation going.

With all that in mind, much effort and funding has gone into crossing Riesling with other German varieties, and even crossing the crosses with Riesling and others. The aim has been to try to perfect a grape that will give the fresh fruit flavours of Riesling, as well as its invaluable susceptibility to botrytis, but with a more reliable ripening pattern. A handful of these have yielded goodish results, but few seriously believe they can take the place of Riesling as Germany's premier performer.

The top classification for German wines, their equivalent of the French *appellation contrôlée*, is *Prädikatswein* (literally, wine with distinction). Within this class, there are five types of wine, measured according to the amount of natural sweetness in them. In ascending order, they are: Kabinett, Spätlese, Auslese, Beerenauslese and Trockenbeerenauslese. The suffix '-lese' means 'picked', and the time of picking is specifically indicated in the prefix, from Spätlese (late-picked, i.e. just after the normal harvesting time) to Trockenbeerenauslese or TBA (meaning berries picked outside – that is, after – the main harvest, which are dried and shrivelled with sugar-concentrating noble rot).

The famous steep vineyards of the Mosel region (below) where the Riesling vines tumble down towards the Mosel river. Such steep sites means hand-picking is the only option at harvest-time.

Any of the first three styles may be fermented out to total dryness to become Trocken (dry) wines, or halfway in the case of wines labelled Feinherb. Some super-sweet berries are left on the vines until nearer Christmas, in some vintages even into the new year, and are picked at the crack of dawn when they are half-frozen. During the pressing, some of the crystals of ice that represent the water content of the grapes are removed and the very sweet juice that hasn't frozen is then fermented. This style is known, for obvious reasons, as Eiswein (ice wine).

The fullest, most concentrated Rieslings have traditionally come from the Rheingau, where the vineyard has long been dominated by Riesling plantings. Here, the best producers make wines that are as expressive of their particular vineyard locations as any illustrious Burgundy *grand cru*.

A non-Trocken Riesling from the Rheingau is generally around 10 per cent alcohol, relatively heady in German terms, and there is a rounded, often honeyed feel to the best of them. Legend insists that the Rheingau was the region where the first noble-rotted wines

were accidentally produced, many years before the technique became known in Sauternes.

To the west of the Rheingau, the Nahe also has a preponderance of Riesling, although here it is a more recent development as a result of the region's standing having risen considerably in the last few years. There are some very promising young growers here now.

The other two neighbouring Rhine regions are Rheinhessen and Pfalz (the latter originally known in English as the Palatinate). Riesling has made great strides in the Pfalz, where an almost tropical aromatic intensity is the house style of the most talented producers, although the wines are still possessed of that traditionally delicate structure and finesse.

To the northwest, and centred on the city of Trier, the Mosel-Saar-Ruwer region produces the lightest, most exquisitely subtle and refined versions of Riesling made anywhere in the world. Alcohol levels may be as low as 7 per cent, and the aromatic profile of the wines so astonishingly rarefied that a sniff at the glass can be like breathing in pure mountain air. The vineyards are planted on vertiginously steep slopes on either side of the river, so any thought of harvesting with motor vehicles is out of the question. Enforced rigorous hand-picking of carefully selected grapes should go some way to explaining the prices.

Vineyards looking down to the village of Ungstein, in the Pfalz region of Germany (above). The traditional style of Riesling wines here is both aromatic and tremendously delicate.

Schloss Johannisberg, looking down over its Riesling vineyards (left), in the Rheingau. Rheingau Rieslings are traditionally the fullest, most concentrated in style.

Alsace

The 15th-century church in the midst of vineyards at Hunawihr, Alsace (above).

Anybody familiar with the wines of Alsace may tend more readily to associate them with the highly perfumed, positively decadent flavours of Gewurztraminer and Pinot Gris than with the steely austerity of Riesling. It is, however, an open secret in the region that Riesling is considered the noblest of them all, partly because the acidity levels it usually attains mean that the resulting wines have a good long life ahead of them. The variety has been here since the 15th century, and today comprises over 20 per cent (and counting) of the vineyard land. Everybody loves Riesling.

It is in the hilly Haut-Rhin district of Alsace that most of the Riesling is concentrated. The best plots are those that are protected from the wind so that the ripening of the grapes is not inhibited, although the climate of this sheltered region is generally much more benign than what German growers have to contend with. Unusually for a fine wine grape, the amount of fruit the vines are permitted to yield under the appellation regulations is quite high, without the wines themselves necessarily lacking anything in full-blown aromatic intensity.

Most Alsace Riesling is made in an assertively bone-dry style, with around 12 per cent alcohol and rapier-like acidity. They are the only Alsace wines that are not especially enjoyable if drunk young, most requiring at least five years to begin to settle down. In their youth, they have a highly strung, quite taut feel on the palate, leavened with some bracing citric fruit, comparable to freshly squeezed lime juice.

In addition to the basic dry wines, there are two designations for sweeter styles. The lighter of the two is Vendange Tardive (meaning late harvest); in a warm late summer the grapes are left on the vines to achieve higher sugar levels that convert to a delicately sweet wine. In the right conditions, ie. damp misty mornings giving way to mild sunny daytime weather, Riesling will botrytize, just as it does in Germany. The hugely concentrated syrupy wines that result are called Sélection de Grains Nobles – among the most appealingly balanced noble-rotted dessert wines in all of France.

Certain of the best vineyard sites in Alsace have been designated *grands crus* since the mid-1980s. These wines should have a noticeable extra dimension of intensity in the flavour, and are inevitably sold for higher prices. Prominent among the best of the *grand cru* sites for Riesling are Hengst, Rangen, Schoenenberg and Sommerberg. Lower yields contribute to their unearthly concentration.

Steeply shelving vineyards form the backdrop to the typically alsacien *architecture of Trimbach's premises at Ribeauvillé, Alsace (right).*

Other Regions

AUSTRALIA

There was once more Riesling in Australia than there was Chardonnay, which may come as a surprise to those who primarily associate Australian white wine with the sun-drenched oaky flavours of the latter grape. Because it needs a certain amount of acidity to give it sharp definition, Riesling is much more successful in the cooler areas of the country, such as the Clare Valley in South Australia and parts of Western Australia such as Mount Barker.

The Australian style is richer and fatter than the European models. In youth, they have pungent lemon-and-lime fruit and oily texture. Sometimes, most notably in wines from Clare Valley, they also display those heady petrol fumes that German and Alsace Rieslings only tend to take on with bottle-age. Despite their smoother angles, the most sensitively made Australian Rieslings still show good acid balance to maintain that sense of freshness without which Riesling wines are lost.

Many growers are more conscientious about their Riesling than they are about any other variety, ensuring its careful handling every step of the way from harvesting to its treatment in the winery, an approach that is paying off handsomely in the depth and ageing potential the wines now boast.

As well as the dry styles, there are also some extremely fine botrytized Rieslings being made in Australia. Indeed, for many people (myself included), these just have the edge, for

thorough-going complexity and balance, over the country's nobly rotted Semillons. Attaining immense levels of concentration, the wines retain their citric freshness, with a flavour profile like lemon marmalade.

NEW ZEALAND

New Zealand's cooler climes should be ideally suited to the production of good dry Riesling. In fact, there was a tendency until fairly recently to make an indeterminate medium-dry sort of wine, with a twangy, not-quite-wholesome fruit quality not a million miles from boiled sweets. The South Island has lately led the way in producing some fresh, clean, impeccably limey Rieslings of great promise. When vintage conditions permit, many producers also make a botrytized Riesling.

NORTH AMERICA

Cooler parts of California and, particularly, Washington State have seen tentative plantings of Riesling, but it's fair to say the grape has not proved the hottest property commercially in the US. Late-picked Washington versions can be sublime, though. Further north, in Canada, Riesling is turning out some convincing wines in the province of Ontario. Some of Canada's fabled Icewines use Riesling; the best can challenge the pick of German Eiswein.

Harvesting Riesling grapes in the depths of winter (above) in Ontario, Canada. The frozen grapes are destined for Canada's fabled Icewine.

Checking the progress of bunches of ripening Riesling (left), in South Australia's Clare Valley, one of the grape's best growing areas.

MERLOT

Historically used in the blended reds of Bordeaux, Merlot's fame is founded on its partnership with Cabernet Sauvignon. Its reputation as a solo performer has been earned more recently.

FOR WINEMAKERS all over the world, Merlot is the significant other of Cabernet Sauvignon, its truest blending friend and stalwart partner. But whereas Cabernet came to be seen internationally as capable of performing in its own right, Merlot was not generally thought to have the wherewithal to fly solo – at least not at first.

Merlot may have been used unblended for industrial quantities of everyday quaffing wine in northern Italy, but in its homeland of Bordeaux, where it originated, the red wines are always blends. Moreover, the first-growth wines of the Haut-Médoc and Graves are all based on a grape mix in which Cabernet Sauvignon predominates.

And yet, there is far more of Merlot planted in Bordeaux than there is of Cabernet. (It is in fact now the most widely planted grape in France.) While it may be a junior partner on the left bank of the Gironde, though, look to the right bank, and we find the origins of its international reach. In the two best areas here, Pomerol and St-Emilion, Merlot has the starring role.

Some Pomerol properties use virtually all Merlot in their reds; the leader of the pack, Château Pétrus, is nearly all Merlot down to the last five per cent or so of Cabernet Franc. You only have to consider the stratospheric prices commanded by Pétrus to realize that Merlot has no need to hide its light under a bushel of Cabernet Sauvignon. The overall percentage of Merlot in the wines of St-Emilion is a little lower, with proportionately more Cabernet Franc, but it is still the capstone variety, prized for its gentler style.

As in all regions where blended wines are the historical norm, producers will mix and match the proportions of Cabernet and Merlot, depending on vintage conditions. Merlot has the advantage of ripening earlier than Cabernet Sauvignon, meaning that late rain or a sudden cool snap at the end of the growing season,

arriving just in time to spoil the chances of great Cabernet, can be at least partially offset by blending in more of the already-harvested Merlot. Even in the better years (such as 1990), Merlot can often out-perform Cabernet in producing a healthy ripe crop.

Stylistically, what Merlot does for Cabernet in the wines of the Médoc is smooth away some of their harder edges. A claret containing, say,

The plump, blue Merlot (right), an early-ripening grape, produces soft, rich wines – often described as 'fleshy' – that harmonize well with the more structured Cabernet Sauvignon.

35 per cent Merlot will have a softer mouth-feel than one where it is limited to a mere 10 per cent. There is an undoubtedly slightly sweeter edge to it than the surlier Cabernet displays.

Outside Bordeaux, Merlot really started to branch out on its own in the California of the 1980s. Varietal Merlot had been produced there prior to this, but the tendency was, as with the Cabernets, to over-extract its tannins. In the latter part of the 80s, softer, gentler Merlots for everyday drinking began to be made. Its role as a red-wine-without-tears saw plantings increase fivefold in the decade from the mid-80s to the mid-90s as Merlot-mania took hold. Washington State also turns out plenty of uncomplicated, velvet-soft Merlot. The result

of that is that knowledgeable wine enthusiasts have stopped treating Merlot as a serious wine. A rethink among producers is now due.

In the southern hemisphere, it has been a conspicuous success in Chile, where the most ambitious Merlots in districts like Rapel are now beginning to rival Pomerol for sumptuous depth of impact. Argentina's plantings are gaining ground too. Outstanding Merlots are cropping up in South Africa, where a spicy, even gamey complexity distinguishes the best.

In Australia, solo Merlot has only lately begun to find its feet. The grape is still more usually seen as a blending partner for Cabernet after the Bordeaux model, an approach common in New Zealand too.

FRENCH ORIGINS
Bordeaux, especially the Libournais on the right bank of the Gironde, which includes St-Emilion and Pomerol.

WHERE ELSE IS IT GROWN?
Throughout central and eastern Europe, from Switzerland to Bulgaria. United States. Argentina. Some in Chile, Australia, New Zealand, South Africa.

TASTING NOTES
At its ripest, soft purple fruits such as blackberries and black plums. In cooler climates, it can have a distinct vegetal streak in it, like French (green) beans or asparagus. If the sun gets to it, there may be a suggestion of dried fruit such as raisins or even fruitcake. Rounded out with oak in the best wines of Pomerol and California, it can also take on a textural richness that has overtones of melted chocolate or possibly Turkish Delight.

France

The fairy-tale Château Ausone (above), in St-Emilion, set amid its vines.

Merlot's French fiefdom is on the right bank in Bordeaux. There, it dominates the communes of Pomerol and St-Emilion. While red wines from the latter district are characteristically composed of around two-thirds Merlot with perhaps just a splash of Cabernet Sauvignon, in Pomerol the proportion may be more like nine-tenths Merlot, with no Cabernet Sauvignon at all.

Differences in character between the wines of the two communes can be quite marked, with the top wines of Pomerol having a seriousness and austerity about them, together with something of the savoury, herbal overtones found in left-bank Cabernet. St-Emilion wines, on the other hand, for all that there may be less Merlot in them, are often softer and more approachable earlier on. Despite the popular assumption that Merlot-based wines mature more quickly than those dominated by Cabernet Sauvignon, St-Emilions and Pomerols can be quite as long-lived as the finest offerings of the Médoc, as witness Château Pétrus.

In 1955, on the centenary of the original Bordeaux classification, St-Emilion endowed itself with a similar league-table of properties. In contrast to the entrenched near-immutability of the left bank, however, the proprietors of St-Emilion undertook to update their classification every ten years. There may be little change from decade to decade, but that is precisely because they know their wines will be

The legendary Château Pétrus, Pomerol (below). Oil burners are still used in the vineyards as late as May to protect the early-ripening Merlot from frost damage.

rigorously reassessed, and so the motivation to maintain standards is compelling. Top spot is shared by two châteaux: Cheval Blanc and Ausone.

Alone among the premier communes of Bordeaux, Pomerol has never been subjected to the trials of classification, and there are no plans for one. The legendary Pétrus would no doubt occupy pole position in any such notional system, followed by the likes of Châteaux Clinet, l'Evangile, Le Pin, Lafleur, Vieux-Château-Certan and Trotanoy.

Less illustrious Merlot-based wines come from what are known as the satellite areas of St-Emilion, a group of small communes that form a northeasterly fringe to St-Emilion itself, and are all allowed to append its name to their own – Montagne, Lussac, Puisseguin and St-Georges. In good vintages, when the grander properties can fetch dizzyingly high prices for their wines, some of the satellite wines can represent exemplary value. The most aromatically attractive, for my money, tend to come from Puisseguin and Lussac.

Elsewhere, Merlot has made great inroads among the varietal wines being produced in the Languedoc under the catchall Vin de Pays d'Oc designation, and it also has a part to play in some of the traditional appellations of the southwest. In Cahors, for example, it performs its time-honoured diplomatic role, tempering the sternness of the Auxerrois and Tannat grapes.

Rest of the World

UNITED STATES

Merlot is the red wine of choice for those California and Washington wine-drinkers who want the richness and structure of a good red, without having to age it until it's soft enough to drink. In that respect, it's very much Cabernet for beginners. The benchmark style is now ripe red fruit with a lick of sweet oak and gentle tannins. Cooler areas of the eastern States, such as the Long Island AVA, are now producing some more complex wines with something of the structure of Bordeaux.

ITALY

It's fair to say that Merlot doesn't enjoy a particularly exalted reputation in Italy, although large swathes of its wine industry – especially in the northeastern areas of the Veneto, Friuli and Piave – would be lost without it. The tendency is to make a juicy, but light-toned wine, perfectly suited to lunchtime quaffing by the carafe. In hotter years, however, and from producers prepared to limit their yields, there can be a little meaty complexity to the wines.

In the hotbed of viticultural dynamism that is Tuscany, one or two of the smart operators are achieving fine results with Merlot. Producers such as Lodovico Antinori, with his varietal Merlot, Masseto, are showing that the variety can make full-blooded, ageworthy wines that are the equals of the monumental Cabernet and Sangiovese super-Tuscans.

CHILE

Merlot is now responsible for most of the greatest red wines of Chile. It was for a long time mistaken in the vineyards for another grape, Carmenère (also found in Bordeaux), and wines labelled Merlot often have a percentage of Carmenère in them. The fruit expression in these wines is little short of stunning. They age well, but are also drinkable at barely more than a year old. Merlots from Rapel have just about the best price-quality ratio of any red wines in the southern hemisphere.

OTHER SOUTHERN HEMISPHERE

The Australasian countries were late starters in the varietal Merlot stakes, the custom having been to blend it traditionally with Cabernet Sauvignon. Hawkes Bay, New Zealand, is

Merlot is the most widely planted red grape variety in Romania (left), making soft, easy-drinking reds.

responsible for some sharply defined, plummy Merlot now. The Barossa Valley and McLaren Vale are good Australian sources.

In South Africa, especially Stellenbosch, the grape has emerged from its eternal partnership with Cabernet to make some outstandingly complex, full-fleshed wines unblended.

OTHER EUROPE

Merlot has traditionally been a source of soft, everyday reds throughout eastern Europe (especially Bulgaria and Romania), and it enjoys particular favour in parts of Switzerland, producing mostly light, easy-drinking wines in the Italian-speaking southern canton of Ticino.

Barrel cellars at Lodovico Antinori (below), Tuscany. Antinori is one of the band of top Tuscan producers creating stunning varietal Merlots.

CHENIN BLANC

Chenin Blanc's wide stylistic repertoire has made it the focal grape variety in the central vineyards of the Loire valley. Put through its paces in Vouvray, it runs the gamut of dry to sweet, and sparkling, wines.

Chenin Blanc (right) is a high-acid grape that favours the cooler climates of the Loire valley. Here, its acidity and susceptibility to botrytis are its keys to success, making fine sparkling wine and exquisite sweet wines that retain a thread of refreshing sharpness.

PERHAPS THE most misunderstood of all the noble grape varieties, Chenin Blanc is the backbone of white winemaking in the Loire valley. While it undoubtedly has a very distinct and recognizable profile in the wines it can produce, it has experienced difficulties in making friends among consumers for two reasons.

One is that, like Riesling, it has a wide stylistic repertoire, ranging all the way from the uncompromisingly bone-dry to luxurious botrytized dessert wines with decades of ageing potential. Nothing wrong with that, except that, in the past, the labelling on Chenin wines from the Loire has been low on information about the style of the wine.

The other hurdle for newcomers to clear is that the drier wines are not over-endowed with the sort of immediately obvious commercial appeal found in young Sauvignon Blanc. Put crudely, they are quite often not very nice. There is an aromatic character to them, but it is composed of rather weird elements – a mixture of brushed steel, old honey and damp. The classic tasting description often heard is 'wet wool'. Add to that the fact that Chenin is nearly always loaded with teeth-grinding acidity, and it is easier to understand why this is not a grape likely to be top of anyone's list of all-time favourites.

Learning to appreciate Chenin requires a more precise knowledge of when to drink the different styles of wines than is the case with most other white wine varieties.

In the Loire, Vouvray is the most important appellation for Chenin. Its wines span the spectrum from dry to sweet, as well as sparkling wine made by the champagne method. The dry wines, increasingly labelled as such (*sec*) these days, can be delicious immediately on release, when they can display exhilarating fruit flavours, and that boldly assertive acid acts as a seasoning in the way that lemon juice does in a fruit coulis. After a year, they seem to lose that fruit and slump into a prolonged sulk;

tasted again at five or six years old, they have developed a honeyed softness that throws that dryness into relief.

In a hotter vintage, the winemaker may choose to leave some of the ripe natural sugars of the grape in the finished wine. This off-dry or medium-dry style is known as *demi-sec*. It can be the most supremely refreshing example of its kind to be found anywhere in France. The delicate note of lingering sweetness tenderizes the prickly acids in a hugely appetizing way.

If the grapes reach a level of sticky-sweet overripeness that the French call *surmaturité*, then the resulting wine is known as *moelleux*. These are not quite the richest dessert wines – they still have that spiky streak of acidity running through them – but they do have a lush coating of honey and caramel.

In years when botrytis has freely developed, some producers may make a fully botrytized wine. This will often be entitled *Sélection*, because it involves selecting only the most extensively shrivelled berries from the vine, for maximum impact. Even then, the layers of concentrated sweetness have a discernible tartness at the centre, so that the overall effect is more toffee-apple than crème brûlée.

Elsewhere in the world, Chenin's malleability has made it something of a workhorse grape. That is certainly the case in the hotter regions of the United States and Australia, where its most widespread use has been as blending fodder, to add a tingle of acid and prevent basic white wines from tasting flabby. It is very extensively planted in South Africa, where it often goes under the alias of Steen. While a lot of it inevitably disappears into the blending vats, some at least is turned into fresh, fruit-filled, even complex whites of almost miraculous crispness, given the climate.

Grapes with naturally high acidity are often a good bet for the production of champagne-method sparkling wine, where a thin, relatively neutral base wine gives the best results. In the Loire, as well as sparkling Vouvray, Saumur is a good source of such fizz, as is the wider regional appellation of Crémant de Loire.

FRENCH ORIGINS
The central Loire valley –
Anjou-Saumur and Touraine.

WHERE ELSE IS IT GROWN?
South Africa. Also California,
Australia, New Zealand, and
a little in Argentina.

TASTING NOTES
When young and dry, tart green
apple and pear, occasionally
something a little more exotic
(passion fruit) in a good year.
Mineral, even metallic, hardness
on the palate, though often with
paradoxical underlying hint of
honey. Can have a dry nuttiness
(walnuts) and an indeterminately
damp smell, like old newspaper
or wet woollens. Sweeter
styles get progressively more
honeyed without losing the
tingly, appley acidity woven
through them.

Loire

An unusually fine summer's day blazes down on the Chenin vines in the tiny AC of Bonnezeaux in Anjou (below), where some of the Loire's finest botrytized Chenins are produced.

Despite its appearance in many areas outside Europe, no region makes more of Chenin Blanc than does the Loire. It is the most important white grape variety in the two central parts of the valley – Anjou-Saumur to the west, and Touraine in the east.

In Anjou, particularly, cultivating Chenin is something of a challenge. So far north, the grape is a notoriously slow ripener and, as summers in these parts are not exactly torrid, a lot of Anjou Chenin is very acerbic and raw-tasting – not a style that would find many imitators beyond France's borders. Then again, that is exactly how the locals like it to taste.

Autumns, though, are damp and warm enough to permit the regular development of the noble rot, botrytis. It is in Anjou that the premier appellations for botrytized Chenin are found: Coteaux du Layon, which encircles the tiny and very fine enclave of Bonnezeaux (an AOC in its own right), and Quarts de Chaume. In the best years, these wines are fully the equal of great

Sauternes and Barsac, because they have that nerve-centre of acidity that keeps them going into a well-balanced old age.

The lesser-known appellation of Coteaux de l'Aubance makes some reasonably good, though much less rich, sweet wines, from grapes that shrivel on the vines but are only rarely tinged with botrytis. Drink them young.

In the west of Anjou is Savennières, the appellation that many consider to be the highest expression of dry Chenin anywhere in the wine world. In their first flush, these intellectually demanding wines make no concessions to drinkability, tasting hard as nails and tightly clenched. Over maybe seven or eight years, they open out into an austere but profoundly beautiful maturity, full of minerals, bitter apples and bracing Atlantic fresh air. The word 'racy', when applied to wine, might have been coined just for Savennières. Within the appellation is a single-ownership AOC called Coulée-de-Serrant, run along biodynamic principles (see entry, Loire section).

Travelling eastwards into Saumur, we enter fizz territory. Sparkling Saumur is made by fermenting the wine a second time in the bottle to produce carbon dioxide, exactly as for champagne. Made only, or almost entirely, from Chenin, it usually has quite a snap to it, and is dead dry. Served well-chilled on a hot day, it makes an appealing aperitif quaff.

In Touraine, the most important appellation of all for Chenin Blanc is Vouvray. Together with its lesser-known and less distinguished neighbour to the south, Montlouis, Vouvray puts the Chenin through its paces, making it dry, *demi-sec*, *moelleux*, botrytized or fizzy, according to taste. Quality is highly variable, and the wines – as elsewhere – are very vintage-dependent, but when it shines, it really shines.

The wines of the best growers in Vouvray constitute an invaluable introduction to this underestimated grape, with which it is worth persevering. You'll find the odd one that has the mildly vomity smell of dried Parmesan, while others are reminiscent of stale nuts. Then suddenly, there'll be one full of green apple tartness, maybe the sharpness of passion-fruit, with honey lurking underneath, finishing with the taste of freshly shelled walnuts, and you've arrived in Chenin country.

Other Regions

SOUTH AFRICA

Chenin, or Steen as it is very often termed, is put to practically the same sort of versatile use in South Africa as it is in the Loire. It's even used in some of the monumental fortified wines for which the Cape was once famous. Although plantings have fallen off in recent years, this is still the country's most widely grown grape.

At one time, the drier styles didn't tend to be that remarkable, being rather neutral, uninspiring house-white stuff. These days, though, that's all changing. Dry Cape Chenin can now fill the mouth with a gum-cleansing feel like biting into a just-picked apple. They have body and definite varietal identity, and they are full of the sharp aromatic definition more logically to be expected from the cool northerly climate of the Loire. Some producers subject their wines to a modicum of oak, which they seem to take in their stride.

Fantastic wines are made from noble-rotted Chenin, when the flavours of tropical fruit, honey, bitter orange peel and barley-sugar all seem to mingle in what are some of the world's most diverting sweet wines.

AUSTRALIA AND NEW ZEALAND

Not many other non-European producers have taken Chenin seriously yet as the base for a varietal wine. There is a tendency to try to make it too rich for its own good by muffling its acidity. Plump, oak-enriched examples crop up in the Swan Valley GI in Western Australia, although the cool climate of New Zealand is a more likely setting for successful Chenin. Some varietal Chenin from the North Island has looked good, but again the tendency is towards a high-extract style.

CALIFORNIA

One or two California wineries have produced convincing varietal dry Chenin, some of it oak-aged. The wines articulate the tart fruit and balancing honey tones of Vouvray, for all that they are appreciably fatter-textured. Otherwise, Chenin goes into everyday blended whites to lend added acidity.

Chenin Blanc, or Steen, vines on the Klein Constantia Estate, South Africa (above). Chenin has been the backbone of the country's white wine production.

Widely spaced Chenin Blanc vines in the Temecula valley, California (left), where the variety is still a minority taste.

VIOGNIER

Viognier's career as an internationally known grape variety has only been very recently established. It is safe to say that, before the early 1990s, the ordinary consumer had probably never heard of it.

THE RISE TO prominence of Viognier over the past decade has been meteoric. Once a niche variety whose name was rarely seen on labels, it is now everywhere, either on its own, or quite often blended in a double-act with Chardonnay. That last detail is a little ironic, as the chief impetus for everybody suddenly deciding to plant the variety was to fulfil the demands of that section of the market that was getting a little tired of subsisting on an unrelieved diet of Chardonnay.

Its spiritual home is in a small appellation at the northern end of the northern sector of the Rhône, called Condrieu. The wines of Condrieu were once one of the wine world's best-kept secrets, and they owed their opulent, perfumed appeal entirely to the Viognier grape. Most often vinified without oak, these are wines that combine the heady, musky scents of ripe orchard fruits (classically apricots) with some powerful spice tones such as cinnamon and cardamom, backed up by big burly texture and high alcohol.

Elsewhere in the region, it is the only permitted grape in the white wines of a micro-appellation within Condrieu, called Château-Grillet, where the wine is made entirely by one producer. It is also, as we saw when discussing Syrah, entitled to form up to 20 per cent of a blend in the red wines of Côte-Rôtie, to which it can contribute an unearthly, often ravishing, layer of floral scent.

When the revolution in French winemaking of the late 1980s established the Languedoc as the nerve-centre of varietal experimentation, Viognier rapidly became one of the favoured grapes of that region. It wasn't that long a journey after all from the northern Rhône, although Vin de Pays d'Oc Viognier is a much simpler and less elegant wine than Condrieu (as well it might be, given the price differential).

As might be guessed from its location in southern France, the variety prefers a fairly warm climate, which is why it has proved particularly suitable for planting in the southern

hemisphere and in the warmer regions of California. The only possible disadvantage to that is that it can lack a little acidity in very warm vintages, which then leaves its fruit flavours tasting slightly mushy. What that in mind, the most conscientious producers pay careful attention to picking times to ensure that the wine retains a freshening lemony streak for balance.

We can perhaps understand why the world was ready for something other than Chardonnay, but why Viognier? The answer to this lies in the immense increase in fashionability that the wines of the Rhône came to enjoy from the 1980s onwards, and which shows no sign of abating. In the northern Rhône especially, Syrah and Viognier played the same pre-eminent role in the vineyards as Cabernet and Chardonnay did elsewhere, and their flavours were seen as usefully distinctive.

Viognier has the structure of the richest Chardonnays, but without needing oak to lend it aromatic personality. It belongs with that category of white wine grapes considered to be naturally aromatic, along with the likes of Gewürztraminer, Riesling and Muscat.

In California, certain quality-conscious producers have achieved results with Viognier that are every bit as gorgeously rich and exotic as the best of Condrieu. There has been a slightly greater tendency to reach for the oak barrel here, but the concentration and extract of the wines is such that they take some judicious wood-ageing in their stride.

The Australians were a little slower off the mark than their American counterparts with Viognier, the variety only starting to become fashionable there in the mid-1990s. Site specification is all. In the hotter districts, the results have been too heavy and clumsy for comfort, but the potential is undoubtedly there, and we can expect to see some more distinguished examples in years to come.

Demand for cuttings of the grape has also rocketed in South America, where both Chile and Argentina are producing convincingly perfumed, unexpectedly subtle Viognier wines with good fruit-acid balance.

Viognier (right) has become undoubtedly one of the most fashionable white grape varieties on the international scene, producing aromatic, spicy wines everywhere from the south of France to the hotter regions of Australia.

FRENCH ORIGINS
Northern Rhône.

WHERE ELSE IS IT GROWN?
Increasingly important in the southern Rhône, Languedoc and Roussillon. Outside Europe, now fashionable in California, Australia, Chile and Argentina.

TASTING NOTES
Its most widely noticed fruit flavour is apricot, which can range from the free-flowing juice and flesh of a fresh ripe Bergeron fruit to the concentrated muskiness of dried Hunzas. Scented white peach may be in there too, and ripe aromatic Comice pear. Supporting that may be subtly delineated spice notes like cardamom, cinnamon or ginger, while the texture of the wine is close-grained and thick like clotted cream. From the hotter regions, it may be distinctly reminiscent of honey-and-lemon throat-soothers.

France

Château-Grillet (above), in its amphitheatre of vines above the river Rhône at Vérin, is one of the smallest appellations in France.

Viognier vines on the Coteau de Vernon (below), from which are made the top wine of Domaine Georges Vernay, long celebrated as one of the most illustrious producers in the whole Condrieu appellation.

The top wines of Condrieu still probably represent the finest expressions of the Viognier grape variety grown anywhere. Other than in the very best Californian examples, it is only really here that the full complexity locked within the grape blossoms forth. For such a small appellation, there is also an intriguing range of styles.

A handful of producers use a touch of oak to round out the texture of the wine and deepen its aromatic impact. It is certainly true that a lick of vanilla, if sensitively applied, can enhance the natural creamy ripeness of the grape in warm vintages, but over-ageing in wood can muddy the waters.

There are also different schools of thought as to how rich and powerful the wine should naturally be, with some preferring an almost delicate, floral style of Condrieu, while others go down the big and blowsy route, emphasizing big alcohol, dense texture and decadently ripe aromas. There are persuasive examples of Viognier in both camps, and indeed it is this very versatility that makes this one of the most fascinating appellations in the whole Rhône valley.

Wholly enclosed with the Condrieu zone is the separate appellation of Château-Grillet which, like certain Burgundy *grands crus*, is exclusively owned by one producer. The style here is quite distinct from Condrieu, with the wine being cask-aged and only released after the next vintage has been made. As a result, the fruit tones are much more muted, leaving just the heftiness of the wine's texture to appreciate.

Many growers in the bulk-producing region of the southern Rhône are now looking to Viognier to add a little aromatic character to their white wines, which have traditionally been rather neutral in flavour. Even so, it is extremely unusual to come across wines that are made from unblended Viognier.

For solo Viognier at kinder prices, it is necessary to head a little further south to the Languedoc, where this grape has become something of a buzz varietal. The wines here don't attempt anything like the complexity of Condrieu, but then the vines themselves are not nearly as ancient. A mouthful of very fresh, apricotty or peachy white, usually unoaked, is to be expected, along with strong alcohol (typically 13.5 per cent), and an often slightly overdone acidic streak with the pronounced flavour of lemon juice. These wines are generally for drinking young, but can benefit from a little ageing to tone down the acidity. They can make a good, if heady, aperitif.

Other Regions

CALIFORNIA

Without a doubt, the best examples of unblended Viognier outside France are being produced in California, specifically in the Napa Valley. Tasted blind, the finest bottlings are all but indistinguishable from best Condrieu, imitating not only the ripe yellow fruits and Indian spices of the Rhône stars, but also their lush, floral, creamy style too. There is also the same debate as to whether oak-ageing suits the wines or not, with exponents of both styles producing some stunning wines. By acclamation, the star winemaker here has been Josh Jensen of Calera, whose small quantities of scintillating wines are as much sought-after (and as hard to find) as the top Condrieus.

At the lower end of the price range, and especially from the northerly Mendocino AVA, there can be a tendency in the wines to that slightly confected honey-and-lemon flavour of proprietary throat-sweets, with all the floral charm and the exotic spice notes missing. However much refined sensibilities may be offended by such tastes, though, these have proved commercially popular wines with the ABC (Anything but Chardonnay) contingent, and plantings of Viognier are on the increase. Quality will undoubtedly continue to improve.

SOUTH AMERICA

Varietal Viogniers from Argentina and Chile have been making their presence felt in the export markets since the late 1990s. The style tends to be big and alcoholic, as elsewhere, but with a little of the honeysuckle charm of Rhône Viognier in the better efforts. Both countries favour an unoaked style over cask-ageing, but with strength prevailing over grace. A strong lemony note underpins the peachy fruit, and the finish may often be quite spirity. Creditable showings have been made by certain of the volume producers in both countries, and we must expect this to be an important varietal in the future.

Joseph Phelps Vineyards (above), at St Helena, in Napa County, California, has been among the trailblazers for varietal Viognier in what many now regard as its second home after the Rhône.

AUSTRALIA

The honey-and-lemon tendency still vitiates too many of Australia's efforts with Viognier, for all that there are plenty of suitable sites for growing it. Top bottlings can have the structure and intensity as those of the Rhône big boys, but without the aromatic finesse or the subtleties to back them up. The McLaren Vale GI has so far been the most promising stamping-ground.

More eye-catching perhaps than varietal Viognier from Australia has been the practice of adding it to Shiraz to produce a southern-hemisphere homage to those Côte-Rôties that have a little Viognier in the blend. There is something peculiar but compelling in finding a waft of clean apricot scent emerging through the inky-dark, blackberry style of strapping Aussie Shiraz. Producers in the Yarra Valley, Victoria, and South Australia's McLaren Vale and Langhorne Creek GIs, have made waves in recent vintages.

A gum tree in the Heggies vineyard of Yalumba (left), in the Eden Valley, South Australia. Viogniers from regions as hot as this usually have the structure and alcohol levels of certain Rhône examples, though perhaps don't always have the same aromatic finesse.

GEWURZTRAMINER

Unique among the white varieties, Gewürztraminer is very much a love-it-or-hate-it grape. Once tasted, never forgotten, its ostentatious, scented, rich character has made it the grape forever associated with Alsace.

WHETHER OR NOT you enjoyed it, your first taste of Gewürztraminer is likely to have made an impression. While a simple Chardonnay may seem shy and retiring in the glass, Gewürz comes screaming out at you with some of the most unearthly and downright bizarre scents and flavours to be found anywhere in the world of wine. So strange can it taste that those encountering it unexpectedly for the first time may wonder whether it has had some other flavouring added to it.

The parent variety seems to be of north Italian extraction, in a grape known simply as Traminer. Its highly scented offshoot, first identified in the 19th century, took its prefix from the German word for 'spice'. By this time, the grape had acquired, by natural mutation, a deep pink skin in place of the green one, and had begun to yield an extraordinarily perfumed juice. Popular in Germany, Gewürz was widely planted in Alsace during the period of the region's absorption into Germany in the late 19th century.

Alsace, now incontrovertibly French, is the variety's first home today. While there are increasingly impressive examples being produced elsewhere, particularly in Germany, they never quite seem to attain the uninhibited aromatic splendour of the greatest Alsace Gewürz. In an especially ripe year, it may combine musky fruit notes like lychee and squishy apricot, with ginger, cloves, talcum powder, and a whole florist's shop of roses, violets and jasmine. It is usually pretty low in acidity, which makes it drinkable quite young, but roaring with alcohol, so that a little – combined with those unsubtle flavours – goes an exhaustingly long way.

Because of its larger-than-life character, Gewürz is constantly in danger of not being taken terribly seriously by those who are used to more restrained flavours in a white wine. In the long dry summers of Alsace, it ripens to a tremendous richness, which accounts for all that alcohol, but even when fermented up to around the 14–15 per cent levels I have seen on some, it still seems to retain a core of residual sugar that leads a lot of consumers to find it too sweet for a supposedly dry wine.

Once the taste is acquired, however, it becomes clear that Gewürztraminer is without doubt one of the classic wine grapes. From a *grand cru* vineyard site owned by one of the top producers in Alsace, its peculiar intensity can be a mightily refreshing antidote to the containerloads of tell-em-apart Chardonnay that the wine market is still awash with. The best Gewürzes will age, although they tend to be the ones that have unusually pronounced acidity to begin with, and there are not too many of these. You can bump up acid levels by picking the grapes earlier, but then you risk losing some of that striking flavour.

The dilemma over picking times is problem enough in Alsace. In warmer climates, it becomes a complete headache. The difficulties of timing it right account for why most efforts outside Alsace have so far failed to match the quality of the best wines produced in this one enclave of northeastern France. That said, some German growers are beginning to achieve convincing results with the variety, especially in the slightly warmer areas of the Pfalz and Baden. New Zealand is giving it its best shot, and there are isolated stars in Chile and the United States. One or two South African examples have been particularly exciting.

For a grape that seems to be telling the winemaker that it wants to be sweet, it comes as no surprise to find that many Alsace and German growers make a late-picked Gewürz in the form of flowery Spätlese and Auslese in Germany, and peach-scented Vendange Tardive in Alsace. When conditions are right, the grape can acquire botrytis, and a fully rotted wine is labelled Sélection de Grains Nobles in Alsace. These are massively dense, opulent dessert wines, tasting like orange and ginger marmalade – one of the great taste experiences. They can age for many years in the bottle.

The unmistakable livery of the Gewürztraminer grape (right). Unlike the green or golden colour of its fellow white grapes, Gewürz sports a dusky pink skin – a fitting outer expression of its flowery, highly perfumed character.

ORIGINS

For the Gewürztraminer specifically, possibly Alsace. For its less intoxicatingly scented forebear, Traminer, probably the south Tyrol area of northern Italy.

WHERE ELSE IS IT GROWN?

Apart from Alsace, it has important bases in Germany and Austria, less so in Spain and eastern Europe. Experimental plantings dotted around the southern hemisphere, and also the United States, particularly the Pacific Northwest.

TASTING NOTES

The list is well-nigh endless. Fruits are usually an eerily precise imitation of ripely juicy lychees, together with overripe peach or nectarine when the flesh is just starting to turn mushy. Some authorities dispute the spice connection evoked in the German word *Gewürz*, but there is nearly always a good sprinkling of ground ginger and often cinnamon, occasionally the scent of whole cloves and even a dusting of white pepper. Flowers are very much in evidence too – violets and rose-petals (often reminiscent of attar of roses, as in Turkish Delight) – and then there is a whole range of scented bathroom products – aromatic bath salts, perfumed soap, talcum powder. Gewürz from regions other than Alsace may present a toned-down version of all that, which may come as a relief to some.

Alsace

Gewurztraminer (spelt without the *umlaut* in France) accounts for just under a fifth of total vineyard plantings in Alsace. It is one of the favoured grapes permitted in the designated *grand cru* areas. Although Riesling is unofficially thought of as the first among this top division by the growers themselves, Gewurz is cherished for the forthright character that has made it the grape most ineradicably associated in consumers' minds with the region as a whole. Blowsy, spicy, exotic Gewurz just is the taste of Alsace.

The grape does exceptionally well on the often rather claggy clay-based soils found in the Haut-Rhin area of Alsace. Its willingness to ripen well in the generally dry vintages of this very sheltered region allows its personality to shine through in the finished wine. In many ways, it is the antithesis in Alsace of the Riesling we looked at earlier, giving more alcohol and less acidity, resulting in a considerably more forward style of wine.

Another quality that marks Gewurz wines out from their counterparts is their very deep

The Clos Windsbuhl vineyard at Hunawihr, owned by Zind-Humbrecht (below). The Gewurztraminer from this site is one of the finest examples of what Alsace Gewurz can achieve.

colour. They usually have a richly burnished golden tone, not dissimilar to the most heavily oaked Chardonnays, a characteristic derived in Gewurz's case not from wooden barrels but from the distinctive pigmentation of the grapeskin. Whereas most white varieties come in conventional shades of green, Gewurz, as befits its gaudy nature, is turned out in a deep pink livery that lends some of its blush to the wine itself, very occasionally showing even as a faint pinkish tinge behind the deep yellow.

In the cooler years in Alsace, Gewurztraminer can seem a rather pale imitation of itself, both in terms of colour and flavours. The vintage of 2001 wasn't particularly good, for example, and the wines' resulting balance was seriously skewed, leaving an overall impression of weight, but without the depth of flavour to carry it off with any grace.

The classification of the *grand cru* sites came into effect in Alsace in the 1980s. While dogged inevitably by controversy over what should be included and what not, it has since emerged

that much of the land that has been incorporated is of sufficient quality to inspire the producers to their greatest efforts. Of the 51 sites, some of the best for Gewurztraminer are Brand, Goldert, Hengst, Kessler, Sporen, Steinert and Zotzenberg, but there are many more.

Wines with those names on the label are undoubtedly worth the extra cost over a bottle of everyday Gewurz. Many producers are in the habit of labelling their wines Cuvée Réserve or something similar, supposedly indicating notably successful batches of a particular vintage, but these terms, unlike *grand cru*, have no legal force.

What is probably more important than anything pertaining to labelling in Alsace is the grape yields. Almost without exception, the best wines, whatever their designation, are sourced from older, lower-yielding vines. Much more

than about 50 hectolitres per hectare, and you're liable to produce a wine that lacks true focus, while some of the finest wines are being vinified off barely more than 25 hl/ha. It may cost twice as much, but then you're buying twice the concentration, and concentrated flavours are what Alsace is all about.

Cooperatives are an important part of the wine scene in Alsace, and vary enormously in quality, but one of the most commercially significant, exporting substantial quantities – the Caves de Turckheim – is one of the most reliable. At the stratospheric end of the spectrum, wines from some of the old-established family vineyards, particularly some of the Vendange Tardive bottlings from *grand cru* sites like Hengst and Goldert, are unutterably exquisite, powerful essences of this most ostentatious grape.

Gewurztraminer grapes left on the vine until November (above), destined for the peach-scented style of Alsace Vendange Tardive.

Other Regions

GERMANY
Although plantings of Gewürztraminer in Germany are by no means extensive, some German growers have achieved notable successes with it in the light-textured, low-alcohol styles for which the country is renowned. It fares better in the warmer regions such as Baden in the south, and the Pfalz, where its best manifestations are brimful of expressive ripe fruit.

UNITED STATES
As others of the Alsace grapes, such as Riesling and Pinot Gris, have thrived in the states of the Pacific Northwest, so Gewürz has also done its bit. Success has come patchily, and the results are not as yet much exported. There are some reasonably tasty examples in Washington State, including a handful of delicate but attractive late-harvest versions.

NEW ZEALAND AND AUSTRALIA
The cooler climate of New Zealand is better for Gewürz than most of Australia (where the grape has often been used simply as blending material for dry Riesling). The North Island regions of Gisborne and Auckland, as well as Central Otago on the South Island, have produced some convincing attempts, but the weight is often lacking, and the perfume more fugitive.

ELSEWHERE
The occasional quietly impressive Gewürz does crop up in other countries, for all that we don't really want Gewürz to be quiet. Chile has some properly scented wines, and one or two South African growers are getting the hang of it rather impressively. It has proved to be a useful blender with Muscat in Penedés in northeastern Spain, especially from Torres.

Matua Valley Winery, set amid its vineyards in the Auckland area of New Zealand's North Island (above). Matua Valley is one of New Zealand's most notable producers of characterful Gewürztraminer.

GAMAY

The one classic grape variety that has stayed close to home, Gamay is synonymous with Beaujolais, that light, fresh, strawberry-fruity red that is mostly designed to be drunk young and lively, but whose best wines will age.

LOOKING AT a map of the world distribution of grape varieties might seem to suggest that Gamay is something of an interloper among our exalted company of 12 noble grapes. A red blob shows a significant concentration of it in eastern France, with only the skimpiest of traces anywhere else. In fact, it gets in because that red blob constitutes one of the world's most individualistic red wine styles – Beaujolais.

Gamay is the only grape used in the making of (red) Beaujolais. Some of it is also grown further north, in the southern stretch of Burgundy known as the Mâconnais, where it's responsible for usually rather indifferent wines bottled as Mâcon Rouge. Elsewhere, it may be blended in a proportion of up to two-thirds with Pinot Noir to make Bourgogne Passetoutgrains. A fair bit is grown in the Loire valley to the west, some as Touraine Gamay, some used in Crémant de Loire pink fizz. On the western flank of the central Rhône, in the Coteaux de l'Ardèche, it makes spicy reds to rival the Grenache-based wines of Côtes du Rhône.

It is on the stern granite hillsides of Beaujolais, however, that Gamay really comes into its own. In addition to basic Beaujolais and Beaujolais-Villages, there are ten villages that are theoretically capable of making the best wine (known as *cru* Beaujolais), and which have their their own appellations within the region. Running north to south, these are: St-Amour, Juliénas, Chénas, Moulin-à-Vent, Fleurie, Chiroubles, Morgon, Régnié, Brouilly and Côte de Brouilly. The last is a peculiar little hill of blue granite that pops up in the middle of the larger Brouilly appellation.

There are some subtle stylistic differences among these ten, but what links them is more important than what distinguishes them, and that is the sunny-natured Gamay grape. Gamay offers the lightest possible style of red wine, full of simple strawberry fruit, fresh sappy acids,

and little or no tannin. Although the best growers do achieve a certain measure of complexity in their wines, and some of the best *cru* Beaujolais can age well for five or six years, most producers are content to turn out oceans of straightforward quaffing wine that reacts appetizingly to chilling for summer drinking.

The light texture of Beaujolais derives from a method of vinification called carbonic maceration, to which Gamay is especially suited. Instead of being crushed in the normal way, which extracts some tannin from the skins and pips along with the juice, the grapes are tipped whole into fermenters from which the air has been driven out with carbon dioxide. The juice starts to ferment inside the whole grapes, until the skins burst from the build-up of gas within them. The grapes at the bottom of the heap are punctured by the weight of those on top, and ferment in the normal way, but that is still gentler than most assisted forms of pressing.

Gamay's suitability for producing cheap, early-drinking, featherweight reds is what inspired the marketing of Beaujolais Nouveau, which continues to this day. Those who feel like imbibing quantities of embryonic, just-fermented, acid-tingling red from the very latest vintage can indulge their passion freely in the third week of November.

There is a movement afoot in the region to introduce greater depth into the wines in an attempt to throw the happy-go-lucky, knock-it-back image of Beaujolais into some sort of relief. Some are using a proportion of normally fermented juice in order to inject a little tannic kick; others are ageing in new oak barrels in a region where such a thing was once anathema. Such courageous swimming against the tide has resulted in top *cuvées* of *cru* Beaujolais that have the gingery, brambly concentration of northern Rhône Syrah (no, really).

External markets are still dominated by the wines of the powerful bulk producer Georges Duboeuf. For once, quantity does not preclude quality because most of the company's wines are good, and easily recognizable by their distinctive flower labels.

Gamay (right) offers the lightest style of red wine, full of simple strawberry fruit, fresh, sappy acids and very little tannin.

About 10 per cent of the vineyard land in Switzerland is planted with Gamay, where it is often blended with the far more widely grown Pinot Noir, and there are one or two producers in California doing their best with it, and achieving reasonable approximations of the style of young *cru* Beaujolais.

By and large, however, Gamay hasn't performed well on soils different to those of its native region. Coupled with the fact that the style of wine it is happiest producing has not been a noticeably fashionable one for red wines in recent years, there isn't the incentive that there is with a variety like Pinot Noir to compete with the best of France. All of which is a shame because, when on song, Gamay is among the most effortlessly charming styles of young red wine. (Its rosés, by contrast, are probably best passed over in silence.)

Misty autumnal scene in Brouilly (left), one of the ten crus of the Beaujolais region.

FRENCH ORIGINS
Beaujolais.

WHERE ELSE IS IT GROWN?
Burgundy, Loire, Rhône. Switzerland and other central European countries. Minute amounts in California.

TASTING NOTES
At its deliriously ripest, fistfuls of pulpy wild strawberries. When very young (as Nouveau, particularly) it can have a synthetic smell like boiled sweets, reinforced by the crunchiness of its acidity in the mouth. That, and related aromas like peardrops (pear candy), banana flavouring and bubblegum, are all fermentation smells accentuated by the fact that no air gets into it while it is vinifying. Some of the richer, meatier *cru* wines can take on the attributes of mature Pinot Noir after five or six years.

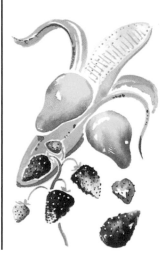

FRANCE

1994
GALET
VINEYARDS
Merlot

PRODUIT DE FRANCE
VIN DE PAYS D'OC
VINIFIÉ ET MIS EN BOUTEILLE PAR
GABRIEL MEFFRE, 84190 FRANCE

75cl ℮

The Loire valley region is famed for its many riverside châteaux of great opulence, like this one (above) at Azay-le-Rideau, on the Indre tributary, southwest of Tours.

The historical pre-eminence of France as the world's foremost wine-producing nation is under threat as never before. As consumers over the past quarter-century have discovered the wines of sunnier climes, with their easily comprehensible labels, pronounceable names, and big, ripe, readily accessible fruit flavours, the country that once lorded it over the whole viticultural world has been left in crisis.

Not only is French wine struggling for market share among what were once its most reliable customers (its slice of the UK retail action finally dropped below 15 per cent at the beginning of the present decade), but the French wine industry itself has become prone to outbreaks of panic. Internecine arguments about quality control, a hostile, even xenophobic, attitude in some quarters to incoming winemakers from abroad, and the clenched-teeth refusal more widely of any acknowledgement that the produce of other wine countries might compare to it, has led its wine industry into a period of sullen retrenchment that can only be wholly self-defeating. Something has to change.

The first straw in the wind came as long ago as 1976, when a young English wine merchant with a business in Paris staged a comparative blind tasting of premium wines from France and California. The American wines, sun-soaked Cabernet Sauvignons and Chardonnays chancing their arms against the French viticultural aristocracy of Bordeaux and Burgundy, emerged as the overwhelming winners, the victory all the sweeter for the fact that the greater part of the tasting panel was composed of French experts. News of the results received very short shrift in the French media (where they were reported at all, that is), but the storm-cones had been hoisted.

In one sense at least, it isn't hard to feel sympathetic to those French *vignerons* who are tired of being reminded of the findings of this tasting, and many thousands of others like it in the years since. They are not intentionally making wines to compete with, rival, imitate or outclass the products of other cultures. Their wines have their own specific identities; they are, at their best, highly individual expressions of their environments, and the practices and

France's appellation contrôlée *regions (right), from the cool vineyards of Champagne to the hotter regions of the Midi in the south.*

1. BORDEAUX
2. LOIRE
3. CHAMPAGNE
4. ALSACE
5. BURGUNDY
6. RHÔNE
7. PROVENCE
8. LANGUEDOC-ROUSSILLON
9. GASCONY & SOUTHWEST
10. JURA
11. SAVOIE & BUGEY
12. CORSICA

philosophies of the winemakers. Then again, it's hard to argue with the miserable brute fact of plummeting market share.

Sooner or later, all what-is-to-be-done? arguments about the French wine crisis get round to raising the question of the AOC system. This is the framework by which the country's wines are graded in quality, with the highest designation – *appellation d'origine contrôlée* – sitting above the progressively humbler *vin de pays* or IGP (*indication géographique protégée*) regional wines and, since 2009, *vins de France*, wines that can be blended from different regions. It's all so complicated, so bureaucratic, and allegedly operates too much like a cartel.

We can safely dispense with this line of argument for a number of reasons. The AOC regulations have been overwhelmingly a force for good since they began to be formulated in the 1930s. They have given legal standing, institutional integrity and binding definition to the best wines of France, in many cases ratifying the status of already celebrated wines, in many others making possible the elevation of the overall quality of a previously humdrum region's production. The system is flexible in that it allows for promotions (from *vin de pays* to AOC, for example), and it is based on empirical observations of which grapes work best in which soils, how they should be vinified, and so forth.

Yes, the system is complicated in the sense that there are hundreds of wine regions to classify, but what's the alternative? Dividing the whole of France into North, South, East and West, and leaving it at that? How is that going to enlighten the consumer? I'm not for a minute suggesting the framework is infallible, and indeed far too many sub-standard wines do slip through the assessments of the regional tasting panels, but the challenge is to make the system work better, not abandon it altogether, as many external commentators (and even some within the French industry itself) keep naively insisting.

There is, moreover, no better argument for the logical force and benign impact of a system of controlled appellations than the fact that every wine-producing country on the planet has either introduced one, or is in the process of doing so. Certainly, the regulations may be looser in Australia, say, than in France, but the geographical principle – the idea that wine is at its best when it tastes as though as it comes from Somewhere rather than Anywhere – has been accepted as a spur to quality all over the viticultural world.

Where I think France is in difficulties at present is the too often uncomfortable gap that exists between the best and the least impressive wines of each area. To its credit, the Bordeaux region, responsible for the lion's share of the country's finest reds, began to look seriously in the 1990s at its often frankly disastrous performance at the lower end of the quality scale, where it has been decisively elbowed aside by riper, fruitier wines from the southern hemisphere. Gradually, the picture here has improved.

What too many consumers find, however, is that when they venture into the market to try one of the many appellation wines, they find themselves choosing between dull generic wines made or bottled by big companies and the almost invariably unaffordable, and much rarer, wines of the most celebrated growers. That creates more of a toxic sense of commercial apartheid than is generated by any of the New World countries.

I remain, indomitably, unrepentantly, a Francophile. When they perform at the top of their game, French wines are regularly among the most exciting in the world. That they should have had to surrender the limelight to other wine countries was always inevitable – and right. But if they become hopelessly marginalized by a combination of implacable indifference on one side of the counter and consumer prejudice on the other, we will have lost one of the Western world's outstanding cultural achievements.

Dusk descends over vineyards in Corbières, in the Languedoc (above).

Ancient presses in the underground cellars at Gaston Huët (above), producer of fine sparkling Saumur, Loire.

BORDEAUX-*Red*

Occupying a position at the pinnacle of world winemaking, the grand châteaux of Bordeaux produce fine clarets and sweet whites in a landscape that could not have been better designed for growing vines.

BORDEAUX-RED

GRAPES: Cabernet Sauvignon, Merlot, Carmenère, Cabernet Franc, Malbec, Petit Verdot

The Bordeaux region lies within the Gironde département. *The Médoc is a narrow strip on the left bank of the Gironde estuary. Upstream, the river Garonne provides the damp climate so suitable for the botrytized wines of Sauternes.*

THE RED WINES OF Bordeaux – or clarets, as they are known in the English-speaking world – have long been synonymous with the popular image of fine wine. If the region's profile has tended to be higher than that of its great rival, Burgundy, that is partly because the trade in fine red Bordeaux has been of paramount international significance, and also because there is just hugely more wine produced in Bordeaux than there is in Burgundy.

At the top of the tree sit the wines enshrined in the 1855 regional classification (more of which below), as well as those from districts considered their equals, notably Pomerol and St-Emilion. It is these that provide the archetype for the notion that red wines improve with age, as they go on developing in the bottle, sometimes for decades, occasionally emerging in parcels from private cellars to be sold at auction, and realizing a tidy profit for the investor.

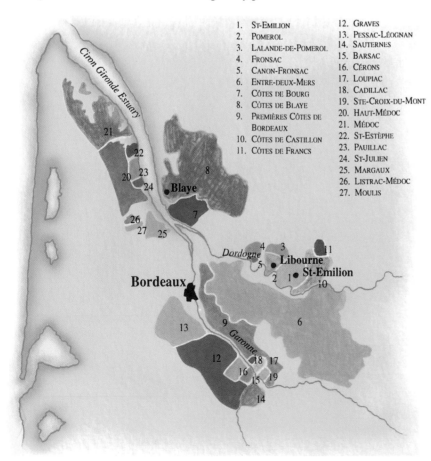

1. ST-EMILION
2. POMEROL
3. LALANDE-DE-POMEROL
4. FRONSAC
5. CANON-FRONSAC
6. ENTRE-DEUX-MERS
7. CÔTES DE BOURG
8. CÔTES DE BLAYE
9. PREMIÈRES CÔTES DE BORDEAUX
10. CÔTES DE CASTILLON
11. CÔTES DE FRANCS
12. GRAVES
13. PESSAC-LÉOGNAN
14. SAUTERNES
15. BARSAC
16. CÉRONS
17. LOUPIAC
18. CADILLAC
19. STE-CROIX-DU-MONT
20. HAUT-MÉDOC
21. MÉDOC
22. ST-ESTÈPHE
23. PAUILLAC
24. ST-JULIEN
25. MARGAUX
26. LISTRAC-MÉDOC
27. MOULIS

Say you don't have a private cellar, though (neither do I). In that case, you can either start your own little collection in the garage, or else buy from one of the many independent wine merchants who specialize in occasional purchases of good mature vintages. But either way, you can't avoid the crucial issue, which is that the overwhelming majority of Bordeaux reds need ageing. Ten years isn't a bad rule of thumb for most; the best may well need considerably longer than that.

During the economic boom-time of the 1980s, a trend for buying claret directly from the château in the spring following the vintage, before it's even been bottled, for delivery at a later date – a deal known as buying *en primeur* – became the smart way to invest. It's certainly cheaper in the long run than waiting until the retailers have bought the wine themselves, and then paying their mark-ups. It is now increasingly coming under fire from within the region for its tendency to provoke winemakers to produce overly forward, upfront wines that will taste good enough to buy at six months old, which is not at all what fine Bordeaux is traditionally about.

Drunk in its youth, a good claret is really wasted. It will be tight and tough in texture, and rigid with tannin. After around five or six years, it can begin to soften up a bit and allow some of the blackcurrant or plum fruit of Cabernet or Merlot grapes to shine forth. Then, in a curious, little-understood development, it will seem to withdraw into a sulky state (known in the lingo as 'dumb'), only blossoming again a few years later, with its fruit still intact, but now deepened with all sorts of complex additional (or 'secondary') scents and flavours.

Great if you can afford it. But if you can't?

That leaves the rest of the market to be mopped up by the everyday produce of the big wine companies, and here is where the problem has traditionally started. Cheap generic Bordeaux can be unattractive at best. Produced from underripe, over-cropped grapes and churned out in bulk for the mass market, it can be vile. That said, the Bordelais have been looking to their laurels since the 1990s, reducing overall production in the region, and even – *quelle horreur!* – studying the Cabernet and Merlot wines of their non-European rivals to see what they might do better.

The Bordeaux classification formulated for the Paris Exhibition of 1855 is a five-tier hierarchy based on the commercial value of the properties listed at the time. It covers only the Haut-Médoc, plus Château Haut-Brion in the Graves. The Graves itself was classified in the 1950s, along with St-Emilion, but Pomerol has never been classified.

To a surprising degree, much of the classification holds good, but properties change hands, expand into new vineyard land, employ new winemakers, and find their standards inevitably fluctuating with the vagaries of successive vintages.

That leaves the individual consumer in the happy position of offering his or her own periodic reassessments. I've rated the properties in the 1855 table below in accordance with the general consensus as to their relative performances over the past 30 years, a period that ranges from difficult vintages like 1984, 1991 and 2002 to the out-and-out stunners like 1982, 1989, 1990, 2000 and 2005.

1855 AND ALL THAT

(Appellation shown in brackets – P = Pauillac, M = Margaux, P-L = Pessac-Léognan, *formerly Graves,* S-J = St-Julien, S-E = St-Estèphe, H-M = Haut-Médoc)

First Growth/1er cru

Lafite-Rothschild (P) ***** Margaux (M) ***** Latour (P) ***** Haut-Brion (P-L) ***** Mouton-Rothschild (P) *****

Second Growth/2ème cru

Rauzan-Ségla, *formerly Rausan-Ségla* (M) **** Rauzan-Gassies (M) ** Léoville-Las Cases (S-J) ***** Léoville-Poyferré (S-J) **** Léoville-Barton (S-J) **** Durfort-Vivens (M) *** Lascombes (M) *** Brane-Cantenac (M) *** Pichon-Longueville, *formerly Pichon-Longueville Baron* (P) ***** Pichon-Longueville Comtesse de Lalande, *formerly Pichon-Lalande* (P) ***** Ducru-Beaucaillou (S-J) **** Cos d'Estournel (S-E) ***** Montrose (S-E) **** Gruaud-Larose (S-J) ****

Third Growth/3ème cru

Kirwan (M) *** d'Issan (M) *** Lagrange (S-J) **** Langoa-Barton (S-J) ****

Giscours (M)*** Malescot St-Exupéry (M) *** Boyd-Cantenac (M) *** Cantenac-Brown (M) *** Palmer (M) **** La Lagune (H-M) **** Desmirail (M) *** Calon-Ségur (S-E) **** Ferrière, *not generally available outside France* (M) ** Marquis d'Alesme Becker (M) **

Fourth Growth/4ème cru

St-Pierre (S-J) *** Talbot (S-J) *** Branaire-Ducru (S-J) *** Duhart-Milon-Rothschild (P) *** Pouget (M) ** La Tour-Carnet (H-M) ** Lafon-Rochet (S-E) *** Beychevelle (S-J) **** Prieuré-Lichine (M) *** Marquis-de-Terme (M) ***

Fifth Growth/5ème cru

Pontet-Canet (P) *** Batailley (P) *** Haut-Batailley (P) *** Grand-Puy-Lacoste (P) **** Grand-Puy-Ducasse (P) *** Lynch-Bages (P) ***** Lynch-Moussas (P) * Dauzac (M) * d'Armailhac, *formerly Mouton-Baronne-Philippe* (P) *** du Tertre (M) *** Haut-Bages-Libéral (P) *** Pédesclaux (P) ** Belgrave (H-M) *** de Camensac (H-M) ** Cos-Labory (S-E) *** Clerc-Milon (P) *** Croizet-Bages (P) * Cantemerle (H-M) ***

The hard way of transporting a barrel through the extensive chai, *or cellar, of first-growth Château Margaux (above).*

Ripe Cabernet Sauvignon grapes being harvested for first-growth Château Latour in Pauillac (below).

GRAVES, ST-EMILION AND POMEROL

Graves This extensive sub-region, lying mostly south of the city of Bordeaux on the west bank of the river Garonne, is named after the gravelly soils that predominate there. Many tasters insist that there is a gravelly, earthy taste in the red wines themselves, and certainly they tend to come clothed in much more austere garb than the lavish finery of the Médoc wines. However, they are quite as capable of ageing, notwithstanding the fact that many producers are attempting to make a more easy-going, early-drinking style of red.

The Graves was classified in 1959, for both red and dry white wines (whereas 1855 applies only to reds). A château is either *cru classé* or it isn't; it's as simple as that. A superior swathe of land in the north of the district was separately demarcated as Pessac-Léognan in 1987, all of the classed growths of 1959 falling within that appellation. (Haut-Brion is the only property whose red also falls within the 1855 classification.) For the reds, they are:

Bouscaut ** Haut-Bailly **** Carbonnieux *** Domaine de Chevalier ***** de Fieuzal *** d'Olivier ** Malartic-Lagravière *** La Tour-Martillac ** Smith-Haut-Lafitte *** Haut-Brion ***** La Mission-Haut-Brion **** Pape-Clément **** La Tour-Haut-Brion ***

St-Emilion Situated on the right bank of the river Dordogne, this is predominantly Merlot country – although not quite to the same degree as Pomerol. The reds are supplemented by the lighter, grassier Cabernet Franc, with only a dash of Cabernet Sauvignon. The style is consequently leaner than in the Médoc, but sharpened by that Cabernet Franc. Ordinary St-Emilion is not that distinguished – many producers have been guilty of over-production – but the top names are worth the premium.

The classification of St-Emilion's reds was drawn up in 1955, but is healthily subject to revision every decade. At the humblest level, Grand Cru is so inclusive as to be all but meaningless. A step up is Grand Cru Classé with around five dozen properties (among which Canon-la-Gaffelière and Clos de l'Oratoire stand out as worthy of ****), and at the top is Premier Grand Cru Classé, subdivided rather prosaically into A and B. Class A consists of just two properties:

Ausone **** Cheval Blanc *****

As of 2006, Class B contains 13:

Angélus **** Beau-Séjour Bécot **** Beauséjour (Duffau-Lagarrosse) **** Bélair-Monange **** Canon ***** Figeac **** Clos Fourtet *** La Gaffelière **** Magdeleine **** Pavie **** Pavie-Macquin **** Troplong-Mondot **** Trottevieille ***

Pomerol Immediately to the north of
St-Emilion, and the only one of the top
Bordeaux districts never to have been classified,
Pomerol's reds are as close to varietal Merlot
as Bordeaux gets. Many have simply the merest
seasoning of Cabernet Franc to add an edge
of ageworthy sternness to what is essentially
pure velvet-soft opulence, the sweetness of
prunes coated in dark chocolate, leading to
a gorgeously creamy finish.

Anybody setting out to play the Pomerol
classification parlour-game for themselves
would have to start out with the hyper-
expensive Pétrus ***** at the top, probably
joined by Lafleur ***** and Le Pin *****.
In the next rank (****) would come Bon
Pasteur, Certan de May, Clinet, La Conseillante,
La Croix de Gay, L'Eglise-Clinet, L'Evangile,
Le Fleur de Gay, La Fleur-Pétrus, Le Gay,
Latour à Pomerol, Petit-Village, Trotanoy
and Vieux-Château-Certan.

CRUS BOURGEOIS/PETITS CHATEAUX/SECOND WINES

Crus Bourgeois Immediately below the five
layers of Médoc *crus classés* are a group of
wines known, in an echo of 18th-century
social stratification, as the *crus bourgeois*.
For the purposes of this category, not only the
Haut-Médoc but also the bottom-line Médoc
area to the north of St-Estèphe comes into
consideration. Many of these properties would
now be included in any redraft of the 1855
classification, including a fair handful from
the less well-known commune of Moulis.

Reliably excellent wines have been produced
in recent years by the following (****):
d'Angludet (M), Chasse-Spleen (Moulis),
la Gurgue (M), Haut-Marbuzet (S-E), Gressier-
Grand-Poujeaux (Moulis), Labégorce-Zédé
(M), Lanessan (H-M), Maucaillou (Moulis),
Meyney (S-E), Monbrison (M), de Pez (S-E),
Potensac (Médoc), Poujeaux (Moulis) and
Sociando-Mallet (H-M).

Next best (***) would be: Patache d'Aux
(Médoc), Ramage-la-Batisse (H-M), Sénéjac
(H-M), la Tour-de-By (Médoc) and la Tour-du-
Haut-Moulin (H-M).

Petits châteaux and other districts Other
important quality districts (with good
unclassified properties known as *petits
châteaux*) are Lalande-de-Pomerol, adjoining
Pomerol to the northeast (Bel-Air, Bertineau
St-Vincent), Fronsac and Canon-Fronsac to the

west of Pomerol (Dalem, Mazeris, La Truffière)
and the various satellite villages to the northeast
of St-Emilion, such as Lussac (Lyonnat),
Puisseguin and St-Georges. Discovering the
best of these lesser-known properties has made
for much happy exploration in recent years.

*Many of the châteaux of
Bordeaux have idiosyncratic
architectural features, such
as the pointed turret (above)
after which Château la
Tour-de-By is named.*

Looking over the medieval rooftops of the City of St-Emilion (below) out towards the vineyards.

The huge area of the Entre-deux-Mers between the Garonne and Dordogne rivers tends to produce pretty rough-and-ready reds under the most basic appellations, Bordeaux and Bordeaux Supérieur. On the right bank of the Gironde, directly opposite the *cru classé* enclaves of the Haut-Médoc, are the Côtes de Blaye and Côtes de Bourg areas. The best vineyards of the former are entitled to the designation Premières Côtes de Blaye, while the much smaller Bourg district is home to some exciting innovators (Civrac's wines have big, concentrated fruit and new oak). The long strip on the right bank of the Garonne, the Premières Côtes de Bordeaux, is responsible for some increasingly satisfying, firm-textured reds.

To the east of St-Emilion are two areas that are among the most unsung (and therefore good-value) sources of classy wine in the whole region: the Côtes de Castillon and Côtes de Francs. Cabernet Franc plays a significant role in the Merlot-based wines, making for some attractive lighter clarets, but there are also wines

of impressive intensity from Pitray, d'Aiguilhe, Robin, Grand-Peyrou, Parenchère, Belcier and Moulin-Rouge in Castillon, and Puygueraud, La Prade, de Francs and Marsau in the Francs. Many of these wines will go the distance in the cellar.

Second wines When the prices of Bordeaux began seriously inflating in the 1980s, much attention came to be focused on the second wines of the principal châteaux. Most producers make a subsidiary wine to their main offering (the *grand vin*), to use grapes that were not thought quite good enough for the flagship wine, or came from vines that were still too young to yield thoroughly concentrated fruit. A ready market emerged for those who may not have been able to afford the *crus classés*, but wanted to gain at least a partial glimpse of their style, and these can be highly rewarding.

The point to remember when considering buying a second wine is only to buy from the best vintages. Top châteaux may be able to make a silk purse out of the sow's ear of an off-vintage, and it should be correspondingly cheaper, so you don't need the second wine. In a super-ripe vintage like 2005, however, when the *grand vin* prices soar out of sight, the second wines represent an affordable alternative.

The following are regularly some of the best (with the main château name shown in brackets):

Les Forts de Latour (Latour), Carruades de Lafite (Lafite-Rothschild), Pavillon Rouge du Château Margaux (Margaux), Bahans Haut-Brion (Haut-Brion), Clos du Marquis (Léoville-Las Cases), Réserve de la Comtesse (Pichon-Longueville Comtesse de Lalande), Marbuzet (Cos d'Estournel), La Dame de Montrose (Montrose), Sarget de Gruaud-Larose (Gruaud-Larose), Lady Langoa (Langoa-Barton), Réserve du Général (Palmer), Haut-Bages-Avérous (Lynch-Bages), La Parde de Haut-Bailly (Haut-Bailly), Grangeneuve de Figeac (Figeac), La Gravette de Certan (Vieux-Château-Certan), La Petite Eglise (l'Eglise-Clinet).

VINTAGE GUIDE

Below is a broad overview of the most recent vintages, as represented by the better wines of each year, plus some earlier stars.

2009 ***** The new century's first decade closed with an absolute stunner. Levels of ripeness, depth and concentration are superb, and the overall balance is well-nigh flawless. Investors (and drinkers too), take note.

2008 *** A difficult growing season with much late picking resulted in a generally patchy picture. Not a classic.

2007 *** Not dissimilar to 2008, with a poor summer undermining the chances of greatness. Gently priced wines should provide good earlyish drinking.

2006 **** Not great for the Merlot wines of the right bank, but Cabernet-based Médoc is generally looking good.

2005 ***** A beautiful vintage of ripe, intense, well-balanced wines that will go the distance for those prepared to keep them.

2004 **** Late picking resulted in big, tannic wines with plenty of alcohol.

2003 ***** The heatwave summer produced a humdinger of a vintage. Not one for purists, maybe, with its colossal alcohol and fruit-preserve intensity, but definitely one for the cellar.

2002 *** A good showing on the left bank, but much of the right bank failed to ripen well.

2001 **** Harvest rains spoiled the chances of some, but this vintage has turned out better than expected, especially in St-Emilion.

2000 ***** A fabulous vintage that has already passed into legend.

1999 ** Very dull (although Mouton is good).

1998 *** Pretty good, though not outstanding.

1997 ** A little better than feared, but basically mediocre.

1996 **** Some classic, austere, ageworthy wines in the Médoc.

1995 **** A very ripe, attractive year, particularly for Cabernet.

1990 ***** Brilliant across the board, with Pomerol the best.

1989 **** Classic claret vintage of well-balanced wines that showed their charms early.

1988 **** Deeply classical wines with intensely ripe fruit and solid structure.

PICK OF THE OLDER VINTAGES: 1986 ****
1983 **** 1982 ***** 1978 ****
1970 **** 1966 **** 1961 *****
1959 **** 1955 **** 1953 **** 1949 ****
1947 **** 1945 ***** 1970 ****
1966 **** 1961 ***** 1959 ****
1955 **** 1953 **** 1949 **** 1947 ****
1945 *****

Despite its venerable history, Domaine de Chevalier, one of the Graves crus classés, has always kept abreast of the times, as witness its state-of-the-art cellars at Pessac-Léognan (above).

BORDEAUX-*Dry White/Rosé*

The dry white wines of Bordeaux have enjoyed a remarkable renaissance in recent years, shaking off their image of being poorly made and dull, and emerging with the kinds of flavours normally only found in America's finest.

BORDEAUX-DRY WHITE/ ROSE

GRAPES: *Sémillon, Sauvignon Blanc, Muscadelle*

BORDEAUX-ROSE

GRAPES: *Cabernet Sauvignon, Merlot, Carmenère, Cabernet Franc, Malbec, Petit Verdot*

THE PAST 30 YEARS have seen a winemaking upheaval in the dry whites of Bordeaux, and one that was sorely overdue. Certain properties, such as Domaine de Chevalier, have always been highly valued for their white wines, and one of the 1855 *crus classés*, Haut-Brion, showed itself as adept at white as at red. The generality, though, for a long time was a rather aimless, unfocused style in the middle rank, and a tidal wave of fruitless, stale-tasting rubbish at the bottom end. These were the least impressive dry whites produced in any of France's classic regions.

The upturn came about via a handful of winemakers – Denis Dubourdieu, André Lurton and Peter Vinding-Diers among them – who began, in the early 1980s, to incorporate a more modern approach to white wine. Better grape selection during harvest, fermenting at controlled temperatures in stainless steel, and considered experimentation with oak-ageing to add an extra dimension to the wines' flavours all paid handsome dividends.

Most importantly of all, the innovators took a long hard look at their grape varieties. Much of the dullness of the bad old days came from overcropped Sémillon being used as a workhorse grape. Some of the most interesting wines have been made from unblended Sauvignon Blanc, but there are exemplary wines now that use both varieties in impressive balance. Look to Pessac-Léognan, and the

wider Graves area, for the best, but even the sprawling Entre-Deux-Mers is brushing up its act these days, and nobody saw that coming.

Occasionally, the wines can taste a little too nervy to me, especially in their youth, and there is often a bit too much oak to suit them. Otherwise, it's all good. A pronounced petrolly pungency characterizes some of the top wines, and the fruit flavours on them, which can mix tropical melon with the apple and lemon scents of Sauvignon, can be astonishing.

Only the Graves has a classification for dry whites, drawn up in 1959. As with its red wines, all of the properties are in Pessac-Léognan, but there are only nine of them:

Bouscaut ** Carbonnieux *** Domaine de Chevalier ***** Couhins ** Couhins-Lurton **** Latour-Martillac **** Laville Haut-Brion ***** Malartic-Lagravière *** Olivier ***

Unclassified fine dry whites from the Graves include: Haut-Brion ***** de Fieuzal ***** Pape-Clement **** Clos Floridène **** La Louvière **** Tour Léognan ****

In the Entre-deux-Mers, the best property without a doubt is Thieuley (****). Elsewhere, the catchall of Bordeaux Blanc applies, and quality is still all over the place, but notably fresh, zippy white is made at de Parenchère (***). Some branded wines, blended from grapes sourced throughout the region, can be fresh and innocent enough (look for Dourthe or Yvon Mau on the label).

Down in the Sauternes region, the top sweet wine producers offer dry whites made from grapes not suitable for Sauternes itself, bottled as Bordeaux Blanc but unofficially thought of as dry Sauternes. Named after the initial letter of the château, they include R (Rieussec), G (Guiraud) and – best of all – Y (Yquem), majestically austere wines with commanding presence on the palate.

The rosé wines of Bordeaux are also much improved, as well they might be since both Cabernet Sauvignon and Merlot make good pink wine. There is more body and riper fruit on them than a lot of rosés from further north. Look out for Méaume, de Bel, de Sours, Clos Fourtet and Roc de Minvielle.

VINTAGE GUIDE

The simpler whites that use a high percentage of Sauvignon are best drunk on release. The top *crus classés* are intended for longer ageing.
2009 ***** Bright, vigorous wines with masses of appetizing fruit. This vintage will repay keeping.
2008 **** Much better than the reds, with attractive balance.
2007 **** Pretty much the same as 08, with fresh, complex, fruit-driven wines.
2006 ***** A great vintage of exciting wines, sure to be long-lived.
2005 ***** Brilliant expressions of both Sémillon and Sauvignon made for fine, classic blends.
2003 **** Exotically perfumed, soft, generous wines of great charm. Drink soon.
2001 **** Very attractive wines from the top châteaux.
2000 ***** Beautifully composed, concentrated whites for ageing.
1996 **** Some lovely creamy, tropical-fruited wines still going strong.
1990/1989 *** Very hot ripening periods meant critically low acidity levels in many wines, so a lot will have had difficulty lasting this long. Only the very best (Haut-Brion, Laville-Haut-Brion and the like) made out-and-out classics.

An ancient windmill presides over vineyards at Gornac, in the Entre-deux-Mers (above).

The gently sloping vineyards of Château Benauge on the border between the Entre-deux-Mers and Premières Côtes de Bordeaux regions (left). Many of the dry whites made in these regions are now much improved.

BORDEAUX-*Sweet White*

Its lofty reputation founded on botrytis, a fungal disease that attacks ripened grapes in late summer and early autumn, the long-lived and intensely rich sweet wine of Bordeaux is the most celebrated of its kind in the world.

BORDEAUX-SWEET WHITE

GRAPES: Sémillon, Sauvignon Blanc, Muscadelle

The Sauternes region of Bordeaux contains some of the most valuable land in the world for producing sweet wines, none more so than at Château d'Yquem (below).

THE FINEST DESSERT wines in the world, whether in Bordeaux or elsewhere, are made from grapes infected by a strain of fungus called *Botrytis cinerea*, widely known as noble rot. Rot normally develops on grapes if the weather turns wet towards harvest-time. This grey rot is the decidedly ignoble sort and, particularly with red grapes, can torpedo any hopes of making great wines. Botrytis, on the other hand, occurs in damp rather than drenching conditions.

Because of its proximity to the Atlantic Ocean, Bordeaux experiences increasingly humid, misty mornings as the autumn comes on, relieved by gentle sunshine during the day. This delicate process of dampening and drying off is the ideal climatic pattern for the encouragement of botrytis on Sémillon grapes. As the berries shrivel on the vine, they lose moisture, meaning that their natural sugars become densely concentrated.

The most celebrated sweet wines on earth come from the southern Bordeaux communes of Sauternes and Barsac. Although the technique was almost certainly discovered in Germany – by accident, of course, like many of the best inventions – it is here that it has been put to the most highly reputed use. Not every vintage produces the right conditions, and the more quality-conscious châteaux simply don't bother making a wine in the off-years.

Quality depends on making painstaking selections of only the most thoroughly rotted grapes. In many cases, proprietors have decided the only way of doing that is by individual hand-sorting, picking only those berries that are completely shrivelled, and leaving the others to moulder a little further on the vine being going through the vineyard again. Several such turns (or *tries* in French) may be necessary to make the most concentrated wines possible. That, together with the long maturation in oak casks that the wines are generally accorded, explains the drop-dead prices that classic Sauternes sells for. It is an immensely labour-intensive wine.

A group of five villages in the southern Graves famous for their botrytized wines – Sauternes, Barsac, Bommes, Preignac and Fargues – was included in the 1855 classification. Together, they now constitute the Sauternes appellation, although Barsac can carry its own appellation as well, if an individual property so chooses. (Just for good measure, it can also be AOC Sauternes-Barsac, if it wants the best of both worlds.)

At the top of the classification, and with a category to itself, rather like the duck-billed platypus, is the legendary Château d'Yquem, for many the supreme achievement in botrytized wine. Fantastically expensive and fabulously rich, its best vintages can last for over a century.

Grand first growth/1er grand cru

Yquem *****

First growth/1er cru

La Tour Blanche **** Lafaurie-Peyraguey ****
Clos Haut-Peyraguey ** Rayne-Vigneau ***
Suduiraut **** Coutet **** Climens *****
Guiraud **** Rieussec ***** Rabaud-Promis
*** Sigalas-Rabaud ***

Second growth/2ème cru

de Myrat ****, *began replanting in 1988 after
coming close to total extinction* Doisy-Daëne
*** Doisy-Dubroca **** Doisy-Védrines
*** d'Arche ** Filhot *** Broustet ***
Nairac ** Caillou *** Suau ** de Malle ***
Romer-du-Hayot ** Lamothe-Despujols *
Lamothe-Guignard ***

Other good properties in Sauternes-Barsac,
but outside the classification, are:
Raymond-Lafon **** Gilette ****
Bastor-Lamontagne ***

In the immediate vicinity of Sauternes are
four less well-known AOCs for botrytis-affected
wines. When the vintage is propitious, they can
produce wines that show something of the
flavours of their more exalted neighbours, while
lacking those final layers of richness that make
Sauternes so fabled. Given that, they are much
more humanely priced. They are Cérons,
Loupiac, Cadillac and Ste-Croix-du-Mont.
Of these, all but Cérons, to the northwest of
Barsac, are on the opposite bank of the river
Garonne to Sauternes. Best properties are
Cérons and Archambeau in Cérons, and
Loupiac-Gaudiet in Loupiac.

Sweet wines from the Premières Côtes de
Bordeaux region, along the eastern side of the
Garonne, are not invariably fully botrytized.
One exception that has provided excellent value
for money in recent years is de Berbec.

VINTAGE GUIDE

If a sweet white Bordeaux has been
conscientiously made, it can easily last a good
20–30 years, and the very top ones are virtually
indestructible. They turn from rich yellow to
burnished orange, and then the distinguished
deep brown of dark sherry, as they age, and
go on selling for phenomenal sums.

2009 ***** Abundant botrytis from late
September on produced wines of staggering
richness, balanced by exemplary acidity.
As close to perfection as sweet wine gets.

2008 *** Not a bad year, but not many wines
have true excitement.

2007 **** Superb Sauternes. Colossal extract
and deep honeyed richness, matched by fresh
acidity. Needs keeping for ages yet.

2006 ** Very variable, even the best remaining
rather simple and only reluctantly sweet.

2005 *** Hard to generalize. Great from
Yquem, Guiraud, Suduiraut, Climens, but
others lack complexity.

2003 ***** A sensational vintage of fully rotted
wines with long lives ahead of them.

2002 **** Sandwiched between two legends,
but full of elegance.

2001 ***** Brilliant, complex, hauntingly
beautiful wines. The best since 1990.

1990 ***** Virtual perfection. Unbelievable
levels of concentration and intensity.

PICK OF THE OLDER VINTAGES: *1989 ****
1988 **** 1986 **** 1983 **** 1976 ****
1967 ***** 1959 ***** 1945 ***** 1937
***** 1929 ***** 1921 ***** 1900 ******

*Autumn vines resplendent
beneath a clear blue sky at
Château Rieussec (above),
one of the best first-growth
properties in Sauternes.*

LOIRE

The river Loire flows through five wine-producing areas, from the Pays Nantais in the west, far inland to Sancerre in the east, each of them boasting very different styles of wine, and offering much good value along the way.

Château de Nozet (above) set in the upper Loire, where Pouilly-Fumé is produced.

PAYS NANTAIS
GRAPES: *Melon de Bourgogne (Muscadet), Folle Blanche (Gros Plant).*

The five wine regions of the Loire valley (below) lie along the banks of the river Loire.

THE LOIRE VALLEY in northern France is a hugely diverse region, encompassing a very broad range of wine styles. Crisp dry whites are usually seen as its strongest suit, but there are medium-dry and lusciously sweet whites, a host of refreshing light reds and rosés, and some of the better sparkling wines made outside Champagne. The Loire is the nation's longest river, rising in central France and disgorging into the Atlantic west of Nantes. To get a coherent view of it as a wine region, it makes sense to subdivide it into five areas, running from west to east.

PAYS NANTAIS
Muscadet The main business of the area around the city of Nantes is Muscadet, which has by far the largest volume of production of any Loire AOC. Made from a single grape variety, Melon de Bourgogne, it is the epitome of a bone-dry, crisp, neutral-tasting white wine. The grape was once grown in Burgundy, as its name suggests, but was imported into Brittany in the early 18th century for its ability to survive frosts.

There are four appellations. Muscadet de Sèvre-et-Maine, in the centre of the region, makes about 75 per cent of all Muscadet, and is generally considered to produce the wines with the most character. Growers with land on the granite hills around St-Fiacre, or in the clay-based soils around Vallet, are good bets for the most interesting offerings. Muscadet Côtes de Grandlieu, centred on a large lake of that name, was demarcated in 1994, and contains a fair amount of sandy soil, which imparts its own aromatic personality to the wines.

The small, more northerly district of Muscadet des Coteaux de la Loire turns out a negligible quantity of undistinguished wine, and the rest is basic AOC Muscadet, not by and large worth dwelling on.

About half of all Muscadets include the words *sur lie* on the label. What this means is that the finished wine was left on its lees (the dead yeast cells left over from fermentation) for up to 12 months. Just as lees-ageing imparts a softer, creamier feel to champagne, so in Muscadet it adds a valuable dimension of textural complexity and some depth of flavour. Always choose a *sur lie* wine. Some producers mature their wines in oak, a high-risk technique for such a light wine, but there are successful examples.

At best, Muscadet has a taut, nervy, high-acid freshness, occasionally with a little fruit (tart green apple, grapefruit) and sometimes a wisp of anise. The bulk-produced stuff smells and tastes of nothing whatsoever. The better ones, believe it or not, will age, taking on a cabbagey, but not unattractive, secondary aroma, while the youthful acidity softens out.

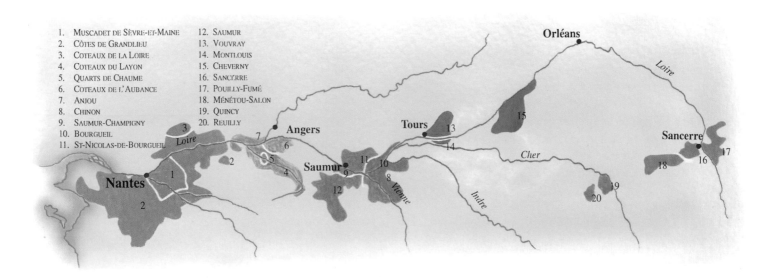

1. MUSCADET DE SÈVRE-ET-MAINE
2. CÔTES DE GRANDLIEU
3. COTEAUX DE LA LOIRE
4. COTEAUX DU LAYON
5. QUARTS DE CHAUME
6. COTEAUX DE L'AUBANCE
7. ANJOU
8. CHINON
9. SAUMUR-CHAMPIGNY
10. BOURGUEIL
11. ST-NICOLAS-DE-BOURGUEIL
12. SAUMUR
13. VOUVRAY
14. MONTLOUIS
15. CHEVERNY
16. SANCERRE
17. POUILLY-FUMÉ
18. MÉNÉTOU-SALON
19. QUINCY
20. REUILLY

PRODUCERS: Sauvion, Luneau-Papin, Métaireau, Dom. de l'Ecu, Ch. de la Ragotière, Landron.

Gros Plant du Pays Nantais The archetypal French local wine, much beloved of the Nantais themselves, but hardly at all exported. Its grape, Folle Blanche, is mostly grown elsewhere for brandy distillation, but appears here in vinified form. Expect highly pronounced (oh all right then, excruciating) levels of acidity in a dead-neutral, squeaky-clean style. Served bone-chillingly cold with the local shellfish, it's a zinger. Look for a *sur lie* wine made by one of the Muscadet growers, such as the reliably good Guy Bossard at Dom. de l'Ecu.

ANJOU

The area south of Angers is the start of Chenin Blanc country, and it's here that some of the great sweet wines of the Loire are made. Chenin submits to botrytis with obliging regularity in these districts, producing finely balanced dessert wines, full of mouth-coating marmalade flavours, but thrown into a state of nervous excitement by a lemony streak of acidity.

Coteaux du Layon The largest AOC for sweet wines regularly produces liquorous but refreshing examples of rotted Chenin. Even in years when there is a lower concentration of botrytis, and the resulting wines are a little less intense, these are generally pretty reliable. Best are labelled Sélection de Grains Nobles. Within the Coteaux du Layon are three separately demarcated AOCs: **Bonnezeaux** to the east, and **Chaume Premier Cru** to the northwest. Within the latter, the enclave of **Quarts de Chaume** can justly be considered a Grand Cru wine, mostly made only when botrytis is sufficiently widespread that only fully rotted grapes need be used. These are exquisitely intense sweet Chenin, with all the majesty of top-flight Sauternes.

PRODUCERS: Ch. de Breuil, Dom. de la Soucherie, Baumard, Ch. Pierre-Bise, Delesvaux, Ogereau.

Coteaux de l'Aubance Northeast of Chaume, this larger AOC produces generally lighter, often non-botrytized sweet wines, but when rot does set in, they may be labelled Sélection de Grains Nobles.

Savennières The best dry white of Anjou is a long-lived, memorably intense Chenin Blanc, brittle in youth, full of mineral purity, but ageing into a stately maturity in the best vintages. They need at least seven or eight

years. Within the appellation are a pair of super-fine enclaves with their own AOCs, **La Roche-aux-Moines** (look for the wines of Soulez) and **La Coulée-de-Serrant**, wholly owned by Nicolas Joly. The latter was one of the pioneers of biodynamic winemaking in France, and the wines are shatteringly pure and concentrated.

OTHER PRODUCERS: Baumard, Pierre-Bise, Ch. d'Epire, Dom. du Closel.

Anjou Blanc Sec The bottom-line AOC for everyday dry white. It is allowed to mix in some Chardonnay and/or Sauvignon with the Chenin, but some opulent straight Chenin is produced in the South African style by fermenting in oak, as at Dom. de Bablut.

Anjou-Villages The better village sites make passable reds from Cabernets Sauvignon and Franc. **Anjou-Villages Brissac** has its own appellation for these in the Aubance.

Anjou Rouge Overlapping into Saumur, these are allowed to use the Beaujolais grape Gamay as well as the Cabernet duo. The Gamays can be charming enough.

Cabernet d'Anjou The best of the AOCs for the considerable quantities of rosé made in the Loire, these can be made from both Cabernets, and tend to be acerbically dry, but with good blackcurrant fruit.

Rosé d'Anjou Made primarily from a local grape, Groslot, often in a demi-sec style, these used to be bog-standard rosés, but some producers (Ch. de Fesles) are now making more attractive, summer-fruited wines to capitalize on the rosé boom. Worth a punt.

Poplar trees break the skyline in vineyards near Vallet (above), Muscadet de Sèvre-et-Maine.

ANJOU
GRAPE: *Chenin Blanc (whites)*

Harvesting Muscadet grapes at Clisson (above), in the Sèvre-et-Maine AC.

*The soaring turrets of
Château Saumur (above),
overlooking the Loire
in Saumur.*

SAUMUR

GRAPES: *Cabernet Franc
(reds); Chenin Blanc
(whites)*

SPARKLING SAUMUR

GRAPES: *Chenin Blanc,
Chardonnay, Sauvignon
Blanc*

TOURAINE

GRAPES: *Cabernet Franc,
Gamay (reds); Chenin
Blanc, Sauvignon Blanc,
Chardonnay, Romorantin
(whites)*

SAUMUR

Two types of wine are important in Saumur –
reds and sparklers. This district and Touraine
make a speciality of the Cabernet Franc grape,
one of the lesser players in red Bordeaux, in the
principal red AOCs. In warm vintages, these
wines have pleasant blackcurrant fruit, a
lightish feel in the mouth (although by no
means as light as, say, Beaujolais), and gentle
tannins. They can mature agreeably for several
years. In less ripe years, though, they can
be pretty depressing, full of bitter green
tannin and hard acid.

Saumur-Champigny Saumur's best reds are
attractive, juicy-fruited wines, their upfront
flavours of summer berries underpinned by
considerable structure. In the good years, they
are worth ageing.

PRODUCERS: Dom. des Roches Neuves, Ch. du
Hureau, Ch. de Villeneuve, Clos Rougeard.

Saumur The less distinguished area around
Saumur-Champigny. Reds are drier and more
astringent, but occasionally summer-ripe
(Filliatreau's are good). One area, **Saumur
Puy-Notre-Dame**, received its own AOC for
reds in 2006. Whites are mainly Chenin with
up to 20 per cent Chardonnay to smooth them
(look for Les Andides).

Coteaux de Saumur Sweet Chenin wines made
in the better years.

Cabernet de Saumur Simple, grassy rosés.

Saumur Mousseux Sparkling Saumur is made
by the same method as champagne, and is
mainly Chenin Blanc, with occasional additions
of softening Chardonnay. From good producers,
such as Gratien & Meyer (who also make a
sparkling rosé from Cabernet Franc), or Bouvet-
Ladubay, they have a tart but refreshing crispness.

TOURAINE

In the west of Touraine, the Loire's most
fascinating, complex reds are made from
Cabernet Franc in three celebrated appellations.

Chinon The best of the three for structure,
balance and ageability, Chinon has been famed
ever since the time of Rabelais. Up to 10 per
cent Cabernet Sauvignon is permitted.
Appealing, complex aromas of raspberries and
anise, with underlying woody notes.

PRODUCERS: Baudry, Couly-Dutheil, Druet.

Bourgueil Rapidly improving from a rough-
and-ready past, these now have good red fruit
along with their earthiness.

PRODUCERS: Druet, Dom. de la Butte, Audebert.

St-Nicolas-de-Bourgueil An enclave within
Bourgueil, the wines are similar in style,
ageworthy in the ripe years, with perhaps
deeper, plummier fruit.

PRODUCERS: Pavillon du Grand Clos, Taluau.
Chenin continues its sway into the area east of
Tours, where its principal stamping-ground is
one of the Loire's world-famous wines.

Vouvray The AOC covers almost every
stylistic manifestation that white wine can adopt
– dry, medium-dry, semi-sweet, botrytized and
sparkling. Despite being very vintage-sensitive,
Vouvray is capable of making some of the most
appetizing Chenin wines in all the Loire. Labelling
is more precise than it used to be, ranging through
Sec (dry), Demi-Sec (medium-dry), Moelleux
(sweet) and Sélection (noble-rotted). Dry wines
are nutty, honeyish but austere at the same time,
while the demi-sec is peachier, gently sugared
but beautifully balanced. Moelleux have the
unctuousness of fruit syrups, while the rotted
wines are all spangling, marmaladey intensity.
Even the dry wines benefit from keeping.

PRODUCERS: Champalou, Dom. des Aubuisières,
Clos Naudin, Pichot, Dom. de la Fontainerie.
Huët makes by far the best Vouvray fizz, a
wine as deeply, yeastily rich and complex
as good champagne.

Montlouis To the south of Vouvray, on the other side of the river. Chenin wines in the same repertoire of styles as its more famous neighbour, but with less finesse.

Cheverny In northeastern Touraine, Cheverny whites may use Chardonnay, Sauvignon or Chenin, but there is also a separate AOC – **Cour Cheverny** – for wines made from residual plantings of a high-acid local grape, Romarantin. The crisp-edged Cheverny reds may use Cabernet Franc, Gamay or Pinot Noir. There is also some sparkling wine with bite.

Touraine The regional AOC is for other reds and whites, usually labelled with the variety. Gamay reds are pleasantly light, those made from the Cabernets have a little more stuffing. Sauvignon whites can be splashed with glorious gooseberry fruit.

UPPER LOIRE

Here, at the eastern end of the Loire, in almost the dead centre of France, Sauvignon Blanc comes into its own for some of the most fashionable of all dry whites.

Sancerre On the left bank, the name that has come to be the reference-point for Sauvignon the world over. They can be intriguing wines indeed, full of intense green flavours of apple, gooseberry, nettles, asparagus and parsley, as well as wisps of beguiling smoke. Best drunk within two years of the vintage. There are also reds and rosés here, made from Pinot Noir, wines that I still struggle to see the point of even in the ripest vintages. The reds are typically very thin and grassy, the rosés barely more than a mouthful of fresh air. PRODUCERS: Bourgeois, Vacheron, Cotat, Mellot, Pinard, Vatan, Gitton, Bailly-Reverdy.

Pouilly-Fumé Facing Sancerre on the right bank of the Loire, Pouilly's wines are made in an almost identical style, perhaps emphasizing that smokiness (as befits the name) a little more in the very best. Some of the most exciting are grown on a type of flint soil called Silex (look for that word on the label), and emphasize stark minerality rather than fruit. The very best are thinner on the ground than they ought to be, given the prices. For the time being, Sancerre is usually a safer bet. PRODUCERS: Bourgeois, Ch. de Tracy, de Ladoucette, Chatelain.

Menetou-Salon West of Sancerre, this AOC offers great crunchy Sauvignon with as much class as decent Sancerre from the best.

Also Pinot reds and rosés.
PRODUCERS: Pellé, Roger, Mellot.

Reuilly Across the river Cher, these are lighter, much less piquant Sauvignon whites, with Pinot Noir reds and (an oddity, this) gentle rosé from pink-skinned Pinot Gris.

Quincy Whites only from Sauvignon, the least distinguished of the Sancerre understudies, but still fresh and sappy when caught young.

Pouilly-sur-Loire A little-seen dry white made from the humdrum Chasselas grape.

OTHER WINES

Haut-Poitou South of the Loire, but north of the ancient town of Poitiers, the Haut-Poitou produces good, simple Sauvignon and Chardonnay whites and Gamay reds.

Crémant de Loire Often impressive champagne-method fizz is made under this designation in Anjou and Touraine from Chenin and Chardonnay, with Cabernet Franc and Gamay for the rosés.

Vin de Pays du Jardin de la France Regional wines made outside the demarcated AOCs, or using non-permitted grapes (often fair quality Sauvignon, Chardonnay, Chenin or Gamay).

VINTAGE GUIDE

Most dry whites are best drunk young. *2009* is good across the board, from Muscadet to the Upper Loire. The best recent vintages for reds have been *2009, 08* and *05*. As with Sauternes, the Loire's best dessert wines last for aeons. Greatest recent vintages are *2007, 05* and *03*.

UPPER LOIRE
GRAPE: *Sauvignon Blanc (whites)*
SANCERRE, MENETOU-SALON AND REUILLY
GRAPES: *Pinot Noir, Gamay (reds/rosés)*

Sparkling rosé, made from Cabernet Franc (left), resting in pupîtres *at Gratien et Meyer, Saumur.*

CHAMPAGNE

The name alone conjures an image of celebration, of romance. The most northerly of France's fine wine regions, Champagne is the source of the world's greatest and most seductive sparkling wines.

NO OTHER WINE in the world comes with quite such an inbuilt, ready-made aura as champagne. With its smart packaging, its world-famous names and the foaming luxuriance of its bubbles, it is the very image of celebration and of luxury. It marks the arrival of good news and the stroke of the new year; it crowns birthdays, anniversaries and weddings. It can alleviate the spirits of the downhearted, and arouse hope at the outset of a grand venture. As Sir Winston Churchill, one of its doughtiest admirers and consumers put it, 'In victory, we deserve it; in defeat, we need it.'

The wines that are produced in France's most northerly vineyard region have, for the better part of the past three centuries been the worldwide reference-point for sparkling wine. Indeed, with the exception of Spanish cava, virtually all other producers of fizz began by referring to their wines as champagne, ciampagna, champanski, or some such. Much tireless litigation has taken place in the Champagne region in recent years to prevent its name from so much as being whispered in the same breath as any other product. Thus there may be no English elderflower 'champagne', no perfumes of that name, not even any official reference to what was once known as the 'champagne method' on the labels of other bottles, even if they were produced in exactly the same way with the same grape varieties. Champagne is a region of northern France, and so it will inimitably stay on pain of litigation.

While consumers go on innocently referring to all sparkling wines as 'champagne', the efforts of the *champenois* to protect their brand are understandable. If an appellation system is to mean anything, it has to define the geographical origin in which a wine may be produced. (An anomaly of the regulations, ironically, is that Champagne is the only AOC that doesn't have to state itself on the label, many producers settling for simply having the C-word in suitably prominent lettering all over it.)

One of the problems that comes with having such an exalted image, though, is that your product is much more hawkishly scrutinized than its humbler competitors are. And

The four vineyard areas of the Champagne region (below), with the warmer Aube valley tucked away to the south.

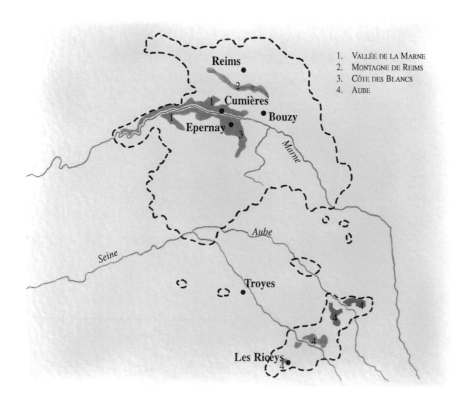

1. VALLÉE DE LA MARNE
2. MONTAGNE DE REIMS
3. CÔTE DES BLANCS
4. AUBE

Reims

Cumières
Bouzy
Epernay

Marne

Aube

Seine

Troyes

Les Riceys

champagne, more than any other French wine, periodically finds itself at the centre of hot political controversy. Most of that controversy in the past 30 years or so has turned on quality, and who has the right to drink champagne.

With the coming of prosperity after the second world war, champagne began very gradually to trickle down the social scale. The industry lost its way somewhat in the 1980s, when consumption in the UK (its premier market) reached unprecedented levels to coincide with a transient economic boom. Some members of the CIVC, its controlling body, felt that the wine was in danger of losing its aura of elite unaffordability. A more or less explicit attempt to ration consumption, using the sledgehammer of price inflation, was just beginning to work when the coming of severe recession did the job for them.

What was so galling about this was that there was suddenly an awful lot of poor champagne out there. After much publicly acrimonious debate, the introduction of a new quality charter in the 1990s set about restoring the region's reputation. An attempt to pretend that there might not be enough champagne to supply the millennium celebrations at the end of 1999 was soon enough rumbled, but contributed to the malign impression that whatever official pronouncements emerge from the regional committee are worth taking with a pinch of salt.

Barrels holding unblended grape must (above). The markings show which area the grapes came from – VZY stands for Verzenay, on the Montagne de Reims.

A blanket of snow covers the walled Clos du Mesnil vineyard owned by Krug (left), planted solely with Chardonnay grapes destined for its prestige blanc de blancs.

The steeply sloping grand cru *Rangen vineyard at the village of Thann (right), Alsace's most southerly* grand cru.

Muscat Muscat is the name of one of the oldest known grape varieties, in fact a many-membered family as opposed to a single variety. Two of the scions are present in Alsace, one of them not surprisingly known as Muscat d'Alsace and the other Muscat Ottonel. No distinction is made between them on the labels. Muscat is one of the great sweet wine grapes, the only one by consensus to actually smell and taste of grapes. Vinified dry, it can be bracingly tart and much thinner in texture than the three varieties listed above. There is very little of it planted compared to the others, but in a good year, from low-yielding vines, it can make a pleasantly sharp, refreshing white with some of the musky spice the region rejoices in.
PRODUCERS: Trimbach, Rolly-Gassmann, Weinbach, Schleret.

Pinot Blanc Not an especially aromatic grape, but definitely an underrated one. Pinot Blanc makes a creamy, slightly appley wine that provides an unstartling introduction to the region for those nervous of plunging headlong

into the giddy waters of Gewurz. Sometimes, in ripe vintages, it might have a suggestion of peach to it. Drunk young, these have far more character than many another unoaked dry white. Not for long ageing. (One of its permitted pseudonyms in Alsace is Klevner or Clevner.)
PRODUCERS: Rolly-Gassmann, Hugel, Mann, Zind-Humbrecht, Trimbach, Weinbach, Deiss.

Sylvaner The speciality grape of Franken in western Germany makes a pungently vegetal, often distinctly cabbagey wine in Alsace. Not the most attractive flavour in the world, but the odd one can have a honeyed quality and unexpected richness. In 2006, it was allowed into the *grand cru* of Zotzenberg, elbowing out Muscat in the process.
PRODUCERS: Zind-Humbrecht, Becker, Weinbach, Ostertag, Seltz.

Auxerrois This is the grape that nobody really talks about, although there is still plenty of it about. Related to Chardonnay, it has tended to be treated interchangeably with Pinot Blanc in Alsace, so that a wine labelled with that latter grape may be blended with Auxerrois (or indeed be nothing but). By itself, it gives very simple, though fairly full-textured wines with a vaguely soapy flavour. (Not to be confused with the red Auxerrois, aka Malbec, of southern France.)
PRODUCERS: Mann, Rolly-Gassmann.

Chasselas Very rarely seen on labels, this undistinguished grape makes extremely light, neutral-tasting wine. Schoffit works miracles with it to produce an impressively lush-textured wine from old vines – worth trying.

Edelzwicker The name used for blends of any of the above grapes (with the exception of Pinot Blanc and Auxerrois). They may be appealing enough, but since the varietals are generally so sharply delineated, there seems little point in drinking one of these if you can have a single-grape wine.

Pinot Noir The only red grape in Alsace makes some mostly very light reds and tiny amounts of rosé. In recent years, it has begun to show some pedigree, nothing like burgundy, to be sure, but still encouraging. There is usually some sharp cherry fruit in it, together with a rustic earthiness, but proper roundness too in the warmer years. When fully concentrated, it can take some oak-ageing.
PRODUCERS: Deiss, Adam, Weinbach, Hugel.

Crémant d'Alsace Alsace makes some of the most impressive sparkling wine in France outside the Champagne region – often a better bet than the Crémants of Burgundy or the Loire. The principal grape used is Pinot Blanc, usually mixed with Pinot Gris, but the small plantings of Chardonnay found in the region go into the sparklers too. The method is the same as that used for champagne, with a second fermentation taking place in the bottle. The result is often attractively nutty, full-flavoured wines of considerable depth. There is also some featherlight Pinot Noir rosé.

PRODUCERS: Dopff au Moulin, Adam, Albrecht, Blanck, Turckheim.

Vendange Tardive This is the less rich of the two sweeter styles of Alsace wine. The name means 'late harvest', to denote grapes that have been left on the vine to overripen, and thereby achieve higher levels of natural sugar. The designation applies only to the first four grapes listed above. They can be utterly delicious, perfectly balanced between the tang of ripe fruits and the lightest trickling of spicy syrup. In the great vintages of 2005 and 2009, they were particularly rich, honeyed and decadently creamy. In lesser years, they can be pretty close to the dry wines, but with a just perceptible extra depth to the texture.

Sélection de Grains Nobles The 'noble' in the name of this category refers to the noble rot, botrytis, which stalks the vineyards in some years and allows the growers to make Alsace's richest and most unctuous wines. They are powerfully alcoholic and glutinously sweet, and should theoretically age beautifully. The only slight vitiating factor is that, particularly in Gewurz and Pinot Gris, the acidity – low enough in the dry wines – can drop even further when the rotted berries are left on the vine for so long. Once again, only the big four grapes can be used, with Muscat by far the rarest.

Alsace Grand Cru The only other AOC in the region, apart from straight Alsace. It has, since 1983, covered the most prestigious vineyard sites, of which 51 have now been demarcated. Maximum yields permitted are 66 hectolitres per hectare, although the better wines are made from crops that are significantly smaller than this. Riesling, Gewurztraminer, Pinot Gris and Muscat are the privileged quartet allowed on most of the specified sites (with Sylvaner getting the nod too in Zotzenberg). Since the individual vineyards are quite distinct from each other in terms of soil, exposure and microclimate, the *grand cru* wines should give us a beguiling insight into the versatility that

Alsace is unquestionably capable of, but they remain for the time being far less fixed in even knowledgeable consumers' minds than the *crus* of Burgundy. Perceptions shift slowly.

VINTAGE GUIDE

Vintages in Alsace remain remarkably even, with the first decade of the 21st century delivering a sequence of very good to great years. *2009 ****** was an absolute cracker, and followed hot on the heels of a pair of vintages that in themselves produced masses of ripe, complex wines. Of those two, *2007 ***** just has the edge over the slightly less concentrated, but still indubitably fine *2008 *****. Buy these recent vintages with confidence. *2005 ****** was an outstanding vintage of harmonious, long-lived wines, while the *2003 ***** heatwave vintage gave us lots of excellent dessert wines, even if the drier wines often lacked balance. Earlier stunners, particularly for dry Rieslings, were *1998 *****, *1990 ****** and *1985 ******.

The village of Riquewihr, dominated by its church spire (above), seen from the Schoenenburg grand cru.

Half-timbered Alsace building (below), Hugel's cellars in Riquewihr.

BURGUNDY

Lovers of great Pinot Noir and classic Chardonnay speak the name with reverence. Burgundy's vinous history dates back for centuries, tied up in the division of land and the role of the négociant.

The autumnal colours of the Charmes vineyard at Gevrey-Chambertin on the Côte de Nuits (above).

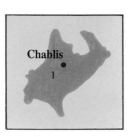

The great names of Burgundy (right) are concentrated in a line north-south between the towns of Dijon and Lyon; Chablis lies alone to the north.

BURGUNDY HAS ALWAYS been the consort to Bordeaux's monarch among the French wine regions. Its red wines in particular have their diehard devotees, just as fine claret does, and there has always been a romanticized comparison between the two. If the claret aficionado is an old-school connoisseur, fastidious, cerebral and contemplative in his approach to wine, the burgundy-lover was more of a wild child, a devotee of hedonistic sensuality, free-spirited and closer to nature.

Passionate controversies have raged and still rage about burgundy, to a degree because of the uncertain quality of so many of the wines. What

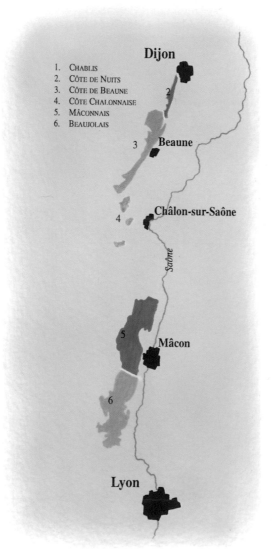

1. CHABLIS
2. CÔTE DE NUITS
3. CÔTE DE BEAUNE
4. CÔTE CHALONNAISE
5. MÂCONNAIS
6. BEAUJOLAIS

Dijon

Beaune

Châlon-sur-Saône

Mâcon

Lyon

makes the debate all the more poignant is that the annual production of fine burgundy is microscopically small compared with the output of Bordeaux. Its premium *grand cru* and *premier cru* wines (the rough equivalent of the classed growths of Bordeaux) come almost entirely from the narrow limestone ridge of the Côte d'Or, less than 30 miles from north to south, and not more than five miles across at its widest point. (Compare that with the oceans of unsold claret that regularly build up in the cellars of the Bordelais.)

The land in Burgundy, which constitutes some of the most costly real estate on the face of the earth, was ruthlessly subdivided over the generations, in accordance with a legal code enacted under Napoleon Bonaparte, which stated that the property of a landowner was to be divided equally among his offspring on his death. Many of these tiny smallholdings are today responsible for producing Burgundy's greatest wines.

They are not, however, the only game in town. Dominating the scene are the large merchant houses, known as négociants, who buy in grapes, and even finished wine, blending them for their own bottlings. If certain of these companies, whose commercial clout after all did much to establish the reputation of the region as a whole in times gone by, are bywords for reasonably good – occasionally scintillating – wines, they can almost never compete with the efforts of the most quality-conscious small growers. Indeed, they rarely try to.

A mood of change has come over Burgundy in the most recent generation, with the result that the wines (the reds especially) are more conscientiously thought about than any other wines in France. There is anything but a consensus as to what the most natural style of Pinot Noir should be here. Some growers emphasize lightness, fruit and charm; others aim for a more dark and brooding style, the kind of wine that delights in making you work hard to become friends with it. There are definite stylistic differences among the various appellations, but the producer's own style is even more crucial.

The white wines of the region are generally more reliable across the board than the reds, not least because Chardonnay behaves more obligingly in most years than Pinot does. If there has been a perceptible shift in philosophies here, it has been to produce more delicate, leaner wines with less overt oak influence, which, in the classiest appellations, I find rather a pity.

To the burgundy-lover (and I am one), there is more of a sense of the soil, of the place the wine comes from, in a good Côte d'Or Pinot or Chardonnay than there is in almost any other wine in the world. It can be heartbreaking to taste the uninspiring generic wines of big companies trading only on the cachet of the famous village names, and even more upsetting that these are likely to be the only wines within reach of the average pocket. It absolutely pays to know who are the better producers, which are the better vintages and – to a lesser extent – which are the better appellations.

This chapter moves from north to south, making its way down through the fabled Côte d'Or towards the large district of the Mâconnais, but beginning – as so many of the best evenings do – with a glass of Chablis.

CHABLIS

Although historically considered to be a viticultural part of Burgundy, the Chablis vineyards lie to the northwest of the main region in the *département* of the Yonne, geographically closer to the southern end of Champagne than they are to the Côte d'Or. As such, they represent one of the most northerly outposts of still Chardonnay wine in the world. Not surprisingly, the style that came to be associated with the area was one of light-textured wines with scything acidity and either complete absence of oak, or only a very restrained use of it.

The appellation's claim to fame is a geological formation of limestone and clay, which it shares with parts of southern England, and which is known as Kimmeridgian (after the Dorset village of Kimmeridge). This is held to endow the wines with their celebrated minerality, an austere hardness that makes them worth ageing for a few years.

The class structure of the wines of Chablis is much the same as in the rest of Burgundy. The top vineyard sites are designated *grand cru*, the next best *premier cru*, and then come the

wines of the basic appellation. In Chablis, this hierarchy is supplemented by a basement category of Petit Chablis, made from land outside the heartland of the appellation, or from vines within it that have not yet attained the minimum age required for Chablis proper.

One of the debates that has consumed the Chablis universe in recent years concerns the question of machine-harvesting. When most or all of your effort is concentrated on making one style of wine, it pays to get it right. And the inherent delicacy of Chablis is such that it benefits hugely from careful hand-picking of only the ripest bunches. Mechanical harvesting for the *grand cru* and *premier cru* wines in particular ought probably to be outlawed altogether.

CHABLIS
GRAPE: *Chardonnay*

Four of Chablis's seven grand cru vineyards (below): looking from Grenouilles towards Vaudésir, Preuses and Bougros beyond.

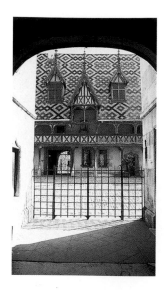

The famous Hôtel de Dieu (above), glimpsed through the entrance to the Hospices de Beaune in the village of Beaune.

Pernand-Vergelesses Delicate whites and slimline reds can both be very attractive when a lighter style is required, but this is not generally the appellation to choose for the full-throttle Burgundy experience. GC: about a quarter of the *grand cru* Corton-Charlemagne lies within this AOC. (8 pc.)
PRODUCERS: Chandon de Briailles, Pavelot, Rollin, Rapet, Laleure-Piot.

Bourgogne Aligoté Some of Burgundy's unsung alternative white wine, Aligoté (from the grape of that name) comes from around Pernand. Expect lemon-sharp acids and spritzy freshness over a softer sour-cream base. (See also Bourgogne Aligoté de Bouzeron, Côte Chalonnaise.)

Ladoix Rarely seen AOC of the village of Ladoix-Serrigny, almost all lean, simple red. Now for the confusing part. GC: about one-eighth of Le Corton (nearly all red) and a tiny part of Corton-Charlemagne (white only) lie within Ladoix, although they are officially the *grands crus* of Aloxe-Corton (see below). Similarly, some of Ladoix's *premiers crus* are claimed by Aloxe, leaving it with 11 pc to call its own.
PRODUCERS: Chevalier, E Cornu, Loichet.

Aloxe-Corton Good muscular reds from the village appellation and a minuscule quantity of underwhelming white. GC: Le Corton (the only *grand cru* for red wines on the Côte de Beaune) may have any one of up to 21 vineyard names attached to it, e.g. Corton-Bressandes, Perrières, Clos du Roi, etc. Corton-Charlemagne (the *grand cru* for whites only) is shared, as above, with Ladoix and Pernand-Vergelesses. (15 pc, some technically in the village of Ladoix.)
PRODUCERS: Tollot-Beaut, Chandon de Briailles, Bonneau du Martray, Méo-Camuzet, Girardin, Coche-Dury, Rapet, Louis Latour.

Savigny-lès-Beaune On the western side of the Côte, this was once considered rather rustic and forgettable, but is now much improved. Still relatively sanely priced. Good red-fruit Pinot, a very little decent white. (21 pc.)
PRODUCERS: Tollot-Beaut, Leroy, Pavelot, Jacob.

Chorey-lès-Beaune Underrated, and therefore generally affordable, reds (and a dash of white). The best have the soft red fruit of good Beaune Pinot, with some depth and ageability to boot.
PRODUCERS: Maillard, Arnoux, Drouhin.

Beaune The village that gives its name to this sector of the Côte. Famous for soft, strawberry-scented reds of great elegance. Also some initially hard, but eventually impressive Chardonnay. (42 pc.)

PRODUCERS: Lafarge, Tollot-Beaut, de Montille, Morot, Drouhin, Champy.

Pommard Classy, long-lived red wines with as much authoritative weight as some Côte de Nuits reds. In the wrong hands, can be a bit heavy, and always expensive for the quality. (27 pc.)
PRODUCERS: Comte Armand, Boillot, de Montille, Lafarge, Girardin, Courcel.

Volnay Top-drawer Beaune Pinot, at best perfectly capturing the combination of creamy red fruit (raspberries, loganberries) with underlying savoury depth. Arguably the finest red of the Côte de Beaune. Expensive, but mostly very fine. (35 pc, five in Meursault.)
PRODUCERS: Comte Lafon, de Montille, Lafarge, Ampeau, Matrot, Potel, Voillot.

Monthélie Suffers from its position between Volnay and Meursault, both of which are better-known, but this is nonetheless a good mainly red village for sturdy, if not noticeably elegant wines. (15 pc.)
PRODUCERS: Comte Lafon, Roulot, Jobard.

St-Romain On the western flank of the Côte, St-Romain makes both white and red, its earthily dry Chardonnays distinctly better than its light, often inconsequential Pinots.
PRODUCERS: Chassorney, Gras, Verget.

Auxey-Duresses A period of instability has been rectified with some gentle, strawberryish Pinots and pleasantly buttery Chardonnays. (9 pc.)
PRODUCERS: Leroy, Diconne, Ampeau, Prunier, Comte Armand.

Meursault First of the five-star white wine villages, and the only one with no *grand cru*. Meursault used to be hugely fat and rich, intensely oaky golden wine full of honey and butterscotch. These days, it's much leaner and more restrained, part of which is owing to over-production. Inexpensive-looking Meursault is likely to be poor value. (19 pc, two of which – Blagny and Santenots – are also for red wine, in which case they don't mention the name Meursault. Santenots then counts as a *premier cru* of Volnay.)
PRODUCERS: Comte Lafon, Coche-Dury, Roulot, Jobard, Ente, Girardin, Bouzereau, Fichet, Jadot.

Puligny-Montrachet The village wines are typically leaner than Meursault, but can be beautifully balanced, creamy and hazelnutty Chardonnay, supported by spicy, toasty new oak. From here on in, all the wines bask to some degree in the reflected glory of the greatest white burgundy of them all, the *grand cru* Le Montrachet, which makes hauntingly powerful, smoky, almondy, mouth-filling Chardonnay at second-mortgage prices. There is a little fairly dull red Puligny. GC: Le Montrachet, Bâtard-Montrachet (both shared with Chassagne-Montrachet – see below), Chevalier-Montrachet and Bienvenues-Bâtard-Montrachet. (17 pc.) PRODUCERS: Sauzet, Leflaive, Carillon, Ente, Ramonet, Larue. For *grands crus*: Dom. de la Romanée-Conti, Colin, Bouchard, Lafon, Leroy, Drouhin's Montrachet Laguiche.

St-Aubin Out west, this emergent AOC is making some fine, smoky, pedigree Chardonnay, and a smaller quantity of light, strawberry Pinot at very attractive prices. Most of the appellation is *premier cru*. (20 pc.) PRODUCERS: Bachelet, H Lamy, Thomas, Larue.

Chassagne-Montrachet Last of the great whites, perhaps the least spectacular for its basic village wines, though they still have the imprint of fine Burgundian Chardonnay, but producing some memorable *grands crus*. Reds are pretty much run-of-the-mill. GC: Le Montrachet, Bâtard-Montrachet (both shared with Puligny-Montrachet), Criots-Bâtard-Montrachet. (50 pc.) PRODUCERS: Blain-Gagnard, Ramonet, Colin, B Morey, M Morey, Niellon, Verget.

Santenay In the south of the Côte, Santenay produces mainly reds of no conspicuous finesse, but can be a satisfying glass of hearty Pinot from the better growers. Good savoury whites. (12 pc.) PRODUCERS: Girardin, Vincent, Muzard, Belland.

Maranges Created in 1988, the AOC unites three villages – Dezize, Sampigny and Cheilly – each followed by the appellation suffix (Dezize-lès-Maranges, etc.), though they may also be labelled simply Maranges. Overwhelmingly red, fairly rustic, but kindly priced. (7 pc.) PRODUCERS: Bachelet, Girardin, Charleux.

Hautes-Côtes-de-Beaune As in the Nuits, there is a scattering of villages among the hills to the west of the sector that take this appellation. Quality is generally good, notably for the soft, cherry-fruited reds. PRODUCERS: Joillot, Jacob, Ch. de Mercey, Caves des Hautes-Côtes.

Côte de Beaune-Villages Red wine appellation that covers most of the Côte, and may be used by any of the individual villages (with the big four exceptions of Aloxe-Corton, Beaune, Pommard and Volnay) or for any wine blended from two or more villages, a practice not much in evidence now. PRODUCERS: Drouhin, Jadot, Lupé-Cholet.

Côte de Beaune The simplest appellation in the area takes in vineyards on the hill overlooking the village of Beaune itself – but not from anywhere else on the Côte, perplexingly. Undistinguished reds and whites.

COTE CHALONNAISE

The large bulk-producing area in the south of Burgundy, the Mâconnais, is separated from the Côte d'Or by a strip of vineyard called the Côte Chalonnaise, which takes its name from the town of Chalon-sur-Saône. As well as producing some basic AOC Bourgogne Rouge and Blanc, there are five important village appellations here. Because their reputations are nothing like as exalted as the villages of the Côte d'Or, these generally represent good value, although they don't have quite the same class. From north to south:

Bouzeron An AOC since 1998, this village appellation is considered the best for the second-string white grape of Burgundy, Aligoté. They should be drunk fairly young to capture their challenging lemon-and-crème-fraîche character. PRODUCERS: de Villaine, Goisot, Mortet, Ente.

Rully The whites and reds of this village have now eclipsed its erstwhile reputation as a source of cheap and cheerful fizz. Its whites are lighter and drier than from the Côte de Beaune, but well-made by and large, as are its simple, plummy reds. (23 pc.) PRODUCERS: Jacqueson, Dureuil-Janthial, Briday, Jadot, Girardin.

COTE CHALONNAISE
GRAPES: *White –*
Chardonnay, Aligoté;
Red – Pinot Noir

Dusk falls over the vineyards of the Hautes-Côtes-de-Nuits AC, in the hills of the Côte d'Or (below).

MACONNAIS/
OTHER WINES

GRAPES: *Red – Pinot Noir,*
Gamay, César, Tressot;
White – Chardonnay,
Aligoté, Pinot Blanc,
Pinot Gris, Sacy

Chardonnay grapes arriving
at the Caves de Buxy
cooperative (below)
in the Montagny AC,
Côte Chalonnaise.

Mercurey The lion's share of Chalonnaise production comes from this village, which is why you will sometimes see the whole sub-region referred to as the Région de Mercurey. Mostly, well-balanced, concentrated reds, though whites are much improved, and can be surprisingly rich. (30 pc.)
PRODUCERS: Ch. de Chamirey, Juillot, de Suremain, Lorenzon, Raquillet, Faiveley.
Givry Predominantly red wines in an impressively scented raspberry style, with good structure. Small amount of intriguingly spicy white. (17 pc.)
PRODUCERS: Chofflet-Valdenaire, Joblot, F Lumpp, Sarrazin.
Montagny Quality in this whites-only appellation is decidedly patchy. Some possess convincing intensity; many taste pretty similar to anonymous Mâcon Blanc-Villages. Absurdly enough, fully half of the land planted qualifies as *premier cru*. (49 pc.)
PRODUCERS: Aladame, Vachet, Roy, Louis Latour, Caves de Buxy.

MACONNAIS

The southernmost district of Burgundy, opposite the town of Mâcon, is in many ways the commercial hub of the region. The majority of Burgundy's cooperatives are found here, and in Beaujolais to the south. Predominantly everyday whites, with one or two stars, the production is very much geared to volume markets, and is easily outshone in many instances by low-priced Chardonnay from elsewhere in the world.

Pouilly-Fuissé A whites-only appellation that carries the quality torch for the Mâconnais as a whole, pricing its wines in accordance with its ambition. At their classiest, they are richly oaked and fleshy, and do display some elegance. Neighbouring appellations of Pouilly-Vinzelles and Pouilly-Loché are not quite in the same class.
PRODUCERS: Château-Fuissé, Guffens-Heynen, Ch. de Rontets, Valette, Ferret, Robert-Denogent, Lassarat, Merlin, Jadot.
St-Véran In the dead south of the Mâconnais, overlapping into Beaujolais and wholly enclosing the Pouilly-Fuissé AOC, St-Véran is a somewhat underrated source of dry, chalky Chardonnay wines with a certain amount of Burgundian flair.
PRODUCERS: Thévenet, Lassarat, Deux Roches, Corsin, Gerbeaux, Jadot.
Viré-Clessé These two villages in the far north of the region were plucked from the humdrum mélange of the Mâcon-Villages in 1999 to form their own AOC. It's Chardonnay only once again, and there are some bravura wines with a deal of showoff oak on them being produced.
PRODUCERS: Bonhomme, Michel, Ch. de Viré.
Mâcon-Villages The umbrella AOC covers a total of 26 villages making white wines, all of which have the right to append their names to the word Mâcon on the label. Some of the better quality are Lugny, La Roche-Vineuse, Montbellet, Uchizy and – tantalizingly – Chardonnay. Prissé has its own AOC.
PRODUCERS: Thévenet, Merlin, Manciat, Barraud, Bret Brothers, Bonhomme.
Below Mâcon-Villages are the basic appellations of Mâcon Supérieur (reds and whites) and simple Mâcon (reds only, mostly from Gamay).

OTHER WINES

The basic appellation for the whole region, top to bottom, is AOC **Bourgogne** – Blanc, Rouge or Rosé. Increasingly, producers are using this to make eye-catching decent varietal wines to hone Burgundy's competitiveness at the affordable end of the market. The whites are often given a little oak, the reds properly endowed with fruit, and the rosés are usually light and evanescently fruity.

Some of the more northerly villages, notably those from the Auxerre region near Chablis – **Chitry**, **Irancy** and **Epineuil** – now have the right to add their names to the Bourgogne designation. In the whites, Chardonnay may be joined by leavenings of Pinots Blanc and Gris,

while reds may add Gamay to the Pinot Noir, together with a pair of historical oddities from near Chablis – César and Tressot.

Bourgogne Passetoutgrains is a regional AOC for a blend of Pinot Noir and Gamay, in which the former should account for not less than a third of the assemblage.

Crémant de Bourgogne The traditional-method sparkling wine can be made from any of the region's grapes, but is principally Chardonnay and Pinot Noir. It can be crisp, palate-cleansing stuff, sometimes with a little depth. The terms Blanc de Blancs and Blanc de Noirs may be used for white wines made from all white grapes or all black grapes respectively. There is also some pleasant Crémant rosé.

VINTAGE GUIDE

Vintage conditions in Burgundy affect the red wines far more than the whites. An off-year for Chardonnay may result in less substantial but perfectly drinkable wines, whereas unripe Pinot Noir may be feeble in colour, flimsy in texture and hopelessly lacking fruit.

REDS

2009 ***** A great vintage that should see many intensely concentrated wines with glorious fruit. Perfect for laying down.
2008 **** Ripe and aromatic, the 08s will repay keeping, with Côte de Nuits reds just shading it.
2007 *** I was less enthusiastic about these than others were. Too many of the wines seem to lack focus, but there are always exceptions.
2006 **** A Côte de Nuits year, if ever there was. Beaune wines seemed to lack grip.
2005 ***** Fabulous. Multi-layered, lush, sexy burgundy wherever you looked. Still worth buying if you come across them.
2003 *** Hard to generalize. A very hot vintage led to too many over-alcoholic wines with tough tannins.
2002 **** Juicy reds with plenty of appealing fruit.
1999 **** A very attractive vintage, with classic Burgundian depth and roundness.
EARLIER HIGHLIGHTS: *1996* **** *1995* **** *1992* **** *1990* ***** *1989* ***** *1988* ****

WHITES

BEST RECENT VINTAGES: *2009, 2007, 2006, 2005, 2004, 2002.*

The rock of Vergisson (above) towers over the Pouilly-Fuissé vineyards, source of Mâconnais's finest white burgundies.

Barrels awaiting the new vintage (left) at Louis Latour's cellars in Aloxe-Corton, Côte de Beaune.

BEAUJOLAIS

Burgundy's southernmost wine region, the huge Beaujolais area, is devoted to the red grape Gamay and one of the winemaking world's most individual red wine styles. The winemakers here offer much more than just Nouveau.

The hilly Beaujolais region (above), the most southerly of Burgundy's wine areas.

BEAUJOLAIS
GRAPES: Red – Gamay; White – Chardonnay

IT IS THE FATE OF Beaujolais never to be taken quite seriously. It is mostly such a lightweight wine that few bother to age it, and most retailers are keen to get rid of last year's stocks before the new vintage arrives. You could sympathize with the region's négociants and growers until you are reminded that they pump out about a third of the entire production every year as Beaujolais Nouveau, which hardly transmits the message that this is a wine worth dwelling on. It remains, I suspect, for a great number of consumers, one of those wines that you might drink one bottle of in any given year.

All this is something of a shame because the wines of many of the *cru* villages age well, but neither their producers nor much of the wine commentariat seem to want you to know that. Admittedly, in its youth – say, six months to a year from the vintage – it can be an incomparably charming wine, its lightness of texture and lack of tannin compensated for by its alcoholic weight (typically around 13 per cent) and the easy, accessible ripeness of its juicy strawberry fruit. But what most Beaujolais lacks in tannin, it more than makes up for in acidity, and it's that raw, crunching tartness – like biting into what you hoped was going to be a nice juicy pear, and finding it as hard as an onion – that too often spoils the enjoyment.

There are moves from some growers to give the *cru* wines more depth and power by varying the vinification method (traditionally carbonic maceration, in which the fermentation takes place within the grape) to allow a little tannin into the wines. Those used to the happy-go-lucky reds of summer may find these wines, which are also sometimes aged in oak, normally a foreign substance in Beaujolais, something of a shock to the system, but they have been among the region's more notable successes.

By and large, though, Beaujolais remains pre-eminently an unchallenging summer tipple, easily made, bottled early and drunk chilled. Most of it is too expensive for what it is, but when growers in the *cru* villages are presented with a ripe vintage of wines that are capable of deepening over six or seven years into a complex,

gamey maturity, then I don't mind the price of admission. Négociants dominate the Beaujolais scene, with the old and reputable house of Georges Duboeuf in the vanguard, but there are many fine small growers to look out for too.

The more basic the quality and the younger it is, the colder Beaujolais should be drunk. Keep the best *cru* wines for longer, and don't chill them at all. These come from ten villages identified as having the best vineyard sites. From north to south, they are:

St-Amour Traditionally drunk on Valentine's Day, of course. Intensely fragrant, but with a hint of Burgundian structure to it as well. It is often one of the best-balanced of the *cru* Beaujolais. PRODUCERS: des Ducs, des Billards, Côtes de la Roche.

Juliénas One of the less charming wines, often rather hard and insufficiently endowed with fruit, but made in a softer style by some. PRODUCERS: Ch. de Juliénas, Pelletier, Tête, Duboeuf Ch. des Capitans.

Chénas At this point, the *cru* wines start becoming bolder and sturdier. These are prime candidates for ageing, being clenched and dour in their first flush of youth, but ageing to a meaty, sinewy richness. PRODUCERS: Champagnon, Lapierre, Piron & Lafont Quartz, Santé.

Moulin-à-Vent The Beaujolais that seems to think it's a Rhône wine, Moulin-à-Vent is always the biggest and burliest of the *crus*. From a good producer, the wines can take ten years' ageing in their stride, but they can be just as enjoyable at three or four years, with ripe blackberry fruit and often a fair bit of tannin. PRODUCERS: Janodet, Ch. des Jacques, Duboeuf Tour du Bief, Santé, Champagnon.

Fleurie Still the best-loved of the *crus* – and therefore often the most expensive. Classic Fleurie is summer-scented with strawberries and roses, light-textured and creamy and soft. A lot isn't. Guy Depardon's atypical wines will shock the purists, but are masterpieces of violetty, gingery, Turkish Delight seductiveness, rounded with barrel-ageing, and needing a decade in the bottle.

PRODUCERS: G Depardon, Verpoix, Chignard, Berrod, Clos de la Roilette, Duboeuf La Madone and Quatre Vents.

Chiroubles Light and attractive wines, not much seen outside France, but worth trying if you come across one.
PRODUCERS: Cheysson, Desvignes, Passot, la Combe au Loup.

Morgon Morgon's wines are famous for their capacity to age very quickly into a light but interestingly meaty Burgundian maturity, an experience worth seeking out. To capitalize on this, some is released with the designation Morgon Agé; it's cellared for 18 months before it hits the market. Even in youth, there is a savouriness to them, and the fruit is often more blackcurrant than strawberry. Best come from a hillside called the Côte du Py, which will be named on the label.
PRODUCERS: Janodet, Desvignes, Aucoeur, Lapierre, Foillard, Duboeuf Jean Descombes.

Régnié The newest *cru*, created in 1988, and it can consider itself very lucky. These are the lightest of the light.
PRODUCERS: Rampon, Durand, Duboeuf des Buyats.

Brouilly Silky-soft, cherry-fruited charmers at their best, the wines of Brouilly are the most approachable of the *crus*. They don't generally need ageing, as their youthful fruit is so exuberant. By far the biggest production of the ten.
PRODUCERS: Ch. Thivin, Ch. de la Chaize,

Lapalu, Michaud, Duboeuf Ch. de Nevers and Dom. de Combillaty.

Côte de Brouilly Hillside vineyards in the middle of Brouilly, but possessing their own blue-granite soil and exposure, consequently making distinctive wine. Deeper cherry fruit and richer texture than Brouilly itself, often with a touch of ginger. Underrated and not much exported.
PRODUCERS: Ch. Thivin, Pavillon de Chavannes, Viornery, Ravier.

Wines from any of 39 villages in the northern part of the region may be sold as **Beaujolais-Villages**, with the village name mentioned if the wine comes solely from that vineyard. These can be delightful, fruity reds for quaffing young. The rest is basic **Beaujolais**, and represents a significant drop in quality. Buy a Villages wine if you're not in the market for a *cru*. There are small amounts of ethereally light **Beaujolais Rosé**, and a smidgen of often pretty impressive, if austere, **Beaujolais Blanc** made from Chardonnay.

As to **Nouveau**, it is the wine of the new vintage, released on the third Thursday of November. In occasional years, it can have a chewy-candy charm, but it mostly stinks of fermentation and is piled with stomach-provoking acids. Yum.
BEST RECENT VINTAGES (but note that Beaujolais rarely has complete disasters): *2009, 2006, 2005, 2003.*

Gamay vines under an autumnal mist in the village of Juliénas (below), one of the more northerly of the Beaujolais cru villages.

RHONE

Overshadowed for centuries by Bordeaux and Burgundy, the Rhône valley is nonetheless the source of formidable spicy, rich reds and intriguing whites from its two distinct areas – the Syrah-dominated north and the mixed culture of the south.

THE RHONE VALLEY consists of two quite distinct viticultural sectors about 30 miles apart, running from Vienne down to Avignon, and referred to simply as Northern and Southern Rhône. Production is predominantly of red wines, and the styles are typically big, hefty, spicy creations that mature as excitingly as the best Bordeaux.

The last 30 years or so have seen a transformation in the Rhône's fortunes. Where once only Hermitage and Châteauneuf-du-Pape were known at all well outside its confines, its many other fine appellations have had the world beating a path to its door. They have also inspired winemakers elsewhere to try their hands with the indigenous Rhône grape varieties, Syrah, Mourvèdre, Grenache, and the white Viognier.

Prices for the top wines have accordingly ascended into the stratosphere, but the good news is that, far more than in Bordeaux or Burgundy, the more gently priced everyday wines are thoroughly reliable. The Rhône thus remains a democratic wine region, where the ordinary customer is far less likely to be fobbed off with undrinkable tat than in the hallowed environs of the Médoc or the Côte d'Or.

NORTHERN RHONE

GRAPES: Red – Syrah; White – Viognier, Marsanne, Roussanne

The Rhône river lends its name to the long stretch of the Rhône valley wine region (below), divided into two distinct viticultural districts – northern and southern Rhône.

NORTHERN RHONE

(from north to south)

Côte-Rôtie What distinguishes the reds of the north from those of the south is that they are made from one red grape, Syrah, whereas the southern wines are always a mix, with Syrah usually a fairly junior partner in the blend. Having said that, Côte-Rôtie is permitted to include up to 20 per cent of the white grape Viognier (see Condrieu below). Not all producers use it, but those who do add a little – and it is hardly ever the full 20 per cent – produce perfumed wines of astonishing intensity.

The AOC name, the 'roasted hillside', refers to its steep, southeasterly exposure on the left bank of the river, where the vines are sheltered from the worst the weather can do, enjoying their own little sun-trap. In the hotter years, Côte-Rôtie is an uncommonly concentrated wine, crammed full of blackberry fruit and tannin, but with layers of spice and chocolate underneath, just waiting for a decade's maturation. It is arguably even more highly prized than Hermitage itself these days, with the inevitable consequence that prices for the wines of the best growers have shot through the roof. At the pinnacle of achievement are the wines of Marcel Guigal, who makes not only straight Côte-Rôtie, but also three exemplary wines from single vineyards (La Landonne, La Mouline and La Turque), for which he charges the earth.
PRODUCERS: Guigal, Jamet, Jasmin, Delas, Rostaing, Cuilleron, Bonnefond, Vidal-Fleury, Duclaux, Gérin, Ogier.

Condrieu The sole grape of this white-wine appellation is Viognier, suddenly internationally fashionable in recent years as an alternative to Chardonnay. Condrieu is its true home, making wines that continue to set the pace for all other growers of the variety. The wines initially seem rather heavy and creamy on the nose, but then a wonderfully musky scent of puréed ripe apricots comes through, followed by subtle spice notes often reminiscent of Indian cooking – ground coriander, sticks of cinnamon, ginger root – but all bound by that thick, clotted-cream feel. Many producers achieve this, moreover,

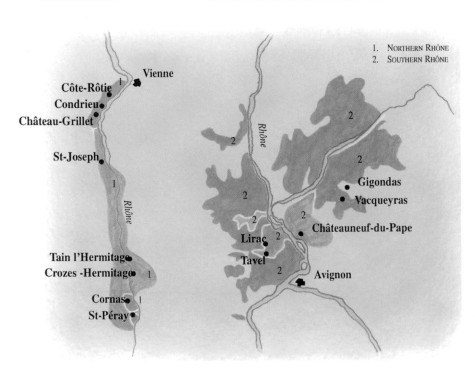

1. NORTHERN RHÔNE
2. SOUTHERN RHÔNE

Vienne

Côte-Rôtie
Condrieu
Château-Grillet

St-Joseph

Rhône

Rhône

Tain l'Hermitage
Crozes -Hermitage

Cornas
St-Péray

Gigondas
Vacqueyras

Châteauneuf-du-Pape

Lirac
Tavel

Avignon

without resorting to oak. Opinion tends to divide on the best moment to drink these wines. I think they are at their best fairly young, up to two years old. Once again, they are expensive, but worth trying at least once. A small amount of sweeter late-harvest wine is made.

PRODUCERS: Vernay, Guigal, Cuilleron, Perret, Villard, Colombo, Monteillet, Pichon, Gaillard.

Château-Grillet Single-vineyard enclave of four hectares within Condrieu, wholly owned by the Neyret-Gachet family and awarded an appellation all of its own. The wine is aged in cask, and is intended to be far longer-lived than Condrieu. At five to ten years, it is full of orange and apricot scents against a mineral background, with notes of golden raisins on the finish.

St-Joseph Red and white wines. The reds may be less distinguished than those of Côte-Rôtie, but do have a raspberry-fruited immediacy to them and some definite ageing potential. Some producers make a practically Beaujolais-like lighter red, but even the heavier ones are nothing like as dense as other northern Rhône reds. Whites are made from a pair of grapes often found together in these parts – the twin sisters Marsanne and Roussanne. There isn't much made in St-Joseph, but what there is is fairly chunky, walnut-dry, but spice-tinged.

PRODUCERS: Chave, Gripa, Coursodon, Graillot, Durand, Jaboulet's Le Grand Pompée.

Crozes-Hermitage The largest output, mostly of red wines, of the north comes from this AOC. Usually considered to be the first rung of the quality ladder, but in fact its wines are remarkably well-made, even at cooperative level, and can therefore represent outstanding value. Peppery, gingery, plummy and firm-textured, they are capable of a few years' ageing. Up to 15 per cent white grapes (Marsanne and Roussanne) may be added to them, though rarely are. The white wines themselves are florally scented, but quite solid and lumpish in texture.

PRODUCERS: Graillot, Ferraton, Fayolle, Combier, Pochon, Les Bruyères, Dom. des Grands Chemins, Darnaud, Cave des Clairmonts.

Hermitage The great hill of Hermitage pops up in the middle of the Crozes appellation, its steeply shelving vineyards forming the AOC of Hermitage itself. Often among the most majestically proportioned red wines made anywhere in France, they are huge, powerfully concentrated, full-on Syrah, with tannin and extract to spare, and demanding the best part

of a decade to begin to unwind. When they do, their fruit remains as vibrantly fresh as the day they were bottled, so that even at 12 years old, they can gush forth blackberries and raspberries in abundance, backed up by dark chocolate and the most savoury herbs – thyme and oregano. Whites, a blend of Marsanne and Roussanne, are rich and weighty, with flavours of roasted nuts and liquorice.

PRODUCERS: Chave, Guigal, Delas, M Sorrel, Faurie, Tardieu-Laurent, Chapoutier, Jaboulet's La Chapelle.

Cornas Enigmatic appellation for densely textured, tannic Syrah reds that never quite seem to open out into the fruit-filled glories of Hermitage. They can often resemble the burlier versions of Châteauneuf-du-Pape, with roasting meat aromas filling out Syrah's black-pepper character, but taking their time to do so.

PRODUCERS: Clape, Voge, Colombo, Allemand, Courbis, Tardieu-Laurent.

St-Péray Mainly noted for rather tough, unfriendly sparkling wine, made from the white Hermitage grapes (plus another fairly rare variety, Roussette), using the traditional method, but lacking elegance. Some strangely cream-cheesy, but often likable, still white is also made, worth trying if you see it.

PRODUCERS: Clape, Gripa, Thiers, Lemenicier.

Vineyards of Côte-Rôtie, 'the roasted slope' (above), on the sunny left bank of the Rhône, overlooking the village of Ampuis.

Picking Viognier grapes at the four-hectare AC Château-Grillet (above), a single vineyard within Condrieu.

Vineyards of Châteauneuf-du-Pape (above), the most famous red wine of the southern Rhône.

SOUTHERN RHONE

GRAPES: Red – Grenache, Cinsault, Mourvèdre, Syrah, Carignan, Gamay; White – Clairette, Picpoul, Bourboulenc, Grenache Blanc, Roussanne, Marsanne, Muscat, Viognier

SOUTHERN RHONE

Châteauneuf-du Pape The most famous red wine of the southern Rhône, named after a palace built for one of the Avignon popes in the 14th century and flattened by Nazi bombers during the war, Châteauneuf always has a symbol of crossed keys embossed on its bottles. It embraces a wide stylistic range, from almost Beaujolais-light to fairly weighty, ink-dark wine with whopping tannic extraction. It always has very high alcohol (14 per cent is quite usual). Principally Grenache, it can draw on 13 varieties, though most producers make do with three or four. The lighter ones can be drinkable

at three years old, but most need at least twice that to begin to lose their tannin. If there is a problem, it's often that the wines are not really about fruit, other than a sort of chewy fruitgum quality.

The white wines come from a cocktail of varieties les by such unlikely stars as Picpoul, Bourboulenc, Clairette and the white version of Grenache. They tend to be fairly neutral in aroma, but fat, structured and alcoholic in the mouth. Ch. de Beaucastel's white has much more character, and is worth keeping for three or four years.

PRODUCERS: Beaucastel, Mont-Redon, Clos du Mont-Olivet, Rayas, Vieux Télégraphe, Bonneau, la Janasse, la Charbonnière, Font de Michelle, Chapoutier, Fortia.

Gigondas A fierce, black-hearted red, often rigidly tannic and head-bangingly alcoholic. It needs plenty of time to soften up, but many of the wines are too austere to make the wait worthwhile. When good, it has a violent liquoricey majesty.

PRODUCERS: St-Gayan, Clos des Cazaux, Raspail-Ay, Santa Duc, Brusset, Moulin de la Gardette, Amadieu, Cassan.

Lirac On the opposite bank of the Rhône to Châteauneuf, this much underrated AOC makes wines in all three colours, all highly reliable. The reds have good fruit and considerable substance, the rosés are agreeably ripe and graceful, and the whites are strong and flavourful.

PRODUCERS: Maby, St-Roch, Lafond Roc-Epine, la Mordorée, Sabon.

Tavel An AOC, unusually, for rosés only. They tend to look more beige than pink, and are not exactly overflowing with fruit. Good with richly sauced crustacean dishes.

PRODUCERS: Genestière, Aquéria, Montézargues, la Mordorée.

Vacqueyras May be red, pink or (very rarely) white. The reds are good, spicy, gingery wines worth keeping for five years.

PRODUCERS: Ch. des Tours, Clos des Cazaux, Monardière, Montirius, Couroulu.

Ventoux Dusty, spicy reds from just south of Vacqueyras, with small amounts of the other two colours.

PRODUCERS: Martinelle, Anges, Cascavel.

Coteaux du Tricastin Mainly reds and rosés with plenty of earthy fruit. One of those appellations that has slowly but surely improved of late.

PRODUCERS: Grangeneuve, St-Luc.

Côtes du Rhône-Villages A whole swathe of villages, from the central Rhône districts of the Ardèche and the Drôme down through the southern section, are entitled to this AOC. Of those, 16 are allowed to append their names to the basic designation, among them Cairanne, Séguret, Sablet, Chusclun and Vinsobres. Quality across the board is quite dependable, and the price is mostly right.

Côtes du Rhône The basic AOC that covers all other villages, including those in the northern Rhône. Styles vary from light and fruity to tannin-driven red, via some delightful rosé, to a scant quantity of vaguely milky white. Quality is all over the place, but the wines are hardly ever pricy. Names to seek are Dom. de la Fonsalette and Guigal.

Other large areas around the southern Rhône make up a fair amount of the annual production. Most is uncomplicated everyday stuff, but there are occasional stars. The **Côtes du Lubéron** is good at hearty reds, as is the **Côtes du Vivarais**. **Costières de Nîmes** is technically in the Languedoc further south, but considers itself part of the Rhône, and its wines can be superbly complex (especially from Mourgues du Grès).

In the central sector are two wine regions, the **Coteaux de l'Ardèche** and the Drôme. The former can be a good source of varietal wines (Duboeuf makes a good Gamay there).

The Drôme encompasses the small but good AOC of **Châtillon-en-Diois**, which makes Gamay reds and Chardonnay and Aligoté whites, as well as an interesting sparkling wine, **Clairette de Die**. Made from a minimum of

75 per cent grapey Muscat blended with the neutral Clairette, it's a refreshing, frothy dead ringer for Italian Asti to the uninitiated.

VINS DOUX NATURELS
These are sweet wine specialities of southern France. They are made naturally sweet by interrupting the fermentation of super-ripe grapes with the addition of spirit to produce a light fortified wine – basically the same method as is used for port.

Muscat de Beaumes-de-Venise The most celebrated of the fortified Muscats is a rich, golden dessert wine, tasting of sweet green grapes and mandarins, with a tongue-coating barley-sugar quality too. They should be drunk young and fresh, and served very well chilled. PRODUCERS: Dom. de Durban, Vidal-Fleury, Jaboulet, Delas, Bernardins.

Rasteau This comes as either red or white, from the respectively coloured versions of Grenache. The red can be good in a rough, young port-like style; the local co-op makes a passable example.

VINTAGE GUIDE
For northern Rhône reds, the best recent vintages are *2009, 2006, 2005, 2003, 2001, 1999* and *1995*.

In the south, the chance for blending means that more vintages are likely to produce something acceptable than if you have to pin all your hopes on the ripening of one grape variety. Good recent vintages are *2009, 2007, 2006, 2005, 2004, 2003* and *2001*.

Harvested Muscat grapes being taken to the local cooperative in Beaumes-de-Venise (below), to make the luscious, rich, golden sweet wine of the same name.

PROVENCE *and* CORSICA

Traditionally known for its pale rosés, the Mediterranean region of Provence now grows a wider and better choice of grape varieties that are bringing some fine reds and whites to market.

PROVENCE

GRAPES: *Red – Grenache, Mourvèdre, Cinsault, Syrah, Carignan, Cabernet Sauvignon, Tibouren, Braquet; White – Clairette, Ugni Blanc, Grenache Blanc, Rolle, Sauvignon Blanc, Marsanne, Terret*

IT IS HIGHLY PROBABLE that the much-loved region of Provence in southeast France was the cradle of French viticulture. Its ancient seaport of Marseilles was founded around 600 BC by Greek settlers, who brought their own wines with them, probably sourced from their colonies in what was eventually to become Rome. Later, when France – as Gaul – had become a major component of the Roman Empire, cultivation of the vine spread slowly westwards and northwards throughout the country from this sun-soaked corner.

Despite the fondness of European tourists, the British foremost among them, for Provence, its wines are still very little known outside the region. That remains a mystery, especially given the unusually high production of rosé wines, a style that has become extravagantly fashionable in the early years of the 21st century. Nearly all the wine is blended from a handful of grape varieties, some of them quite obscure, which means that Provence doesn't have varietalism on its side. But there is much healthy experimentation in the region, and its wines are worth trying.

Côtes de Provence By far the biggest AOC, covering the whole region, Côtes de Provence embraces a number of totally diverse areas in

a broad sweep that runs from near Aix-en-Provence down via the coast at St-Tropez and back up to a mountainous enclave north of Nice. The greater part of the production (fully 80 per cent) is pink wines – known locally as 'little summer rosés' – targeted specifically at the tourist hordes, and sold in peculiar skittle-shaped bottles. The wines are largely based on the Midi varieties Grenache and Cinsault, but there is a good-quality local grape, Tibouren, that is used on its own by some producers, and makes characterful rosés that are a cut above the norm.

Reds have traditionally been based on the rather dull ubiquitous southern grape, Carignan, although since the 1980s, it may constitute no more than 40 per cent of the blend. Cabernet Sauvignon and Syrah are beginning to play significant roles in the vineyards instead. Only a small amount of white wine is made, but it can be unexpectedly fragrant and good.
PRODUCERS: la Courtade, Ott, Richeaume, Rimauresq, Cressonnière.

Coteaux d'Aix-en-Provence The area around the old university town of Aix-en-Provence produces wines in all three colours, which are quite as varied as those from the main regional AOC, but at a higher overall standard of quality. Its performance has been on a steady upward trajectory since it was demarcated in the 1980s. Again, Cabernet and Syrah are beginning to make their presences felt, and some of the reds from this westernmost part of Provence have a tantalizingly claret-like profile. Rosés account for about a third of the output, while whites are very few and far between.
PRODUCERS: Vignelaure, du Seuil, les Bastides, les Béates.

Les Baux de Provence Demarcated from the above AOC in 1995, Les Baux is a mountainous outpost of highly individual red and rosé wines, some of them from relatively recently planted vineyards. Cabernet and Syrah combine to do their stuff once more among the more traditional Provençal varieties, and encouragingly around 85 per cent of the appellation is run along organic or biodynamic lines. Indeed, so

The broad sweep of the Provençal wine region, running from the cooler inland hills along the sun-soaked but Mistral-blown Mediterranean coast (below).

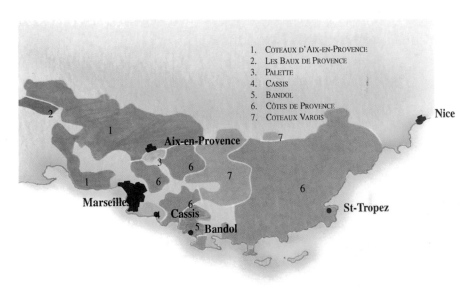

1. COTEAUX D'AIX-EN-PROVENCE
2. LES BAUX DE PROVENCE
3. PALETTE
4. CASSIS
5. BANDOL
6. CÔTES DE PROVENCE
7. COTEAUX VAROIS

great is the local commitment to these methods that growers are lobbying for them to be made a stipulation of the AOC regulations.
PRODUCERS: Mas de Gourgonnier, Romanin, Terres Blanches, Hauvette.

Bandol Potentially the weightiest and most ageworthy reds in Provence come from this coastal appellation that also makes some good savoury rosé and a little crisp, appley white (some containing a dollop of Sauvignon Blanc). The reds have to be cask-aged for a minimum of 18 months, and they must include at least 50 per cent of the distinguished Mourvèdre grape, to achieve a dense-textured wine full of black plum fruit and herbs. They are slowly but surely acquiring a reputation outside the region – largely thanks to the first-named producer below – and represent a serious alternative to mid-range Bordeaux.
PRODUCERS: Tempier, Pibarnon, Pradeaux, Gaussen, Vannières.

Cassis Nothing to do with the blackcurrant liqueur of the same name, this tiny AOC a little further westwards along the coast from Bandol makes mainly white wines from a fascinating grab-bag of southern Rhône varieties – Marsanne among them – and Sauvignon Blanc. Mainly sold locally, they can be quite sturdy, but often possessed of an uncommonly beautiful aromatic allure. Reds and pinks use proportionately about as much Mourvèdre as those of Bandol.
PRODUCERS: Best is Clos Ste-Magdeleine.

Bellet Perched high up in the hills to the north of Nice, near the border with Italy, Bellet is seldom seen outside Provence. Because of its altitude, this is a cooler area, and the small production of reds, whites and rosés reflects that in noticeably higher acid levels. The grape varieties are shared with parts of western Italy, so that the Rolle of Bellet's whites is Vermentino to the Italians, while the Braquet used in its pinks is called Brachetto over the border. Outposts of Grenache and Cinsault make their appearance in the reds.
PRODUCERS: Ch. de Bellet, Ch. de Crémat.

Palette An historic enclave near Aix-en-Provence, about 75 per cent of which is owned by one property, Ch. Simone. In addition to the usual southern grape varieties, there are some microscopic plantings of all but forgotten local grapes on very aged vinestock, producing reds, whites and rosés. Reds and rosés can both make quite an impact in the best years.

Coteaux Varois Named after the *département* of the Var in which it is located, this AOC was carved out of the Côtes de Provence in 1993. The usual mixture of southern grape varieties is employed to mostly good effect, although the whites can be a shade dull.
PRODUCERS: Triennes, Miraval, Alysses.

CORSICA

The Mediterranean island of Corsica may be French-controlled, but its vine culture owes much to neighbouring Italy. Once the source of basic slosh that went into the European wine lake, it set about radically improving its ways in the 1980s, with cautiously encouraging results to date, and an interesting spread of styles.

Corsica has a wide range of grapes, including the reds of the southern Rhône and Languedoc, as well as more fashionable international varieties. In the white Vermentino (known as Rolle in Provence) and two characterful reds (Nielluccio and Sciacarello), it has a handful of good indigenous grapes.

Only a small percentage of the island's production goes under one of the nine AOCs available. They are **Patrimonio**, **Ajaccio**, the island-wide **Vin de Corse** (all making emphatic use of the local grapes), five subdivisions of Vin de Corse – **Coteaux du Cap Corse**, **Calvi**, **Figari**, **Porto Vecchio** and **Sartène** – and a separate AOC for a *vin doux naturel*, **Muscat du Cap Corse**.

About 60 per cent of Corsican wine is made by powerful cooperatives as Vin de Pays de L'Ile de Beauté.

Carefully tended vines at Dom. Clos Ste-Magdelaine (left), in the hot coastal hills of Cassis.

Houses tumble down the hillside (above) in the Corsican town of Sartène that gives its name to the local AOC, Vin de Corse Sartène.

LANGUEDOC-ROUSSILLON

Better grape varieties and modern technology are assisting producers across Languedoc-Roussillon in their efforts to move away from everyday plonk to greater quality, with clean, stylish varietal wines.

Tradition bush-trained vines near Caramany in Côtes du Roussillon-Villages (above). Behind are the Pyrenees.

France's largest wine region (below), taking in Languedoc and the Côtes du Roussillon – once known as the Midi – which touches the Spanish border.

THE CENTRAL-SOUTHERN swathe of France that is comprised of the twin regions of Languedoc and the Côtes du Roussillon – often referred to as the Midi – is where the most dynamic developments in the recent history of French wine have been taking place. This is the traditional grape-basket of France, and too often in the past simply a backwash area of over-production. Now it is the scene of frantic innovation, inspired to a significant degree from the 1990s on by the technical input of wine consultants from other countries.

A debate of gathering ferocity has been going on as to whether roving winemakers, with their technocratic ways, jetting in from Australia and elsewhere, and stopping just long enough to oversee the harvest, the grape-crushing and the vinification, are not guilty of homogenizing the taste of these wines. There has been some militant resistance on the part of local growers to superstar investors from the English-speaking world hoping to buy up land, and grow something akin to California Merlot in the rolling hills of southern France.

The potential of the Languedoc has nonetheless begun to emerge. Some of its key appellations were only upgraded to AOC status in the past 20 years, while a lot of the running has been made by growers working outside those regulations. These latter have been

planting varieties that were not previously the norm in the region – Cabernet Sauvignon, Chardonnay, Sauvignon Blanc, even the odd outbreak of Pinot Noir. In consequence, the Languedoc is – with the exception of Alsace and its handful of traditional white grapes – the best bet for the varietally minded wine-lover starting out in France.

Vin de Pays d'Oc The Languedoc has done a smart job since the 1980s of turning wine tradition on its head by bottling much of its best wine under the catchall generic designation of *vin de pays*. Theoretically inferior to wines of AOC status, these would-be 'country wines', in many cases, put the produce of the appellations to shame in terms of quality. Prices for the most ambitious rose rapidly, as growers realized that an oak-aged Cabernet Sauvignon could fetch more in the market than Fitou.

The climate down here is more reliable than in most of the classic French regions, with relatively low rainfall and less severe spring frosts. Deep, blackcurranty Cabernets are nearly always better than cheap Bordeaux, Chardonnays range from the lightly oaked and lemony to strapping young things full of butterscotch and cream, while Sauvignons can be improbably crisp and fresh for such a warm climate. Soft juicy Merlots, peppery-plummy Syrahs, ripely apricotty Viogniers and the odd, rather lost Pinot Noir fill out the picture. PRODUCERS: Skalli-Fortant, Clovallon, Val d'Orbieu, Denois, Lurton.

Vin de Pays de l'Hérault If there were to be a *grand cru* of the *vins de pays* in the south, it would surely go to an estate called Mas de Daumas Gassac in the eastern Languedoc district of the Hérault. Here, powerfully aromatic whites, thick, strong, mountainous Cabernet-based reds of uncompromising intensity, and a delightful, madeira-like sweet wine, Vin de Laurence, have ripped up the formbook. Quality is on a definite upswing across the Hérault, though, and there are increasing numbers of stars. PRODUCERS: Mas de Daumas Gassac, Limbardié, Grange des Pères, Ch. Capion.

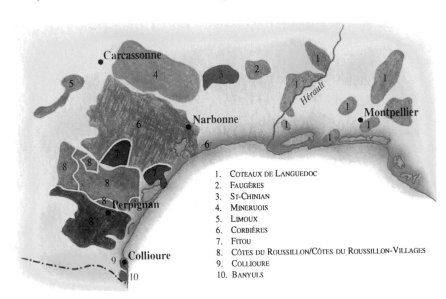

1. COTEAUX DE LANGUEDOC
2. FAUGÈRES
3. ST-CHINIAN
4. MINERUOIS
5. LIMOUX
6. CORBIÈRES
7. FITOU
8. CÔTES DU ROUSSILLON/CÔTES DU ROUSSILLON-VILLAGES
9. COLLIOURE
10. BANYULS

Coteaux du Languedoc A rather sprawling AOC for some of the best village wines of the Hérault, flanked by the eastern edge of the Aude and the western fringe of the Gard *départements*. The painstaking process of subdividing the Coteaux into recognizably distinct districts has been under way for some years, and includes the areas of Grès de Montpellier, La Clape, Pézenas, Pic-St-Loup, Picpoul de Pinet, Terrasses de Béziers, Terrasses du Larzac and Terres de Sommières. Within these, individual *crus* to look out for are Quatourze (La Clape), Cabrières (Pézenas) and Montpeyroux and St-Saturnin (Terrasses du Larzac).

The overall picture here is improving all the time, with Grenache, Syrah and Mourvèdre staking a claim to a larger share of the red blends, at the expense of the humdrum Carignan, and making some fragrant, pale pink rosé. Whites from Picpoul de Pinet have been impressive in a muscular, solidly textured way, while Clairette du Languedoc is a white of uncommon versatility, ranging in style from light, dry and neutral to heavily sweet and oxidized. Take your pick.

PRODUCERS: Mas Jullien, Prieuré St-Jean-de-Bébian, Clos Marie, Peyre Rose, Lacroix-Vanel.

Working our way around in a southwesterly arc from just north of Cabrières, the other appellations for unfortified wines in Languedoc-Roussillon are as follows:

Faugères Demarcated in 1982 out of the Coteaux du Languedoc, Faugères makes soft, berryish reds from Syrah, Grenache, Mourvèdre and a maximum proportion of 40 per cent Carignan. Small amount of fairly ordinary rosé. Excellent value.

PRODUCERS: Alquier, Barral, Estanilles, Lorgeril.

St-Chinian A little further west in the foothills of the Cévennes, St-Chinian shares the same history and grape varieties as Faugères, with light rosés and perhaps a little more heft to the reds, which can be impressively long-lived.

PRODUCERS: Cazal-Viel, Rimbert, Mas Champart, Berlou co-op.

Minervois As for Faugères and St-Chinian, with the addition of a little white. Quality here has steadily improved since it gained its AOC in 1985. Reds in particular can now be richly aromatic and ageworthy. Best wines come from a *cru* called La Livinière, which may be stated on the label, and represent excellent value.

PRODUCERS: Ste-Eulalie, Villerambert-Julien, Oupia, Senat, Clos Centeilles.

The old farmhouse at Mas de Daumas Gassac (above), star of the Vins de Pays de l'Hérault.

Cabardès North of Carcassonne on the cusp of Languedoc and the southwest, this AOC (since 1999) is allowed to use both Midi and Bordeaux grapes for hearty, meaty reds and rosés.

PRODUCERS: Jouclary, Cabrol.

Côtes de la Malepère West of Carcassonne, and very similar in style to Cabardès, this became an AOC in 2005.

PRODUCERS: Cave du Razès, Matibat.

Limoux Created in 1993 for white wines, Limoux represents a determined attempt to give the oaked-Chardonnay brigade a run for their money, so much so that oak-barrel treatment is compulsory. There are also plantings of Chenin Blanc and a crisply appley local variety, Mauzac. Since 2005, reds are permitted too from Merlot, Malbec and the Midi grapes.

PRODUCERS: Sieur d'Arques, d'Antugnac.

LANGUEDOC-ROUSSILLON

(PLUS OTHER NATIVE VARIETIES)
GRAPES: Red – Carignan, Grenache, Cinsault, Mourvèdre, Syrah, Merlot, Cabernet Sauvignon, Malbec; White – Clairette, Rolle, Terret, Bourboulenc, Picpoul, Muscat, Maccabéo, Marsanne, Viognier, Sauvignon Blanc, Chardonnay

Bush vines growing high in the hills of the Côtes du Roussillon (above), with the snow-capped Pyrenees and the Spanish border in the near distance.

Blanquette de Limoux/Crémant de Limoux
The former is the traditional sparkling wine of the region, made by the traditional method, but claiming an older lineage than champagne. Blanquette is a synonym for the local Mauzac grape, although there can be 10 per cent of Chardonnay or Chenin. Since 1990, any wine that contains up to 30 per cent of those, plus Pinot Noir, is Crémant.
PRODUCERS: Collin, Martinolles, l'Aigle.
Corbières One of the larger and more famous Languedoc AOCs covers a range of good, sturdy, often spicy reds, as well as small amounts of white and rosé from southern varieties. Includes a *cru* village, Boutenac. These are now some of the more fascinating, and fairly priced, examples of modern French winemaking. Buy with confidence.
PRODUCERS: les Ollieux, Voulte-Gasparets, Caraguilhes, Lastours, l'Anhel.
Fitou The oldest AOC in the Languedoc lies on the border of Languedoc and Roussillon, in two separate zones that are divided by part of

Corbières. There is still a fair amount of roughly undistinguished Fitou around, but the best is as good as Corbières now, a herb-tinged, sinewy red.
PRODUCERS: Mont-Tauch, Bertrand-Bergé, Roudène, Nouvelles, Lerys.
Roussillon/Côtes du Roussillon/Côtes du Roussillon-Villages The area south of Perpignan, bordering on Catalan country, is home to some rather more run-of-the-mill offerings. By far the best of these three designations is the last, which is for red wines only, and comprises the northern section of Roussillon, nearest to Fitou. Individual village names to look out for are Caramany, Latour-de-France, Lesquerde and Tautavel.
PRODUCERS: de Jau, Gauby, Mas Amiel, Cazes.
Collioure A coastal AOC of vertiginously steep vineyards, making some remarkable, thoroughly original reds in an ultra-ripe, expansive style, mainly from Grenache and Mourvèdre. Some rosé and white.
PRODUCERS: Mas Blanc, la Rectorie, Clos de Paulilles.

OTHER WINES

There are a number of *vins doux naturels* produced in this region, both white and red. Winemaking techniques are the same as those for Muscat de Beaumes-de-Venise (see entry, Rhône), and the whites here all use either of two strains of Muscat. Frontignan, together with three other Muscats suffixed respectively by de Mireval, de Lunel and de St-Jean-de-Minervois, all use the Muscat Blanc à Petits Grains grape, and produce lightly fragrant, barley-sugar sweet wines of varying degrees of intensity. The chunkier, less attractive Muscat d'Alexandrie is permitted as well in Muscat de Rivesaltes, made north of Perpignan.
PRODUCERS: la Peyrade (Frontignan); Mas de Bellevue (Lunel); Clos Bagatelle (St-Jean-de-Minervois); Cazes (Rivesaltes).

Sweet red wines, usually made entirely or predominantly from Grenache, are made in **Rivesaltes, Maury** to the west of Fitou, and **Banyuls,** down on the Roussillon coast and overlapping with Collioure. Of those, Banyuls is about the best, with sweet strawberry fruit and a heady perfume sometimes reminiscent of good ruby port, but much less aggressive on the palate. Maury is characterful too, though.
PRODUCERS: Mas Blanc, la Rectorie (Banyuls); Mas Amiel (Maury).

GASCONY *and* THE SOUTHWEST

These small wine areas, scattered from Bordeaux down to the Spanish border,
offer a diverse and exciting range of wines that have been little influenced by
passing fashions. These winemakers are proud of their traditions.

WHEREAS MOST OF the appellations of the sprawling Languedoc region make use of the same basic collections of red and white grapes for their wines, a much more diverse picture prevails in the southwest. There is an umbrella trade organization for the wines of the southwest, but each AOC retains its own fiercely guarded identity, and many have one or two local grape varieties they are proud to call their own.

They also have a culinary tradition to be proud of. After Burgundy, this is probably the most celebrated gastronomic corner of France, home of magnificent pork and poultry, Toulouse sausages, duck confit, foie gras, sheep's-milk cheeses, prunes and armagnac.

The producers have been considerably less susceptible to the influence of foreign technologists around these parts than further east, and are consequently more fearful that their often little-known wines will continue to be swept aside in the varietal mania that has overcome the world markets. However, there remains at least a sporting chance that the next generation will discover Petit Manseng and

Négrette grapes, and then the southwest will have its day at last.

Wending our way circuitously down from just south of Bordeaux to the far southwest corner, the main appellations are as follows:
Bergerac/Côtes de Bergerac The first few AOCs in the immediate vicinity of Bordeaux were once considered part of its overall catchment area. They use the same grape varieties (chiefly Cabernet Sauvignon, Merlot and Cabernet Franc for reds and rosés, Sauvignon Blanc and Sémillon for whites). Bergerac and the theoretically slightly superior Côtes de Bergerac are to the east of the Côtes de Castillon sector of Bordeaux, on the river Dordogne. There are a few stars here, though a lot of the wine is pretty basic stuff from the local cooperative.
PRODUCERS: la Jaubertie, Bélingard, Tour des Gendres, l'Ancienne Cure.
Montravel/Côtes de Montravel/Haut-Montravel Traditionally a white-wine AOC at the western end of Bergerac, mainly planted with Sémillon. The three designations refer to dry, semi-sweet and very sweet wines respectively.

Château de Crouseilles peering majestically over its vineyard in the Gascon red-wine enclave of Madiran (above).

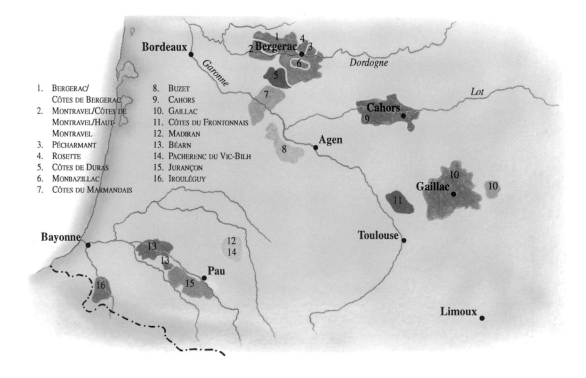

1. BERGERAC/ CÔTES DE BERGERAC
2. MONTRAVEL/CÔTES DE MONTRAVEL/HAUT-MONTRAVEL
3. PÉCHARMANT
4. ROSETTE
5. CÔTES DE DURAS
6. MONBAZILLAC
7. CÔTES DU MARMANDAIS
8. BUZET
9. CAHORS
10. GAILLAC
11. CÔTES DU FRONTONNAIS
12. MADIRAN
13. BÉARN
14. PACHERENC DU VIC-BILH
15. JURANÇON
16. IROULÉGUY

The scattered appellations of Gascony and the southwest (left), from Bergerac, close to Bordeaux, down to Irouléguy on the border with Spain.

**GASCONY &
SOUTHWEST**

*GRAPES: the Bordeaux
grape varieties and a
wide collection of local
varieties further south.*

*The old face of Cahors,
in the Lot valley (below),
an area once renowned
for its 'black wine'.*

The dry Montravel wines are best, and much
improved of late. Montravel may also now be
red, from at least 50 per cent Merlot.
PRODUCERS: Jonc Blanc, du Bloy, Puy-Servain.
Pécharmant Red wines from Bergerac itself,
using Bordeaux grapes with a preponderance
of Merlot. Overall quality is high, classy and
claret-like.
PRODUCERS: Tiregand, Chemins d'Orient.
Rosette Sweet-wines AOC overlapping into
Pécharmant and using Sémillon, but now sadly
dwindling towards extinction.
Côtes de Duras South of the Dordogne, the
Duras makes some passable wines in the style
of simple Bordeaux. The best shots are the
Sauvignon whites, which can be agreeably
crisp and clean.
PRODUCERS: Chater, Petit Malromé.
Monbazillac One of the southwest's unsung
stars is the potentially glorious botrytized wine
of Monbazillac. While Sauternes prices soar,
this AOC further east along the Dordogne looks
a ringer for great dessert wines at affordable
prices. Sensational vintages in the late 1980s
brought its name to a wider audience. Made
from noble-rotted Sémillon, with Sauvignon
and flowery Muscadelle, the best are full of
golden, honeyed richness.

PRODUCERS: Tirecul-la-Gravière, Grande
Maison, Haut-Bernasse, Theulet.
Saussignac Tiny AOC for sweet Sémillon-
based whites, just west of Monbazillac. Of no
great pedigree, though Ch. Court-les-Mûts
produces a reasonably good one.
Côtes du Marmandais An AOC since 1990,
the Marmandais straddles the river Garonne,
south of Bordeaux. It makes principally reds
(with a smidgen of rosé and white) in a
no-nonsense, easy-drinking style. The Bordeaux
varieties are allowed to constitute up to
75 per cent of the red blends, the remainder
made up of Syrah, Gamay, the rough-natured
southwestern grape Fer Servadou, and a
Marmandais speciality, Abouriou. A couple
of co-ops account for the bulk of production.
Buzet Although south of Marmandais, Buzet
returns to the Bordeaux varieties for all
colours of wine. Once again, the cooperative
predominates, but its versatile range (look for
its Baron d'Ardeuil) is good. The austerely
concentrated reds are often as structured as
cru bourgeois claret.
Cahors Situated northeast of Agen, Cahors
spans the river Lot. Historically one of the more
famous southwest names, it was once known
as the 'black wine' because the grape juice was
boiled to concentrate its colour. Now more
sensitively vinified, it is made from a minimum
70 per cent of the Bordeaux variety Malbec
(known locally as Auxerrois), backed up by
Merlot and a fierce local grape Tannat, used
only in judicious dashes. Light red fruits and
modest tannins are the hallmarks of the wines
now, but many have an intriguing violetty
note too, and a lingering spicy sizzle.
PRODUCERS: Triguedina, Clos de Gamot,
Haute-Serre, Lamartine, les Rigalets.
Gaillac A large AOC northeast of Toulouse, Gaillac
makes a wide range of styles, from bone-dry
as well as slightly sweet whites, via some
sparkling wine using an old, single-ferment
rural method, to firm full reds. Its proximity
to Limoux means that Mauzac is an important
variety, and the dry whites and fizzes have the
same sort of tart, green-apple bite to them. It's
supplemented by local grapes Len de l'El and
Ondenc, as well as a soupçon of Sauvignon.
The fizzes may be either just pétillant (Gaillac
Perlé), or fully re-fermented and released with
the yeast sediment still sloshing around in them.
Reds include the local Duras and Fer Servadou,
together with Syrah and Gamay, as well as the

big three Bordeaux varieties. There is a tendency to produce sturdy, oaky reds now, which require keeping.

PRODUCERS: Plageoles, Labarthe, la Ramaye.

Fronton Distinctive reds made from the local grape Négrette, which has a deliciously savoury pepperiness to it, fleshed out with the two Cabernets and Fer Servadou. Better than most country reds for sheer concentration and personality. Also makes a small amount of rosé.

PRODUCERS: Baudare, Bellevue-la-Forêt, Cahuzac.

Tursan Roughish, everyday reds from the muscular Tannat grape and the Cabernet duo, rosés from the Cabernets, and oak-matured white based on local variety Baroque.

St-Mont All shades of wine, dominated by the reliable Caves de Plaimont cooperative. Reds and pinks use Fer Servadou and Tannat, as well as the main Bordeaux trio; indigenous white grapes include such delights as Ruffiac and Courbu, among others. Some highly interesting flavours and oak experimentation are to be found, but quality remains uneven.

Madiran The unforgivingly brutal Tannat grape comes into its own in these fiery reds that always need a few years to soften, but never quite lose the power to intimidate. When fully ripe, they are spicily elegant. The two Cabernets are used to provide some fruit relief.

PRODUCERS: Montus, Aydie, Capmartin, Berthoumieu, Ch. de Crouseilles.

Béarn To the west of Madiran, and using the same grapes for reds and rosés. These are softer than Madiran, but not particularly characterful. Lapeyre makes a good one.

Pacherenc du Vic-Bilh A separate AOC within Madiran for generally sweet white wines made from the local grapes Ruffiac, Courbu and Gros and Petit Manseng, together with Sauvignon and Sémillon. Depending on the vintage conditions, Pacherenc may be made dry, but its sweeter wines made from grapes left to shrivel on the vine can be occasionally as distinguished as the sweet wines of Jurançon.

PRODUCERS: Aydie, Labranche-Laffont.

Jurançon Much underrated AOC south of Pau, making white wines principally from a blend of the twin varieties Gros Manseng and Petit Manseng (the latter the better for its piercing pineapple and apricot aromas), together with some Courbu. The wines may be refreshingly dry and full of tropical-fruit ripeness, or

lusciously sweet from raisined grapes, as in Pacherenc. Excellent value.

PRODUCERS: Uroulat, Cauhapé, Lapeyre, Souch.

Irouléguy Practically on the Spanish border in the Pays Basque, this far-flung AOC takes in a number of young vineyards carved out of the Pyrenean rock by growers motivated by great regional pride. Tannat raises its wild head in the reds and rosés, but is tempered by the Cabernets, while the whites use the Jurançon varieties. As elsewhere, the regional co-op makes a fair amount of the wine, but Arretxea and Brana are also good.

Vin de Pays des Côtes de Gascogne Surplus grapes not used in the production of armagnac, the brandy of the southwest, go into white wines under this regional designation. Much comes from Ugni Blanc and is yawningly dull, although there is also some Sauvignon and both Mansengs to add aromatic appeal, and even a little Chardonnay and Sémillon. They should all be drunk young and fresh. There are smaller quantities of red and rosé too, with an equally broad palette of grapes to choose from – the three main Bordeaux varieties, plus Malbec, Tannat, Négrette, Duras and Fer Servadou. Styles tend to be on the lighter side, crisp but not especially memorable.

PRODUCERS: Tariquet, Brumont, St-Lannes, Caves Plaimont.

The stunning Château de Monbazillac (above). The finest sweet wines of Monbazillac can rival those of Sauternes.

Cabernet Sauvignon grapes arriving at the Buzet cooperative (above). The Bordeaux varieties are used to make concentrated claret-style reds.

JURA, SAVOIE *and* BUGEY

To the east of Burgundy lie the three little-known regions of Jura, Savoie and the Bugey. Tucked up against the French Alps, the areas are dominated by white wines, and the unique styles of vin jaune *and* vin de paille.

THESE THREE EASTERLY regions are among the most obscure and insular of all France's wine-growing areas. Not much of their wine is exported, and what is makes few compromises to modern tastes.

JURA

The remote high-altitude vineyards of the Jura, not far from the Swiss border, harbour some of France's most individual wines. They do crop up in minute quantities on the export markets, but tend to be highly priced, and the house style of the region is not an especially fashionable one. That said – *vive la différence*.

There are two regional specialities – *vin jaune* and *vin de paille*. The former, 'yellow wine', is made in a similar way to dry sherry, in that it matures in cask for six years under a *voile*, or film, of yeast culture. As the wine oxidates, it turns yellow. About one-third also evaporates. The resulting wine is heavy-textured, dry as chalk-dust and alcoholic – rather like fino sherry, in fact. *Vin de paille*, 'straw wine', is equally rare and made from raisined grapes dried on straw mats. These are rich, powerful wines, capable of some bottle-age. Both these wines are only made in certain years and in small quantities, and are therefore pricy. Much of the *vin de paille* is found in Arbois, while *vin jaune* reigns supreme in L'Etoile and Château-Chalon.

Arbois The greatest volume of Jura wine is produced under this AOC in the northern part of the region, centred on the town of the same name. They may be red, white or rosé, and there are three important local grapes: two red varieties – Trousseau, which gives a deeply rich if unsubtle wine, and thin-skinned Poulsard, quite the opposite and good for rosés – as well as a white, the gloriously musky Savignin, a relative of Gewürztraminer.

Pinot Noir and Chardonnay are also grown, the latter more extensively in recent years. Some of the wine is made sparkling by the traditional method, and labelled Crémant du Jura, while wines from the best village, Pupillin, are allowed to add its name as a suffix.
PRODUCERS: Puffeney, Tissot, Maire.

Côtes du Jura The central and southern parts of the region take this AOC, but make the same broad range of styles from the same grapes as Arbois. Ch. d'Arlay is a good producer of *vin jaune*.

L'Etoile Tiny AOC largely represented by the local co-op, specializing in hazelnutty *vins jaunes* from Savagnin. Also straight white, and sparkling wine.

Château-Chalon The only AOC entirely for Savignin *vins jaunes*, Château-Chalon sits on a little hilltop, remaining completely aloof from the modern world. Wine is only made in years when the producers deem the harvest good enough to bother.
PRODUCERS: Bourdy, Berthet-Bondet, Macle.

The vineyards of Jura and Savoie (below) lie on the lower slopes of the French Alps, close to the Swiss border.

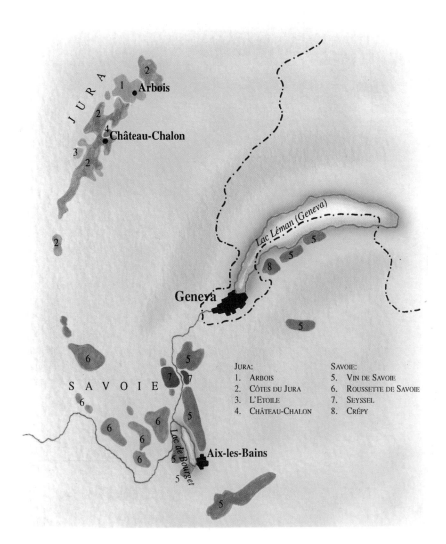

JURA:
1. ARBOIS
2. CÔTES DU JURA
3. L'ETOILE
4. CHÂTEAU-CHALON

SAVOIE:
5. VIN DE SAVOIE
6. ROUSSETTE DE SAVOIE
7. SEYSSEL
8. CRÉPY

Macvin du Jura A fortified style in any colour, Macvin gained its AOC in 1991. It is unfermented sweet grape juice to which a slug of marc du Jura (grapeskin spirit) is added.

SAVOIE

Lying due south of Geneva, Savoie is home to some indigenous grape varieties. Many of its wines have character, but are not much exported.
Savoie The overall AOC for any wine produced within the *départements* of Savoie and Haute-Savoie. Most are whites and are made from the local Jacquère grape in a crunchy-fresh style, supported by Chardonnay, some of the northern Rhône's Roussanne, and the neutral-tasting Chasselas much favoured in Switzerland. Reds use Pinot Noir and Gamay, as well as a local variety called Mondeuse, which makes something a little fleshier than the light-bodied norm. Seventeen privileged villages may add their names to the basic designation; they include Apremont, Abymes, Montmélian and Chautagne.
Roussette de Savoie The Savoyards consider the Roussette (aka Altesse) to be their best white grape. It has its own AOC throughout the region. The wines have a diverting floral perfume, and should be drunk young to catch their tingling acidity at its freshest. In four villages – Frangy, Marestel, Monterminod and Monthoux – the wines must be 100 per cent Roussette; elsewhere, they can be up to 50 per cent Chardonnay.
Seyssel Small AOC taking in dry white wines from Roussette and the local Molette. There is also a sparkling version, Seyssel Mousseux, based on Molette, but which has to contain at least 10 per cent of Roussette.
Crépy Chasselas makes the wines of this dry-whites appellation, and jolly dull they are too.

BUGEY

Just west of Savoie, in the Ain *département*, is the Bugey. Historically part of Burgundy, it now constitutes a mini-region of its own, its grape varieties marking its identity as a sort of cross between Savoie and the Jura. Finding any outside the region is something of a teaser, though some make it as far as Lyon.
Bugey The main designation covers the whole region. An entire range of styles is made, from aromatic, crisply textured dry whites, through delicate rosés, to lightish reds using Gamay, Pinot Noir and also some Mondeuse. There are additionally two styles of fizz – lightly prickly (Pétillant) and fully sparkling (Mousseux). Much praise has been heaped on the region's Chardonnay varietals. Cerdon is perhaps the best of the handful of village names that may appear on the labels. A separate AOC, **Roussette du Bugey**, is for whites made entirely from Roussette (Altesse).

JURA
GRAPES: *White – Savagnin, Chardonnay;*
Red – Trousseau, Poulsard, Pinot Noir
SAVOIE
GRAPES: *White – Jacquère, Roussette, Molette, Roussanne, Chasselas, Chardonnay;*
Red – Mondeuse, Gamay, Pinot Noir

VIN *de* PAYS

The vin de pays *designation was created to encourage production of higher quality, easy-drinking red, white, and rosé wines, 'country wines' that display the character of their region.*

MANY FRENCH WINES – about a quarter of the annual production – fall below the top category for quality wine, *appellation contrôlée*. *Vin de pays* (literally 'country wine') is a designation drawn up in the 1970s to denote wines that had some sort of regional identity, but for one reason or another, perhaps because the grower was using grapes not officially sanctioned in the locality, or perhaps because the vines were too young under the appellation regulations, didn't qualify for AOC status, but were better than the basic slosh.

The most primitive quality category of all is straightforward French wine (*vin de France*), the labels of which will usually have scarcely more information than a brand name and the information that it's from France. *Vin de pays*, intended in its way to be as representative of regional characteristics as the appellation wines, should be several rungs up the ladder from *vin de France*, and most of it is.

There are three levels of *vin de pays*, depending on how specific the individual producer wants, or is able, to be. At the broadest, most inclusive level, the designation may cover a whole region, such as the commercially pre-eminent Vin de Pays d'Oc, the regional VdP for Languedoc-Roussillon (and now the most geographically extensive single wine designation in the world).

Then there are VdPs that use the name of the *département*, such as Alpes-Maritimes in Provence, Gers in Gascony or l'Hérault in the Languedoc. To use these, the wine must have been sourced from grapes grown entirely within that *département*. Within the confines of those, there are local VdP areas, based on named patches of vineyard land, particular hillsides, geographical features, and so forth (such as the Coteaux de l'Ardèche in the Rhône valley, a subdivision of the larger, departmental Ardèche VdP). These are the districts that are best qualified to be elevated to AOC status in due course, as indeed many have been in the past 20 years.

To qualify as a *vin de pays*, the wines must be made from certain grape varieties, and are not to be blended with wines from other areas. Many of them are single-varietal wines and, as such, are virtually the only French wines so labelled outside the Alsace region. At the outset of the *vin de pays* revolution, this facility enabled the producers to compete with wines labelled Chardonnay, Merlot and so on from the

Vins de pays *that use the name of a* département, *such as Ardèche (below), must contain grapes sourced only from within that district.*

rest of the world. Gradually, however, it has promoted recognition of some of the lesser-known varieties, such as Viognier and Marsanne of the northern Rhône, giving consumers a hint of the kinds of flavours previously only familiar to drinkers of Condrieu or white Hermitage.

Because the bulk of it is produced in the south of France, about three-quarters of all *vin de pays* is red, although the second most important area is the Loire, where much of the white *vin de pays* is produced.

REGIONAL VIN DE PAYS

Vin de Pays d'Oc Stretching across the Languedoc-Roussillon region of southern France, this is by far the most commonly seen *vin de pays*. A whole cocktail of what are now international grape varieties is grown here, and styles range from crisp, nettly Sauvignon to big, burly Cabernet. Wines can be blends of more than one variety, with the components stated on the label in descending order of their proportions in the bottle. Some of these combinations are innovative mixtures that are not permitted within any of the regional AOCs, hence their apparently lowlier designation, but quality of the best can be little short of stunning.

Vin de Pays du Jardin de la France The so-called Garden of France is the regional designation for the whole of the Loire valley. Varietally labelled white wines from Chardonnay or Sauvignon Blanc are common, and can be engaging enough in a fairly simple style.

Vin de Pays du Comté Tolosan This covers much of the southwest, with wines that are generally blends of two or more of the regional grapes. Whites are distinctly underwhelming, but there are some reasonable reds that tend to be on the light side.

Vin de Pays de Méditerranée Wines from Provence and the southeast.

Vin de Pays des Comtés Rhodaniens The designation for the whole of the Rhône valley.

DEPARTMENTAL VIN DE PAYS

Among the more important of the departmental *vin de pays* are **Vin de Pays du Gers** (in Gascony), **Vin de Pays de l'Hérault**, **Vin de Pays de l'Aude** and **Vin de Pays du Gard** (within the Pays d'Oc region), **Vin de Pays du Var** and **Vin de Pays de Vaucluse** (in Provence) and **Vin de Pays de Charente-Maritime** (which is part of the Cognac region of western France).

SOME LOCAL VIN DE PAYS

Vin de Pays des Coteaux de l'Ardèche The region in between the northern and southern sectors of the Rhône has proved to be a highly reliable source of varietal reds and whites, and might expect to promoted to AOC before long, although its present spread of grape varieties – Syrah, Gamay, Merlot, Cabernet Sauvignon, Viognier, Chardonnay and Sauvignon Blanc – will be hard to rationalize into one overarching set of regulations.

Vin de Pays des Côtes de Thongue A good source of spicy reds from within the Hérault, northeast of Béziers.

Vin de Pays des Côtes Catalanes Sturdy whites and herb-tinged, concentrated reds from Roussillon in the deep south.

Vin de Pays des Côtes de Gascogne Mostly crisp, clean, herbaceous whites from the armagnac production area in the southwest.

These vineyards of Château Capion, in Hérault (above), grow Cabernet Sauvignon, Chardonnay and Merlot for Vin de Pays d'Oc.

Hand-picking of grapes near Reuilly in the upper Loire (above), destined for one of the region's comparatively rare red vins de pays.

Grapes growing in the spectacular Ardèche gorge for use in the region's highly regarded Vin de Pays des Coteaux de l'Ardèche (left).

EUROPE, AFRICA AND THE EAST

The 11th-century Castillo de Milmanda (above), owned by the famous winemaking family, Torres, in Catalonia.

Picking grapes for Vinho Verde (above), on Portugal's 'Green Coast'.

When the first edition of this book was published, back in 1996, I reported that the world of wine was convulsed by a struggle for supremacy, billed as France versus the New World. Varietalism (naming wine after the grape variety or varieties it contained) was king. Serious consumers had grown tired of the often badly made and boring wines of the rest of Europe and, other than the abiding French classics, had largely bailed out of Europe, and were chasing the easy-drinking wines of the sunnier (and largely English-speaking) parts of the viticultural world.

In the years since that diagnosis, things have changed considerably. The picture has become productively more complicated, and there are signs of hope springing up all over, not just in the old European heartlands, but in some surprising new quarters too.

The single biggest factor influencing the way wine is made, sold and indeed talked about is the development of the theory of *terroir*. *Terroir* is a famously untranslatable French word for the entire mass of geographical, climatic and cultural circumstances in which a wine (or speciality food) is produced. It is the main reason that an unoaked Chardonnay grown in the *département* of the Yonne in northern France tastes like Chablis, while one grown in the Santa Ynez Valley, California (or, for that matter, a little way south of the Yonne in the Mâconnais) doesn't.

At one time, producers outside Europe congratulated themselves on the fact that they were not in hock to the pettifogging regulations of the continental wine bureaucracies, but by the mid-1990s, that attitude was discernibly shifting. Now producers all over the Americas, Australasia, South America and South Africa

were beginning to demarcate the specific locations of which their wine industry was comprised. Now there were AVAs, GIs and WOs to match the European AOCs, DOCs and so forth. Which meant, did it not, a wholesale victory for the *terroir*-based appellation systems of Europe?

Well, yes and no. If we struggle to define *terroir* precisely, that is at least partly because it isn't in itself a wholly stable concept. This is a point that receives too little acknowledgement among its defenders (of whom I am unequivocally one). Tradition is important in wine, but dynamism, innovation, a wholesale commitment to learning from mistakes and moving on, are even more so.

One of the principal drivers for reform, and one that is bound to become more important, is climate change. If the appellations of southern Europe are going to become hotter and drier over the next generation, that will have profound implications for what happens in their vineyards. Certain grape varieties will become unfeasible. At worst, whole vineyard regions may have to be abandoned, to be replaced by new ones in northern Europe.

Even more than global warming, though, for the time being, is the Herculean effort being made by the ever-expanding European Union to harmonize the respective quality systems in place among all its wine-producing member countries. What that enterprise often foundered on was the attempt to reconcile the irreconcilable, to cater for all the niceties of individual national systems within a roughly recognizable overarching structure.

If there is one complaint consumers have about the various appellation systems, it is that they are too complicated. The everyday drinker accepts that he or she doesn't need to memorize the names of every last one of the hundreds of denominated wines in each country, but it is often the structure itself that baffles. As I write, they are just in the process of abandoning a little-used intermediate classification in French wines (VDQS, *vin délimité de qualité supérieur*) that sat awkwardly in between AOC and *vin de pays*. It only accounted for about one per cent of total production, but justifying its existence was always a headache. Now they need to do something about the subdivisions and sub-subdivisions within the *vin de pays* framework.

Similarly, by the end of the first decade of the 21st century, Italy had saddled itself with a system that began with *vino da tavola* (the entry-level table wine designation that nonetheless included some of the greatest wines of Italy, produced outside the DOC regulations), went on up through the *vin de pays* equivalent, IGT, and on to the top wines awarded DOC, the analogue for the French AOC. Except that DOC itself was further subdivided into around three dozen DOCGs, theoretically super-dooper wines, the absolute *crema* – except that they happened to include Albana di Romagna, a snoozingly dull white made near Bologna.

From 2009 onwards, Italy creditably began the long, potentially fraught process of streamlining all that into two broad categories, a regional country-wine designation to be known as IGP, with a rationalized DOP category for the upper echelon. Noses were put out of joint right and left as many wines were reclassified, but the end-result will be a more readily accessible set-up – and one that, with any luck, will obviate the need for further tinkering in the forseeable future.

Italy remains the great *terra incognita* of European wine, a country festooned top to toe with interesting indigenous grape varieties (and a few depressing dullards too, to be sure), and yet one that barely registers in the high-street retail trade beyond the over-familiar names of bulk producers of Chianti, Valpolicella, Soave and deracinated Pinot Grigio. But grapes like Sangiovese, Nebbiolo, Barbera, Dolcetto, Negroamaro, Aglianico and Primitivo (that last the European precursor of California's Zinfandel) should be on the radar of any self-respecting wine-lover.

As should Spain's Tempranillo, Verdejo, and a handful of others. Spanish wine is struggling to emerge from its traditional bad habits, which included over-ageing many red wines in cask until they tasted well and truly past it. I worry that too much regional identity is being sacrificed here to international winemaking theory, but we'll see. In the meantime, sparkling cava has suddenly got good.

Portugal has more indigenous grapes than Spain, despite its much more limited production. Some talented small producers have emerged all the over the country, with regions like the Alentejo, Ribatejo and the Douro pointing the way. For me, the best thing about the Portuguese wine industry is that it remains, among the advanced winemaking countries, by far the least wedded to varietal thinking. Why churn out more tankerloads of Chardonnay and

Cabernet when you have such sumptuous and inimitable native styles to call on? It's a self-defeating strategy they've resisted.

Poor old Germany is in real trouble. It has to find a way of convincing the world to try its premium Rieslings, list them in restaurants and bars, and drink them at the table – in other words, rebuild the world from the ground up. They remain its strongest suit, but who will buy? Meanwhile, neighbouring Austria capitalizes on its greater diversity, and the novelty value of its wines, to win new converts.

The countries of the former Soviet bloc have had mixed fortunes since its breakup in the early 1990s. For a while, Hungary forged ahead, while Bulgaria fell spectacularly back. Moldova began to emerge, while Romania may have been sitting on some of the best-kept secrets of the lot. In time, Russia and Georgia will become important players. Once again, there are plenty of fascinating grape varieties, and some (though by no means enough) outside investment.

Greece continues to lag inexplicably behind, long ripe for promotion to Europe's second division, but never quite getting there. I expect the handful of quality producers on Malta to elevate its small but exciting wine industry to international acclaim before too long.

Outside Europe, there are exciting things afoot in east Asia, where Japan, Thailand and (most promisingly of all) China are working out how to apply international know-how to the biggest untapped domestic audiences for grape wine left on the planet. Watch this space.

Autumn arrives in the vineyards of Germany's Mosel region (above), above the town of Piesport.

The dramatic modernist bodega (below) was built in 1918 for the Spanish producer Raimat.

ITALY

The invading Greeks called it Oenotria, the land of wine. Italy has remained steeped in viticulture, has an extravagantly diverse range of styles, and today usually produces more wine than any other country in the world.

VITIS VINIFERA, the wine-grape species, has been growing on the Italian mainland since several centuries before the birth of Christ. For a long time, the archaeological orthodoxy was that invading Greeks brought the vine to Italy in the era before the rise of the Roman Empire. It is now known that some tribal cultures, notably the Etruscans whose domain extended along the western coast of the peninsula, already possessed viticultural knowledge, and that the Greeks did little more than introduce new vine varieties to southern Italy when they arrived.

The clue to the central importance of viticulture in the ancient world is in the name that the Greeks gave to their new territory, Oenotria (land of wine). Over the centuries that followed, Roman ingenuity extended the possibilities of winemaking considerably, until it had far surpassed the Greek model. Wines of particular vintages came to be valued, as did the wines of specific regions, such as Lazio, Campania and Toscana (Tuscany).

Wherever the conquering Roman armies went, they took their vine-growing expertise with them, to keep their troops supplied with better wines than were locally available in such benighted outposts as Spain, France and even Britain. As Greek civilization entered its long decline, Italy became the heartland of European wine culture in the ancient world.

Nowadays, in terms of volume, Italy remains in most years the most significant wine producer in the world, knocking France into second place. Wine is still central to Italian family life, in a way that has all but vanished among modern urban families in France. No part of Italy is a no-go area for the vine, from the Tyrolean north to the Calabrian south, not forgetting the islands of Sicily and Sardinia. There are now over one million vineyard holdings throughout the country, an astonishing figure for its size. To a great and overarching extent, Italian agriculture just is wine.

Ongoing efforts simultaneously to refine and simplify the Italian wine classification system are a sign of progress. When the DOC system was drawn up in the 1960s, it did little more than acknowledge which wines were most commercially important, regardless of quality. That began to change in the early 1990s, when a genuine attempt to ensure quality within the regulations was initiated, with maximum yields and minimum ripeness levels specified, and wines that fell within the top DOCG category expected to pass muster among professional tasting panels.

The customary styles of many Italian wines have played an unfortunate part in holding the country back in the international markets. Most of the traditional dry white wines, to be frank, are pointless, boring, vapid creations that might taste agreeable enough if knocked back well-chilled at lunchtime while you're on holiday

Italy's foremost agricultural industry is grape-growing. Vines are planted across the country, from the northern borders to its heel in the south (below).

1. PIEDMONT
2. VALLE D'AOSTA
3. LIGURIA
4. LOMBARDY
5. TRENTINO-ALTO ADIGE
6. VENETO
7. FRIULI
8. EMILIA-ROMAGNA
9. TUSCANY
10. THE MARCHES
11. UMBRIA
12. LAZIO
13. ABRUZZI
14. MOLISE
15. PUGLIA
16. CAMPANIA
17. BASILICATA
18. CALABRIA
19. SICILY
20. SARDINIA

there, but have no obvious role in world viticulture now. The breakout success in recent years, Pinot Grigio, made across a whole swathe of northern Italy, has mostly only succeeded in replacing the watery white wines of the north with a watery white wine with a varietal name on it.

Reds were always better, but too often marked by what is technically known as volatile acidity, and which, bluntly simplified, meant there was more than a faint air of vinegariness to them. Many of the reds were anaemically pale and thin – not just the Merlots of the northeast either, but much of what flowed out of the Chianti region too.

Much of this is now receding into a past worth forgetting, while the true treasure-trove of Italian viticulture, its cornucopia of fine indigenous grape varieties, comes to the fore. Wines made in central Italy outside the DOC regulations, those that came to be known as the super-Tuscans, pointed the way out of the quality impasse, encouraging the production of better wines at the more affordable end of the scale. And just as Italian domestic cooking has been the single most important influence on global food fashion since the demise of French haute cuisine, so the world wants something to drink with it. And there remains no better accompaniment to tomato-based pasta dishes, Italian cured meats, risottos, gnocchi, pesto, Italian cheeses, even pizza, than Italian wine.

The pages that follow reflect the classification system as it existed up to 2010. It can be assumed that DOC (*denominazione di origine controllata*) and DOCG (*denominazione di origine controllata e garantita*) wines will eventually fall within the DOP (*denominazione di origine protetta*) category, with IGT (*indicazione geografica tipica*) regional wines becoming IGP (*indicazione geografica protetta*). It'll all be much simpler – honestly.

PIEMONTE

The northwestern region of Piemonte (Piedmont in English), in the foothills of the Alps, is one of Italy's premium wine-growing districts. Styles range from the lightest of whites through delicate sweet sparklers to thundering, fabulously complex reds of great longevity. They are listed here alphabetically.

Arneis A DOC since 1989 for white wines made from the grape of the same name. They are made of sterner stuff than many Italian dry

whites, with a fruit like fresh pears, often mixed with a discernible hint of almond. Grown in the Langhe hills around Alba, and also in Roero to the northwest of the town, where it becomes DOCG. One of Italy's better whites.
PRODUCERS: Giacosa, Vietti, Prunotto, Deltetto.
Asti Formerly known as Asti Spumante, the famous frothy sweet fizz produced around the town of Asti is one of Italy's classic styles, a DOCG no less. Made from Moscato, low in alcohol (usually about 7 per cent) from a procedure that involves chilling it to halt the fermentation, and full of the flavours of ripe green grapes and sugared almonds, it is one of the most approachable sparkling wines in the world. Quality is extremely reliable.
PRODUCERS: Fontanafredda, Contero, Bera, Martini & Rossi.
Barbaresco This and Barolo (see below) are the two most important reds produced from the excellent Nebbiolo grape. Centred on the eponymous village, the Barbaresco DOCG is often held to produce slightly more elegant Nebbiolos than Barolo, but the difference is pretty subtle. These are huge, tannic, exotically scented wines, monstrously tough in youth, but ageing well to a savoury, chocolatey maturity. Single-vineyard wines can be monumental.
PRODUCERS: Giacosa, Gaja, Pio Cesare, Sottimano, Rocca, La Spinetta, Ceretto.
Barbera d'Alba/d'Asti/del Monferrato The Barbera grape, suffixed by any of these regional names, produces a sharply acidic but agreeably cherry-fruited red that is usually fairly light in both body and alcohol, though barrel-aged wines are becoming more common. Otherwise best drunk young and fresh, its undeniable potential as a variety has carried it to the vineyards of California.
PRODUCERS: Voerzio, Aldo Conterno, Giacomo Conterno, Bertelli, Prunotto, Correggia.

The Barbaresco DOCG (above) in Piedmont, the foothills of the Alps.

Scything poppies in springtime (above) in Barolo.

PIEDMONT:
ARNEIS
GRAPE: *Arneis*
ASTI
GRAPE: *Moscato*
BARBARESCO
GRAPE: *Nebbiolo*
BARBERA D'ALBA/ D'ASTI/DEL MONFERRATO
GRAPE: *Barbera*
BAROLO
GRAPE: *Nebbiolo*

BRACHETTO D'ACQUI
GRAPE: *Brachetto*
DOLCETTO
GRAPE: *Dolcetto*
FAVORITA
GRAPE: *Favorita*
FREISA D'ASTI/
DI CHIERI
GRAPE: *Freisa*
GATTINARA
GRAPES: *Nebbiolo, Bonarda*
GAVI/CORTESE DI GAVI
GRAPE: *Cortese*
MOSCATO D'ASTI
GRAPE: *Moscato*
SPANNA
GRAPE: *Nebbiolo*

LOMBARDY:
OLTREPO PAVESE
GRAPES: *Red – Barbera,*
Bonarda, Croatina, Uva
Rara, Pinot Nero; White –
Riesling Italico, Pinot Bianco,
Pinot Grigio
VALTELLINA
GRAPE: *Nebbiolo*
FRANCIACORTA
GRAPES: *Red – Cabernet*
Sauvignon, Merlot, Pinot
Nero; White – Chardonnay
LUGANA WHITE
GRAPE: *Trebbiano di Lugana*

High on the alpine slopes of
Valle d'Aosta, vines are often
still trained up traditional
low pergolas (above).

Barolo King of the Piedmontese reds, Barolo is one of Italy's most travelled DOCG wines, even though it's often very difficult to know when to drink Barolo to catch it at its best. In its youth, it is absolutely rigid with tannin, although its colour starts to fade surprisingly quickly. It then acquires an extraordinary range of flavours that includes violets, black plums, bitter chocolate and wild herbs, but even at 20 years old (when it may be quite brown), it obstinately refuses to let go of that heavyweight tannin. In the main, its growers have refused to compromise with modern tastes, so that Barolo remains one of the world's most gloriously unreconstructed red wines. Best vineyard sites (e.g. Ginestra, Monfalletto, Arione) may be specified on the label.
PRODUCERS: Giacomo Conterno, Bartolo Mascarello, Giuseppe Mascarello, Sandrone, Roberto Voerzio, Einaudi, Altare, Ceretto.
Brachetto d'Acqui Light red or rosé wine from the aromatic Brachetto grape, often slightly spritzy to add a dash of character.
Carema Tiny DOC for lighter Nebbiolo reds, in the far north.
Dolcetto Eleven DOCs in Piedmont make red wines from this grape. They include Dolcetto d'Alba (the best), Diano d'Alba, Dolcetto d'Acqui, Dolcetto d'Asti, Ovada, Monferrato and Langhe Monregalesi. There is also a DOCG for it in Dogliani. The wine is a bright purple, light-bodied, exuberantly fresh product, crammed with blueberry fruit, for drinking young. A more gently priced alternative to Beaujolais.
PRODUCERS: Giuseppe Mascarello, Vajra, Ratti, Bongiovanni, Chionetti, Pecchenino.
Erbaluce di Caluso Light, fairly soft dry whites, some fizz, and a famed but rare golden dessert wines (Caluso Passito), made from the not especially distinguished Erbaluce grape.
PRODUCERS: Ferrando, Orsolani.
Favorita White variety making pleasantly lemony wine on both banks of the Tanaro.
Freisa d'Asti/di Chieri A pair of DOCs, the latter very near Turin, for an intensely scented, light, floral red. Can be sparkling.
Gattinara Most important of the lesser-known DOC reds based on Nebbiolo. Intense, potentially long-lived wines.
PRODUCERS: Travaglini, Antoniolo.
Gavi/Cortese di Gavi Ambitiously priced dry whites from the herbaceous Cortese grape. Held in preposterously high esteem locally, hence its outlandish price. Gavi di Gavi is the top wine, with some creamy, nutty substance to it.

PRODUCERS: Chiarlo, La Scolca, Giustiniana.
Grignolino Light quaffable varietal red made near Asti, almost as fruity as Dolcetto.
Moscato d'Asti Made in the same region and from the same grape as Asti, but less fizzy and even less alcoholic (5 per cent is typical). An appetizing mouthful of citric freshness.
PRODUCERS: Ascheri, La Caudrina, La Spinetta, Bava, Giacosa, Saracco.
Ruchè Small DOC making full-bodied, herbal-scented reds in the Monferrato region.
Spanna Widely used synonym for Nebbiolo, often seen on richly textured reds from a number of localities.

VALLE D'AOSTA
The far northwestern corner of Italy is occupied by a small river valley bordering on both France and Switzerland. Wines produced here are made from a number of native grapes, backed up by a smattering of Nebbiolo and Moscato, and plantings of Burgundy and Alsace varieties. They are almost all consumed locally.

LIGURIA
An arc-shaped mountainous region that runs along the Mediterranean coast of northwest Italy, Liguria's main commercial centre is Genoa. It isn't particularly significant in terms of exports, and some of its traditional wines, such as syrupy dessert wines made from raisined grapes, are dying out. **Cinque Terre** is a dry white based on the local Bosco grape, usually blended with Vermentino. Rossese is an important native red variety, and has its own DOC, **Dolceacqua**, in the west of Liguria. Some Dolcetto is produced in the DOC of **Ormeasco**, and is known by that name there.

LOMBARDIA
Centred on Milan, Lombardia runs from the Alpine border with Switzerland down to the river Po, which forms its southern extremity. It is geographically the largest of Italy's wine regions, and has been in recent years one of the quality leaders.
Oltrepò Pavese In classic Italian fashion, this name covers almost any style of wine, only some of which qualifies for the DOC. The best is a good sturdy red based on Barbera, while the dry whites from Riesling Italico (not the noble Riesling) are largely forgettable. Traditional-method fizzes use the Pinot family.
PRODUCERS: Frecciarossa, Verdi, Montelio.

The castle of Soave (left), in the Veneto, that gives its name to one of Italy's most famous dry white wines.

Drying grapes for Amarone and Recioto (above) at the Masi winery, in Veneto's Valpolicella DOC.

Valtellina The largest volume of Nebbiolo in Italy is produced in this DOC near the Swiss border. As well as basic DOC Valtellina and the slightly better DOCG Superiore version, there are four recognized sub-regions for the better wines: Inferno, Grumello, Sassella and Valgella. These are much lighter than Piedmont Nebbiolo, but the best do attain a purity of fruit and staying-power on the palate. Some powerful wine is made from shrivelled grapes fermented until fully dry, labelled Sforzato.

Franciacorta Created a DOCG in 1995 for potentially excellent traditional-method sparklers. Still wines are labelled DOC Terre di Franciacorta, and tend to use classic French varieties and techniques.
PRODUCERS: Ca' del Bosco, Bellavista, Cavalleri, Berlucchi.

Lugana White DOC for dry wines based on a local variant of the dreaded Trebbiano grape. The odd one has a little herbaceous snap to it. Zenato is a good producer. (Lugana overlaps into the Veneto region.)

TRENTINO-ALTO ADIGE
Hard by the Austrian border is Italy's northernmost wine region. The Alto Adige is known to the Austrians, as well as the many German-speaking Italians in these parts, as the Südtirol. The lower half of the region takes its name from the city of Trento. It's a portmanteau region, like Languedoc-Roussillon.

In the last 30 years, producers here have made a name for the region by making some light but impressive wines from international varieties, most notably the two Cabernets, Merlot and Pinot Noir, as well as Chardonnay, Pinot Gris and Pinot Blanc.

Some of the Chardonnay is barrel-aged and has carved itself a niche in the international market for oaky white wines, but prices have sometimes been too stiff for their own good. Local red varietals of particular note are the sour-cherryish **Marzemino**, the richly chocolatey Lagrein (which can make sinewy reds such as **Lagrein Dunkel**, as well as graceful rosés known as **Lagrein Kretzer**), and the blackcurranty Teroldego, which has its own DOC in **Teroldego Rotaliano**.
PRODUCERS: Ferrari, San Leonardo, Haas, Lageder, Tiefenbrunner, Walch.

VENETO
The Veneto is the major wine-producing region of northeast Italy, extending from east of Lake Garda across to Venice and up to the Austrian border. There are some important DOCs and commonly recognized names like Soave and Valpolicella, but overall quality is dogged by excessive production and some ill-considered matching of grape varieties to vineyard sites. However, the Veneto is putting its house in order, and some enterprising growers are beginning to realize the region's potential.

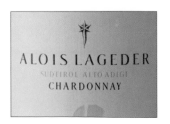

Cases of Soave leaving the packing shed (right).

VENETO:
BARDOLINO

GRAPES: Red – Corvina, Molinara, Rondinella

BIANCO DI CUSTOZA

GRAPES: White – Trebbiano Toscano, Garganega, Tocai Friulano

BREGANZE

GRAPES: Red – Cabernet Sauvignon, Cabernet Franc, Merlot; White – Tocai Friulano, Pinot Bianco, Sauvignon Blanc, Chardonnay

PIAVE

GRAPES: Red – Merlot, Cabernet Sauvignon; White – Tocai Friulano, Verduzzo

SOAVE

GRAPES: White – Garganega, Trebbiano di Soave, Chardonnay, Pinot Bianco

VALPOLICELLA

GRAPES: Red – Corvina, Molinara, Rondinella

Bardolino Featherlight reds from a trio of local grapes, for drinking young and fresh but not lingering over. Wines labelled Superiore should have a bit more oomph. The rosé version is called Chiaretto.

PRODUCERS: Masi, Le Vigne di San Pietro.

Bianco di Custoza Mostly neutral dry whites from a cocktail of grapes, none of them of much character. Some have a little tutti-frutti personality, if you try hard enough.

PRODUCERS: Le Vigne di San Petro, Gorgo.

Breganze One of those DOCs making waves by trying out international varietals, though there is plenty of ordinary stuff too. The reds made from the Bordeaux blend can be extraordinarily good. Maculan is the best producer by some distance.

Gambellara Dry whites that bear a marked resemblance to Soave, from the same grapes. Blandly inoffensive.

Piave The area immediately behind Venice produces large quantities of indifferent varietal wine, the lion's share of it thin, grassy Merlot.

Prosecco di Conegliano/di Valdobbiadene Named after its principal grape, Prosecco can be a still dry white, but its more celebrated manifestation is as a sparkler, using the Charmat method in which the second fermentation is induced in a large tank before bottling. Once useful mainly for mixing with peach juice to make the famous Bellini cocktail, Prosecco has now come up in the world, with more complex, elegant wines, in many cases rivalling Spanish cava.

PRODUCERS: Carpenè Mavolti, Bisol, Adami.

Soave One of Italy's most famous dry whites, synonymous for too long with the bone-dry, totally neutral, flavour-free image of Italian white wine. Very gradually, Soave is getting better. Some of it now has a little Chardonnay in it, and some is cautiously oak-aged. At its best, and with plenty of the traditional Garganega grape in the blend, it can be a deeply appealing, gently silky white with a touch of almond paste and a faintly toasty note, perfect with lunchtime salads. **Recioto di Soave** is a sweet but austere version made from raisined grapes.

PRODUCERS: Pieropan, Anselmi, Prà, Ca' Rugate, Coffele, Suavia.

Valpolicella A red wine DOC that covers a multitude of styles, from very dilute pinkish wines of no great character to deliciously concentrated, berryish, chocolatey reds of considerable ageing potential. As well as the basic style (and the slightly stronger Superiore version), there are some high-octane traditional Valpolicellas produced from grapes that have been dried on straw mats. **Recioto** is a silky-sweet version that can resemble port, while **Amarone** (DOCG since 2009) is fermented out to full dryness, is hugely alcoholic (often 15–16 per cent, without fortification) and almost painfully bitter – its name coming from the Italian for bitter, *amaro*. **Ripasso** is a sort of compromise, an ordinary Valpolicella that has been allowed to run over the skins of grapes used to make Amarone or Recioto. These can be good too, though.

PRODUCERS: Allegrini, Quintarelli, Masi, Tedeschi, Le Ragose, Dal Forno, Bussola.

FRIULI

The easternmost wine region of Italy borders Austria to the north and Slovenia to the east, forming part of the Adriatic coastline that extends down to Trieste. It is sometimes known as Friuli-Venezia Giulia. This is another region that has achieved some notable successes with international varieties, and the main production within DOC regions such as **Collio** or the **Colli Orientali** is of varietally named wines.

Best reds so far have been Cabernet Sauvignon and Merlot, particularly from the commercially important DOC of **Grave del Friuli**, Cabernet Franc from Collio, and local grapes Refosco, which makes a sharp-textured but appetizing red, and spicy Schioppettino. Successful dry whites have been Pinot Grigio, the tantalizingly flowery Tocai Friulano, crisp Sauvignon, and even some subtly perfumed Gewürztraminer. The improving DOC of

Isonzo has scored with most of these varieties too. There are also a pair of very rare, austerely almondy, golden DOCG dessert wines made by the raisining method, one from a grape called **Picolit**, the other – a stern tannic white called **Ramandalo** – from Verduzzo Friulano. Snap them up if you see them, but expect to pay.
REGIONAL PRODUCERS: Borgo Magredo, Pecorari, Puiatti, Edi Kante, Colmello di Grotta.

EMILIA-ROMAGNA

A sprawling region south of the river Po, comprised of Emilia in the west and Romagna on the Adriatic coast, with the ancient city of Bologna at its heart, Emilia-Romagna is one of the bulk-producing wine regions of Italy. Very little of the wine is of DOC standard, and much of it is drunk in a slightly fizzy state, whatever the provenance. The epitome of this tendency is **Lambrusco**, which comes in all colours but is usually sparkling, high in acidity and of often dreadful quality.

A hillside district bordering on Lombardia, in the northwest of the region, the Colli Piacentini, is one of the better zones for quality wines. **Gutturnio** (made from Barbera and Croatina grapes) is a good hearty red, and there are some refreshing white varietals, including Sauvignon Blanc. Down in the southern part of Romagna, **Albana di Romagna** is noteworthy only for being the first white wine to receive the DOCG, a questionable choice for an unexceptional wine made from the workaday Albana grape. Some steadily improving red wine is made from Sangiovese, the great red grape of Tuscany. Labelled **Sangiovese di Romagna**, it is best drunk young while there is still a bracing acid edge to it. Try Cesari's.

TOSCANA

Along with Piedmont, Tuscany is the most significant part of Italy in quality wine terms, and occupies a special place at the cultural heart of the country. In addition to the beautiful old cities of Florence and Siena, the rolling landscape of olive trees and vines is one of the best-loved on the European tourist trail.

For many newcomers to wine in the 1960s, Chianti – usually sold in straw-covered bottles – came to be synonymous with Italian red wine. More than in any other region, however, it was here that the *vino da tavola* revolution really took off, with the launch of a generation of wines made without reference to the DOC

stipulations. These proved once and for all that Italian growers are capable of producing world-class wines. Many are superb.

Bolgheri The Tuscan wine scene was transformed in the 1970s with the release of the first vintages of Sassicaia, brainchild of the Incisa della Rochetta family. Blended from the two Cabernets, it was an explicit attempt to produce a premium wine in the image of a classed-growth Bordeaux. For all there are no Italian varieties in it, it does still taste quintessentially Tuscan, the rich cassis-and-plum fruit always having a savoury edge like bitter herbs. It was a mere *vino da tavola* until 1994, when the Bolgheri DOC was drawn up to include it. The rest is history.
PRODUCERS: Ornellaia, Le Macchiole, Grattamacco, Satta, Poggio al Tesoro.

Brunello di Montalcino Created single-handedly by the Biondi-Santi family in the late 19th century, Brunello is made from a particularly fine clone of Sangiovese. It is only since the second world war that any other producer has made Brunello. One of Tuscany's greatest reds, it's deeper and richer than Chianti, full of sour black cherries and pungent herbs, and capable of long evolution. It has to be aged for three years in cask under the regulations (which many feel is too long). Prices are stratospherically high. A separate DOC, **Rosso di Montalcino**, has been created for wines released at one year old; these represent excellent value.
PRODUCERS: Biondi-Santi, Talenti, il Poggione, Castelgiocondo, La Gerla, Case Basse.

Merlot vineyard in the Bolgheri DOC (above), destined for the 'super-Tuscan' Tenuta Ornellaia.

TUSCANY: BOLGHERI
GRAPES: *Red – Cabernet Sauvignon, Cabernet Franc*
BRUNELLO DI MONTALCINO
GRAPE: *Red – Sangiovese*

CARMIGNANO
GRAPES: *Red – Sangiovese,
Cabernet Sauvignon*
CHIANTI
GRAPES: *Red – Sangiovese,
Cabernet Sauvignon,
Canaiolo; White –
Trebbiano, Malvasia*
**VERNACCIA DI SAN
GIMIGNANO**
GRAPES: *White – Vernaccia,
Chardonnay*
**VINO NOBILE
DI MONTEPULCIANO**
GRAPES: *Red – Sangiovese,
Canaiolo; White –
Trebbiano, Malvasia*
VIN SANTO
GRAPES: *White – Trebbiano,
Malvasia, Pinot Grigio,
Pinot Bianco, Sauvignon
Blanc, Chardonnay*

IL BIANCO
DECUGNANO
A.D. 1212
2009

*Grapes hanging from the
rafters (above) to dry out
for the sweet Tuscan wine,
Vin Santo.*

Carmignano Cabernet Sauvignon was allowed into Carmignano before it gained admittance to any other Tuscan red. The proportion isn't huge, but the Sangiovese is generally ripe enough not to need the extra dimension of intensity conferred by Cabernet. Impressive quality has been rewarded by elevation to DOCG. Capezzana is a highly reliable producer.

Chianti Inevitably for such a high-volume wine region, Chianti spans the quality range from heavenly wines of tremendous, often oak-powered concentration down to vapid, thin apologies for red wine that have only undermined it over the years. Part of the problem is that the boundaries for the region are much too inclusive. It consists of seven sub-zones: Chianti Classico (the heart of the region between Florence and Siena), Chianti Rufina in the northeast, Chianti Montalbano, and four hillside areas named after the cities they adjoin – Colli Fiorentini (Florence), Colli Senesi (Siena), Colli Aretini (Arezzo) and Colli Pisane (Pisa). Of these, only the first two are generally dependable for quality, and will always carry their regional names.

Wines given longer in cask from any of the sub-zones are labelled Riserva, not necessarily an infallible indicator of a fine wine, since much Chianti is too frail to withstand long periods in wood. The traditional Sangiovese and Canaiolo blend has been joined by Cabernet, but the allowance of the white grapes Trebbiano and Malvasia has only hindered the production of quality wine, and many of the better producers don't bother with them.

Typically, Chianti was always an orangey-red wine with an aroma of dried berry fruits, perhaps some plum tomato, and savoury herbs, feeling quite sharp on the palate from high acidity and a faint peppery edge. Modern production methods are now seeing wines with much richer colour and riper fruit, some with obvious Cabernet presence.
PRODUCERS: Volpaia, Fonterutoli, Villa di Vetrice, Isole e Olena, San Polo in Rosso, Fontodi, Selvapiana, Frescobaldi, Querciabella.

Galestro Water-white, low-alcohol, flavourless dry white used for mopping up the surplus Trebbiano no longer used in Chianti. Malvasia can add some interest.

Vernaccia di San Gimignano The local Vernaccia grape forms the basis for this highly prized, but low-volume white wine made within sight of the famous towers of San Gimignano.

Elevated to DOCG in 1993, it may now contain up to 10 per cent Chardonnay. At its best, it has an intriguingly waxy feel and attractive almond-paste character. Too much falls blandly short.
PRODUCERS: Teruzzi & Puthod, Casale-Falchini, Vagnoni, Cesani.

Vino Nobile di Montepulciano There is a grape called Montepulciano, but it doesn't feature in this DOCG made in the hills southeast of Florence from the classic Chianti grape mix (minus Cabernet). The wines can be powerfully intense, with strong purple fruit and a dash of liquorice, but they tend to stop just short of the pedigree of top Chianti. Two years' cask-ageing is mandatory. Again, the better producers ignore the white grapes. Younger wine may be released as **Rosso di Montepulciano** under its own DOC.
PRODUCERS: Avignonesi, Trerose, Boscarelli, Dei, Poliziano, Salcheto.

Vin Santo Undoubtedly the best manifestation of the undistinguished white grapes of Tuscany is as Vin Santo, a tawny, often lusciously sweet raisined wine. The grapes are hung up or laid out in the warmest part of the winery to lose their moisture. A small amount is fermented out to a nutty dryness like the driest sherry. There are DOCs for Vin Santo throughout Tuscany (one of the best being **Colli dell'Etruria Centrale**), some permitting the use of non-Italian varieties. Long cask-ageing of the wines is the norm, and many are made in a deliberately oxidized style, but retain an attractive orange-peel-and-walnuts allure.
PRODUCERS: Isole e Olena, Avignonesi, Selvapiana, Fontodi, Bindella.

LE MARCHE

An eastern region on the Adriatic coast, with the city of Ancona its main commercial centre. Its best wines are a pair of red DOCs, **Rosso Conero** and **Rosso Piceno**, made from blends of the eastern Italian grape Montepulciano with Tuscany's Sangiovese. (In the case of Rosso Conero, the former predominates, while Rosso Piceno must be not less than 60 per cent Sangiovese.) Both are full-bodied, spicy reds with notable ageing potential. Verdicchio is the regional white grape, most often seen in **Verdicchio dei Castelli di Jesi**, one of those uninspiringly neutral-tasting whites that Italy seems to specialize in (although the best producers coax some peanutty aromatic quality out of it). **Verdicchio di Matelica** is a superior, rarer version. Garofoli makes an oak-aged Verdicchio of impressive concentration. The house of Umani Ronchi is a reliable regional producer.

UMBRIA

Wedged between Tuscany and the Marches, the small landlocked region of Umbria is centred on the city of Perugia. Its most famous wine is **Orvieto**, which lays claim to a distinctive local grape variety in Grechetto, swamped in too many wines with admixtures of Trebbiano and Malvasia. It comes in three basic styles, a simple dry wine (*secco*), which often has the tartness of Conference pears, a medium-sweet, in-between version (*abboccato*), and a fully sweet, often rotted dessert wine (*amabile*). Overall quality isn't great, but Decugnano dei Barbi shines out.

Torgiano is the best red wine, now classified a DOCG. It is made from Sangiovese in a dense, concentrated style (look for Lungarotti's wines). **Montefalco** is a DOC near Assisi for Grechetto-Chardonnay whites, as well as Sangiovese reds blended with a little of the local variety, Sagrantino. Vinified alone in this region, this latter grape also has its own DOCG, **Sagrantino di Montefalco**.

LAZIO

Lazio is the region surrounding Rome, chiefly responsible for large quantities of indifferent white wine, the most famous of which, **Frascati**, is one of Italy's best-known names. Trebbiano and Malvasia hold sway here too, so most Frascati is fairly dull stuff. Decent producers include Colli di Catone and Fontana Candida. Drink young to catch their tangy, crème fraîche character. The most overbearingly named wine in Italy, **Est! Est!! Est!!! di Montefiascone**, is also Trebbiano-based, and rarely tastes as if it justifies one exclamation mark, let alone six. Some Cabernet and Merlot is grown in this region, but otherwise there are no particularly remarkable reds.

ABRUZZI

The reputation of this mountainous region on the Adriatic coast, south of the Marches, rests on a trio of DOC wines, one of each colour. The red, **Montepulciano d'Abruzzo**, is by far the more famous of the two. Made from the grape of the same name, it is always a softly plummy, low-tannin, easy-going wine with a strange but unmistakable waft of sea air about it. Despite its strong reliability, it has never become expensive

on the export markets, and is often a surefire bet for a modestly priced Italian red with more depth than most of its equals. Umani Ronchi and Masciarelli make fine ones. **Cerasuolo** is the deeply coloured rosé version.

The white, **Trebbiano d'Abruzzo**, is hampered by its name alone. It is mostly actually made from a southern variety with the rather splendid name of Bombino, but the less reputable Tuscan Trebbiano may also be used. Valentini has single-handedly made a name for this DOC with a hazelnutty dry wine of quite uncommon intensity.

MOLISE

Small and quantitatively unimportant region south of the Abruzzi, specializing in *vini da tavola* from international varieties such as Chardonnay and Riesling. **Biferno** is a regional DOC for wines in all three colours, the reds and rosés based on the Montepulciano grape, the whites on Bombino, Trebbiano and Malvasia.

Bottles of Montepulciano d'Abruzzo being packed at the Illuminati winery in eastern-central Italy (below). The wine is regularly one of the country's most reliable and reasonably priced reds.

*Vines compete for space
with houses on the coastal
cliffs at Amalfi (above),
in Campania.*

PUGLIA

The heel of Italy, Puglia incorporates the Adriatic port of Bari, and is responsible for one of the largest annual productions of any of the country's wine regions. Only a small proportion of this is of DOC standard, however. The extreme southeastern province of Salento is where the finest reds come from. Here, the spicily exciting Negroamaro grape is the claim to fame. Its best DOC is **Salice Salentino**, a richly plummy, often interestingly honeyed red wine of enormous appeal. (Candido's Riserva is especially good.) There are now also two white wines here, the straight **Bianco** containing a minimum 70 per cent Chardonnay, and one made from **Pinot Bianco**. Negroamaro also crops up in the wines of **Copertino**, **Squinzano** and **Brindisi** among others, sometimes given extra bite with another local grape, Malvasia Nera. These are good meaty reds.

Primitivo di Manduria makes colossally alcoholic reds from the Primitivo grape (aka Zinfandel in California). **Castel del Monte** is another DOC with its own local red grape, the intriguing Uva di Troia. Otherwise, the grapes of Abruzzi are relatively important for reds and whites, and there is the usual smattering of international varieties.

CAMPANIA

The Neapolitan southwest has the most venerable winemaking tradition of any part of Italy, but the lowest percentage of wine qualifying as DOC. And yet the DOC areas have undoubted potential. **Taurasi** DOCG is a fierce and exciting, if tannic, red made from a fine local variety, Aglianico. **Falerno del Massico** is a newish DOC seeking to recreate the lost glory of Falernian, the much-revered wine of classical antiquity; the red is a blend of Aglianico and the local Piedirosso with Primitivo and Barbera. Early indications are that it is promising enough to investigate.

The main white DOCGs are **Greco di Tufo**, a mildly lemony wine of some charm, and **Fiano d'Avellino**, which can have a haunting taste of ripe pears. Both are named after their grapes. **Lacryma Christi del Vesuvio** is one of the region's more famous wines, appearing in both red and white versions, both fairly underwhelming. Another interesting local white grape is Falanghina, often vinified as a varietal. Mastroberardino is the reference name among Campania producers.

BASILICATA

This very poor southern region makes only minuscule quantities of wine. Far and away its best shot is the DOC **Aglianico del Vulture**, from the red grape of that name. Here it is grown in vineyards around the extinct Vulture volcano, and produces an astonishingly lush-textured wine with a lovely coffeeish aroma, worth seeking out.

CALABRIA

Cirò is the only DOC wine you might see outside the region that forms the toe of Italy's boot. Based on the local Gaglioppo grape, the full-bodied reds and rosés may, as with many other Italian reds, be blended with some white grapes, inevitably including Trebbiano. On the south coast, a rather sophisticated DOC dessert wine, **Greco di Bianco**, is produced from semi-dried Greco grapes.

SICILIA AND PANTELLERIA

The island of Sicily is one of the most copiously productive regions of Italy. Much of its produce is of no more than table wine standard, but there are isolated pockets of improving quality which suggest that Sicilian wines may well one day be among Italy's finest.

Its most celebrated product is the fortified wine **Marsala**, produced in the west of the island. In common with southern Europe's other classic fortified wines, it remains one of the great original wine styles, quite unlike any other. Various methods of fortification are used, including a rather clumsy one that uses cooked concentrated grape juice, *mosto cotto*. The best grades of Marsala, however, **Superiore** and **Vergine**, are not permitted to use this method.

Styles range from the austerely dry (*secco*) to the liquorously sweet (*dolce*), but common to all of them is a smoky, almost acrid, burnt-toffee tang that is Marsala's unique selling-point. These days, much of it is consumed in tiramisu and zabaglione, but the best Marsalas, such as those from de Bortoli, deserve to be appreciated on their own as stimulating alternatives to the more familiar after-dinner tipples.

Two of the white grapes used in Marsala make good dry unfortified IGT wines elsewhere on the island. They are **Inzolia** and **Catarratto**, both capable of producing lightly aromatic wines of some character. **Nero d'Avola** is the best of the native red grapes, and blends containing a healthy percentage of it are often among the best. The wines are robust and savoury in style, with blackberry fruit and a suggestion of spice.

Regaleali is one of the leading producers of quality Sicilian wines. Its reds can be monumentally complex and ageworthy, as can Corvo Rosso, a long-lived, excitingly spicy IGT red made by Duca di Salaparuta. Settesoli, the main co-op, makes some decent simple reds.

The tiny island of Pantelleria, halfway between Sicily and Tunisia, has revived one of the legendary dessert wines of history in **Moscato di Pantelleria**, made from dried Moscato grapes given delicious richness with oak-ageing. Try it if you're on vacation.

SARDEGNA
Sardinia's wine production continues to be hampered by its very insular approach to marketing, and the ridiculously high yields permitted under the DOC regulations for what could otherwise be interesting wines.
Cannonau is one of the most important red varieties (claimed by some to be related to Grenache), and can make an inky, full-bodied red where yields are restricted. **Monica** produces a much lighter, sharper, Beaujolais-like red for early drinking.

Nuragus is one of the more significant white grapes, but its wines tend to the classic Italian neutrality, partly again because of over-cropping. **Vernaccia di Oristano** can be a diverting curiosity for those on holiday – a bone-dry, nutty, often oxidized white that may remind you of a basic fino sherry.

OTHER CLASSIC WINES OF ITALY
As the redesigning of Italy's wine classification system continues apace, one of its central concerns has been to draw into its embrace all those quality wines that were being produced outside the regulations as *vini da tavola*, but actually comparable to the most illustrious wines of France. The ground-breaking Sassicaia is now DOC Bolgheri, as is Ornellaia. The other wines listed here have all been designated IGT Toscana. A lot depends on whether the individual producers care to play a part in the official system. Many don't as yet.
Balifico (Castello Volpaia): Sangiovese-Cabernet Sauvignon blend aged in French oak.
Cepparello (Isole e Olena): Attractively ripe varietal Sangiovese fleshed out with new oak.

Flaccianello della Pieve (Fontodi): 100 per cent Sangiovese similar in style to Cepparello, but with more obvious Tuscan bitterness to it.
Grifi (Avignonesi): Sangiovese-Cabernet Franc from a fine Vino Nobile producer.
Ornellaia (Lodovico Antinori): Massively concentrated blend of Bordeaux grapes, built for long life.
Sammarco (Castello dei Rampolla): Predominantly brambly Cabernet with a dash of Sangiovese.
Solaia (Piero Antinori): Cabernet-Sangiovese of great distinction, full of classical intensity.
Tignanello (Piero Antinori): A Sangiovese-Cabernet blend, Tignanello is a hugely exciting, long-lived red that combines gorgeously ripe purple fruits with chocolatey richness.

RECENT VINTAGES FOR REDS
It remains tricky to generalize about Italian vintages, as there is such microclimatic variation from one site to the next. But here goes.
Piedmont: 2009 **** 2008 **** 2007 **** 2006 **** 2005 **** 2004 ***** 2003 **** 2002 ** 2001 ***** 2000 ****
Tuscany: 2009 **** 2008 **** 2007 **** 2006 ***** 2005 **** 2004 ***** 2003 **** 2002 * 2001 **** 2000 ***

Ancient farmhouse in the hills of Basilicata (above), surrounded by ploughed land ready for planting with new vines.

Sicilian vineyard (below) planted on black volcanic soils in the shadow of Mount Etna.

SPAIN

A proud winemaking tradition, and the producers' commitment to quality, are placing Spain at the forefront of Europe's great wine nations. Freshness and fruit are now the bywords for the best wines, rather than old-fashioned wood flavour.

The castle of Peñafiel (above) perches above the vineyards of the dynamic Ribera del Duero region.

Renowned for its sherries and oaked wines, the arrival on Spain's map of new wine regions is bringing impressive still and sparkling wines to the market (right).

MODERN SPAIN has more land devoted to vine cultivation than any country in the world, although its average annual production is normally behind those of both Italy and France. Part of the explanation for that paradox lay traditionally in the abnormally low yields that its vines produced, a situation that has been rectified to some degree in the modern era.

Its viticultural industry has slowly but surely come to terms over the past 30 years with what the modern world expects of wine. The old habit of according extended cask-ageing to both red and white wines tended to see off any fruit, with the result that wines labelled Gran Reserva often tasted like museum-pieces. Today, there are vibrant, fresh wines bursting out all over, based on indigenous grape varieties. Tempranillo and Garnacha still lead the pack, but Bobal, Albariño and Loureiro are coming up on the inside track.

The classification system in operation has been taken more seriously in Spain than it often has in parts of Italy. It has equivalents of *vin de table* and *vin de pays* in *vino de mesa* and *vino de la tierra*, respectively, while the appellation wines are DO (*denominación de origen*). An upper level, the rough equivalent of Italy's DOCG, has been created in DOCa (*denominación de origen calificada*), but has been used sparingly so far, with only Rioja, Priorat and Ribera del Duero being elevated. An innovative category, *vino de pago*, has been established for the best single-estate wines, so far only applying to the regions of Castilla-La Mancha and Navarra.

In sherry, Spain has one of the great, and now jealously protected, fortified wines of Europe, easily a match for port and madeira in its versatility and complexity. There is even decent wine being made these days in the Balearics.

1. RIOJA
2. NAVARRA
3. RIAS BAIXAS
4. RIBEIRO
5. VALDEORRAS
6. EL BIERZO
7. TORO
8. RUEDA
9. CIGALES
10. RIBERA DEL DUERO
11. CHACOLI DE GUETARIA
12. CALATAYUD
13. CAMPO DE BORJA
14. SOMONTANO
15. TERRA ALTA
16. COSTERS DEL SEGRE
17. PRIORATO
18. TARRAGONA
19. CARIÑENA
20. CONCA DE BARBERÁ
21. PENEDÉS
22. ALELLA
23. AMPURDÁN-COSTA BRAVA
24. MÉNTRIDA
25. LA MANCHA
26. VALDEPEÑAS
27. UTIEL REQUENA
28. VALENCIA
29. ALMANSA
30. JUMILLA
31. YECLA
32. ALICANTE
33. MONTILLA-MORILES
34. MÁLAGA
35. CONDADO DE HUELVA
36. JEREZ

All that can go wrong now is climate change reducing much of the interior of Spain to unproductive desert. Perish the thought.

RIOJA

Spain's most visible export wines for years have come from the Rioja region surrounding the river Ebro in the north of the country. The red wine in particular, with its strawberry-flavoured fruit and smooth, creamy texture derived from ageing in oak, became a much-loved style in the 1970s, and it remains the pre-eminent Spanish red for many drinkers. When the new super-category of DOCa wines was created, Rioja was its first recipient, reflecting its importance in Spanish wine history.

The region is subdivided into three districts: the Rioja Alta, west of Logroño (generally held to produce the wines of highest pedigree); the Rioja Baja, southeast of the same town; and the Rioja Alavesa, which forms part of the province of Alava, in the southern Basque country. All three regions make reds, whites and rosés, the last known as rosados in Spanish.

The hierarchy of classification for the wines depends on the length of maturation in barrel and bottle they receive before being released on to the market. At the bottom of the pile, young new wine may be released as **Joven** (meaning 'young'). It can have a delicious, sweet-cherry appeal, and responds well to chilling.

Crianza wines must be aged for one year in barrel and a further year in bottle before release. Many commentators feel that this is probably the optimum period for most wines, producing an oaky red that still retains some decent fruit. **Reserva** spends a year in barrel, but a further two in the bottle, while **Gran Reserva** is aged for at least two years in wood before being held in the bottle for a further three.

Traditionally, the type of wood favoured for the production of both red and white Rioja was American oak, which gives a much more pronounced sweet vanilla flavour than the softer French oak. More producers are now turning to French coopers, however, in order to achieve a subtler wood influence in their wines, and the innovation seems to be paying off in the form of more balanced wines.

Tempranillo is the principal grape of the reds, contributing flavours of summery red fruits to young wines, but often turning fascinatingly gamey (almost like Pinot Noir) as it ages. It is supported mainly by Garnacha (Grenache),

which usually lends a spicy edge and some structure to the softer Tempranillo, as well as Graciano and Mazuelo, with a little Cabernet Sauvignon in the wines of producers who always had historic plantings of it.

As to white Rioja, or **Blanco**, there are two distinct schools of thought. The traditional preference is for heavily oaked and deliberately oxidized wines of golden-yellow hue. They often smell tantalizingly like dry sherry, yet possess a bitter tang like dried citrus peel. Sipped in small quantities, they can be impressive wines to mull over, but you'd be mulling over them a long time before the word 'refreshing' suggested itself.

The newer style is all about squeaky-clean fermentation in stainless steel, at low temperatures, to maximize fruitiness and freshness. Often made entiely without the use of oak, these light, lemony wines may not be as imposing as their barrel-fermented cousins, but they do cater more obviously to modern tastes. Rioja's white grapes are the relatively neutral Viura (often seen unblended in the modern styles) and the muskier, more headily perfumed Malvasia.

The **Rosado** can be utterly charming, a little too alcoholic for its own good perhaps, but crammed full of just-picked summer berry fruit. Served properly chilled, it can be a great accompaniment to meaty tapas.

PRODUCERS: La Rioja Alta, Artadi, Montecillo, Marqués de Murrieta, López de Heredía, Remírez de Ganuza, Marqués de Cáceres, Marqués de Riscal, Faustino, Remelluri, Baron de Ley, Marqués de Vargas.

Oak barrels piled up outside the winery at Rioja producer Bodegas López de Heredía (above).

RIOJA

GRAPES: *Red – Tempranillo, Garnacha, Mazuelo, Graciano; White – Viura, Malvasia*

Splashes of red mark the autumnal vineyards of Valdeorras (above), where increasingly characterful wines are being created.

NAVARRA
GRAPES: Red – Garnacha, Tempranillo, Cabernet Sauvignon, Merlot;
White – Viura, Chardonnay
RIAS BAIXAS
GRAPES: Albariño, Treixadura, Loureiro, Caiña Blanca
RIBEIRO
GRAPES: White – Treixadura, Torrontés, etc;
Red – Garnacha, etc.
VALDEORRAS
GRAPES: White – Palomino, Godello, etc; Red – Garnacha, Mencía, etc.
EL BIERZO
GRAPES: Red – Mencía
TORO
GRAPES: Red – Tinto de Toro

NAVARRA

Just to the east of Rioja, but also on the river Ebro, is the increasingly fashionable DO region of Navarra. While Navarra grows essentially the same grapes as neighbouring Rioja, its wines are quite different. There has been increasing interest in incorporating some of the classic French varieties into the more ambitious oak-aged wines, so that it is not uncommon to see a white wine labelled Viura-Chardonnay. Unlike the traditional oaky wines of white Rioja, these are much fresher, with a gently buttery quality reminiscent of the lighter whites of Burgundy.

Navarra makes a much higher proportion of rosado than Rioja, and most of it benefits from attractively juicy strawberry fruit and exemplary freshness. Red wines range from the relatively light in style, a little like midweight Côtes du Rhône, to seriously weighty, world-class wines from the aspirational producers. There is also some sweet Moscatel.
PRODUCERS: Chivite, Inurrieta, Ochoa, Magaña, Nekeas, Príncipe de Viana, Camino del Villar.

RIAS BAIXAS

Rias Baixas has lately been one of the more talked-about regions of northern Spain. Situated in Galicia in the northwest, its reputation has been founded on some unexpectedly fragrant, concentrated dry white wines, mainly based on a fine local grape variety called Albariño. The DO is subdivided into three areas: Val de Salnes on the western coast; O Rosal and Condado de Tea on the Portuguese border; and Soutomaior and Ribera de Ulla near the city of Pontevedra. As in much of the rest of Spain, the typical yields are low, and although other varieties are permitted in the wines, including the scented Loureiro, they don't generally account for much of the blend. Quite expensive, but highly attractive.
PRODUCERS: Lagar de Fornelos, Codax, Lagar de Cervera, Condes de Albarei, Terras Gauda, Lusco do Miño, Besada, La Val.

RIBEIRO

The region's name means 'riverside', and the vineyards occupy the land around the river Miño, which extends up from northern Portugal. There is some fairly inconsequential red, but – as in Rias Baixas – the main business is white wine, and here quality is much improved of late. Some recently established plantings of Torrontés are adding character to the whites. This is a florally aromatic grape with strong notes of orange blossom and roses (now starring in many Argentinian wines). Often blended with Treixadura.

VALDEORRAS

Small region in the east of Galicia that is progressing slowly but surely from making dull, bland plonk to wines of burgeoning character. Palomino, the sherry grape, has long been the curse of northwestern whites, but is now being replaced by more promising varieties such as the local Godello, which gives good, modestly aromatic, dry whites. The ubiquitous Garnacha goes into many of the reds, but some attractively grassy, fresh-tasting reds are being made from the native Mencía grape, in a style not dissimilar to the lighter reds of the Loire valley, but with gentler acidity.

BIERZO

Just to the northeast of Valdeorras, the Bierzo DO is also beginning to explore its potential. The main focus of interest so far is good ripe Loire-like reds made from the local Mencía grape. More richly structured wines come from the Palacios family vineyards.

TORO

The wines of Toro are produced in some of the most inhospitable conditions of any of Spain's vineyard regions. Planted at high altitude along the river Duero, the grape responsible for the thunderously powerful Toro reds, Tinta de Toro, is a local mutation of Spain's premier red variety, Tempranillo. Alcohol levels are typically at least 13.5 per cent, but the wines mostly wear it well, the thick, liquoricey flavours of the grape more than adequately rounding out the spirity finish. Insignificant quantities of weighty rosado and white are also produced.

PRODUCERS: Numanthia-Termes, Fariña, Telmo Rodriguez.

RUEDA

A DO region since 1980, Rueda makes white wines only, and has now carved out a reputation for some of the freshest and tangiest dry whites in all of Spain. The native variety here is Verdejo, which gives snappy, herbaceous whites with good texture. It is sometimes given a little citrus tang with a dash of Viura, but more often brought into focus with a sharp dose of nettly Sauvignon Blanc. Straight Rueda must be at least 50 per cent Verdejo, while wines labelled Rueda Superior have to contain a minimum of 85 per cent of the grape. Oak-aged wines can be surprisingly good.

PRODUCERS: Marqués de Riscal, Belondrade y Lurton, Sila, La Vieja, de Medina.

CIGALES

North of the river Duero, Cigales is not much known to the outside world. It principally makes dry rosados and a little red from the two main red grapes of Rioja.

RIBERA DEL DUERO

For many, this dynamic, forward-looking DOCa (since 2008) region is now at the head of the Spanish pack. Across the board, its carefully crafted wines are highly dependable, and its producers have absorbed the lessons to be learned from global trends in premium red wine production. Its principal variety is another local variation of Tempranillo, Tinto Fino, often appearing unblended. Controlled plantings of some of the Bordeaux varieties are permitted in specific sectors of the region, and a little plummy rosado is produced too. A proportion of juice from the local white grape, Albillo, may be used to soften the intensity of the red wine, but the DOCa regulations don't yet extend to the production of white wines. One superstar producer has provided much of the impetus, but there are now dozens of quality names here.

The best wines of Ribera del Duero have concentrated blackberry or plum fruit, and usually a fair amount of oak influence. This can be either the exotic vanilla of American oak or the more muted, subtler tones of French. The system of ageing in cask and bottle is analagous to that of Rioja: Joven, Crianza, Reserva and Gran Reserva.

In the west of the region is a property called Vega Sicilia, which makes an enormously opulent, totally individual range of red wines, using Tinto Fino with the French varieties and a modicum of Albillo. Valbuena is a five-year-old oak-aged red with an astonishing and unforgettable mixture of perfumes – orange essence, loganberries and milk chocolate. Unico is its top wine, made only in the most promising vintages. The wine is released at about ten years old, after undergoing an elaborate ageing procedure in various types of wood (including large old casks that allow a fair amount of oxygen to seep into the wine) and in bottle. It has been fairly compared to the top classed growths of Bordeaux, in majesty if not in flavour.

OTHER PRODUCERS: Pesquera, Aalto, Carraovejas, los Capellanes, Aster, Moro.

CHACOLI DE GUETARIA

A tiny DO region (Spain's smallest) in the Basque country to the west of San Sebastian. Its mainly white wine is light and spritzy, and made in such modest quantities that it isn't really viable as an export product. The equally light red is even rarer.

RUEDA
GRAPES: White – Verdejo, Viura, Sauvignon Blanc, Palomino
CIGALES
GRAPES: Red – Tinto del País (Tempranillo), Garnacha
RIBERA DEL DUERO
GRAPES: Red – Tinto Fino (Tempranillo), Garnacha, Cabernet Sauvignon, Merlot, Malbec; White – Albillo

The church of Santa Maria la Mayor in Toro (left). On Spain's high central plain, the wine region of Toro makes big, powerful reds.

The 17th-century castle of Raimat, in Catalonia (right), where the Raventos family has extensive high-altitude vineyards.

CHACOLI DE GUETARIA
GRAPES: *White – Hondarrabi Zuri; Red – Hondarrabi Beltz*
CALATAYUD
GRAPES: *Red – Garnacha, Tempranillo, Mazuelo, Graciano; White – Viura, Malvasia*
CAMPO DE BORJA
GRAPES: *Red – Garnacha, Cariñena, Tempranillo; White – Viura*
CARINENA
GRAPES: *Red – Garnacha, Tempranillo, Cariñena; White – Viura, Garnacha Blanca, Parellada*
SOMONTANO
GRAPES: *Red – Moristel, Garnacha, Tempranillo, Cabernet Sauvignon, Merlot; White – Viura, Alcañón, Chardonnay, Chenin Blanc, Gewürztraminer*
TERRA ALTA
GRAPES: *White – Garnacha Blanca, Macabeo; Red – Garnacha*
COSTERS DEL SEGRE
GRAPES: *Red – Tempranillo, Garnacha, Cabernet Sauvignon, Merlot, Pinot Noir; White – Chardonnay, Parellada, Macabeo*

CALATAYUD

In the Aragón region on the river Jalón, Calatayud is dominated by cooperative producers, but not much geared for export. The varieties are essentially the same as for Rioja, and the wines come in all three colours, the unsubtle, alcoholic reds being the surest indicator of local taste.

CAMPO DE BORJA

Stunningly alcoholic reds are the speciality of this DO near the town of Borja in the province of Aragón. Made mainly from Garnacha, they also incorporate the other Rioja varieties, along with the big two Bordeaux grapes and a little Syrah. Again, cooperatives rule the roost, and again, most of the wine is drunk in the vicinity.

CARINENA

Much the most promising so far of the DO regions of Aragón, Cariñena – southwest of Zaragoza – is named after the grape variety that originated and once flourished here. (It's the same grape as Rioja's Mazuelo and France's Carignan.) Garnacha is these days the star of the show for the big opulent reds in which the region specializes and, as in other parts of Aragón, they can attain spine-tingling levels of alcohol. Some Tempranillo is often blended in to soften the impact. Whites are largely fresh and clean, and some use a little of the Chardonnay-like Parellada grape more typically associated with the white wines of Penedés further east. A small quantity of Spain's traditional-method sparkler, cava, is made in Cariñena and isn't bad either, although it too is more at home in Penedés.
PRODUCERS: San Valero, Añadas, Victoria.

SOMONTANO

A healthily outward-looking DO region in the Pyrenean foothills to the east of Navarra, Somontano makes reds, whites and rosados from a tempting mixture of local grapes (including the indigenous red Moristel and Parraleta, and white Alcañón), and a catholic range of French varieties, including some convincingly perfumed Gewürztraminer and full-bodied Chardonnay. As in Cariñena, a small amount of cava is produced.
PRODUCERS: Blecua, Enate, Laus, Irius.

TERRA ALTA

As its name suggests, Terra Alta is a high-altitude vineyard region in the west of Catalonia, currently making the familiarly northern Spanish shift from heavy fortified wines to light dry whites in the modern idiom. Reds are galumphing Garnachas in the old unsubtle jammy style.

COSTERS DEL SEGRE

Split rather messily into six separate sub-regions, Costers del Segre has made waves outside Spain, despite its starting life as inauspicious desert land. The six zones are: Artesa, Valls de Riucorb, Garrigues, Raimat and (since 1998) Pallars Jussà and Segrià, the last entirely encircled by Raimat. The principal exporter has been the Raimat winery in Lleida (Lérida), which makes a range of fine varietals, from softly velvety Tempranillo to densely meaty Merlot, as well as some Chardonnay fizz of impressive richness, and Franco-Spanish blends with Cabernet Sauvignon. Prices have stayed sane, with the result that this is definitely a region worth watching.
OTHER PRODUCERS: Castell del Remei, Cusiné.

PRIORAT

Practically a legend in its own right, Priorat makes one of the most uncompromising styles of red wine anywhere in Europe. Yields from the older vines in the region are minuscule, and the rules specify a minimum alcoholic strength of 13.5 per cent for the wine to qualify as DOQ (the Catalan for DOCa). The result is not hard to imagine – fiercely concentrated, heady stuff, with a pugnacious peppery edge to it, capable of ageing for many years in the bottle. It's predominantly Garnacha and Cariñena, although French varieties are being planted here too, with stunning results. Worth a flutter for one of the unique tastes of Spain.
PRODUCERS: Mas Doix, Scala Dei, Finca Dofi, Clos Mogador, Clos Erasmus, Cims de Porrera.

TARRAGONA

After once enjoying a reputation for sweet red port-style wines, Tarragona now contents itself largely with producing unambitious blending material for bulk producers elsewhere. Its limited local wine production, in all three colours but mostly white, is quite forgettable.

CONCA DE BARBERA

Considered virtually a western extension of Penedés, Conca de Barberà produces some pleasantly fresh dry whites from the Catalan varieties (see Penedés below), as well as some hearty blended reds, rosados from the local Trepat grape, and a great deal of sparkling cava. The region became a DO in 1985, and has since benefited from substantial investment from the Penedés giant, Torres.

PENEDÉS

The largest of the DO regions of Catalonia, Penedés has two main claims to fame. It is the centre of the cava industry, and it is the base of one of the most successful wine dynasties of Europe – the house of Torres.

Cava is a peculiarity in terms of its regulations, in that it can technically be made elsewhere in Spain; the DO is not specific to Penedés. In practice, most of it is made in this northeastern region near Barcelona. The method used is the same as that for champagne, but the grapes are nearly all native varieties: Parellada, Macabeo and Xarel-lo. In addition to those, Chardonnay is being grown to a much greater extent than hitherto, although it is by no means taking over. The rosados use Garnacha and the local Monastrell, and may also now use Pinot Noir. Cava has to be aged on its yeast lees for a minimum of nine months (or two years for vintage cava), but in practice, many houses age it for significantly longer.

Once upon a time, much of it was bedevilled by disturbing, rubbery off-flavours, but that syndrome is now receding rapidly into the past. In fact, cava is on one of the most exciting quality upswings of all Spanish wine, with many producers both big and small producing deeply elegant, complex, toasty sparklers, as well as some lemony-light wines that make perfect aperitifs. The rosados have improved hugely too, the best having sensational raspberry fruit and graceful texture. Some are now boldly aiming, in both style and price, to give champagne a run for its money, and are frankly often capable of outshining some of France's famous names.
PRODUCERS: Raventos i Blanc, Codorníu, Gramona, Rovellats, Torello, Jané Ventura.

The pioneering work of the late Miguel Torres established Penedés as the most outward-looking wine region in the country. He planted international grape varieties alongside the indigenous ones, in many cases blending them together, creating a formidable and enduring reputation in the process for both his company and the region.

Among the more successful Torres whites are the basic Viña Sol (a reliably straightforward, clean house white), Fransola (mouth-wateringly crisp Sauvignon and Parellada), Viña Esmeralda (a honey-and-lemon, off-dry blend of Muscat and Gewürztraminer), and Milmanda (a buttery oaked Chardonnay in the Burgundian style).

The notable reds include Gran Sangre de Toro (earthy Garnacha, Cariñena and Syrah), Atrium (a soft varietal Merlot), Mas Borràs (a classically cherry-scented, gamey Pinot Noir), and Mas La Plana (a premium bottling of intensely dark, austerely tannic Cabernet Sauvignon). At the top of the tree is Reserva Real, a Bordeaux blend for long ageing. (Torres also produces a rather good Gran Reserva brandy.)

Jean León is another grower of note to have followed the international varietal trail here. His Chardonnay, Merlot, Cabernet Sauvignon and Syrah are made in the thoroughly modern style, with lashings of ripe, vibrant fruit and unabashed levels of oaky richness.
OTHER STILL WINE PRODUCERS: Can Rafols dels Caus, Albet i Noya, Puig i Roca.

PRIORATO
GRAPES: *Garnacha, Cariñena*
TARRAGONA
GRAPES: *Red – Garnacha, Cariñena; White – Macabeo, Xarel-lo, Parellada, Garnacha Blanca*
PENEDES
Numerous Spanish and French red and white varieties

Old Garnacha and Cariñena vines yield powerful, heady reds that have drawn attention to the small Priorato region in Catalonia (above).

ALELLA

Alella is a tiny DO north of Barcelona, in which the Marqués de Alella cooperative is the predominant producer. The output is attractive dry whites, in which the assertive character of Xarel-lo (here known as Pansa Blanca) is frequently softened with a modicum of Chardonnay, as well as sparkling cava labelled Parxet, which may also contain a freshening dash of Chenin Blanc. A varietal Chardonnay and Viognier are also made.

AMPURDAN-COSTA BRAVA

This is a small DO situated on the opposite side of the border to the French Côtes du Roussillon. Nearly all the wine made here is drunk *in situ* – mostly simple rosados for the tourist market. There are also some rustic reds and, this being Catalonia, some cava from the traditional grapes. A recent innovation is rush-released Vin Novell, an Iberian answer to Beaujolais Nouveau. Er, no thanks.

MENTRIDA

A DO region immediately to the south and west of Madrid in central Spain, Méntrida's principal business is rough-and-ready Garnacha reds of no obvious pedigree. However, the excellent winery of Marqués de Griñón is also situated near here. Since 2003, it has had its own *vino de pago* DO near Toledo, **Dominio de Valdepusa**, and the wines, including stunning varietal Cabernet Sauvignon, Petit Verdot and Syrah, as well as a premium bottling, Eméritus, a blend of all three, are among the most fabulously rich and opulent Spanish reds of all.

LA MANCHA

The largest DO region in Spain is also the largest individual appellation in Europe. La Mancha occupies the broiling, arid dustlands of the centre of Spain from Madrid down to Valdepeñas, about 125 miles from top to bottom. The pre-eminent grape variety grown here, the white Airén, is actually the most extensively planted wine grape in the world. Given that it's grown virtually nowhere outside Spain, that gives some idea of the sprawling vastness of La Mancha's vineyards.

Once seen as a workhorse area, dedicated as much to producing alcohol for industry as everyday table wines, La Mancha is now set on an upward course to quality. The Airén, previously dismissed as boringly neutral, turns out to make quite refreshing, simple, lemony whites in the right hands, and since the predominant red grape is Tempranillo (here adopting another of its many pseudonyms, Cencibel), the prospects for classy reds too are good. They are generally somewhat lighter than those of Rioja, but have the pronounced strawberry fruit of the grape, together with appealingly smooth contours. The cosmopolitan duo of Cabernet and Chardonnay are beginning to make their presences felt, reflecting the scale of ambition among many of the small proprietors.

In short, La Mancha is set fair to prove that, even in the world of wine, big can be beautiful. It is expected, however, that sooner or later the region will have to be broken up into more manageable chunks.

VALDEPENAS

Valdepeñas is the southernmost outpost of the huge central plateau of La Mancha. Its wines are thought sufficiently distinctive to merit a separate DO, and the growers have been quicker off the draw in penetrating the export markets than their neighbours to the north. Red wines from Cencibel (Tempranillo) are the main business. Often given long cask-ageing, and labelled as Reserva or Gran Reserva, they can suffer from an excess of petrolly oak flavours on a basically rather light fruit base, but the better producers are managing to achieve better balance. Some straightforward, thin dry white is also made from Airén, but a fair amount of it, depressingly enough, goes into the red wines below Reserva level, reducing them to insipid irrelevance.
PRODUCERS: Los Llanos, Solis, Megía.

UTIEL-REQUENA

In the province of Levante, to the west of Valencia, Utiel-Requena's speciality is the Bobal grape – a good red variety that yields fairly beefy wine with a distinctive raisiny flavour. The reds can be a little clumsy, but the rosados are improving, and can be agreeably refreshing on a hot day. Mustiguillo is the outstanding producer and has, since 2003, had its own country wine designation in **Vino de la Tierra El Terrerazo**.

VALENCIA

The eastern port of Valencia lends its name to a DO region inland from the city. White wines run the gamut from dullish dry wines, made from the less than inspiring local Merseguera grape, to the well-known sweet wine, Moscatel

---

ALELLA
GRAPES: White – Pansa Blanca, Chardonnay, Chenin Blanc
AMPURDAN-COSTA BRAVA
GRAPES: Red – Garnacha, Cariñena; White – Xarel-lo, Macabeo
MENTRIDA
GRAPES: Red – Garnacha
LA MANCHA
GRAPES: White – Airén, Chardonnay; Red – Cencibel (Tempranillo), Cabernet Sauvignon
VALDEPENAS
GRAPES: White – Airén; Red – Cencibel (Tempranillo)
UTIEL-REQUENA
GRAPES: Red – Bobal, Tempranillo
VALENCIA
GRAPES: White – Merseguera, Muscat of Alexandria; Red – Monastrell, Garnacha

de Valencia. The Moscatel doesn't undergo normal fermentation, but is made by adding grape spirit to freshly pressed Muscat juice (a style known as *mistela* in Spanish). Red wines can be surprisingly thin and acidic when made from the Garnacha variant grown in these parts (rosados are better), but the Monastrell grape produces a firmer, beefier style of red. PRODUCERS: Cambra, Gandia.

ALMANSA

A relatively unimportant Levantine DO that has concentrated much of its effort hitherto on making blending wine for other regions. When it does bottle its own red wines, they tend to the heavyweight end of the spectrum. Varietal Tempranillos are the best bets, but the conscientiously made blends of Piqueras are pretty good.

JUMILLA

Much the same applies in Jumilla as for neighbouring Almansa. A lot of blending wine is produced, alongside some strong-limbed Monastrell reds and Merseguera whites that lack excitement. Improvements are afoot, though, particularly among the red wines. El Nido is the go-to producer, but there are also impressive wines from Castillo.

YECLA

Another DO making large quantities of blending wine, with a vast cooperative at the centre of operations. Big beefy reds are the name of the game once more, supplemented by weedy Merseguera whites.

ALICANTE

The typical Levantine pattern of giant cooperatives producing mainly blending wine is repeated in the Alicante DO, which extends inland from the coastal city of that name. A sweet fortified wine, **Fondillón**, using the same ageing method as in sherry, brightens the picture a little, and Tempranillo is beginning to lend some sophistication to the generally rustic reds.

THE ISLANDS

The holidaymakers of the Balearic islands are kept well supplied with wine by the **Binissalem** and **Plà i Llevant** DOs on the island of Mallorca. Two indigenous grape varieties, plus Catalonia's white grapes, make some simple whites, gluggable rosados and increasingly good reds.

Among the Canaries, there are a total of 11 DOs (including **Lanzarote**, where the sweet Malvasia can prove a hit in small doses), with fresh dry whites and juicy reds aplenty.

ALMANSA
GRAPES: Red – Monastrell, Garnacha, Tempranillo
JUMILLA
GRAPES: Red – Monastrell; White – Merseguera
YECLA
GRAPES: Red – Monastrell, Garnacha; White – Merseguera
ALICANTE
GRAPES: Red – Monastrell, Garnacha, Bobal, Tempranillo; White – Merseguera
BINISSALEM
GRAPES: Red – Manto Negro; White – Moll, Xarel-lo, Parellada

La Mancha, in the hot, arid centre of Spain (below left). This vast vineyard area is Europe's largest single appellation.

GRAPES: *Palomino,*
Pedro Ximénez, Moscatel

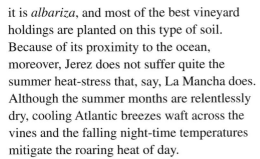

The finest vineyards of the
sherry region, as here at
Osborne's Viña el Caballo
west of Jerez (below), are
planted on chalk-white
albariza *soil.*

SHERRY AND OTHER FORTIFIED WINES

The province of Andalucía, in the south of
Spain, is home to a range of traditional fortified
wines, the most celebrated of which is sherry.
At one time, fortified wines were produced all
over Spain, but as the fashion gradually shifted
towards lighter table wines, so the other regions
abandoned their frequently poor efforts, and
Jerez and its satellites cornered the market.

It is, alas, a dwindling market. Tastes have
changed, and the image of sherry has suffered
both from its preferment by drinkers of a certain
age, and its exasperating association with
inferior products from elsewhere that had no
moral (or now legal) right to the name. Neither
has the preponderance of simple sweet styles
of the real thing much helped. People have a
tendency to grow out of cream sherry. Since
1996, the word 'sherry' has at least been
reserved rightfully for the first of the fortified
wines discussed below.

Sherry The wine takes its name from the city
of Jerez de la Frontera in Andalucía, but the
region also encompasses the major towns of
Puerto de Santa María and Sanlúcar de
Barrameda. These are the three principal
locations for the maturation of the region's
wines. Their quality rests fundamentally on the
geology of the Jerez DO. The soil at the heart
of the region is a mixture of limestone, sand
and clay that looks deceptively like chalk, so
blindingly white does it glare at you in the
brilliance of a summer day. The local name for

it is *albariza*, and most of the best vineyard
holdings are planted on this type of soil.
Because of its proximity to the ocean,
moreover, Jerez does not suffer quite the
summer heat-stress that, say, La Mancha does.
Although the summer months are relentlessly
dry, cooling Atlantic breezes waft across the
vines and the falling night-time temperatures
mitigate the roaring heat of day.

Palomino is the main grape variety in sherry
production. Nearly all the wines, from the palest
and driest up to the most liquorously treacly, are
based on that grape. The variable element lies in
how the producers decide which lots of the base
wine will end up as which style.

After the light Palomino base wine has
completed its fermentation, it is fortified with
grape spirit up to anything from 15 to 20 per
cent alcohol. Generally, the lighter fortification
will be used for wines that are destined to be
sold as **fino**, the palest, most elegant version
of dry sherry. This is because fino sherries are
matured in casks underneath a film of naturally
forming yeast called *flor*, derived from wild
yeasts that are present in the atmosphere of the
cellars. The *flor* protects the developing wine
from the influence of too much oxygen, and
also imparts a characteristic nutty taste (like
fresh peanuts) to classic fino. Fortification
above 15 per cent will inhibit the growth of *flor*,
which is why fino sherries are lower in alcohol
than darker and sweeter styles.

Sometimes the *flor* doesn't quite form a solid
enough layer to produce fino. It breaks up and
sinks to the bottom of the cask, and the more
direct exposure to oxygen causes the wine's
colour to darken. This becomes the style known
as **amontillado**. (The best amontillados are
still bone-dry, the popular conception of it
as a medium-sweet style being derived from
commercial brands that have been sugared up.)

The heaviest, darkest version of sherry is
oloroso, which is fortified to the highest
alcoholic degree of all, and is aged with
maximum oxygen contact so that the colour is a
deep burnished brown. Most olorosos are given
a sweetening dose of juice pressed from raisined
grapes, Pedro Ximénez (or PX) giving the best
quality, although Palomino may be treated in
this way too. As with amontillado, however, there
is a certain amount of totally dry oloroso made,
labelled oloroso seco. Austere and intense,
with a flavour of bitter walnuts, it is one of
the greatest taste experiences wine can offer.

Other sherry styles commonly encountered are **palo cortado** (which is a kind of naturally evolved median stage between amontillado and oloroso, generally given some sweetening), **cream** (sweetened, blended brown sherries, eternally typified by Harvey's Bristol Cream) and **pale cream** (a sweetened fino epitomized by Croft Original). **Manzanilla** is the official name of fino sherries matured in the town of Sanlúcar de Barrameda. They are popularly supposed to have a distinct salty whiff of the local sea air in them, and on a good day, with a spanking-fresh bottle, they really seem to.

Some houses make a speciality of bottling their raisined **PX** wine unblended. The result is an oleaginous, nearly-black essence of mind-blowing sweetness, so glutinously thick that it can scarcely be swirled in the glass. Everybody should try at least a mouthful, but it is admittedly hard to know what to do with a whole bottle. Its more or less dignified fate is to be used as a very grown-up kind of ice-cream topping.

The traditional method of sherry maturation, now extensively abandoned by many houses, was the so-called *solera* system (or fractional blending). This consisted of massed ranks of barrels containing wines that dated back a century or more. With each bottling, a third of the wine would be drawn off the oldest barrels, which would then be topped up with wine from the next oldest, and so on up to the youngest at the top of the pile, which would be topped up with newly made wine.

Given the painstaking labour involved in operating and maintaining such a system, it isn't entirely surprising that modern economics have decreed the abandonment of it in many cases. Wine that has been aged in a *solera*, however, will be labelled with the date of the oldest wine in it; there will thus be some 1895 wine in a bottle so labelled, but only a microscopic amount.

A note about serving the different types of sherry: Fino and manzanilla sherries *must* be served well-chilled, or they will taste lifeless, but no other sherries should be. Equally as important with the paler sherries is to drink them promptly after opening, as soon as you would drink leftover white wine. They aren't that much stronger, after all.

BEST SHERRIES: FINO: Tio Pepe, Don Zoilo, Hidalgo, Lustau, Williams and Humbert, Valdespino Inocente.

MANZANILLA: Barbadillo Príncipe, Hidalgo La Guita, Don Zoilo, Valdespino, Lustau Manzanilla Pasada (an older, darker version than the norm).

AMONTILLADO: Gonzalez Byass Amontillado del Duque, Valdespino Tio Diego and Coliseo, Hidalgo Napoleon, Lustau Almacenista.

OLOROSO: Gonzalez Byass Matúsalem and Apostoles, Valdespino Don Gonzalo, Williams and Humbert Dos Cortados, Lustau Muy Viejo Almacenista.

PX: Valdespino, Hidalgo, Garvey.

Montilla-Moriles A region to the northeast of Jerez that makes entirely analogous styles of fortified wine to sherry. However, it is generally somewhat behind the best sherries in terms of quality because of its inland location and less promising soils, and also the fact that the main sherry grape Palomino has not been able to make itself at home here. The wines can be good though, and are always cheaper than the corresponding sherry.

PRODUCERS: Alvear, Pérez Barquero, Toro Albalá, Garcia Hermanos, Aragón.

Málaga Made in the hinterland behind the Mediterranean port of the same name, the fate of Málaga stands as a salutary warning to what can happen to an original and inimitable style of wine when nobody wants to drink it any more. In the 19th century, it was highly revered, particularly in Britain where it was known as Mountain, owing to the steep hillside locations of its vineyards. By the end of the 20th century, hardly anybody had heard of it, and the last major producers in the region were close to shutting up shop. At the death, it was reprieved, as news of its possible demise caused a modest resurgence of interest. Made from PX and Moscatel, it is usually mahogany-coloured, and has a gentle raisins-in-caramel sweetness that is somehow never cloying. López Hermanos is a great producer.

Condado de Huelva To the west of Jerez towards the border with southern Portugal, Condado de Huelva is now sunk in obscurity as far as the outside world is concerned. Some fortified wine is still made, based on a grape called Zalema. There's a kind of fino that develops under *flor* called Condado Palido, and a darker, oloroso-type wine, Condado Viejo, aged in a *solera* system. The emphasis is slowly shifting, though, towards the production of an unfortified table wine, Vino Joven, and white-wine vinegars.

MONTILLA-MORILES

GRAPES: *White – Pedro Ximénez, Muscat of Alexandria*

MALAGA

GRAPES: *White – Pedro Ximénez, Airén, Muscat of Alexandria, Palomino*

Fino sherry is matured in oak butts (above) under a film of flor, *a natural yeast that imparts a characteristic nutty taste to classic fino.*

PORTUGAL

Shaking off its old-fashioned attitudes, Portugal has rediscovered its greatest treasure – a range of exciting grape varieties – to prove that it can produce more than the world's top fortified wines.

THE EMERGENCE OF PORTUGAL into the international limelight in the past 30 years has been one of the more heartening stories in European wine. For centuries, it occupied a place at the top table on the strength of its two famous fortified wine styles, port and madeira. The latter, particularly, was responsible for opening up Atlantic trade in the period prior to the war of independence in what was to become the United States. And as for the British, they had always drunk port (having more or less invented it), firstly as a matter of

patriotic observance during the regular bouts of hostilities with the French, but also as a matter of national taste.

Nobody really paid much attention to the unfortified table wines of Portugal, though. And, to be brutally honest, they weren't much worth paying attention to. You might drink them on holiday in the Algarve, but they weren't a taste you acquired. The whites were flat and often musty. The reds might be palatable, but there was better in Spain, Italy and France.

That state of affairs has been swept away completely. Investment funds began to flow when Portugal joined the European Union in 1986. The flying winemakers flew in, like they do, and were sensible enough to work with the grain of what they found. And what they found was a benign climate, much influenced by coastal breezes, great soils, and – best of all – a cornucopia of fascinating indigenous grape varieties. These last make it possible to say that, apart from the still emergent Greek wine industry, Portugal is, among the Old World wine countries, the least in hock to international varietalism. If you don't know Portuguese wines, now's the time to come on in.

The classification of the wines follows the four-tier system that EU regulators devised on the basis of the original French model. At the top, the equivalent of *appellation contrôlée* is DOC (*denominação de origem controlada*). Then comes IPR (*indicação de proveniencia regulamentada*), a sort of waiting-room category for promotion to DOC; *vinho regional* for regional wines like the *vins de pays*; and finally simple table wine, *vinho de mesa*.

VINHO VERDE

This is Portugal's largest DOC region by far, up in the northwest corner of the country around Porto. The sheer volumes produced and exported have made Vinho Verde one of Portugal's better-known wines internationally. At least, it's the white version that is popular; many consumers are unaware that just over half of all Vinho Verde is red, probably because the

At their best, traditional aged Portuguese reds (above) are liquoricey and spicy in character.

1. VINHO VERDE
2. PORTO/DOURO
3. DÃO
4. BAIRRADA
5. OESTE
6. RIBATEJO
7. BUCELAS
8. COLARES
9. PALMELA
10. ARRÁBIDA
11. ALENTEJO
12. ALGARVE
13. SETÚBALMOSCATEL
14. CARCAVELOS
15. MADEIRA

Portugal offers a striking range of wine styles (right), the two most renowned – port and Vinho Verde – coming from the north.

VINHO VERDE

GRAPES: White – Loureiro, Trajadura, Arinto, Avesso, Alvarinho; Red – Vinhão, Azal, Espadeiro, etc.

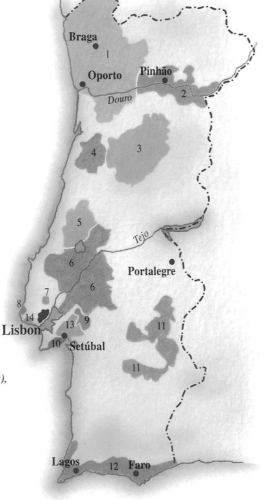

Portuguese keep nearly all of it to themselves. The name means 'green wine', not, as is often thought, in reference to the greenish tinge in many of the whites, but to the fact that the wine, both red and white, is released young for quick consumption. Its youth means there is usually a slight pétillance, even a positive sparkle, in many bottles (indeed, some wines are deliberately carbonated before bottling), as well as generous dollops of raw, palate-scouring acidity. Fruit? Don't ask.

Most wines are blends of various local grapes, and each sub-region has its own particular specialities, Loureiro and Trajadura for example being especially favoured in the central part of the DOC. The whites are a simple, bracing, lemony slap to the tonsils that can be appealing enough at the height of summer. Sensitive souls may gag on the reds, however, which are astringently dry as well as slightly fizzy, not a combination familiar from any other European wine.

PRODUCERS: Tamariz, Aveleda, Azevedo, Soalheiro, Baguinha.

DOURO

Named after the river Douro, which has its origin in Spain (as the Duero), the Douro valley's most celebrated product is port (see pages 176–177), but the DOC for the region as a whole also encompasses some exciting unfortified wines. Growers here are not exactly short of choice when it comes to the right grape to grow on each patch – they have nearly 100 at their disposal, including all the varieties used in port for a start.

Just as Spain has its premium red wine in Vega Sicilia, Portugal has Barca Velha, launched in the 1950s by the port house of Ferreira. It is a complex, subtly spicy red made only in the best vintages and given long cask-ageing – a profound and inspired wine.

Notable successes have been achieved with blends of international varieties such as Cabernet Sauvignon, but the non-traditional grapes are not allowed DOC status, the wines taking the regional designation, Terras Durienses. There has been a slight tendency to the over-enthusiastic use of oak from some producers, but better balance is now emerging across the board. Reds can be sumptuously deep, herb- and spice-scented beauties, while whites from vineyards planted higher up can be florally perfumed and fresh.

If there has been a problem during this initial period of heady experimentation in Douro, it has tended to lie in over-eager extraction of tannin in the red wines. We take the point that they are intended for ageing (and can easily take a decade in their stride at best), but they are after all meant to be table wines, not vintage port.

PRODUCERS: Ferreira Barca Velha, Crasto, Vale Meao, Côtto, Galvosa, Chryseia, Vale Dona Maria, Casal de Loivos.

DÃO

Dão, a large mountainous DOC just to the north of central Portugal, makes one of the higher-profile red wines, as well as a small quantity of fairly undistinguished white. The reds were bedevilled in the past by sloppy winemaking, and even now can be dried out and robbed of their fruit by extended cask-ageing. When good, though, they can show that spicy, liquoricey appeal that characterizes the country's best reds. The whites were also traditionally over-aged, but there are now real aromatic trail-blazers from companies like Sogrape and Quinta das Maias.

PRODUCERS: Pellada, São João, Roques, Vegia, Aliança, Sogrape Quinta dos Carvalhais.

The port house of Ferreira has gained a reputation for a fine red wine, from grapes grown on the steep hillsides (above) of the Douro valley.

DOURO
GRAPES: Red – Touriga Nacional, Tinta Roriz, Tinta Cão; White – Gouveio, Malvasia, Viosinho
DÃO
GRAPES: Red – Touriga Nacional, Bastardo, Tinta Pinheira, Tinta Roriz, Alfrocheiro Preto, etc; White – Encruzado, Bical

A timeless scene outside the 19th-century adega (above) at Bairrada's most innovative producer, Luis Pato.

BAIRRADA
GRAPES: Red – Baga;
White – Maria Gomes, Bical
ESTREMADURA
GRAPES: Red – Arruda
RIBATEJO
GRAPES: White – Fernão
Pires, Arinto;
Red – Periquita

BAIRRADA

To the west of Dão, the Bairrada DOC shares some of the same problems as its neighbour, in that its production has been dominated by poorly equipped cooperatives using rather backward vinification methods. The picture is slowly brightening, however, as more of the small growers decide to cut out the co-ops and bottle their own wine.

Three-quarters of Bairrada is red, and the main grape, Baga, is one of Portugal's more assertive red varieties, although since 2003, a clutch of other Portuguese and international grapes may now be blended in. Clumsily vinified, it can be depressingly tannic and rough, but the smarter operators are coaxing some ripe plummy fruit out of it and showing its potential. White Bairrada, given a gentle touch of oak by one or two producers, can be splendidly smoky and appley, but the majority is still fairly bland. That remains hard to account for as its main grape varieties, Maria Gomes and Bical, are good ones.

This is also the region in which the Sogrape company makes its famed Mateus Rosé. Originally a sweetish pink fizz, it has now gone fashionably drier, with clean, peachy fruit that makes it a respectable proposition on a hot day. PRODUCERS: São João, Aliança, Sogrape, de Sousa, Baixo, Campolargo.

ESTREMADURA

Quantitatively the most important region of Portugal, this western coastal region north of Lisbon encompasses nine DOCs and a number of IPR regions. **Alenquer** is a quality DOC with mature plantings of the local red Castelão, Trincadeira, Touriga Nacional and Aragonez (Spain's Tempranillo) grapes, with some French interlopers, such as Cabernet and Syrah, mingled in. Other constantly improving DOCs include **Arruda**, **Obidos**, **Torres Vedras** and **Lourinhã**. Good IPR wines come from **Encostas d'Aire** and **Alcobaça**, but much of the wine is still given the regional designation, **Lisboa** VR, after the capital city. Monte d'Oiro is one of the producers setting the pace.

Bucelas is a tiny DOC to the south of Arruda. It came perilously close to extinction in the 1980s, when there was just one producer, Caves Velhas, remaining. There are now a handful of new estates determined to restore its historically lofty reputation. It makes white wines only in a light, crisply acidic style from the Arinto grape, which also crops up in white port, together with Esgana, which (as Sercial) is one of the four noble grapes of madeira. Traditionally, the wines were kept for many years in bottle, for all that their grape varieties seem to be telling us to drink them young.

Colares is another of the DOC minnows, perched high on the wind-battered clifftops above the Atlantic Ocean, northwest of Lisbon. Its claim to fame, the noble Ramisco grape, makes some fine, concentrated, ageworthy reds, both on the coast as well as further inland. Whites, based on Madeira's Malvasia, are fairly heavy and less interesting.

RIBATEJO

Inland from Estremadura, also north of Lisbon, Ribatejo also contains a patchwork of IPR districts. From north to south, these are **Tomar**, **Santarém**, **Chamusca**, **Almeirim**, **Cartaxo** and **Coruche**. The potential for outstanding quality here is manifest. The main red grape, Periquita (locally called Castelão Frances) is a good one, giving deeply coloured, spicy wine, while the whites are based on Fernão Pires (aka Maria Gomes in Bairrada). They can be enticingly fresh and floral, and even lightly oaked from those with the resources.
PRODUCERS: Casal Branco, Lagoalva de Cima, Cadaval, Fiuza & Bright.

SETUBAL

Palmela, in the northern part of the Setúbal peninsula, was made a DOC in 2003, incorporating the former IPR of Arrábida, and has gradually made a name for itself as a quality region. The fine red Periquita grape makes intriguingly spicy, peppery wines with good plum and raisin fruit, as well as a small amount of fresh rosé.

The *vinho regional* here is labelled **Peninsula de Setúbal** (formerly Terras do Sado), and includes a slew of excellent savoury reds and scented whites. Some of Portugal's best large companies are based here, including DFJ Vinhos, José Maria da Fonseca and the Pegôes co-op. Sparklers are also becoming a speciality. This is a region to watch.

The **Setúbal** DOC is for fortified sweet Muscats (see page 179).

ALENTEJO

In the southeast of the country, not far from the Spanish border, the Alentejo region has become one of the hottest names on the Portuguese wine scene. Indeed, this was where the quality revolution really began. Much experimentation has taken place, and the evident standard of the predominantly red wines speaks for itself. The Alentejo is divided into eight sub-regions, all

formerly either DOCs or IPRs in their own right, but which were amalgamated into the overall Alentejo DOC in 2003. From north to south, these are: Portalegre, Borba, Redondo, Evora, Reguengos, Granja-Amareleja, Vidigueira and Moura. The VR wines are labelled **Alentejano**.

Grapes are all first-class, with reds led by Aragonez, Trincadeira, Moreto and Periquita, the whites by the gently spicy Roupeiro, and there is the usual crowd of well-controlled French interlopers among them. Careful site selection and judicious oak-ageing are the hallmarks of the best efforts in what is for me Portugal's most dynamic region.
PRODUCERS: João Portugal Ramos, Esporão, JM de Fonseca, Bacalhôa, Malhadinha Nova, Mouchão, Cortes de Cima, Mouro.

ALGARVE

The southern coastal strip of Portugal may be much-loved as a holiday destination, but it hasn't tended to produce much in the way of quality wine. It consists of four DOCs – from west to east, **Lagos**, **Portimão**, **Lagoa** and **Tavira** – mostly making burly reds of no particular charm. Wines from the Vida Nova estate, owned by Sir Cliff Richard, might just change that. A long-forgotten pale dry fortified wine is still made by the local cooperative.

BUCELAS
GRAPES: *White – Arinto, Esgana Cão*
COLARES
GRAPES: *Red – Ramisco; White – Malvasia*
PALMELA
GRAPES: *Red – Periquita*
ARRABIDA
GRAPES: *Red – Periquita, Espadeiro, Cabernet Sauvignon, Merlot; White – Moscatel de Setúbal (Muscat of Alexandria), Arinto, Esgana Cão, Chardonnay*
ALENTEJO
GRAPES: *Red – Aragonez, Trincadeira, Moreto, Periquita; White – Roupeiro*

Ripe bunches of Periquita grapes (below) destined for Tinto da Anfora, a blended red from the Alentejo region.

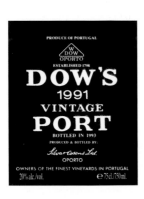

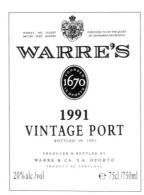

Taylor's Quinta de Vargellas, source of one of the most successful single-estate ports (above).

PORT

The origins of port, as of all fortified wines, lie in the need to stabilize light table wines and protect them from spoilage during long sea voyages. When the English merchants found themselves having to pay punitive tariffs to import French wines, as a result of the 17th-century wars with France, they turned to Portugal as their next best source. The thin white wines of northern Portugal (the modern Vinho Verde DOC) were not much to anyone's taste but, venturing into the Douro valley, the importers chanced upon the fiery red brews of what was to become port country.

Imported in barrel, the wines had inevitably spoiled by the time they reached England, and so the shippers learned to add a little brandy to them in order to preserve them. At this point, therefore, port would have been a potent but dry wine. It wasn't until some while later that the English began systematically adding the brandy before the red wine had finished fermenting. That stopped the yeasts dead in their tracks before all of the grape sugar had been consumed, and so port became naturally sweet as well as strong. A legendary fortified wine was born.

Today, the fortifying agent is a more neutral, colourless grape spirit rather than actual brandy, but the production process is otherwise not

much changed from the 1600s. In the mid-18th century, in a drive to protect port from poor imitations from other regions, the Douro valley was demarcated as the only area that could produce genuine port. It was thus the first ever denominated appellation, predating the French system by about 180 years.

Of all the European fortified wines, port is the most confusing to the unsuspecting. The following is a summary of the range of port styles now offered.

Ruby The most basic style of all, blended from the produce of several harvests and aged for no more than a couple of years. Many shippers produce a house brand that may or may not call itself Ruby (the term is somewhat debased now), but if it has no other description, this is what it will essentially be.

Vintage Character If ever a wine term were ripe for abolition, it is Vintage Character port. These are basic rubies, aged for longer (about five years on average) that theoretically have something of the depth of flavour of true vintage port. In practice, they simply never do, and if you're going to trade up from basic ruby, it is far more advisable to move on to the next category, Late Bottled Vintage.

Late Bottled Vintage (LBV) Unlike Vintage Character, these really are the produce of a single vintage, which will be specified on the label. They are basically the years that are not quite deemed good enough to make true vintage port, but the quality is nonetheless generally good. They are aged for between four and six years, and the best ones will have been bottled without being filtered, so that the wine throws a sediment and requires decanting. Some companies filter their LBVs in order to avoid the need for that, largely because many consumers wrongly imagine that decanting is more technical than it is (see page 15). Buy an unfiltered LBV in preference to a filtered one; the flavours are far more resonant and complex.

Vintage port At the top of the pyramid, vintage port is the product of a single year, stated on the label as with ordinary table wine, that is bottled after two or three years' cask-ageing. Each shipper must decide within two years of the harvest whether the wine of a particular year is going to be fine enough to be released, unblended, as a vintage port. This is known as 'declaring' the vintage. Good years such as 2003 may result in a universal declaration among the major shippers. Vintage port requires ageing in the bottle by the customer, and will always throw a sediment. Some, such as the relatively light 1980, will only need a few years; other vintages, like the legendary 1977, may take a quarter of a century and more before they are ready for drinking.

Single quinta Vintage wines made from the grapes of single estates or quintas. Since these grapes normally play a part in a shipper's best vintage port, the single-estate wines tend to be produced in the marginally less good years, but quality is still fine (above LBV in most cases). Names to look for are Quinta do Bomfim from the house of Dow, Quinta de Vargellas from Taylor, and Quinta da Cavadinha from Warre.

Crusted port So called because it forms a crust of sediment in the bottle, crusted or crusting port is a kind of cross between vintage port and LBV. It is not the produce of a single year, but is treated like a vintage port and bottled unfiltered. The style is a speciality of the British-owned port houses, and is intended as an economically kinder alternative to true vintage port.

Tawny port Traditionally a basic blended port that is aged for several years longer than ruby, so that its colour drops out and the flavour goes almost drily nutty with oxidation. Some tawny is now made by simply adding a little white port to the base of paler red wines to lighten the colour.

Aged tawny These are invariably true tawny ports, aged for many years in cask. The difference from basic tawny is that the label will state the average age of the wines that have gone into the blend, calculated in multiples

of ten. A 10-year-old tawny, such as the perennially superb example from Dow, may well be the optimum age. Twenty-, 30- and 40-year-old wines will increase correspondingly in price, but may yield diminishing returns as to appreciable complexity.

Colheitas A *colheita* port is essentially a vintage tawny. The wines from a single year receive a minimum of seven years in cask, so that their colour fades. Many are only released at grand old ages, and the prices – compared to early-bottled vintage port – can look immensely attractive.

White and rosé port Among the cocktail of 80-plus grape varieties that are permitted in port are a few white ones. Some houses produce a port solely from white grapes (largely Arinto, Gouveio, Malvasia and Viosinho), which is fortified by the same method as the red. They may be dry or sweet and are not particularly great wines. The dry white has nothing like the pedigree of good fino sherry, for instance, but can be appealing served well-chilled in small quantities. Rosé port is the latest innovation, but not one that was crying out to be introduced.

BEST NAMES IN PORT: Dow, Taylor, Graham, Cálem, Fonseca, Warre, Ferreira, Niepoort, Burmester. Quinta do Noval makes a famously brilliant vintage wine called Nacional from ancient vines, selling at a once-in-a-lifetime price.
PORT VINTAGES: 2008 ***** 2007 ****
2005 **** 2004 **** 2003 *****
2000 ***** 1997 *** 1994 **** 1991****
1985 **** 1983 **** 1977 *****

Back-breaking manual harvesting in the terraced vineyards of Quinta do Bomfim in the Douro (above).

A traditional barco rabelo sails through Oporto (below), on the Portuguese coast. These boats were used to carry the pipes of port down the Douro to the port houses.

MADEIRA

The history of madeira is perhaps the single most remarkable example of human dedication to the cause of fine wine. The island of Madeira is a volcanic tropical outcrop in the Atlantic Ocean, nearer to the coast of north Africa than to the Portugal of which it forms an autonomously governed province. Its soil contains a great quantity of ash from a conflagration that raged across the island many centuries ago, and its mountainous terrain means that its vineyards are among the most inaccessible in the world.

Like port, Madeira's wines were once light table wines that came to be fortified so that they might better survive long sea transportation. In the case of madeira, though, the shippers stumbled on an extraordinary discovery. Carried aboard the great trading vessels of the Dutch East India Company, the wine's voyage east was a more arduous matter than simply ferrying port from northern Portugal to the south of England. It was noticed that, when the wine arrived in India, it was unspoiled; in fact it was positively improved. So, just for good measure, the shippers left some to complete a round trip back to Europe, and that turned out even better.

No other wine has ever, before or since, proved so improbably masochistic. It sailed the heaving oceans in raging heat for weeks at a time, the barrels clattering around in the hold, and nothing could destroy it. For many decades, every bottle of madeira sold had been on this round-the-world cruise, until a way was found to simulate those conditions in its place of origin.

In the 19th century, a maturation system known as the *estufa*, or stove, was introduced. The *lagares* – the storage houses in which the wine is aged – were equipped with central-heating systems, hot-water pipes that ran around the walls (or occasionally through the vats of wine themselves) in order to cook it, as it had been in its maritime days. Some wines known as *canteiros*, reputedly the best, were cooked by simple exposure to the tropical summer sun.

Simple blended madeira is often based on a red grape variety called Tinta Negra Mole that used also to find its way into any of the four varietal styles of madeira. These must now, as a result of intervention by the European Union, be made up of no less than 85 per cent of the named varietal, although Tinta Negra Mole itself has now been accepted as Madeira's fifth varietal, which seems fair enough.

All of Madeira's agriculture, including its vineyards, is planted in terraces on sheer hillside land such as this (right). The fearsome gradients mean that any form of mechanized harvesting is out of the question.

The white varietal wines are, from lightest and driest to richest and sweetest, **Sercial**, **Verdelho**, **Bual** and **Malmsey** (the last name being an anglicized corruption of Malvasia). Even at its very sweetest, madeira always has a streak of balancing acid running through it to complement the amazing flavours of molasses, toffee, Christmas cake, sweet spices, dates and walnuts. There is also often a telltale whiff of mature cheese about it, rather like old dry Cheshire, and just to complete its range of peculiar attributes, it generally has a distinct green hue at the rim.

Labels may state the age of the blend (ten-year-old is significantly more rewarding than five), or may use such vague-sounding, but in practice fairly precise, terminologies as Finest (about three years old), Reserve (five), Special Reserve (ten) or Extra Reserve (15).

A small quantity of vintage-dated madeira is made, which sells for a fraction of the price of vintage port. As the history of this fabulous, unique wine suggests, it is virtually indestructible. Definitely worth trying.

BEST NAMES IN MADEIRA: Blandy, Henriques & Henriques, Barbeito, Cossart Gordon, Rutherford & Miles, Leacock.

SETUBAL

Three variants of the Muscat grape, the main one Muscat of Alexandria, make a port-method sweet fortified wine on the Setúbal peninsula, **Moscatel de Setúbal**. After the fortification, the skins of the grapes are left to infuse in the new wines for several months, so that a particularly pronounced aroma and flavour of fresh Moscatel grapes is imparted to it. It is usually aged in cask for five years before bottling, though some premium wines are given up to 25 years' maturation, resulting in a nuttily oxidized, deep brown wine. Most examples taste fairly heavy on the palate, but some attain the graceful balance of the best southern French fortified Muscats. JM da Fonseca makes excellent ones. Wines with less than 85 per cent Moscatel in them are labelled as simple **Setúbal**.

CARCAVELOS

Decreasingly important coastal DOC just west of Lisbon that once tried to rival port as a producer of quality fortified wine. The wines are made in much the same way, from both red and white grapes, and generally resemble basic tawny. Quinta dos Pesos is a recently established estate determined to keep the flame alive.

Traditional thatched A-frame houses, like this one at Palheiros (below), are a characteristic feature of Madeira's vineyards.

GERMANY

Germany's wines have struggled to earn respect abroad in the modern era, yet the country's conscientious producers can offer the very best of fine, light wines in a whole range of styles.

Germany's famous wine regions hug the river Rhine and its tributaries, along the southwestern borders (below). Saale-Unstrut and Sachsen are two additions since the fall of the Berlin Wall.

IMAGE PROBLEM? What image problem? Everybody knows that Germany produces some of the finest light fermented drinks in the world. Indeed, it set the European standard, and remains an enviable beacon of integrity when set against the mass-produced stuff churned out to satisfy everyday tastes elsewhere in Europe. That's right. German beers are second to none.

Wine? That – sadly, agonizingly, notoriously – is another story. It hardly seems necessary to rehearse again the long decline of German wine over the 20th century. War reparations following the Treaty of Versailles in 1919 devastating a wine industry that had enjoyed a continent-wide reputation for quality since the Middle Ages. The invention of a new product (sweetened-up slop, to be sure, but a unique style anyway) in order to move in on the

undemanding end of the market. The graduation of international taste to dry, full-bodied, barrel-fermented white wines and sturdy, ultra-ripe reds when all you've got is delicately lacy white wines that nearly all have some degree of sweetness to them. What's a wine producer to do? People always enjoy a glass of fizz, perhaps, but then even your sparkling wines are mostly rubbish.

All in all, the modern wine world has been more of a challenge for Germany than it has been for any other established wine-producing country. The first signs of a way out of the impasse began to emerge in the early 1990s. If the world wanted dry wines, German winemakers would produce them. Early attempts at fermenting out the Rieslings to full dryness were often grotesque, unbalanced and painfully bitter, but with the right varieties in the right sites, decent dry whites are now being produced. They're not world-shattering, but they don't taste unripe any longer.

What's more encouraging is that the best growers – and Germany has some of the most talented winemakers on the face of the earth – have excelled in the past couple of decades at extending their range, and modernizing their approach. There are wines being made along the Mosel, in the Rheingau, the Pfalz and the Nahe, by no means exclusively from Riesling, for which only the word 'beautiful' will do. 'But what do we drink them with?' is the parrot-cry of the food-and-wine chatterati. Don't drink them with anything if nothing seems to work. Drink them on their own, if you prefer, but drink them. They're too good to miss.

The only problem you'll encounter is finding any, since most high-street retailers, restaurants and wine-bars bailed out of quality German wine a long time ago. And that, which returns us to the whole question of image, really is what you call a problem.

A wine classification system comparable to the French standard was established in 1971. At its lowest level, is the basic table wine, *Deutscher Tafelwein*, to be avoided here as elsewhere. A step up is the *vin de pays* category,

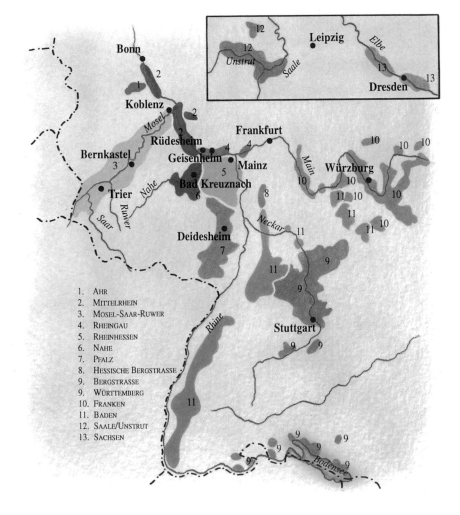

1. AHR
2. MITTELRHEIN
3. MOSEL-SAAR-RUWER
4. RHEINGAU
5. RHEINHESSEN
6. NAHE
7. PFALZ
8. HESSISCHE BERGSTRASSE
9. BERGSTRASSE
9. WÜRTTEMBERG
10. FRANKEN
11. BADEN
12. SAALE/UNSTRUT
13. SACHSEN

Landwein, which may come from any of 19 large demarcated regions. Above that is QbA (*Qualitätswein bestimmte Anbaugebiete*, 'quality wine from a specified region'). This is the volume category, covering 13 regions, in which the juice of underripe grapes may be sweetened to increase the final alcohol level.

At the top is *Prädikatswein*, formerly QmP (*Qualitätswein mit Prädikat*, 'quality wine with pedigree'). These wines are subdivided according to how much natural sugar the harvested grapes possess; they must not be artificially sweetened. In ascending order of sweetness, they are: Kabinett, Spätlese, Auslese, Beerenauslese and Trockenbeerenauslese. The separate category Eiswein ('ice wine' made from frozen ultra-ripe grapes picked in the dead of winter) also counts as *Prädikatswein*. It usually falls somewhere between the last two categories in terms of sweetness.

Dry wines are labelled Trocken, the semi-dry Feinherb (the latter term unofficially replacing the original Halbtrocken).

It remains true that its Rieslings are still Germany's best shot, but there are other varieties to contend with, many of them grown in different regions. In an effort to find grapes that will ripen more dependably than Riesling in the cold northern climate, viticultural researchers have produced crossed varieties, and even crossed the crossings. The results have been decidedly mixed, and remain mostly specific to Germany. Grapes familiar from elsewhere are a safer bet, but you'll need to know their German names – Weissburgunder (Pinot Blanc), Grauburgunder or Ruländer (Pinot Gris), Spätburgunder (Pinot Noir) and, more recognizably, Gewürztraminer.

OTHER GRAPES

Silvaner Particularly valued in the Franken region around Würzburg, Silvaner is one of the best of the uncrossed grapes after Riesling. An earlier ripener, it gives wines with a whiff of cabbage leaves when young, but that can age to a silky, honey-laden maturity.

Müller-Thurgau A Riesling-based mix, this was the first of the crossings, developed in the 1880s. So grateful were the growers for its early-ripening properties that they fell upon it with unconfined zeal, to the extent that it became Germany's most widely planted grape, a position it no longer occupies. Indeed, it could have been the Holy Grail, were it not for the

fact that the wines it produces are unspeakably dull and watery. Unbelievably, though, new plantings of it are still being established.

Kerner One of the more successful new varieties, Kerner is a crossing of Riesling with the red Trollinger. It at least makes a crisp, lime-zesty wine with at least some of the elegance of the real thing, but plantings are declining.

Scheurebe A Riesling-Silvaner cross, Scheurebe has, when properly ripe, a distinct flavour of grapefruit, with the corollary that, if the summer hasn't been kind, its wines are agonizingly tart. In the right conditions, however, it gives excellent noble-rotted dessert wines of piercing intensity.

Rieslaner Probably the best of the Riesling-Silvaner crossings, the clumsily named Rieslaner can be stunning, full of almost tropical fruit from the best growers. Mostly only found in the Pfalz and Franken, it's a shame it hasn't become more widely favoured.

Bacchus Crossed from two other crossings, and with Riesling and Silvaner in its parentage, this can be an exhilarating aromatic variety, as some English growers have discovered. In Germany, it is of declining importance, planted mainly in Franken.

The sundial (above) that gives the terraced Wehlener Sonnenuhr vineyard, one of the Mosel's premier sites, its name.

A misty winter morning dawns over the vineyard of Schwarzerde, near Kirchheim, Pfalz (above). German wines have to survive some of the severest cold-weather conditions in the world.

The village of Zeltingen (above), caught between the Mosel river and the steeply rising vineyards.

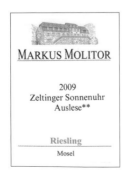

Dornfelder A fine red variety produced from two other crossed grapes, Dornfelder has made inroads into various German regions, particularly along the Rhine. Its wines can be light and cherryish, a little like young Beaujolais occasionally, but with less alcohol. Some producers are attempting to coax a fuller, richer style from it suitable for oak-ageing.

Blauer Portugieser Not a Portuguese grape despite the name, it gives rather coarse reds with high acidity, and is now in decline.

Lemberger Known as Blaufränkisch in neighbouring Austria, this is a good, characterful red grape that produces light, but appetizingly spicy, even violetty wines with plenty of fresh acidity. Plantings of it are on the up.

Trollinger Planted mainly in the Württemberg region, Trollinger (known as Schiava in northern Italy) is a quality red grape that produces light, redcurranty wines, often with a gentle hint of nutmeg to them.

THE REGIONS

Ahr This small northerly wine region, lying just south of the city of Bonn, specializes in red wines, mostly from Spätburgunder (Pinot Noir). They are inevitably light, in both texture and colour, as a result of being grown in such a marginal climate, but there are increasing numbers of good examples, notably from late-picked grapes that retain a gentle natural sweetness. The region's production is dominated by cooperatives, but Meyer-Näkel is a one of a handful of skilful smaller winemakers. There is also some Riesling, but it's losing ground as a percentage of total plantings.

Mittelrhein A small production area that extends from Bonn to south of Koblenz, the Mittelrhein is two-thirds Riesling – a high proportion for any German region. Vineyards are planted on both banks of the Rhine, often on steep hillsides. Pinot Noir is increasingly important here. Quality is good, but most of the wine is drunk *in situ* by the locals – or by tourists, as this is one of the most unspoiled parts of Germany. Toni Jost is a fine Mittelrhein winemaker who is exporting some of his sharply defined, exciting Rieslings.

Mosel The Mosel valley runs southwest of Koblenz, down past the city of Trier, and stops short at the intersection where Germany borders Luxembourg and France. The region also embraces two small tributaries of the river Mosel, the Saar and the Ruwer. It includes some of the most historically celebrated vineyards in German wine history, many of them located in the Bernkastel district in the centre of the valley. These are some of the world's most dramatically sited vineyards, clinging vertiginously to sheer hillsides on either bank of the river, completely inaccessible to any form of machine-harvesting. Here the Riesling achieves some of its great glories, wines that are almost miraculously subtle expressions of the variety, extremely low in alcohol and yet possessed of a fragile purity all their own.

The best vineyard sites (preceded by their village names) have been Erdener Treppchen, Wehlener Sonnenuhr, Graacher Himmelreich, Bernkasteler Doktor, Brauneberger Juffer and Piesporter Goldtröpfchen. Some of these, notably Piesport, have suffered by association with bland, mass-market products that are blended from the general district (or *Bereich*). Always choose a single-estate wine in preference to anything else.

Around the Saar, Wiltinger Scharzhofberg, Ockfener Bockstein and Ayler Kupp are the leading vineyards, while Maximin Grünhaus and Eitelsbacher Karthäuserhofberg are the jewels in Ruwer's crown.

PRODUCERS: Egon Müller (Scharzhofberger), Haag, Dr Loosen, von Schubert, JJ Prüm, Thanisch, Saarstein, Pauly-Bergweiler, Molitor.

Rheingau The Rheingau mostly occupies the right bank of the Rhine to the east of the Mittelrhein region. In some ways, it represents the nerve-centre of German winemaking. Rheingau boasts some of the most highly regarded wine estates in the country, growing a great preponderance of Riesling. At Geisenheim, the viticultural research institute has been responsible for so much of the work in creating new vine varieties.

A range of disparate vineyard conditions makes up the Rheingau. Around Rüdesheim, steeply shelving slaty soils produce some ethereally light Rieslings, while more robust wines, known and much favoured once as 'hock', come from the more gently contoured land around Hochheim.

At the heart of Rheingau production is a group of about four dozen winemakers calling itself the Charta Association. To qualify for the seal of approval (look for an emblem of twin arches embossed on the brown bottles), Charta wines must pass a rigorous taste test, which only Rieslings may enter. It is a quality initiative that other German regions would do well to emulate.

The two most famous properties are the ancient estates of Schloss Vollrads and Schloss Johannisberg. In a region dominated by small producers rather than cooperatives, the names of outstanding individual growers are a better guide to quality than the vineyard sites themselves. Look out for the following.

PRODUCERS: Breuer, Johannishof, Künstler, Domdechant Werner, Kloster Eberbach, Leitz, Kesseler, Schönborn, Reinhartshausen.

Rheinhessen South of the Rheingau, the Rheinhessen is where a lot of the mass-market wines of Germany originate. Half of all Liebfraumilch is made here, and there are other regional names that will be familiar to English-speaking consumers, such as Niersteiner Gutes Domtal. Much of Germany's acreage of crossed grape varieties is planted in the Rheinhessen too, with Müller-Thurgau leading the way. Production is much larger than in the Rheingau, and this is not by and large a quality region. There are, however, always exceptions, increasingly so in the production of surprisingly sturdy reds from Spätburgunder and Dornfelder. Silvaner also makes good wine, although less of it than it once did.

PRODUCERS: Villa Sachsen, Guntrum, Heyl zu Herrnsheim, Keller, Wittmann.

Nahe The Nahe region, named after its river, lies to the west of the Rheinhessen. It is a fine, and considerably under-recognized, player on the German wine scene, its best estates as good as those in the Rheingau or Mosel. Some astonishingly concentrated Rieslings are made within the vicinity of the town of Bad Kreuznach, with Müller-Thurgau and Dornfelder making up most of the rest of the plantings. A concerted campaign to raise the profiles of the best growers has helped; it's also driven prices up, but this is still one of the best-value regions in Germany.

PRODUCERS: Dönnhoff, Diel, Crusius, Plettenberg.

A tiny patch of red earth at the foot of the towering Rotenfels cliff (above) at Bad Münster, in the Nahe, yields intensely flavoured wines.

Assmannshausen, at the western end of the Rheingau (below). This wine region, like Burgundy, can trace an unbroken history back to the early days of the Benedictine and Cistercian monks.

Decorative architecture typical of Germany's wine villages (above).

Weingut Müller-Catoir Haardt/Pfalz
Müller-Catoir
Bürgergarten Riesling

Looking down over the town of Würzburg on the river Main in Franken (right), from the Marienberg vineyard.

Pfalz Once known in English as the Palatinate, the Pfalz is a fast-improving and dynamic region to the south of Rheinhessen. The range of grapes grown is very broad. Not only Riesling, but Dornfelder, Spätburgunder, Grauburgunder and Gewürztraminer are all producing good things. Among the best villages are Deidesheim, Ruppertsberg and Wachenheim, but impressive wine is proliferating all over the Pfalz now. Some of the new-style Pinot Noir reds could give some négociant burgundy a run for its money these days; not only do they have richness and body, but they can often match Burgundian Pinot for alcohol too. Decent sparkling wine, known in Germany as Sekt bA, is also becoming something of a speciality.

The very best Pfalz estate is Müller-Catoir, whose range of varietals is frankly world-class. Not only does it make breathtaking Rieslings and Rieslaners, as well as some convincingly spicy Gewürz, but the estate has even been known to cajole some display of personality from that old dullard, Müller-Thurgau.
PRODUCERS: Müller-Catoir, Lingenfelder, Bürklin-Wolf, Bassermann-Jordan, von Buhl, Köhler-Ruprecht.

Hessische Bergstrasse Germany's smallest region, to the east of Rheinhessen, does not export much of its wine, but quality is impressively high. About half the vineyard is Riesling, and the better growers manage to achieve levels of concentration similar to those around Hochheim. This has been one of the sectors of Germany that has wholeheartedly embraced the latter-day trend for fermenting out wines of *Prädikat* standard to Trocken or Feinherb styles. Vineyards owned by the state of Hesse are producing some of the best wine, including sumptuous Eiswein; Simon-Bürkle is a commendable individual estate.

Württemberg A large region centred on Stuttgart, Württemberg is not greatly renowned beyond its own boundaries. Riesling and Kerner are the principal white varieties, Trollinger the main red. The region in fact specializes in red wines, with some also made from Spätburgunder, Lemberger and Schwarzriesling (the last better known as Champagne's Pinot Meunier). Trollingers are light in both colour and body, but have an attractive, summery, red-fruit nature.

Franken The region through which the river Main runs was traditionally famous as the mainstay of the Silvaner grape, although that now only accounts for about a fifth of the area under vine. The local taste is for austerely dry wines, the best of which come in a flat round bottle called a *Bocksbeutel*. Nowadays, Müller-Thurgau has, somewhat depressingly, made inroads into the vineyards, but there are also some delicately floral wines from that much-crossed variety Bacchus. The wines are exported to some degree, but prices tend to be off-putting.
PRODUCERS: Wirsching, Ruck, Juliusspital.

Baden The principal region of southwest Germany , just over the border from Alsace, Baden has been on most people's lists as one of the more exciting European wine regions of recent years. It encompasses a long stretch between Franken and the border with Switzerland, with some vineyards situated in the vicinity of Lake Constance (or the Bodensee in German). Although there is a fairly high percentage of Müller-Thurgau in the vineyards, there is also fine, boldly delineated Riesling, musky dry Grauburgunder, spicy Gewürztraminer and – perhaps most promising of all in these warmer southern climes – plenty of intensely ripe, deeply raspberryish Spätburgunder, some of it benefiting from oak influence.
PRODUCERS: Königschaffhausen co-op.

Saale-Unstrut One of two small regions that fell within the boundaries of the former GDR (East Germany), Saale-Unstrut is named after the two rivers at whose confluence it lies. Müller-Thurgau, Weissburgunder, Silvaner and others are used to make dry, relatively full-bodied wines, but the region wasn't much blessed with investment by the old state authority, and it can still only be considered emergent as yet. Lützkendorf is a producer worth noting.

Sachsen The most northerly and easterly wine region in Germany, Sachsen (Saxony in English) is centred on the old city of Dresden, its vineyards planted along the banks of the river Elbe. Like Saale-Unstrut, it makes dry

white wines from good varieties, but the prospects for quality wine are noticeably higher. Müller-Thurgau rules the roost, but Riesling, Weissburgunder, Gewürztraminer and Grauburgunder all play their parts. The wine is mostly made by a single large cooperative of numerous small growers, but Zimmerling is a good solo performer.

SPARKLING WINES

German sparkling wine covers a multitude of sins. It comes in four basic categories, the best of which is **Sekt bA** (*Sekt bestimmter Anbaugebiete*), which must come from one of the 13 QbA districts, indicated on the label (e.g. Pfalz Sekt bA). Most is made by the Charmat or tank method. Wonderfully fresh, lime-scented sparkling Rieslings at all levels of sweetness are getting better and better.

Deutscher Sekt is a step down, and may be blended from anywhere in the country. Basic **Sekt**, which accounts for about 90 per cent of German fizz, lacks the adjective Deutscher for the simple reason that it contains wines from other countries, mainly the unwanted slosh of Italy, Spain and France. Lowest of the low is carbonated **Schaumwein**, the most unbelievably atrocious fizzy wine made anywhere.

RECENT GERMAN VINTAGES: 2009 ****
2008 *** 2007 ***** 2006 ****
2005 ***** 2004 **** 2003 ****
2002 **** 2001 ***** 2000 **

Netting keeps birds off the sweet shrivelled Riesling grapes left on the vine after harvest to botrytize (above), in the Ungeheuer vineyard at Forst, in the Pfalz.

UNITED KINGDOM

A mechanical harvester at work at Denbies, in Surrey (above), the UK's largest producer at 250ha.

Most of the UK's vineyards (below) are clustered in the southeast, and are tiny, averaging less than one hectare.

In the relatively short period of the last 30 years, the UK's wine industry has developed dramatically. It may not ever become prolific but when the weather is kind, the quality is there.

WINEMAKING in the British Isles was revived at a purely speculative level in the years following the second world war. For a long time, it was a rash hobbyist's pursuit, which involved rummaging through the back cupboard of Germany's experimental grape laboratories to find varieties that might care to ripen in the famously damp summers. The amount of investment needed to establish a vineyard meant that the resulting produce had to be sold at prices that made the wine look like a luxury item, compared to Muscadet or Bulgarian Merlot.

Quantities were tiny, so most of the wine was sold out of the vineyards themselves. Where anything was produced in sufficient quantity for one of the high-street multiples to take them, they belly-flopped commercially. The labels looked frumpy, the wines had names like Huxelrebe and Madeleine Angevine in a world of Chardonnay and Cabernet, and the tastes were something else. The French winemaker who commented with a sniff that English wine tasted of rain wasn't far wrong (although he perhaps hadn't tasted a great deal of Muscadet lately). Slow sales meant that a lot of wineries routinely offered light white and rosé wines for sale at six and seven years old, long past their notional sell-by dates.

If the British are noted for anything, though, it is the dogged refusal to know when they're beaten. Painstaking experimentation continued throughout the 1980s, and then in 1992, the national output of wine exceeded 25,000 hectolitres, which is the magic figure above which the European Union requires a country to institute an appellation system. So the UK is now divided into two appellations – **England** and **Wales**. Anything else is UK Table Wine (avoid like the plague), or Regional Counties wine if it includes non-*vinifera* grapes.

That marked some sort of coming of age, but the single biggest story to happen to English wine since then has been fizz.

SPARKLING WINES

The soils of whole swathes of southern England are part of the same geological chalk deposit as is found in Champagne. A cool climate is auspicious for yielding just the kind of low-alcohol, high-acid base wine that good fizzes need, and all three of the champagne grape varieties – Chardonnay, Pinot Noir and Pinot Meunier – have proved they will grow in England.

The result is a generation of sparkling wines that are every bit as good as decent champagne. They have the same toasty warmth, depth and concentration of their French cousins, whether vintage or non-vintage, and even though the prices are scarcely any different, the best wines are fully worth the outlay. The rosés, arguably, need a bit more work (many still taste rather heavy and solid), but the whites are little short of fabulous. When one of the champagne houses turns up, as it has, to buy four hectares of prime Hampshire real estate, England's sparkling wine producers can fairly claim to have arrived.

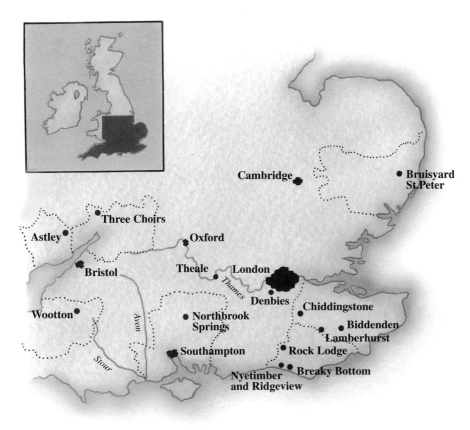

Three Choirs
Astley
Oxford
Bristol
Theale
London
Wootton
Denbies
Northbrook Springs
Southampton
Rock Lodge
Nyetimber and Ridgeview
Breaky Bottom
Lamberhurst
Biddenden
Chiddingstone
Cambridge
Bruisyard St.Peter

Look especially for the wines of Nyetimber and Ridgeview (both from West Sussex), Camel Valley (Cornwall) and Theale (Berkshire), but there will be many more stars in the years to come.

OTHER WINES

Otherwise, Britain's cool, damp northerly climate means that the range of grape varieties that can be successfully grown, even given some climatic warming, is pretty narrow. There may be the odd heatwave, it's true, but vines need to keep producing year after year to earn their keep, and from where I'm sitting writing this on the south coast of England, I'm looking out of the window at the fourth wet August in a row. That's not good.

On the other hand, if there has been a reasonable summer, followed by a dampish, misty autumn, botrytis can set in, and there have in the opening years of the 21st century been some astonishing noble-rotted dessert wines. They could even cause the next wave of excitement, to follow up the success of the sparklers.

The single most important determining factor in the style of an English or Welsh wine is the grape or grapes it contains. Regional characteristics are not sufficiently sharply delineated as yet. The great tragedy, in a sense, of UK winemaking is that Riesling – hero of the German vineyards – just won't ripen here, which is where all those crossed grapes come into play. The following are some of the most commonly planted.

Seyval Blanc Seyval is something of an albatross to the English wine industry, in that it's a hybrid variety. This means that it has some non-*vinifera* parentage, thus outlawing it within EU rules from any appellation wine. As a varietal, it gives generally dull, thin, neutral-tasting wine, and is best blended with grapes that have a little more to say for themselves. The fact that it has gained in vineyard share to become the country's most planted grape can only hold English wine back.

Reichensteiner A three-way cross, Reichensteiner can occasionally make an exotically scented (and often slightly sweet) varietal. Some have achieved partial success with it by giving it a period in oak.

Müller-Thurgau The widely planted German workhorse grape was once England's most common variety, but it has lost ground since the 1990s. This is no bad thing, as its wines are no more thrilling than they are in the Rheinhessen.

Some producers add a little sweetening to it before bottling to create a more commercially appealing style. Enough said.

Bacchus A cross involving Silvaner, Riesling and Müller-Thurgau, Bacchus is quite a good grape. At its best, it has the flowery hedgerow scents that somehow suit English wine.

Other good white grapes include the perfumed Schönburger and Ortega, a little grapefruity Scheurebe, a pinch of Gewürztraminer, and growing quantities of good old Chardonnay – not all of which is going into the sparklers.

Red wines account for only about a quarter of the overall production. Germany's Dornfelder is doing well, the hybrids Rondo and Regent have produced some surprisingly robust, beefy reds, and we may one day see some exciting varietal results with Pinot Noir.

Only a tiny amount of wine is made in the south of Wales, most of it consumed locally. Monnow Valley in Monmouth has made some good, crisply refreshing whites.

Breaky Bottom, in Sussex (above). Frost and birds are two menaces facing growers.

CENTRAL EUROPE

Led by Austria, the wine regions of central Europe – stretching from Switzerland to Slovakia – are becoming increasingly important in the global arena. Internationally familiar grape varieties will help them to compete.

This highly ornamental gateway (above) leads to the wine cellars of Gustav Feiler at Rust, in the Burgenland region of eastern Austria.

T HE CENTRAL EUROPEAN countries, some of them former members of the old Soviet bloc, were of only marginal importance to the international wine scene at one time but, with the exception of Switzerland, all the countries on these pages are now members of the European Union. Things are changing fast, as their wine industries are brought within the purview of continental regulations, and improvements in quality – dizzyingly rapid in some instances – have followed. Foreign consultants have played their parts, and as the old wine countries of western Europe have in many areas begun to seem arrogantly distant from the ordinary consumer, these new kids on the block are poised to dazzle. They just need to find adventurous consumers prepared to try them.

Austria's vineyards lie in the eastern half of the country (right), producing mainly full-bodied dry white wines, now being joined by some rapidly improving reds. Around the Neusiedlersee lake in Burgenland, the regular occurrence of noble rot provides some of Europe's best-value dessert wines.

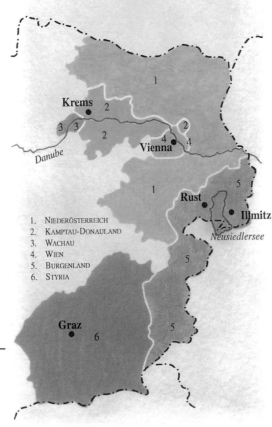

Krems

Danube

Vienna

Rust

Illmitz

Neusiedlersee

1. NIEDERÖSTERREICH
2. KAMPTAU-DONAULAND
3. WACHAU
4. WIEN
5. BURGENLAND
6. STYRIA

Graz

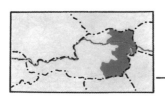

AUSTRIA

The vineyard regions of Austria are almost all located in the eastern half of the country, along its borders with the Czech Republic, Slovakia, Hungary and Slovenia. Germanic as well as French grape varieties are grown, but being that much more southerly than most of Germany's wine regions, Austria is able to produce a wider spectrum of wine styles in a more benign climate.

Its classification system has been a work in progress ever since Austria joined the EU. Originally modelled on the German system, it consists of *Tafelwein* and *Landwein* at the lower end, above which is a *Qualitätswein* category for 16 demarcated regions (comparable to Germany's QbA), and then *Prädikatswein*, the major difference being that Kabinett wines (the sweetness category below Spätlese) are not included, but sit in their own category. In the Wachau district of Lower Austria, a three-tier classification for dry wines consists of (in ascending order of ripeness and potential alcohol) Steinfeder, Federspiel and Smaragd.

So far, so Germanic. Austria is also in the process of instituting a geographically based classification too, on the model of the French appellations. The category has been given a Latin title (there's posh): Districtus Austriae Controllatus (DAC). There are seven of these to date: Weinviertel, Mittelburgenland, Traisental, Kremstal, Kamptal, Leithaberg and Eisenberg. Each may grown only certain designated grapes, mostly Grüner Veltliner and/or Riesling for whites, Blaufränkisch for reds.

GRAPES AND WINE STYLES

The local grape made good in Austria is Grüner Veltliner; it occupies just over a third of all vineyard land. The wine it yields is quite unique, mediumweight to hefty on the palate, with an extraordinary dry spice like white pepper, and often quite biting acidity. It's fair to say the less carefully balanced ones can be more of a mouthful than you're expecting from a dry white wine, but they lack nothing in personality.

Otherwise, among whites, there's Müller-Thurgau (slowly being abandoned), Weissburgunder (Pinot Blanc), Chardonnay, Gewürztraminer, Ruländer (Pinot Gris), a dash of Sauvignon Blanc, and growing amounts of Riesling. Another white grape widely grown in these parts, Welschriesling (which has nothing to do with the real Riesling), occupies nearly a tenth of the Austrian vineyard. Normally, a clumsy oaf of a grape, it has achieved some improbably tasty results here. Then there are Rotgipfler and Zierfandler, the Rosencrantz and Guildenstern of Austrian wine, which together go into a peculiarly heavy wine called Gumpoldskirchner, made just south of Vienna.

Red varieties are the indigenous Zweigelt, which gives an often purple-hued wine with a Dolcetto-like taste of blueberries. The German varieties Blaufränkisch and Blauer Portugieser also appear, as well as some impressive Cabernet Sauvignon and Pinot Noir (often termed Blauerburgunder). St Laurent is a central European grape gaining a reputation, now making gently spicy, raspberryish reds in the style of classic meaty burgundy.

Before its emergence as a producer of fine dry wines, though, Austria was noted for its botrytized dessert wines. These are mostly produced around the Neusiedlersee, a large shallow lake on the border with Hungary. Conditions for the development of noble rot are so obliging most years that they enable Austria to sell its sweet wines for much less than the top German examples. The categories for dessert wines are essentially the same as Germany's, including Eiswein, though with one extra classification – Ausbruch – inserted between Beerenauslese and Trockenbeerenauslese. Another sweet speciality is Strohwein (straw wine), made from naturally overripe grapes that are dried on straw mats, as in the production of Spanish *mistela* or the French *vin de paille*.

REGIONS

Niederösterreich (Lower Austria) The northernmost wine zone, north of the Danube. Its wines are mostly dry or medium-dry whites from Grüner Veltliner, Riesling and Welschriesling. Kamptal, on the western fringe, makes richly intense Grüners and racy Rieslings, while Wachau has sharply defined Rieslings (some botrytized) to rival those of the Rhine valley. PRODUCERS: Brundlmayer, Loimer, Nigl, Nikolaihof, Malat, Salomon, Winzerhaus.

Wien Vienna is a little wine region in itself, unique among European capitals. Grüner, Riesling and Weissburgunder are the best wines, nearly all drunk locally. Traditional taverns known as *Heurigen* are cheery hostelries in the city's outskirts, where growers sell the wines of the new vintage, half-fizzing and still cloudy from the tank. Look for Wieninger's.

Burgenland On the Hungarian border, this is the region that includes the Neusiedlersee. A versatile range of dry table wines is made here, as well as fabulously opulent dessert wines from grapes such as Welschriesling, Gewürztraminer, the local Bouvier, and others. Dry whites take in firmly textured Weissburgunder, as well as creamy oaked Chardonnay and gooseberryish Sauvignon, while Zweigelt and Blaufränkisch reds are often packed with savoury spice, increasingly barrel-matured. One or two growers have produced breathtakingly concentrated Cabernet Sauvignon. PRODUCERS: Kracher, Opitz, Umathum, Velich, Feiler-Artinger.

The imposing white church gives its name to the village of Weissenkirchen (above) in the Wachau region of Austria, source of some of the country's finest Riesling wines.

Trimly tended vineyards cluster around the village church at Conthey (above), in the Valais, western Switzerland.

Through the heart of Europe stretches a band of cool vineyards (right). Once under the rule of empires and some now emerging from communist control, they produce mainly white wines.

Steiermark (Styria) The southernmost sector. It's predominantly white wine country and, while extensive, only accounts for a modest fraction of the national output. The style, whether for Sauvignon, Chardonnay (often known by the pseudonym Morillon), Gewürztraminer or dry Muscat (Gelber Muskateller) is extremely dry, often tart, with sharply emphasized acidity. In the west, around Graz, a red grape called Blauer Wildbacher makes Schilcher, a highly regarded rosé.
PRODUCERS: Gross, Polz, Tement.

SWITZERLAND

The wine-growing areas of Switzerland are concentrated near the country's borders – with France in the west, Germany to the north and Italy in the south. Its wines are not exported in any great quantity, and tend to be horrifyingly expensive even *in situ*. Unless a path to better value can be found, they are only ever likely to have curiosity status in external markets.

Around the continuation of the river Rhône in the west, the Valais and Vaud regions specialize in French varieties, although the favoured white grape, **Fendant** (Chasselas to the French), is not much prized in its mother country, yielding a thin, unassuming, sometimes minerally, but not conspicuously fruity white. Sylvaner does well here, and there are isolated outposts of Chardonnay and Pinot Gris.

Pinot Noir, the most planted grape with 30 per cent of the land, makes reasonably ripe light reds, sometime in a blend with smaller proportions of Gamay. These are labelled **Dôle** in the Valais, **Savagnin** in the Vaud. A white version of the Valais blend, **Dôle Blanche**, is made by avoiding maceration. East of France's Jura is Neuchâtel, where the local claim to fame is a delicate Pinot Noir rosé, **Oeil-de-Perdrix** ('partridge-eye').

Ticino in the south is the Italian-speaking sector. Here production is overwhelmingly dominated by **Merlot** reds, some light and grassy, others with a bit of sinew to them, helped along by judicious application of oak.

LUXEMBOURG

Müller-Thurgau (known here as Rivaner) and a pallid-tasting variety called Elbling are joined by most of the Alsace varieties in Luxembourg's vineyards. Nearly all the wine is white, with a little Pinot Noir for frail rosés, and is labelled by variety. There is just one AOC, **Moselle Luxembourgeoise**. Perhaps the most interesting wine is **Crémant de Luxembourg**, a denomination that came into effect in 1991 for the country's traditional-method fizz, both white and rosé. Quality is good, but you'll probably have to go to the Grand Duchy to taste it.

CZECH REPUBLIC/SLOVAKIA

Both halves of the former Czechoslovakia are emerging, blinking, into the modern wine world after decades of insularity under the state-controlled Soviet bloc system.

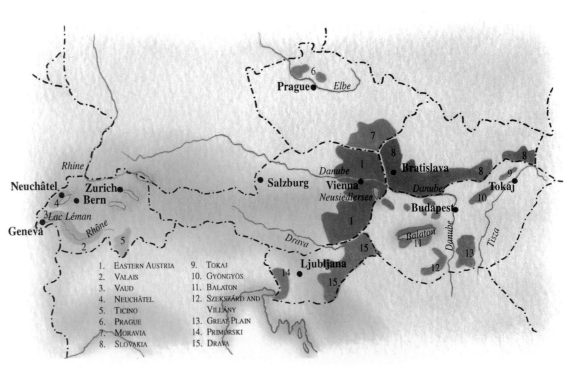

1. EASTERN AUSTRIA
2. VALAIS
3. VAUD
4. NEUCHÂTEL
5. TICINO
6. PRAGUE
7. MORAVIA
8. SLOVAKIA
9. TOKAJ
10. GYÖNGYÖS
11. BALATON
12. SZEKSZÁRD AND VILLÁNY
13. GREAT PLAIN
14. PRIMORSKI
15. DRAVA

The Czech Republic is the lesser of the two players as yet. Its vineyards are largely concentrated in the southeastern region of Moravia, on the Austrian and Slovak borders, although an insignificant quantity of wine is made north of Prague.

International varietals to look for are Cabernet Sauvignon and Pinot Noir for reds, and Sauvignon Blanc, Pinot Blanc, Riesling and Traminer (as in Gewürz) for whites. Sporadic plantings of the Austrian Grüner Veltliner, together with Müller-Thurgau, are responsible for quite a lot of Czech white. St Laurent makes appetizingly rustic red, and the violetty Blaufränkisch crops up as Frankovka.

Slovakia's vineyard regions extend in a virtually unbroken line along the country's southern borders, all the way from Austria to Russia. Varieties are mostly as in the Czech Republic. A local curiosity is the Irsai Olivér grape, which makes fragrantly graceful white wines, with more than a whiff of scented soap about them, especially in the Nitra region – strange but attractive. Pinot Gris does well too.

HUNGARY

Hungary was once famous only for Tokaji, occasionally great, often stalely oxidized, brown dessert wines that can bear an uncanny resemblance to sherry. Produced in the northeast of the country, they are made in a range of styles, from basically dry to lusciously sweet. Tokaji is matured in large casks under a film of naturally formed yeast comparable to the *flor* of the Jerez region (hence the similarity to sherry).

The sweeter styles, labelled Aszú, involve an addition to the base wine of rotted grapes pounded into a paste. They are measured out in custom-made hods called *puttonyos*; the label states the number added (from three up to a sticky-sweet seven). Tokaji Essencia, sweetest of all, appears only in occasional vintages, and is made from free-run juice cask-aged for at least five years. Inward investment in the Tokaji region in the last few years, including French and German interests, has gone a long way to restoring the wines to their former exalted reputation.

As well as Tokaji, Hungary's table wines are gaining ground. Most of the major varieties of Burgundy, Bordeaux and Alsace are now planted here, and are yielding encouraging results. Chardonnay (both oaked and unoaked) and Sauvignon Blanc have been particularly good, in the easy-drinking style.

Native white grapes include the Furmint and Hárslevelü used in Tokaji, but also in some straight dry whites, and the crisp but unremarkable Ezerjó. The principal red is Kadarka, which makes beefy reds in the southern regions to the west of the Danube, such as Szekszárd and Villány. It's also the backbone of the famous Egri Bikavér (Bull's Blood). Blaufränkisch is successful as well; it's known in Hungarian as Kékfrankos.

SLOVENIA

The northwestern province of the former Yugoslavia became an independent country in 1991. It was from here that one of the biggest-selling wine brands of the 1970s hailed – the palatable, but desperately ordinary, Lutomer Laski Rizling, made from the Welschriesling grape. These days, Slovene wine production is trying hard to enter the international quality league with a range of classic varietals. Expertise and influence are being absorbed from neighbouring Italy and Austria, in the Primorska and Podravje regions respectively. Sipon (Hungary's Furmint), Sauvignon Blanc, Cabernet Sauvignon and Merlot are all doing well, while the best of the Muscat family – Muscat Blanc à Petits Grains – can make refreshing, simple sweet wines.

Vineyards at Nova Gora in Slovenia (above), one of central Europe's emergent wine nations.

Checking on the development of sweet Tokaji in the mould-coated cellars of the Tokaji Wine Trust, Hungary (above).

EASTERN EUROPE

Through the great empires of the Greeks, Byzantines and Ottomans who crossed eastern Europe, the vine has flourished and faded. Centuries on, winemaking is again enjoying a new momentum.

The swathe of eastern Europe, crossing Bulgaria, Romania and Moldova, Turkey and Greece (below), offers a vast range of styles and native grape varieties.

As WE MOVE TOWARDS the eastern fringes of Europe, we are nearing the birthplace of wine itself, the first homeland of the winemaking grape, *Vitis vinifera*. If things had all turned out differently, then Greece would have been the pre-eminent wine country in Europe ever since classical antiquity.

But it didn't happen that way. The Greeks took their expertise into Rome and other parts of southern Europe, and the Roman Empire carried it on northwards and westwards. In time, the native varieties of what was to be France became the most highly prized of all wine grapes, the vineyards in which they grew were carefully delineated, and French wine ascended to greatness.

In the Middle Ages, Greece became part of the Byzantine Empire. The fateful decision of the Byzantine emperor Alexius to grant favourable trading status to the Venetian Republic in 1082, exempting the goods of Venice from export duties, undermined Greek winemaking more or less at a stroke. When an enterprise becomes obsolete because others are able to practise it

more cheaply, the inevitable decline is accompanied by a critical loss of skills and knowledge. So it was with Greek wine.

As the collapsing Byzantine Empire was in due course overrun by Ottoman Turks, the fate of Hellenic wine was sealed. The nation that had, in large measure, taught Europe the art of vinification saw its viticulture regress to a state of helpless infancy that was to endure right up to the most recent generations. Only now are the first tentative steps towards a reconstitution of Greek viticulture being taken. The going is heavy, and the acute devastation caused by the credit crisis of recent years can hardly help matters, but somewhere at the end of the tunnel is the light of a competitive modern wine culture that, I believe, will one day be at least as successful and exciting as that of Portugal has been.

In the eastern countries formerly in the Soviet sphere of influence, a quality wine industry was viewed as something of a luxury when the agricultural sector as a whole was so chronically fragile. The one exception was to be Bulgaria, where an experiment in flooding western markets with heavily subsidised state-produced wines was to be one of the more conspicuous economic successes of the Soviet era.

Today, eastern Europe, most of it absorbed into the European Union, is struggling to keep pace with developments in the southern hemisphere. The auguries are ultimately favourable, though, not least because of the mass of potentially interesting indigenous grape varieties found all over the area.

GREECE

When Greece joined the EU in the 1980s, it had already put in place an appellation system so devotedly modelled on the French that it had appropriated the French terms *appellation contrôlée* and *vin de pays*. As in other countries, the better wines that have been treated to cask-ageing are labelled either Réserve or Grande Réserve. Table wines, including branded wines of dubious repute, make up much of the rest. There are now around 30 appellations throughout the country, from Macedonia in the

1. MACEDONIA	13. TROODOS
2. THRACE	14. ISTANBUL
3. EPIRUS	15. IZMIR
4. THESSALY	16. ANKARA
5. PELOPONNESE	17. KHAN KRUM
6. CEPHALONIA	18. SUHINDOL
7. PAROS	19. HASKOVO
8. SANTORINI	20. DAMIANITZA
9. SAMOS	21. MURFATLAR
10. LEMNOS	22. COTNARI
11. RHODES	23. TEREMIA
12. CRETE	

north down to the island of Crete, with Greek terminology now elbowing aside the expropriated French.

Macedonia and Thrace The northern regions are especially noted for red wines. Xinomavro is the main indigenous red grape, making intense, oak-aged, raisiny reds in **Náoussa** and **Goumenissa**. One of the first reds to be taken seriously in the early stages of Greek wine was Château Carras (now Porto Carras), from the slopes of Mount Meliton on the Thraki (Thracian) peninsula. It was conceived as an authoritative Greek version of classic claret, brought into being with French expertise, and based on good Cabernet Sauvignon. Although many feel it isn't now what it was, it at least spawned the Côtes de Meliton appellation, and launched a period of feverish experimentation with blending local and French grapes.

Epirus and Thessaly Vineyards are rather thinly spread over the central regions of Greece. In the west, not far from the Albanian border, a local variety called Debina makes a slightly pétillant white wine at **Zitsa**. On the Aegean coast, the Xinomavro grape crops up again, this time in a blended, cask-aged red, **Rapsani**, made in the shadow of Mount Olympus. Further south, **Ankhíalos** is a crisp dry white made from native grapes Roditis and Savatiano, a successful combination also much favoured in retsina (see below).

Peloponnese The southern peninsula is home to more of Greece's appellations than any other zone. The extensive vineyards of Patras in the north produce wines that span the stylistic spectrum, from **Patras** itself, a light dry Roditis white, through fortified **Muscat of Patras** (made in the same way as French *vin doux naturel*), to the fairly widely known **Mavrodaphne**, Greece's answer to port. Mavrodaphne is the eponymous main grape in it, and the vinification method is the same as for port. Extended cask-ageing is the norm, although the wine tends to retain its deep red colour. The best (try Kourtakis) are a rich and robust match for good LBV.

At **Nemea** in the northeast, another good red grape, Agiorgitiko, comes into its own, making full-bodied, concentrated, oaky reds at high altitudes. Some of the less good wine from this region is made slightly sweet.

On the central plateau of **Mantineia**, some of Greece's more arrestingly original wine is made from Moschofilero, one of the rare varieties of

grapes that may accurately be classed as pink, rather than red or white. Most of the wine is a highly scented, viscous white full of musky orange aromas, like a heavier version of dry Alsace Muscat. The pigmentation of the skin means that a period of maceration can yield a full-fruited rosé.

Greek islands In the Ionian Sea off the west coast of Greece, the island of **Cephalonia** makes its own versions of the fortified wines of Patras, as well as a strong-limbed, heavy-going varietal white from the northern Italian Ribolla (here called Robola).

Hot and dry, Cephalonia, in the Ionian Sea (left), makes both fortified and varietal white wines.

Picking Cabernet Sauvignon on the slopes of Mount Meliton, in Thrace (below), for the Château Carras red. Styled on claret, this wine marked the birth of Greece's modern wine industry.

*Pruning vines (above).
Old-fashioned methods still
rule in many of Cyprus's
remote hilltop vineyards.*

*Almond trees in blossom
among the vines in the
foothills of the Troodos
mountains (below), home of
Cyprus's legendary fortified
sweet wine, Commandaria.*

The Cycladean islands of **Paros** and **Santorini** each have their own respective appellations, the former for a red wine blended from the red Mandilaria grape with some white Malvasia, the latter for a dry, refreshingly crisp white made from the local Assyrtiko.

Greece's most celebrated fortified Muscats, from the top-flight Muscat Blanc à Petits Grains, come from two islands in the Aegean. **Muscat of Samos**, from the island just off the Turkish coast, is the better-known, and comes in a range of styles from gently sweet to an almost unbearably concentrated nectar, made from fully raisined grapes. The version most often seen abroad is somewhere in the middle, a *vin doux naturel* like Muscat de Beaumes-de-Venise. Further north, **Lemnos** makes a similar style of sweet wine, as well as a small quantity of dry wine for local consumption, and a resinated Muscat wine made like retsina.

Rhodes has a trio of appellations, representing different wine styles. The dry white is made a grape called **Athiri**, the red is from the **Mandilaria** seen on Paros, and there is also the inevitable dessert **Muscat**.

Crete, which has been making wine since early antiquity, has a good showing of native grape varieties. **Peza**, in the centre of the island, is the principal appellation, making both red

and white wines from grapes such as red Liatiko and white Vilana.

PRODUCERS: Kostas Lazaridis, Antonopoulos, Gerovassiliou, Kourtakis, Evangolos Tsantalis.

Retsina The wine that was entirely synonymous with Greece in the early days of mass tourism, and for many, the very definition of the phrase 'acquired taste'. The style is based on techniques that date back to classical times, when stone wine jars were lined with pine resin in order to preserve their contents. Today, retsina is a simple dry white wine that has had lumps of resin, from the Aleppo pine, infused in it during fermentation. It's made all over Greece, but mainly in the area around Athens to supply the tourist industry. Served extremely cold in sherry-like quantities, it can be an interesting aperitif, but a little does go a very long way. There's a rosé version too now.

CYPRUS

Winemaking on the island of Cyprus has not covered itself in glory in the modern era. Production is largely cornered by large industrial concerns whose installations are located near Limassol for easy export, a worryingly long way from the hillside vineyards. But there are very tentative signs of improvement, encouraged by the country's accession to the EU.

Two indigenous grapes dominate the vineyards. Mavro makes good fresh reds for drinking young. Xynisteri is a bit of a rough diamond that is theoretically capable of dry whites with some aromatic personality. Plantings of southern French varieties, plus Chardonnay, may well point the way forward for now. Sodap is a good volume producer.

As in other Mediterranean regions, Cyprus has a once-legendary, but now little-known, dessert wine. **Commandaria**, a fortified sweet wine made from sun-dried Mavro and Xynisteri grapes, is made in the foothills of the Troodos mountains. It is aged for a minimum of two years in cask – often much longer – arranged in some cases in a *solera* system. It became a legally protected name only in 1993.

The fortified wines once sold as 'Cyprus sherry' were mostly best forgotten, but there is some fino-style matured under *flor* and aged in a *solera* system, which is quite like the best examples of the real thing. These are worth seeking out if you're on vacation there.

MALTA

Still in its infancy, winemaking on Malta looks
to have a bright future. Since 2007, it has had a
European classification system, and is producing
carefully crafted, well-defined varietals and
blends from Italian grapes such as Vermentino,
Zibibbo and Sangiovese, as well as Merlot,
Syrah and Chardonnay, and a handful of local
specialities such as the cherryish red Gellewza,
grown both on Malta itself and the second
island, Gozo. There are even traditional-method
Chardonnay sparklers. Tourists should look for
the wines of Meridiana, Delicata and Marsovin.

TURKEY

Turkey's viticultural history goes back at least
to Biblical times, when – as the story has it –
Noah established the first vineyard on Mount
Ararat after the Flood. Excavations in the area
have lent strong support to the theory that some
of the very earliest systematic wine-growing did
arise here. Today, there are plantings of some of
the southern French grapes, and even Riesling
and Pinot Noir, in the west of the country,
while Anatolia produces wines from mainly
indigenous varieties that are better able to
withstand the climatic extremes.

The Doluca company makes some half-decent
reds and whites, but for the time being, there is
nothing like the level of expertise, or will, to get
Turkey off the ground as a serious producer, and
state-controlled plonk for the tourists dominates
the picture. But all it may take is one or two
far-sighted foreign investors (and perhaps that
long-coveted accession to the EU), and grape
names like Papazkarasi and Oküzgözü may
be on all our lips.

BULGARIA

Bulgaria's phenomenal export success in the
1970s and 80s was built on a winemaking
tradition among the most venerable in the
world. The Ottoman interdiction on alcohol
consumption during the period that Bulgaria
came under its sway contributed to a certain
decline, but it was undoubtedly the investment
in state-owned vineyards that communist
Bulgaria initiated in the years after the second
world war that set the ball rolling once again.

A combination of uprooting and neglect,
coupled with the economic upheaval that
followed the reforms of the post-Soviet era,
led initially to troubled times. As the vineyards
were sold back into private hands, the result was
a considerable setback in terms of quality.

Gradually, things are rallying, though.
Bulgaria's accession to the EU in 2007 has
helped, and a system of GCAOs (Guaranteed
and Controlled Appellations of Origin)
has emerged from the country's five main
wine zones – Eastern, Northern, Southern,
Southwestern and Sub-Balkan. There are
currently 40 designated GCAOs, which may
only grow approved grape varieties.

*Melnik, in the torrid
southwestern region of
Harsovo, Bulgaria (above).
The native Melnik grape
makes characterful,
dark reds for ageing.*

*A truckload of freshly picked
Chardonnay at Blatetz
(below), in the Sub-Balkan
region of Bulgaria.*

At Cernavoda, east of Constanta in Romania, the vineyards lie alongside the canal (above).

The varieties with which Bulgaria shot to prominence, and which are still planted extensively, were classic French reds led by Cabernet Sauvignon and Merlot, together with a small amount of Pinot Noir. Whites include reasonable Chardonnay, Sauvignon Blanc (which tends to lack aromatic definition), and rather flabby Riesling.

These are supplemented by some fine native red grapes such as Mavrud and Melnik, which both give appetizingly meaty wines, and Gamza, which turns out to be the same as Hungary's Kadarka. Native white grapes are less inspiring, and include a variety called Dimiat, of no noticeable character, which has been crossed with Riesling to produce Misket, but still contrives to be pretty tasteless. Welschriesling is there too.

There are considerable climatic variations among the regions, the Northern having the most temperate conditions, while the Southwestern, bordering Greece, is fairly torrid. Some of what are now the GCAO districts established solid reputations with particular varieties over the years when the wineries were state-controlled, achievements that have formed the backbone of the new regulations. These

include the often distinctly claretty Cabernets of **Rousse** and **Svishtov**, the voluptuously plummy Merlots of **Stambolovo**, and the fiery Mavruds of **Assenovgrad**.
PRODUCERS: Bessa Valley, Suhindol, Boyar.

ROMANIA

The vineyard regions of Romania are comprehensively scattered across the country, from Teremia in the west to Murfatlar on the Black Sea coast. The vast majority of wine produced, even since Romania's entry to the EU in 2007, is still consumed within its borders, although there is a driving will to fashion an export industry.

Western investment has begun to flow, and so have plantings of international varieties. In time, Romania could well become the most reliable producer of quality wine of all the old Soviet bloc countries. Its climate is far more dependable than that of Bulgaria, for example, and it does have some excellent indigenous styles of wine.

Cabernet Sauvignon has been established extensively throughout the country, far more so than in Bulgaria, while Pinot Noir was the first varietal to make western commentators sit up

and pay attention to Romania's potential. There are also plantings of Merlot, Burgundy's Aligoté, Sauvignon Blanc and Pinot Gris. Two versions of a white grape called Fetească represent the most widely planted varieties of all, and are used in some of the sweet wines in which Romania has a long and distinguished tradition.

Tămâioasă and Grasă are the two native ingredients of **Cotnari**, the country's greatest and most assertively flavoured botrytized dessert wine, which is made in the northeast of Romania, near the border with Moldova.

North of the capital Bucharest, the **Dealul Mare** region has made waves with its often sensational Pinot Noirs. At their most carefully vinified, they can be uncannily close to the style of good village burgundy. Greater input from outside investors may well result in some world-class Romanian Pinot before too long. Cabernet and Merlot make hearty reds in Babadag and Istria nearer the Black Sea. Lower down on the coast, **Murfatlar** also has a venerable dessert wine tradition, but its wines are less opulent than those of Cotnari, being much less prone to noble rot.

MOLDOVA

Moldova retains strong cultural ties to Romania, and speaks its language. Its vineyards are hugely extensive and, like its western neighbour, it looks set fair to ascend the quality scale in time. A very broad range of grape varieties is grown, including most of the major French names, some Russian varieties such as the white Rkatsiteli and the red Saperavi, plus a few of its own. Cabernet, Chardonnay and Sauvignon have inevitably been the first successful Moldovan wines seen in the west.

As well as promising table wines, Moldova has a long-established tradition in sparkling wine, together with some high-potential fortified styles, some similar to sweet sherry, others to the Liqueur Muscats of Australia.

GEORGIA

The oldest wine-producing region in the world, Georgia's South Caucasus is extensively planted with two eastern specialities, Rkatsiteli (which makes crisp, clean whites) and Saperavi (for fresh, black-cherry reds, which can also have guts and ageing potential when treated carefully). **Khvanchkara**, a semi-sweet red, is one of the country's more diverting styles, reputedly a favourite of Stalin's, and there are some decent fortified wines.

UKRAINE

Crimean reds were once celebrated far beyond the boundaries of Ukraine, and may come to be once again if the investment currently flowing in begins to pay dividends. Widely planted international grapes include Cabernet Sauvignon, Riesling, Chardonnay, Merlot and Burgundy's Aligoté.

As elsewhere in eastern Europe, there is an age-old tradition of sweet wines, many from Muscatel (in which style Massandra is considered a reliable name), and the sweetness tendency extends to the production of sparkling wines with plenty of sugar.

Russia and **Belarus** are also significant wine producers, but are not yet focusing on western markets to any degree. Visitors to the old USSR may recall the great quantities of Soviet sparkling wine, fancifully termed *shampanskoe*. Despite the name, it was made by a variant on the tank method. It is still produced in gargantuan quantities, mainly from Chardonnay, Aligoté and Pinot Blanc, and is more often than not surprisingly palatable.

Hay-making in the Tîrnave region, in central Transylvania, Romania (left). The high, cool vineyards produce mainly white wines.

Gigantic fermentation tanks at the bulk-producing Sliven winery, Bulgaria (above), typify the large-scale postwar investment the country conferred on its wine industry.

(Above) State-of-the-art sparkling winemaking at Domaine Chandon, in Napa Valley, owned by champagne house Moët & Chandon (right). The fertile valley floor of Napa Valley is considered by many to be the state's premier site for Cabernet and Chardonnay.

The **Sonoma Valley** AVA itself includes some of California's oldest wineries, such as Buena Vista (established in the 19th century by a Hungarian migrant pioneer) and Sebastiani. Running north to south, the valley is blessed with subtle gradations of microclimate as it moves away from the cooling influence of the Bay. This means that a highly disparate range of grapes can be grown. At the southern end, it takes in a section of the celebrated **Carneros** region, which it shares with Napa County (see below).

One of the cooler Sonoma AVAs is the **Russian River Valley**. The impact of the morning fogs that roll in off the Bay is most keenly felt here, with the result that Pinot Noir is notably successful (especially from practitioners like Williams-Selyem, Dehlinger, Iron Horse, Marimar Torres and Rodney Strong). Chardonnay can be superbly balanced from the likes of De Loach, and there is fine sparkling wine too.

Dry Creek Valley AVA, formed around a little tributary of the Russian River, is making a name for itself with some sharply delineated Sauvignon from Preston and Dry Creek Vineyard, as well as one of the more memorable Zinfandels from Quivira.

The **Northern Sonoma** AVA is an important redoubt of E&J Gallo, planet Earth's largest wine producer. While the discriminating may be tempted to dismiss the produce of such a large powerful corporation, there are one or two decent wines among the premium bottlings of red varietals, especially Zinfandel and Cabernet. OTHER SONIMA PRODUCERS: Ravenswood, Laurel Glen, Kenwood, Matanzas Creek, Sonoma-Cutrer, Flowers, Simi, Jordan sparkling wines.

Napa If California is the premier state for American wine, the Napa Valley is its regional frontrunner. So much land has been planted with vines that the region is almost at capacity, forming a virtual grape monoculture. The Napa is the Côte d'Or of California, if such comparisons can be risked. Like Burgundy's prime patch, it is barely more than 20 miles from end to end, but embraces a dizzying degree of climatic variation. As with Sonoma, the southern end near the Bay is relatively cool and foggy, while the northern end at Calistoga is fiercely hot.

The overall **Napa Valley** AVA was organized into a plethora of smaller appellations from the 1990s onwards, based on the main towns along the valley highway. There are 15 at the time of writing. Cabernets and Merlots are made along this trail, varying in style as much because of their geographical location and altitude as because of the philosophies of individual winemakers.

The qualitatively important **Stag's Leap District** lies just to the north of town of Napa, and includes fine Cabernets and Merlots from

Stags' Leap Wine Cellars, Clos du Val and Shafer. **Howell Mountain** in the east of Napa is where La Jota makes some sensationally concentrated Cabernet. **Mount Veeder**, between Napa and Sonoma, has distinguished Chardonnays and Cabernets from the Hess Collection, and **Wild Horse Valley**, east of Napa itself, is turning out to be a good site for gracefully balanced Pinot Noir.

OTHER NAPA PRODUCERS: Newton, Silverado, Caymus, Phelps, ZD, Silver Oak, Diamond Creek, Heitz, Groth. Top premium wines come from Screaming Eagle, Dominus and Opus One. Good sparklers include Schramsberg and Cuvée Napa.

Carneros The Carneros district overlaps the southern ends of the Napa and Sonoma regions, and forms a distinctive AVA of its own. Being immediately to the north of the Bay, its climate is continually influenced by dawn fogs which often don't clear until around mid-morning. They mitigate the ferocious heat of summer to such a degree that Carneros qualifies as one of the coolest areas on average in all of California.

It shot to prominence in the 1980s for a handful of exquisitely crafted Pinot Noirs and Chardonnays from such wineries as Acacia, Saintsbury and Carneros Creek. The quality of the Pinots in particular – angular in youth, but packed with deep red fruit and roasted meat intensity – served notice that the citadel of Burgundian Pinot was about to be stormed.

Carneros has developed a reputation as a good producer of sparkling wines as well, with the champagne house Taittinger (Domaine Carneros) and cava producer Codorníu (Codorniu Napa) representing the European vote of confidence.

Sierra Foothills The foothills of the Sierra Nevada mountain range that forms the border with the state of Nevada encompass some of the oldest vineyard land in California, dating from the Gold Rush that began in 1849. Within the overall **Sierra Foothills** AVA are five sub-divisions. **El Dorado** County forms one, within which is the smaller, promisingly named **Fair Play** AVA, while Amador County to the south takes in **Shenandoah Valley** and **Fiddletown**. The usual diversity of grapes is grown, but the acreage of Zinfandel vines is among California's more venerable. The **North Yuba** AVA includes the Renaissance winery, famed for delicate Rieslings and Sauvignons and a totally contrasting Cabernet – a pitch-black study in rip-roaring tannins.

Livermore Valley East of the Bay in Alameda County, the **Livermore Valley** AVA was historically famed for its Bordeaux-style white blends, but has since followed the path of California diversity. One of the Livermore's oldest wineries is Wente Brothers, founded in 1883, and acclaimed now for its best *cuvées* of Chardonnay, as well as some tasty sparkling wines.

Santa Clara Valley South of Alameda, the **Santa Clara Valley** is now rather more about micro-electronics than wine, although it was one of the first AVAs.

Santa Cruz A coastal district south of San Francisco, the **Santa Cruz Mountains** AVA has been a whirlpool of innovative ferment on the California scene. This was one of the first regions to try producing great Pinot Noir, its proximity to the ocean making its climate cool enough not to overstress that notoriously fragile grape. Now all sorts of grapes have moved in, many of them under the creative aegis of Randall Grahm at the Bonny Doon winery. Plantings of Marsanne, Roussanne, Syrah, Grenache and Mourvèdre, just as everyone else was going hell-for-leather with Cabernet, earned Grahm the nickname of the Rhône Ranger, and helped to blaze a particularly fruitful trail. His entertainingly off-the-wall labels and wine names announce some genuinely original wines, marked by crystal-clear definition and great intensity.

Clos Pegase, in the Napa Valley (above). This striking modern building contains not only the winery but an art gallery too.

New vines waiting to bud against a stark California landscape at Au Bon Climat, Santa Barbara (above).

Vineyards of Wente Brothers in Livermore Valley (above), east of San Francisco Bay in Alameda County.

Paul Draper has been the other Santa Cruz colossus, producing monumental Cabernets and Zinfandels under single-estate names. More mainstream but still brilliant Cabernets and Chardonnays have come from Mount Eden, Ahlgren and Kathryn Kennedy, with gorgeously expressive Pinots from David Bruce.

San Benito San Benito is a smallish inland wine region west of Fresno, whose brightest star is Calera Vineyards, sole proprietor in the tiny **Mount Harlan** AVA. Calera's offerings include hauntingly scented Mills Pinot Noir, lovely, buttercream Chardonnay, and one of the most extraordinary Viogniers made anywhere outside Condrieu. It sells for about the same sort of giddy price as Condrieu, but the aromatic intensity and great length of the wine are powerfully persuasive.

Monterey County Monterey on the Central Coast is marked by both coolness and aridity, so that grape-growing has always been something of a challenge. Notwithstanding that, the county is one of the more densely planted California regions. Cool-climate grapes such as Pinot Noir, Riesling and even Chenin Blanc are now doing well here. Within the overall **Monterey** AVA, there are three flagship zones that represent Monterey's premier league: **Chalone** (overlapping into San Benito), **Arroyo Seco** and **Carmel Valley**. The first of those is home to Chalone Vineyards, maker of benchmark Chardonnay, surprisingly full Pinot Blanc and richly gamey Pinot Noir.

San Luis Obispo A little further south along the coast from Monterey, this county covers the climatic extremes, with the most highly

regarded wines tending to come from the cooler coastal areas, such as the **Edna Valley** AVA. The Edna Valley winery makes pace-setting Chardonnay here. North of Edna is the large elevated plain of **Paso Robles**, where the fiercer conditions are better for Cabernet and Zinfandel. South of Edna Valley, in the Arroyo Grande Valley AVA, the champagne house Deutz has established one of its overseas outposts, Maison Deutz.

Santa Barbara The southernmost of the Central Coast wine counties is fog-shrouded Santa Barbara, not far north of Los Angeles. Its best vineyards congregate in two AVAs – **Santa Maria** and **Santa Ynez Valley**. Both enjoy the cooling influence of the ocean and make good showings of Pinot Noir and Chardonnay, much as Carneros does, as well as some crisply textured Sauvignon and Riesling. Au Bon Climat and Sanford wineries set a tough standard with their effortlessly concentrated, raspberry-fruited Pinots, while Zaca Mesa has done improbably good things with Syrah, and Byron Vineyards scores highly for Chardonnay, Pinot Blanc and Pinot Gris.

In the south of California, three regions of no enormous viticultural significance are Riverside County (which includes the **Temecula Valley** AVA), San Diego County (including the tiny AVA of **San Pasqual Valley**) and the inland Imperial Valley.

PACIFIC NORTHWEST

Three states in the far northwest of the USA have emerged in recent years from the long shadow cast by California's premier wine status. Of the three, it is Oregon, with its challenging climatic circumstances, that has generated the greatest excitement so far, but Washington State is making a strong showing as well, and inland Idaho will surely have a lot to offer future generations. Despite the favourable press they continue to receive, we still don't see enough of these wines in Europe.

Oregon Although *Vitis vinifera* vines were first planted in Oregon over a century ago, it is only comparatively recently that the state's potential as a quality wine producer has begun to bear fruit. There was some scepticism from the neighbours in California as to how likely it was that Oregon would turn out at all well, but early vintages of Eyrie Vineyards Pinot Noir, one of the great trailblazing American wines, were instrumental in proving them wrong.

Pinot Noir, the goal of aspirant winemakers everywhere at the time, became the Oregon buzz wine *par excellence*, so much so that for a while it looked as though there might be a surfeit of growers producing mediocre Pinot when they could be more profitably growing something easier. Where stunning Pinots have emerged, they have more often than not been made in the gently savoury, fruit-driven but attractively light style of the Côte de Beaune, rather than anything bigger and burlier. Alsace varieties have done remarkably well, providing dry, spicy, fragrant wines from Riesling, Gewürztraminer and – most successfully of all – Pinot Gris.

One long valley area dominates Oregon production – the **Willamette Valley** AVA. It occupies a northwestern corner of the state, near the Pacific coast, and enjoys the kinds of cool growing conditions that are to be found in parts of northern France. All of the finest Oregon producers are located here. The **Dundee Hills** is an especially propitious sub-regional AVA within the Willamette.

Adelsheim, Ponzi and Eyrie make full-blown, creamy Pinot Gris, and Eyrie is also tops for Chardonnay with its subtle, baked-appley Reserve bottling. As to the celebrated Pinot Noirs, Elk Cove, Bethel Heights, Ponzi, Argyle, Beaux Frères and Domaine Drouhin (owned by the Burgundy négociant house) all make state-of-the-art, sweetly cherryish, but ageworthy wines.

Washington State In volume terms, Washington's production of *vinifera* wine is a very distant third in the American stakes, but some feel it's first runner-up for quality. The two halves of the state are, climatically, chalk and cheese. While the seaward side has temperate, dampish conditions, the eastern half has sweltering summers and unforgivingly cold winters.

Notwithstanding that, nearly all the vineyard land is in the east, where the overall **Columbia Valley** AVA accounts for most of the wine produced. An important sub-region of Columbia – the **Yakima Valley** AVA – is home to some of the state's oldest vineyards.

Cabernet, and particularly Merlot, have proved themselves adept at coping with the climatic torments of eastern Washington, and generally yield round, emphatically fruity wines that are drinkable quite early. Riesling, perhaps surprisingly, does well, and can produce outstandingly graceful dry and medium-dry styles; it seems a shame that the variety isn't especially popular among American consumers.

The inevitable Chardonnay, however, sells like hot cakes, and good, gently buttery stuff it is too. Semillon, not previously much lauded in the USA, has carved out a niche for itself; the style is a little like the minerally-dry unoaked examples of Australia's Hunter Valley.

Half of all Washington production is accounted for by one giant combine, Ste. Michelle Wine Estates, which puts out wines under a number of labels, such as Columbia Crest, Chateau Ste. Michelle, Snoqualmie and so forth. Quality is reasonable, if rarely idiosyncratic. Best of the smaller wineries include Delille, Quilceda Creek, Matthews, Hogue and Kiona (the last, in the Red Mountain AVA, is a specialist in late-harvest sweet wines from the Alsace varieties Gewürztraminer and Riesling, and also makes a Chenin Blanc ice wine).

Idaho Washington's eastern neighbour shares much the same climate as the Columbia Valley, except that Idaho's vineyards are planted at very high altitudes, making winter conditions here extremely severe. High-acid white varieties do better than Chardonnay, so Riesling and Chenin Blanc can be impressive. Against all the omens, Cabernet is now yielding some reassuringly ripe reds. A single high-volume producer, Ste. Michelle, rules the Idaho roost, and its wines are generally good. However, most of the state's production doesn't travel much further than Washington State.

Oregon's cool Willamette Valley (above) dominates the state's wine industry, with the top producers clustered at the northern end of the valley.

While Oregon's vineyards lie close to the ocean, Washington's major wine regions are in the east, where the temperatures are more extreme, as in neighbouring Idaho (below).

1. WILLAMETTE VALLEY
2. COLUMBIA VALLEY
3. YAKIMA VALLEY

OTHER STATES

New York State New York viticulture only really got under way in the early years of the 19th century, not much before California's, although the eastern state had of course been settled for much longer. Native American vine species dominated the wine industry into the most recent era, but that has now substantially changed, and New York is now the second most productive wine state in the USA (although, to put that into perspective, we're talking about four per cent of all American wine, as against California's 89 per cent).

The principal growing region is the **Finger Lakes** AVA, a group of long thin bodies of water in the centre of the state, south of Rochester. **Long Island** also has fairly extensive vineyards, and a pair of AVAs, **The Hamptons** and **North Fork**, within the overall regional designation. The cooler climates of these regions are beginning to produce some heartily encouraging, attractively balanced alternatives to the sun-soaked wines of Napa and Sonoma, their winemakers working with the grain of the climatic conditions.

Riesling vines of Idaho's main producer, Ste Chapelle (above).

Vineyards spreading towards the water's edge in New York State's Finger Lakes AVA (right).

Chardonnay has performed well, making appealing, lean, nutty whites that can stand a little oak. Classically steely Riesling is good enough to turn America's wine-drinkers on to that much underrated variety, and Cabernet-based blended reds have had something of the angular austerity of decent Bordeaux. Red grapes that do well in cooler conditions, though – including Pinot Noir and Cabernet Franc – will likely turn out to be the real stars.

Good producers include Fox Run, Anthony Road, Lamoreaux Landing and Wagner in Finger Lakes, and Bedell, Lenz and Pellegrini in Long Island.

Texas The Lone Star state develops apace, and now has eight AVAs, its most important one being the northerly **Texas High Plains**. Its wine industry is essentially a creation of the 1970s, when the Llano Estacado winery set the ball rolling, making Cabernet, Chardonnay and Sauvignon near Lubbock. In their wake have followed the likes of Fall Creek, McPherson, and the ambitious Ste Genevieve – a joint venture with a Bordeaux négociant. Good results are being posted with southern French

varieties such as Syrah and Viognier, as well as plantings of Spanish and Italian grapes like Tempranillo and Sangiovese.

Virginia Despite the fact that it has an uncompromisingly hot climate, some are tipping Virginia, with its six AVAs, as a forthcoming story in American wine. Unusually, given the pretty torrid conditions, it has proved itself most adept so far at white wine. The Chardonnays are luscious enough to give the best of California a run for their money, while Viognier, Semillon and Riesling also look promising. Reds are improving too, though, with Petit Verdot and Cabernet Franc among the likely stars of the future.

Other states poised to cause a stir in wine circles are **Missouri**, **Maryland**, **Pennsylvania** and **North Carolina**, but there is at least one winery in every single state of the Union now.

Going way out on a limb, you might enjoy some of the blueberry and rhubarb wines of **Alaska**, but they're probably beyond the scope of this book.

A coming region is the state of Virginia (above), where new plantings of classic white varieties are proving successful.

FOX RUN

VINEYARDS™

Riesling

Finger Lakes Table Wine

2008

Grown, produced and bottled by Fox Run Vineyards Inc., Penn Yan, N.Y. 14527 • 750 ml • Alcohol 12% by volume

CANADA

Canada first attracted attention for its award-winning Icewines. Now, with plantings of popular international varieties, the country's producers are surging forward with an impressive range of styles.

Harvesting frozen Vidal grapes (above) in winter for Canada's speciality, icewine.

Canada's two important wine-growing regions are divided by the vast country itself, with Ontario on the east coast, bordering New York State, and British Columbia on the west.

WHILE OTHER EMERGENT wine countries have targeted European markets with huge sales drives and promotional campaigning, Canada has quietly been developing its own industry at a rate that suits itself. Like New York State, it has made the necessary transition from reliance on ghastly hybrid grape varieties to *Vitis vinifera* types, although the harsh northern climate has made varietal and site selection much trickier than they have been in the States.

The Canadian summers are benign enough, but wintertime reliably brings several degrees of frost in most vineyard districts, which can be highly dangerous for the dormant vines. A clutch of French varieties has been established, though, mainly in Ontario and British Columbia, and even though many of the vines only came into full production towards the turn of the century, early showings have been highly encouraging.

Above and beyond the dry varietals, Canada's major speciality has been icewine, made in the same way as it is in Germany and Austria. After all, if you have sub-zero winters

as a matter of course, you may as well put them to good use. The grapes are left to overripen on the vine, and then freeze as night-time temperatures start to plummet with the onset of winter. When the frozen berries are harvested, they are quickly pressed so that the ice-pellets of water remain behind in the presses, and the sweetly concentrated juice runs free.

Riesling has been, not unexpectedly, a favoured variety for icewine, but the other main grape is one of those hybrid varieties. Vidal isn't the most likely star turn for dry white wine, but has consistently yielded some of the most lusciously concentrated examples of Canada's icewine. It easily attains the kind of sugar levels found in all but the very sweetest German and Austrian versions of Eiswein. Good acidity balances the apricot-syrup sweetness of the wines, so that, although irresistibly easy to drink on release, they are also capable of ageing in the bottle.

So proficient a specialist at the icewine style has Canada become, indeed, that experiments with red icewine are now being tried. Cabernet Franc has been the leading grape so far, but the

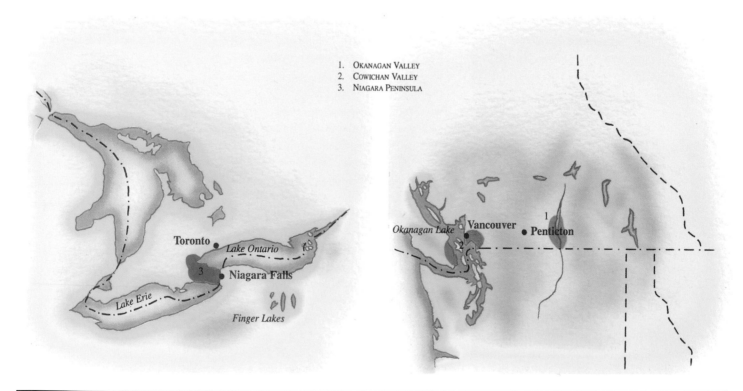

1. OKANAGAN VALLEY
2. COWICHAN VALLEY
3. NIAGARA PENINSULA

Toronto
Lake Ontario
Lake Erie
3 Niagara Falls
Finger Lakes

Okanagan Lake Vancouver Penticton

Pilliteri winery in Ontario has also branched out into Cabernet Sauvignon and even Shiraz icewines at the dawn of the new century. Red icewines tend to be quite delicately coloured and structured, but with lush aromas of red fruit purées and rose-petals. Try them with lighter chocolate-based desserts if you happen to come across them.

For dry wines, Chardonnay and Riesling are the best whites so far, but Gewürztraminer and Pinot Gris have also shown promise, while gently savoury Pinot Noir, cranberryish, Loire-style Cabernet Franc and lightly plummy Merlot have been the more successful reds. There is a certain amount of light-textured Cabernet Sauvignon from pioneering producers in British Columbia, but too much still tastes too thin to be convincing.

Canadian winemakers instituted an appellation system in 1988, the Vintners Quality Alliance. To make the VQA grade, wines must be sourced entirely from grapes grown in the defined regions, and to have achieved minimum levels of ripeness. Anything labelled 'Cellared in Canada' will have been made at least partly from the juice of imported grapes, a naïve and foolish practice that will surely undermine the efforts of winemakers working within the painstakingly elaborated VQA system.

Canada's vineyards are located in four of its provinces, of which the first two shown here are by far the most important for quantity.
Ontario The province that borders New York State has similarly cool, marginal growing conditions. A degree of natural protection is afforded by a high ridge overlooking the main vineyard area that mitigates the worst effects of the climate. Riesling is a star performer here, from crisp dry styles to the celebrated icewines, and Chardonnay too achieves good things in the style of steely Chablis, as well as softer, gently oaked examples. Pinot Noir grown in these cool climes may very well turn out to be among North America's finest.

It was in Ontario's **Niagara Peninsula** that the modern Canadian wine industry got going, with the innovative Inniskillin winery's first plantings in the 1970s. Its standard bottlings of Chardonnay and Riesling are still highly reliable, well-made wines.
PRODUCERS: Clos Jordanne, Hidden Bench, Tawse, Château des Charmes, Henry of Pelham.
British Columbia Whereas most of Canada's vineyards lie in the Atlantic east of the country,

the western province of British Columbia, way out on its own Pacific limb, is also participating in the quality wine movement. The **Okanagan Valley** in the southwest of the province is where the best vineyards are found. Good varietals have been produced from Alsace grapes such as Pinot Blanc and Gewürztraminer, as well as Riesling of course. Delicate Chardonnays are good when not smothered with oak. Reds from the Bordeaux grapes are improving, but icewines are the cream of the crop.
PRODUCERS: Mission Hill, Black Hills, Sumac Ridge, Road 13.
Quebec and Nova Scotia The other two eastern provinces to make wine have only a sparse scattering of vineyards. So far, they are largely dedicated to the production of wines from hybrid grape varieties, although there are incipient plantings of Chardonnay.

The beautiful Okanagan Valley in British Columbia (above) is carving a name for itself for Alsace grape varieties.

SOUTH *and* CENTRAL AMERICA

Led by the great successes of Chile and Argentina, South America has become an important player in the southern hemisphere. Mexico, from where vines initially headed south with the Spanish, is also enjoying a revival.

ALTHOUGH WILD VINES flourished in Central America just as they did in the north, there is no indication of any systematic wine production in pre-Columbian times. It took the arrival of Spanish and then Portuguese colonists to develop intensive viticulture in the central and southern sectors of the Americas. A rapid southward march from Mexico, down through Peru, Chile and Argentina, carried the wine grape into those areas familiar to us today.

Argentina produces the highest volume of wine of all the Latin American countries, despite the fact that it was Chile that initially made all the running in the export markets from the late 1980s onwards. What galvanized the progress of Chile to international renown was

Climatically, Chile and Argentina offer the best wine-producing conditions in South America (below). There are also pockets of vineyards in Brazil and Uruguay.

1. BAJA CALIFORNIA
2. SONORA
3. HERMOSILLO
4. QUERETARO
5. ACONCAGUA
6. CENTRAL VALLEY
7. MENDOZA
8. RIO GRANDE DO SUL
9. CARPINTERIA
10. CERRO CHAPEU

the arrival of some big European names in its vineyards. The early pace was set with sensationally rich, concentrated Cabernet Sauvignons and Merlots, as well as some fine, opulent Chardonnays. There was some often rather feeble Sauvignon, and that was basically it for quite a while. Greater diversification in the vineyard is now paying dividends, though, with Pinot Noir, Syrah and Viognier all turning out some stunners now.

The unique selling point of Chilean wine for some years was the fact that, alone among significant wine-producing countries, it was never invaded by the vine louse, phylloxera (see page 205). Chile's main protection lay in the circumstances of its geography. Since the country is, in essence, one long narrow Pacific coastal strip, nearly all of its soil is sand-based. And sand is the one type of soil in which phylloxera doesn't survive. Furthermore, the natural bulwark of the Andes mountains prevented what limited outbreaks of phylloxera arose in Argentina from spreading westwards.

Thus it is that Chilean wines might fancifully be said to taste something like the wines of a century and more ago, although you might be rather dismayed if you found your bottle of Curico Valley Cabernet Sauvignon had been made with the primitive vinification techniques of a hundred years ago.

While Chilean wines began to take the world by storm, Argentina's wine industry bided its time. Its growers were much less hidebound as to the varietals they produced. Malbec, one of the minor varieties in red Bordeaux, is accorded a status in Mendoza that it doesn't quite enjoy anywhere outside Cahors (see southwest France). The perfumed white variety Torrontés, a relative of the one grown in Galicia in northwest Spain, is very widely planted, and can make intensely fragrant wines with clearly defined acidity.

These two countries between them are now making some of the most reliable – and also some of the most interesting – wine in the whole southern hemisphere. While there is the same impetus here as elsewhere (especially

New vineyard plantings of Cabernet in Chile (left). Vines do not need grafting on to phylloxera-resistant roots as the pest cannot thrive in the sand-based soils.

All over central Chile, new vineyard holdings are being established, making the country currently the most dynamic in South America (above).

in Chile) to produce isolated superstar wines selling at crazy prices to satisfy the premium end of the market, the commitment to providing the export markets with good to great wines at prices all of us can afford has never wavered.

The consequence is that the price-quality ratio of South American wines is unmatched anywhere on the planet. Chile's Cabernets and Merlots are considerably better than the same varietals from the Languedoc at the same prices. Argentina's best Torrontés can be had for a fraction of the price of the equivalent, spicy-flowery white varietals of Alsace. This is a cause for unalloyed celebration.

Brazil, despite its scale, has not so far been geared for a serious export push, other than to one or two of its neighbours. Hybrid grapes have been a big drawback, but so has finding the right sites for the good grapes. Even within the colossal Brazilian interior, this latter has not been the most straightforward of tasks, owing to the enervating heat and humidity most of the country endures. The southerly regions, which are decisively milder, will produce the best wines in due course. Sparkling wines, to everyone's surprise, are showing exciting potential.

Mexico, the only other wine producer of significant scale in Latin America, is where the whole American wine story started. Planted by Spanish conquistadors in the 1500s, the country's vineyards had gone into a seemingly terminal decline by the 20th century, as native wine was elbowed aside in the marketplace by tequila, mezcal and beer. The cautious beginnings of a remergence, fuelled in part by Mexican migrant workers returning from stints in the California vineyards with a taste for wine, are now upon us. Southern French red varieties, as well as one or two minority stars such as Petite Sirah, have yielded some superlative results, and the only way is up.

ARGENTINA

The vast majority of Argentina's vineyard land is in the western province of **Mendoza**, in the foothills of the Andes. This is a very arid region, and depends greatly on irrigation from melting mountain snow, which runs through the vineyards in carefully laid trenches to prevent them from becoming terminally parched.

As in other emerging wine countries, the quality revolution in Argentina has been led by investment in new technology, with wineries being built nearer to the vineyards themselves, and equipped with temperature-controlled fermentation facilities. Then too the second-division grape varieties that once prevailed – among them Criolla, Cereza, Pedro Giménez (nothing to do with the PX grape of the sherry region) and the humdrum Muscat of Alexandria, used to make rather leaden sweet wines – have begun to cede vineyard land to the viticultural aristos.

Fine white wines are being made from florally perfumed Torrontés, juicy Chardonnay and Semillon, and some powerful, apricot-and-citrus Viognier that works well when not overcropped.

Ploughing the old-fashioned way (above) in Argentina.

(Right) Three-quarters of Argentina's wines, and the finest, come from the western province of Mendoza, in the foothills of the Andes. Of the other four regions, Salta is producing the most notable wines.

Mendoza

Buenos Aires

1. MENDOZA
2. SAN JUAN
3. LA RIOJA
4. SALTA
5. RIO NEGRO

For reds, Malbec leads the field. On its own, it can produce excellent midweight to full varietal reds, with plenty of meaty structure and some ageing potential, the perfect accompaniment to the prodigious quantities of beefsteak consumed in Argentina. Some growers have been successfully blending it with Shiraz or Merlot. Shiraz on its own has been outstanding too. Italian grapes such as Nebbiolo, Barbera and Sangiovese do well in this climate, as does Spain's Tempranillo. Cabernet Sauvignon adds to a rollcall that would make up most people's list of pedigree red varieties.

Mendoza This is where about three-quarters of all Argentinian wine is made, and where all of the companies that have so far come to notice in the export markets are based. The **Luján de Cuyo** district south of the city of Mendoza and the high-altitude vineyards of the **Uco Valley** have been the two most exciting districts to date.

The much-favoured Malbec heads the list of grapes planted, and is supported by Barbera, Sangiovese, Tempranillo and Cabernet. By and large, Mendoza Malbecs are rich, opulently damsony reds, with pronounced but controlled tannins and fairly overt oak influence. The Cabernets can be denser and darker still, often reminiscent of good *cru bourgeois* Médoc, while Syrah/Shiraz can be monumentally, spicily intense. White wines have featured fine, lightly buttery Chardonnay (some with beautifully weighted oak), solidly ripe, scented Viognier, and even a little Sauvignon.

PRODUCERS: Cateña, Norton, El Retiro, Terrazas de los Andes, Cobos, Clos de los Siete, Weinert.

San Juan The area north of Mendoza is important in terms of volume, but not yet of the quality to balance it. With a much less forgiving climate to contend with than the Mendozans, San Juan wineries have largely contented themselves with supplying the domestic market.

La Rioja The scattered vineyards of La Rioja lie to the northeast of San Juan. Although this is where Argentinian wine probably started, there isn't much to stimulate the imagination now. Flabby Muscats are not exactly the mood of the moment. La Riojana co-op has better wines.

Salta The northwestern province of Salta is currently producing the best Argentinian wine after Mendoza. Here, some gloriously ripe Cabernet and Malbec are appearing, and the speciality Torrontés comes into its own. Etchart makes a fine example at Cafayate in the Calchaquí Valley, all orange-blossom and cinnamon on a crisp, appley base. Colomé is another good producer.

Rio Negro and **Neuquén** These two regions in the southern swathe of Argentina known as Patagonia look to have perhaps the best potential of all. The cooler climate and more propitious soil types are making them a happy hunting-ground for new investors. White varietals such as Torrontés, Sauvignon, Chenin and Chardonnay could well be among Argentina's finest, while sparkling wine production was given a substantial fillip in the 1990s by the arrival of a posse of Champagne VIPs with money to spend.

BRAZIL

Brazil's viticultural history fits the general pattern of most of the Americas. Colonists (Portuguese in this case) and missionaries planted the vine, slow vineyard expansion led to hybrid grapes churning out basic plonk by the 19th century, with foreign investment arriving in the late 20th century to encourage the planting of Chardonnay and Cabernet.

In Brazil's case, though, the progress has been more halting than it has elsewhere, despite the fact that it is now in the top three South American producers. Most of the Brazilian landmass is simply too tropical for *Vitis vinifera* vines to cope with, with raging humidity and extremely high rainfall presenting an insuperable challenge even for the eminently adaptable Chardonnay. Only the more temperate areas are suitable for viticulture, which is where Rio Grande do Sul, the deep south of Brazil, comes into play. In regions like **Serra Gaúcha** and **Frontera**, the latter near the borders with Uruguay and Argentina, the best results so far are being achieved.

For the time being, the problem remains that less than one-tenth of Brazil's vineyards are planted with *vinifera* grapes, the rest being a mixture of native species and hybrids. Pre-eminent among them is a grape called Isabella, which carpeted the vineyards of California in the dim distant past. None of these grapes will produce world-class wines, and one can only hope they start receding before too long.

Irrigation channels in a Mendoza vineyard (below). The water is sourced from the melting snowcaps of the Andes mountains.

Huge old oak fermentation vats at a vinery in Rio Grande do Sul, Brazil (above).

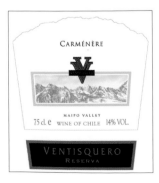

Chardonnay and most of the Bordeaux varieties, red and white, represent the future. Plantings of Pinot Blanc and Gewürztraminer look a little more optimistic, but who knows? Initially, the wines tended to be made in a rather light and inconsequential style, with not-quite-ripe whites and featherlight reds predominating, as though in compensation for any potential overripeness the climate might deliver. That tendency is gradually being overcome, and better-balanced wines are emerging.

Perhaps surprisingly, there is a thriving – and growing – sparkling wine industry. Made mainly to cater to local tastes at first, it has now begun to attract attention with a range of styles from refreshingly dry to delicately sweet. Significantly, champagne giant Moët & Chandon has a commercial interest here, just as it does in Argentina.

The next decade will undoubtedly see a much bigger export push for Brazil's wines. Substantial quantities are presently being sold to Russia, but the US and western Europe are firmly in Brazilian sights. Big players so far have been the Aurora and Palomas companies.

CHILE

The meteoric rise of Chilean wine in both European and North American markets in the late 1980s was one of the more sensational (and also more salutary) tales of latter times. One of its premium Cabernet Sauvignons, from the Los Vascos winery in Rapel, got sent to Bordeaux, where it muscled in among the top châteaux and set their annual wine-fair alight. Breathless notices in the French press called it 'Chile's *premier cru*'. And so Chile found itself hailed as the hot new property.

Certain members of the international wine aristocracy had, to be sure, been convinced of the potential of Chile's vineyards as far back as the 1970s, when the Torres family of Catalonia bought some land. Eventually, Bordeaux first-growth Château Lafite bought into Los Vascos, and soon there was California money coming in too. At the time, it felt like a case of too much, too soon, as the wines that emerged from this initial stampede turned out to be good enough, but ultimately rather limited in terms of their stylistic range.

Meanwhile, at the other end of the market, Chile looked like it was in danger of going too enthusiastically down the bargain-basement route, looking to mop up custom driven away from the other southern-hemisphere countries by rising prices. Fortunately, the story had a happy outcome, and Chile has since balanced the best of both worlds to emerge as, for my money, the most consistently rewarding winemaking country south of the Equator.

THE GRAPES

What has been fascinating since the 1990s has been to see the meeting of northern- and southern- hemisphere thinking that Chile's staple varietals display. Many wines are made in a distinctly French style, the Cabernets with austere, backward tannins in their youth, the Chardonnays showing tantalizingly subtle oak seasoning and taut acidity. Others have nailed their colours to what we used to think of as the New World mast, with voluptuous, blackcurrant-essence Cabernets and muscular, wood-driven Chardonnays big on vanilla and alcohol.

Sauvignon used to be a perennial problem in that what a lot of growers had in their vineyards was not the true Sauvignon Blanc, but an inferior cousin of the grape called Sauvignonasse. That has been largely rectified now, and Chilean Sauvignon usually offers a glass of crisply acidic, often distinctly Loire-like white tasting of goose-berries and asparagus, although where grown in the hotter regions, it can lack fruit and focus.

First-class Merlot is often Chile's trump card. The best wines have enveloping aromas of black fruits, evolving to well-hung game as they age, many of them withstanding comparison with good Pomerol. Even the Reserve wines have remained very competitively priced for their outstanding quality. One can only wish they wouldn't release them quite so young (they're frequently on the market even before their first birthdays), but then they are very supple and drinkable in their youth.

Chile has oodles of Semillon, but that has traditionally gone into roughly made plonk for domestic consumption. Small quantities of Riesling make fresh, simple, dry wine not too far from the New Zealand style, while Viognier is getting in on the fashion for big aromatic whites, with a little delicate Gewürztraminer tagging along behind.

Among the other reds, encouraging things are happening with Pinot Noir. Rather a lot is still made in a fiery, full-throttle style with surprising levels of tannin, but better-balanced wines may yet be good enough to compete with California's finest eventually. Syrah looks potentially very exciting, and is amply equipped in the warmer vineyard sites to produce richly concentrated wines. Also in the 'richly concentrated' bracket are reds from a grape called Carmenère (another wholesale misidentification once had this grape tagged as Merlot, partly because it turns out to be planted in Bordeaux too). Often blended with Merlot and/or Cabernet, Carmenère produces a thickly opulent, liquoricey wine with plenty of ageability.

Rosés in particular have been a notable success story in recent years. Made from the richer red varieties, such as Cabernet, Merlot and Syrah, they are full of juicy summer fruit, a little alcoholic perhaps, but far more satisfying than many of the pallid rosé styles of the northern hemisphere.

THE REGIONS

Most of Chile's vineyards lie in the climatically benign central section of the country, immediately south of the capital, Santiago. The smouldering heat of summer is mitigated to a significant degree by the proximity of the vineyards to the cooling influence of the Pacific Ocean. Irrigation is as widely practised here as it is in Argentina,

Cabernet grapes arriving at the Santa Rita bodega (left), in Chile's Maipo Valley.

A long narrow strip of land caught between the Pacific and the Andes, Chile (below) is blessed with sandy soils. The vineyards lie mainly in the centre of the country, where the climate is benign.

with mountain meltwater flowing through the soil. And no description of Chilean viticulture would be complete without mention of the celebrated fact that these mountain-protected, sandy vineyards are a no-go zone for the dreaded phylloxera.

Aconcagua/Casablanca The northernmost region for export wines is the Aconcagua, south of Santiago, incorporating the Aconcagua and Casablanca valley sub-regions. Cabernet Sauvignon is the grape best suited to the arid, broiling conditions in the former, where it achieves massive, pitch-black concentration in the premium wines.

To the southwest, nearer the coast and the city of Valparaiso, the Casablanca district has been the main talking-point of Chilean wine in recent years. Here, the climate is much cooler, so much so that frosts in the spring are not at all uncommon, and the summer swelter is constantly mitigated by ocean breezes. Here, a range of sharply defined varietals (notably from the eponymous Casablanca winery) has made the running, with some gorgeously aromatic, positively *alsacien* Gewürztraminer and melon-scented Sauvignon in among the tropical-fruited Chardonnays, beautifully balanced Pinots and well-built Cabernets, the last stuffed with brooding tannins and chewy damson fruit. PRODUCERS: Casablanca, Ventisquero, Concha y Toro, Cono Sur, Casas del Bosque, Montes.

Valparaiso • Aconcagua
Santiago •

1. ACONCAGUA
2. CASABLANCA
3. MAIPO
4. RAPEL
5. MAULE   Curicó •
6. BIO-BIO

Maule

MONTES ALPHA
Cabernet Sauvignon
2007

Stainless-steel tanks at Montes winery, in Maule's Curicó area (above), symbolic of the investment in and influence of modern technology in Chile.

Next south is **Rapel**, comprising the two valley districts of Cachapoal and Colchagua. The latter has been a conspicuous presence on the export markets, with brilliant Merlots, distinctive Cabernets and innovative Pinots. In Cachapoal, California's Clos du Val has invested in a winery called Viña Porta, which is making some first-division reds (including robust Pinot Noir) and Chardonnays.

The **Maule** area is cooler again than Rapel, and includes the important wine centres of **Curicó** and **Lontué**, both of which are good for white wines, crunchy Sauvignons as well as lightly creamy Chardonnays. In Maule itself to the south, Merlot has long shown real class as a varietal (as has Carmenère, which we used to think was the same thing), along with some fresh, sappy Sauvignon.

PRODUCERS: Almaviva, Cousiño Macul, Carmen, De Martino, Quebrada de Macul, Canepa, Santa Rita (Maipo); Casa Lapostolle, Ventisquero, Anakena, Misiones de Rengo (Rapel); Gillmore, Caliboro, Valdivieso, Echeverria, Miguel Torres (Maule/Curico).

Bio-Bio The largest wine region, Bio-Bio, south of the Central Valley, is also the least interesting to date. It is considerably cooler and damper than Maule to the north, and is mostly carpeted with a dull pinkish-red variety called País (aka Criolla Chica in Argentina, where it produces much the same style of thin, tasteless semi-red). Undoubtedly, though, there is potential for the classic grapes, as soon as more of the big companies venture this far south. Concha y Toro has planted some Gewürztraminer here, to see what happens.

Central Valley South of Aconcagua, the vineyards of the Central Valley and its various sub-regions are concentrated midway between the Andes and the Pacific. At the northern end is **Maipo**, just south of the capital. Cabernet is king once again, but there are convincing Sauvignons too, and the Chablis grower William Fèvre has set up shop here.

The long-established Santa Rita winery produces an ultra-reliable range of basic varietals and Reservas, including top Cabernets. There's even a Zinfandel from the enterprising Canepa winery. One bastion of ancestral tradition is the Cousiño Macul estate, which makes Antiguas Reservas Cabernets that can age for 20 years to a gamey, claret-like venerability. Not to be missed.

MEXICO

When the conquistadors arrived from Spain in the wake of Columbus's voyages of discovery, Mexico was where they started their long triumphal sweep through Central and South America. Wherever anyone settled, vineyards were planted, so that something like the life back home could be replicated in the brave new Spanish world. The wine may not have tasted much like the produce of the motherland, but at least it was wine.

Wine production has always taken a back seat to distillation in Mexico, and the fiery spirits tequila and mezcal were supplemented by grape brandy. Mexico actually produces one of the world's largest export brandies, Presidente, and much of the country's vineyard yield is destined for the stills. However, strengthening flickers of domestic interest, followed by the usual sporadic foreign investment, have created the bare bones of a modern wine industry.

Since the Spanish also once occupied what is now California from their Central American base, it should come as no surprise to find most of the vineyard land concentrated in the north of the country near the United States border. The Mexican state of **Baja California** is its premium growing area. Along with the other main northern region, **Sonora**, this is where most of the wines with any chance of competing internationally will come from.

Southern French red varieties make up much of the vineyards, together with outposts of American continental grapes both old and new, including the historically significant Mission (Chile's País), a variety called Petite Sirah (nothing to do with Syrah, but actually another dark-skinned French grape, Durif), and a spot of Zinfandel.

Petite Sirah has shown particular promise in producing a thick savoury red at the commercially important LA Cetto winery, which also makes excellent Cabernet Sauvignon. Plantings have not mainly been of the more distinguished varieties, though there is some Chenin, Viognier and Chardonnay. Sparklers may one day get a foot in the door, if the presence of the Spanish cava company Freixenet is anything to go by. As well as LA Cetto, Santo Tomás and Casa de Piedra have been among the better producers.

URUGUAY

If Brazil doesn't emerge to join Chile and Argentina as the next big South American wine country, then Uruguay could well be in the frame. The usual drawback of widespread hybrid vines is present, but a very broad-minded range of international *vinifera* varieties now offsets them. Just as Argentina has its Malbec, so Uruguay has made an intriguing speciality of one of the lesser-known southern French grapes in Tannat, the often brutal red menace of Madiran (see southwest France). Uruguayan Tannat, however, seems better suited to its surroundings, and the Castel Pujol offering, which spends several productive months in oak barrels, is a beauty – full of ripe purple fruits and dark chocolate richness.

Vineyards are planted in most parts of Uruguay, with those at **Carpinteria** in the centre of the country and **Cerro Chapeu** near the Brazilian border showing the most exciting promise. In the **Canelones** region in the south, the Pisano winery makes a fine range of reds from French varieties. The industry has a long way to go before it can think seriously of exporting in any quantity, and a lot more investment is needed, but given the current outside interest in South America, that should certainly come.

Other South American wine producers, of no real significance outside their own national boundaries, are **Peru** (which was once the dominant source of wine on the continent), **Bolivia**, **Ecuador** and **Venezuela**.

An old timber-roofed wine bodega at Ensenada, Baja California, Mexico (above).

Traditional low-trained vines in Uruguay (left). Viticulture is practised all over the country.

SOUTH AFRICA

After a century of political strife, the South African wine industry is developing fast. The potential for quality wines is vast and expanding, and exciting times lie ahead for the country's most ambitious winemakers.

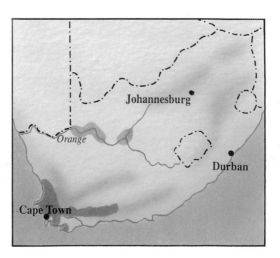

The Cape of Good Hope has always been the focus of wine-growing in South Africa (below). Even so, inland from the cooling Atlantic and Indian oceans, the climate here can still be hot and humid.

1. OLIFANTS RIVER
2. SWARTLAND
3. PAARL
4. DURBANVILLE
5. CONSTATIA
6. STELLENBOSCH
7. ELGIN
8. WALKER BAY
9. WORCESTER/TULBAGH
10. ROBERTSON
11. KLEIN KAROO

VITICULTURE WAS among the very first enterprises of the Dutch settlers who arrived on the Cape of Good Hope in the mid-17th century. We don't know what grapes they brought with them, though it seems likely the cuttings would have come from Bordeaux. Early results were not exactly seized on with glee when they made their way back to the Netherlands, but a start had been made. What first put Cape winemaking on the map was one of those legendary dessert wines with which vinous history is strewn.

Constantia was the name of an estate near Cape Town planted by a colonial governor, Simon van der Stel, barely 40 years after the new territory had been claimed by the Dutch. It made sweet wines in both colours from grapes that were left to overripen and then dry out on the vine – a rudimentary version of the *passerillage* process still practised across much of southern Europe. There is some uncertainty as to whether they were fortified, although analysis of the contents of antique bottles opened in the 1990s suggests not, at least where they were intended for local consumption. (Some of the wines transported overseas may, however, have been fortified to preserve them, as was the developing practice at the time.) The wines took Europe by storm. In the 18th and

early 19th centuries, they enjoyed a reputation so exalted indeed that higher prices were paid for them than for any of the classic dessert or fortified wines of Europe.

If this was South African wine's early historic claim to glory, and a long enough moment in the spotlight at that, it was to be brutally extinguished from the latter half of the Victorian era onwards. The abolition in 1861 by the UK, then the colonial power on the Cape, of preferential treatment for goods coming in from outposts of the Empire forced South Africa's wines to compete, all but hopelessly, with wines being imported from much closer to home on the European continent. What need for wine merchants to pay for expensively imported Constantia when there were port, sherry and madeira readier to hand? The Cape export trade to its chief target market began to wither.

As the decline set in, it was aggravated by the depredations of the vine pest phylloxera, swinging through the Cape in the 1880s on its triumphal world tour. Many vineyards had to be uprooted, but even what was left was now producing at a rate that couldn't be absorbed either domestically or by export sales. A kind of forerunner of the European wine lake of the 1970s was the result, a surplus stagnant pool of unwanted wine that largely went to waste.

Something resembling a solution to that emerged in 1918 with the foundation of the Koöperatieve Wijnbouwers Vereniging (KWV).

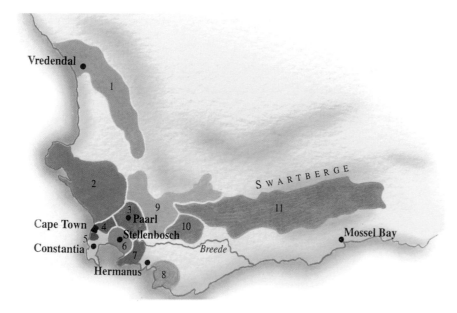

This huge organization was set up specifically to exercise a stranglehold over the South African wine industry, which it did with brutal efficiency until the 1990s. In many ways, it represented an outline of the European regulatory authorities, in that it declared what could be planted where, how much of it could be produced, and what the growers could sell it for. It worked, but at the cost of steamrollering diversity. For many years, the only wines seen in export markets were from the KWV.

Excess production, where it wasn't distilled into brandy, was often fortified to produce a range of wines – some resembling port, others madeira – that became minor Cape specialities. The table wines were generally thin and acidic, the whites based on the Cape's number one variety, Chenin Blanc, the reds on Cinsault.

The next calamity was entirely self-inflicted. Ruthless imposition of racial segregation during the apartheid era prompted a worldwide trade boycott of South African goods. Wines that had been only a minority percentage of the market anyway now basically failed to sell, their cause not at all helped by the fact that those consumers who were prepared to try them were regaled with an unrelieved diet of the KWV's insipid slosh.

With the political settlement of 1994 came the long-awaited denuding of the powers of the KWV. Small private growers began to plant the varieties they chose, inward investment started to flow, and in a few short years, South Africa has moved in among the other southern hemisphere giants and ruffled a few feathers. Complex varietal wines made from a broad canvas of grapes have achieved luminous intensity in a breathlessly short time, and there is a generation of sensational sparkling wines able to compete with the best from any continent.

The rather baggy appellation system that South Africa inaugurated in 1973 has gradually been honed into a fitter state of precision in recent years. The basic designation is Wine of Origin (WO), which is subdivided into progressively more defined areas. Geographical Units are the largest and least meaningful, but are divided further into Regions, then Districts, then Wards. Only the last really resemble the demarcations of the French AOC system, with appellations such as Elgin being identified for their specific *terroirs*. Wines labelled by grape variety must contain at least 85 per cent of that variety, and vintage-dated wines must be composed of at least 85 per cent of that year's wine. All this is encouraging.

Harvesting Sauvignon grapes at Klein Constantia (above), in the Cape.

The manor house at Klein Constantia (below), the smallest of the three producers that make up the small, yet famous, Constantia wine region.

*Looking out across the
stunning Paarl region from
Fairview Estate (above).
Paarl produces the full
range of South African
wine styles.*

THE GRAPES

In a country whose climate is so propitious for
the production of concentrated, rich red wines,
it may comes as a surprise to learn that no less
than 82 per cent of the vineyard was planted
with white varieties as recently as the late
1990s. That picture rapidly changed over the
following decade, as the Cape began to win
plaudits for its Bordeaux-style blends and
Shiraz, and there is now virtual parity between
reds and whites.

Chief among the whites is Steen (what most
of the rest of the world, and now many of the
winemakers themselves, know as Chenin
Blanc). It is encouraged to perform to the full
range of its versatility here, just as it does in
France's Touraine. Its repertoire ranges from
almost excruciatingly sharp, young dry wines,
through fuller, richer, more substantial wines
that have some of the palate profile of unoaked
Chardonnay, to the ever-popular off-dry idiom
(like demi-sec Vouvray) at which the grape
excels, and all the way up to honeyed, liquorous
dessert wines made from grapes picked after
the main harvest.

Colombard, a French import from the
Cognac region, was traditionally important in
South Africa's brandy industry too, and is often
used to make light dry whites. As a varietal,
however, it has little character other than a
waxy, sweetcorny coarseness not designed to
endear it to the Chardonnay set.

Chardonnay itself is spreading like wildfire,
as – just ahead of it – is Sauvignon Blanc,
which, in some of the cooler areas, is turning
out some superbly complex, smoky Loire-style
wines. These are among the country's best
white wines, increasingly showing better
balance than the Loire's traditional main rivals
in New Zealand. Riesling (once labelled as
Weisser Riesling to distinguish it from a
dreadful French variety, Crouchen, which
had inappropriately become known as Cape
Riesling) makes decent, lime-scented dry
wines and some sweeties. Both of the two
main Muscats are used for producing sweet
and fortified wines and, promisingly, some
growers are achieving highly impressive
results with Gewürztraminer, especially in
the Paarl region.

waft of burning rubber coming off it and a crude metallic aftertaste. At best, the lighter versions have a fruit flavour of little pippy berries like cranberries or redcurrants. Made in the more lavish idiom, from the better producers, it can be almost Rhône-like, with lush raspberry fruit and sinewy density of texture, reflecting one half at least of its parentage.

The Cape pantheon of red grapes also includes a French variety long since abandoned in its homeland. Pontac, named after one of the more illustrious families in Bordeaux history, is actually rather a rustic grape. Left to its own devices, it doesn't amount to much, but it was one of the minor components of Constantia, and is still grown on part of the old estate in readiness to play a role in the wine's resurgence.

Vergelegen's highly functional cuvier *(below) in Stellenbosch, where viticulture dates right back to the Dutch colonists' arrival in the 17th century.*

As to red grapes, Cabernet Sauvignon has come on in leaps and bounds. For a while, South Africa was burdened with rather inferior clones of Cabernet, meaning that its varietal wines from that grape often tasted oddly weedy, unclean and rubbery, but better clonal selection has now transformed it. It is often blended Bordeaux-style with Cabernet Franc and Merlot. Merlot itself is making some gorgeously intense, plummy reds on its own. Shiraz is coming up on the inside track, a real contender to match some of the pedigree Shiraz of Australia, and there are increasing quantities of quality Pinot Noir. Smatterings of Gamay and Zinfandel may produce interesting reds in time.

South Africa's equivalent of California's Zinfandel, a red grape it can call its own, is Pinotage, a crossing of the once ubiquitous Cinsault with Pinot Noir. If that sounds like a rather clumsily arranged marriage, many would agree. There are a number of Pinotage styles: simple rosés, light Beaujolais-like reds, and deeper, often barrel-aged versions. The uncomfortable truth is that the vast majority of it is unpleasantly coarse and ugly wine, with a

Immaculate vineyard rows at Klein Genot wine estate in Franschhoek (below), a quality WO within the Paarl region.

THE REGIONS

Most of South Africa's wine regions are located in the southwest of the country, where the vineyards benefit to greater and lesser degrees from the cooling maritime influences of both the Atlantic and Indian Oceans. Most of the interior is too hot for successful viticulture, although there are some recently established vineyards around the Orange River in the centre of the country. Although winters are usually damp and windy, the growing season is characterized by prolonged hot and arid weather conditions. Irrigation is routinely practised in most Cape vineyards, albeit not quite to the extent that South American growers have to resort to.

The following guide to the regions moves anti-clockwise around the Cape.

Olifants River Primarily a source of bulk wine for distillation, the mountainous Olifants River area is home to several of the major Cape cooperative producers. The biggest of these, Vredendal, is actually one of the better practitioners, with some appetizing Chardonnays and Sauvignons. Its Goiya Kgeisje is an early-bottled, fruity-fresh Sauvignon-based white, its flavours presenting considerably less of a challenge to European tongues than its name. Sweet Muscat wines are locally popular. Red wine production is only a marginal activity, though Vredendal does a Cabernet Franc.

Swartland The blackish scrubland of this large, mostly very hot region gives the area its name ('black land'). Notwithstanding the heat, Sauvignon Blanc is curiously one of its best varietals, as in the smoky, nettly Reuilly or Quincy lookalike from the Swartland cooperative, for example. Pinotage does well, achieving some of its more concentrated wines here. A measure of how promising this sort of climatic context is for thick-skinned red varieties that can take more ripening than most is the success of Tinta Barocca. One of the mainstay grapes of port production, it makes an intriguing, plums-and-pepper varietal at the Allesverloren estate.

Paarl With Stellenbosch, this is one of the Cape regions that made early headlines in the export trade. It is where the once all-powerful KWV is based, and still represents the epicentre of the whole South African wine enterprise. One of the hotter regions as a result of lying completely inland, Paarl nonetheless produces the full range of South African wine styles, from crisp, light dry whites and sparklers to full, long-lived reds and excellent fortified wines, as well as some of the country's premium brandies.

All of the major varietals are made in Paarl. The Nederburg estate is one of the largest private producers, making some succulent Chardonnay and minty, chocolatey Cabernet Sauvignon. Fairview Estate is representative of the modern South African outlook, making an impressively diverse range of top varietals. These include enterprising reds such as peppery Mourvèdre and Petit Verdot, steely Chenin Blanc, peachy Viognier, and a particularly well-crafted Riesling, which often comes close to the fullness and weight of Alsace versions.

Villiera does good perfumed Gewürz, as well as sensationally intense Sauvignon (often with as much exuberant fruit as New Zealand growers typically obtain), while Backsberg makes creditable Chardonnay and Merlot. The Glen Carlou estate is notable for one of the Cape's best Pinot Noirs to date, with a headily perfumed Turkish Delight quality, as well as persuasively Burgundian Chardonnay.

In the southeast of the region is a valley enclave called **Franschhoek** (meaning 'French corner', after its original settlers). Many of Paarl's best wines come from here. High flyers so far have been Dieu Donné, whose superb Chardonnay is in the buttered-green-bean Côte de Beaune mode, La Motte with its brambly Shiraz, and the excellent Boekenhoutskloof, which has superlative premium bottlings of Cabernet, Syrah and Semillon, as well as an affordable mid-priced range called Porcupine Ridge. Clos Cabrière is a specialist in traditional-method fizz.

Meerlust Estate in Stellenbosch (left), with the Helderberg mountain beyond.

Modern equipment and new oak barrels (above) at Klein Constantia.

The KWV still makes its sherry-style fortifieds in Paarl, maturing the dry ones under a *flor*-style yeast layer and putting them through a *solera* system. Its portfolio doesn't stop at wine, however, but goes on to encompass several spirits, as well as the once popular Van der Hum, a kind of South African Grand Marnier whose name translates as something like 'Whatshisname'.

Durbanville Like many another small vineyard region that lies in the shadow of a major city, Durbanville's existence is being threatened by the urban expansion of Cape Town. It hasn't consequently played a significant role in South Africa's wine renaissance.

Constantia The old, sprawling estate where South Africa's historically greatest wines were made was initially broken up and divided among three proprietors, the largest of them – Groot Constantia – state-owned. Constantia went on to be considered a WO in its own right, though, and there are currently nine wineries based here. Of the privately owned estates, Steenberg has wonderfully edgy Sauvignon and luxurious, intense Merlot, while the smallest of them all, Klein Constantia, has so far proved itself the most visionary. As well as producing splendid modern varietals in the shape of Sauvignon and Chardonnay (together with an improving Bordeaux-blend red), it has been the first to make a serious attempt to revive the fortified Constantia of blessed memory, rechristened Vin de Constance. Recent efforts have been little short of sensational.

Stellenbosch Viticulture in the coastal Stellenbosch region, south of Paarl, dates back to the first generation of Dutch colonists. Today, it is home to more of South Africa's first-division wine estates than any other district. Benefiting from their proximity to the ocean, the vineyards of Stellenbosch regularly produce the best-balanced red wines of the Cape. At the heart of the region is the headquarters of the Republic's principal viticultural research institute.

Blended reds, often using all three main Bordeaux varieties are very often a better bet than varietal Cabernet. Warwick Farm's Trilogy is a fine blend, as are the sumptuous Rubicon from Meerlust, Paul Sauer from Kanonkop, and the sleek, sublime Faithful Hound from Mulderbosch.

Kanonkop also makes one of the more charming Pinotages. Neethlingshof is an enterprising producer, making an aromatic Alsace Gewürztraminer varietal, as well as an expressive late-picked Riesling, Maria.

Sauvignon Blanc from the Uitkyk estate is impressive, while Thelema has won plaudits for its rounded, golden Chardonnay and a seductively silky Merlot of great power and presence. Avontuur's Reserve is one of the more ripely concentrated Cabernets. Mulderbosch's Sauvignons are packed with varietal intensity – either oak-fermented or *au naturel* – and the Chenin Blanc has pleasing density of texture as well as aromatic lift. Stellenzicht makes a coffee-scented oaked Syrah, plus some luscious dessert wines, including a botrytized Riesling labelled Noble Late Harvest.

OTHER PRODUCERS: Beyerskloof, Grangehurst, Jordan, Rustenberg, Vergelegen, Simonsig, De Trafford.

Barrel cellar of Graham Beck Winery in the Robertson region (above), renowned for its Madeba Sauvignons.

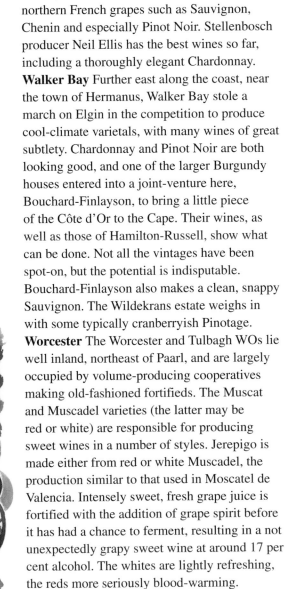

Elgin One of South Africa's newer regions, following the recent trend for planting vineyards at higher altitude in order to benefit from cooler growing conditions, the WO ward of Elgin is turning out to be a good source of varietals from northern French grapes such as Sauvignon, Chenin and especially Pinot Noir. Stellenbosch producer Neil Ellis has the best wines so far, including a thoroughly elegant Chardonnay.

Walker Bay Further east along the coast, near the town of Hermanus, Walker Bay stole a march on Elgin in the competition to produce cool-climate varietals, with many wines of great subtlety. Chardonnay and Pinot Noir are both looking good, and one of the larger Burgundy houses entered into a joint-venture here, Bouchard-Finlayson, to bring a little piece of the Côte d'Or to the Cape. Their wines, as well as those of Hamilton-Russell, show what can be done. Not all the vintages have been spot-on, but the potential is indisputable. Bouchard-Finlayson also makes a clean, snappy Sauvignon. The Wildekrans estate weighs in with some typically cranberryish Pinotage.

Worcester The Worcester and Tulbagh WOs lie well inland, northeast of Paarl, and are largely occupied by volume-producing cooperatives making old-fashioned fortifieds. The Muscat and Muscadel varieties (the latter may be red or white) are responsible for producing sweet wines in a number of styles. Jerepigo is made either from red or white Muscadel, the production similar to that used in Moscatel de Valencia. Intensely sweet, fresh grape juice is fortified with the addition of grape spirit before it has had a chance to ferment, resulting in a not unexpectedly grapy sweet wine at around 17 per cent alcohol. The whites are lightly refreshing, the reds more seriously blood-warming.

The **Tulbagh** district WO, to the northwest of Worcester, has produced some of the most admirable sparkling wines yet in the form of Krone Borealis Brut from the Twee Jonge Gezellen winery, despite the fact that this is not theoretically the right sort of climate for fizz.

Robertson Another of South Africa's up-and-coming WOs, Robertson is located well back in the hot and steamy hinterland, its vineyards heavily dependent on irrigation. Nonetheless, it has emerged as a premier-league producer of white wines rather than red. Pre-eminent among these are Chardonnays, with plenty of fleshy, chunky Colombards and more of that super-ripe, eminently fortifiable Muscat and Muscadel.

De Wetshof is leader of the pack for Chardonnay, its Danie de Wet *cuvées* aged on their lees to produce an indulgently rich, buttercream style with powerful appeal. Van Loveren's are almost as good. Sauvignons from this region are now exhibiting plenty of lush tropical fruit, replete with convincing gooseberry character from the Springfield and Graham Beck estates. Beck also makes fine unoaked Chardonnay called Waterside, and one of the region's more conspicuously successful sparklers. Among reds to look out for are the full-blooded Shirazes of the Zandvliet estate, and Springfield's Bordeaux blends and varietal Cabernets. Bon Courage makes fine dessert wines.

Klein Karoo Sprawling landlocked region where fortified Muscadels are best suited to the indomitable heat, though a few producers are chancing their arms with dry varietal table wines. Sauvignon Blanc may be the best bet.

Mossel Bay Like Walker Bay and Elgin, this easterly coastal area is a relatively new wine region, located to benefit from the ameliorating sea breezes, in this case blowing in from the Indian Ocean. Cool-climate varieties are what the growers have put their faith in, with Pinot Noir at the pinnacle of ambition as usual, supplemented by Riesling and Sauvignon Blanc. Given time to find a foothold, the wines should be excellent.

Orange River To the west of the landlocked state of Lesotho, the Orange River region is South Africa's climatically fiercest wine area, its riverside vineyards further from maritime influence than any on the Cape itself. Volume production is the chief activity; since the vines have to be so intensively irrigated, the amount of fruit they bear is correspondingly far too high for true quality.

SPARKLING WINES

So important had South Africa's current generation of sparkling wines become by the 1990s that a new country-wide term, Méthode Cap Classique (MCC), was instituted to classify the best. It denotes any sparkler produced using the traditional secondary bottle-fermentation method of champagne.

Many of these quality sparklers are made from the classic blend of Chardonny and Pinot Noir, while others may have a dash of Loire-like Chenin and even Sauvignon Blanc in them, but the overall quality is frankly breathtaking. Indeed, these may well be, along with those of southern England, the best such wines made anywhere outside Champagne itself. Given that the traditional method only started being used to any significant degree in South Africa in the 1980s, the progress is all the more astonishing.

Although fizz is made in many different WOs, including some of the warmer districts of Stellenbosch, the wines retain good crisp acidity and freshness in their youth. What has been so striking about many of the releases, however, is the yeast autolysis characters they display. Autolysis is the name for the biochemical interchange that takes place within the wine as it undergoes its second fermentation in the bottle. As the active yeasts die off, the dead cells impart a distinctive aroma and flavour to

the wine, a kind of toasty, wheatgrain character reminiscent of freshly baked bread. The more pronounced it is, the longer the wine must have spent maturing on its lees before being disgorged, and there is no surer sign that a sparkling wine producer means business than prolonged maturation of its wines.

That said, some of the wineries are now finding themselves tempted to release their wines too young to cope with the growing demand. This is a shame, but not exactly unknown of course within the Champagne region itself. Rosés could generally do with a little more fruit, but some are beginning to appear in a reasonably attractive, elegant style. Vintage-dated wines will in time be the classiest of all.

PRODUCERS: Twee Jonge Gezellen (Krone Borealis Brut), Cabrière Estates (Pierre Jourdan Brut and Blanc de Blancs), Bergkelder (Pongracz), Graham Beck (Graham Beck Brut), Simonsig (Kaapse Vonkel), Bon Courage (Jacques Bruére Brut Reserve), Steenberg (MCC Brut 1682), Villiera (Tradition Brut), Boschendal (Grande Cuvée Brut).

Pressing Chardonnay grapes (above) destined for the Cap Classique sparkler, Madeba Brut, at Graham Beck Winery in Robertson.

This gleaming white, intricately gabled façade (left) belongs to the manor house of the Boschendal estate in Franschhoek, Paarl.

AUSTRALIA

Leaders in the triumphal march of the varietal movement, Australia's winemakers have taken Chardonnay and Cabernet Sauvignon, added Shiraz to the list, and recreated them in styles all of their own.

Australia's vineyards run in a swathe across the southeast of the continent, as well as popping up in enclaves in Western Australia and on the island of Tasmania.

OF ALL THE NEWER, non-European winemaking countries, Australia is the least in thrall to European ways of doing things. Its wine industry is scarcely any older than that of the USA, and quite considerably younger than South Africa's. (Some of the earliest imported vine cuttings came from the Cape.) The country had no wild vines, and so its industry didn't – unlike California's – have to go through the painful process of ridding itself of hybrid varieties. The slate it started with was blank and clean.

Barring the odd sighting of rough-and-ready fortified wines (mostly imitations of port), Australian wines were virtually unheard-of in the northern hemisphere as recently as the early 1980s. The first experimental cuttings of Chardonnay and Cabernet were only just going into the Australian dirt in the 1970s, when California's best were already winning prizes in French tastings. How, then, did Australian wine go from a tentative trickle to an almighty Eureka-style gush within one decade?

It was all a question of style. Winemakers in the Barossa and Hunter Valleys, in the Adelaide Hills and Victoria, taught the non-specialist wine consumer varietal recognition by making the wines thus labelled so easy to love. They removed the red-hot, mouth-furring tannins from Cabernet, and the razor-like acidity from a lot of traditional Chardonnay, and marinated them both in the sweet vanillin of brand new oak, and the world came running.

What helped to fuel this recipe for success was the wine-show system in Australia. All the country's wine-producing states regularly hold their own regional competitions, the results of which – rather like the UK's International Wine and Spirit Competition – have a galvanizing effect on the sales of wines that win medals. Many producers were driven by the competition phenomenon to craft wines made in a big, brash, love-me-or-leave-me style that would enable them to stand out in a lineup of their stylistic rivals.

These wines not only impacted on the show judges; they also exercised a siren-like allure for British and American retail buyers. By the early 1990s, nearly every bottle of Australian wine you opened tasted sweetly overripe, the over-maturity of the grapes accentuated by a lathering of oaky richness, all building up on the palate to an alcohol blast at the end that was like being punched in the head.

Along with the eggyolk-yellow Chardonnays came a raft of Cabernets, Shirazes, and blends thereof. These were red wines that had none of the harsh tannin or volatile sourness of French or Italian reds and, as such, they won over many of those who didn't think they liked red wine at all. Some of these wines were stunning in their depth of fruit and genuine complexity, but an awful lot of the others (mainly unblended Shiraz) tasted like overboiled jam, with gummy, cloying texture and a synthetic, un-winey aftertaste.

There were sparkling wines that tasted of ripe summer fruits, mango-scented whites and strawberry-perfumed rosés, selling for as little as a third the price of non-vintage champagne, for all that they weren't necessarily made by the traditional method and might be more likely to contain Semillon and Shiraz than Chardonnay or Pinot Noir. In time, these would be followed by more genuinely sophisticated fizz.

Behind them came a phalanx of fortified wines, Liqueur Muscats unlike any other *vins de liqueur* on earth, headily redolent of crystallized tangerine and creamy milk chocolate. It all added up to a non-stop scattergun strategy, and it worked like a dream.

The result of Australia-mania has been that the country is unable by quite some distance to supply the worldwide demand for its wines. They may still turn up their noses at them in continental Europe, but American and (especially) British consumers can't get enough of them – literally.

At present, in my view, the Australian wine industry is a great unanswered question. It established a solid bridgehead for itself into the global wine village more quickly and decisively than was achieved by any other emergent nation in wine history. The question is: which way does it go now? There is a tidal wave of crude-tasting, cheap Australian varietal wine on the world markets. They may have taken the oak out of the Chardonnay, but it still tastes sweet. Most Pinot Noirs remain maladroit offerings with hardly an iota of the elegance cool-climate New Zealand has achieved. Cheap Shiraz can be one of the unwisest ways of spending your money when you're dropping into the wine-shop for a simple hearty red to go with tonight's dinner.

Opening the vintage (above) at the annual Barossa Festival, in South Australia.

Morning sunlight over the northern slopes of the Great Dividing Range (below), in Victoria.

Margaret River (above)
is one of Australia's cooler
wine-growing regions.

Australia is hardly short of outstanding producers, from the pioneering Penfolds wines to the most talented growers in the Clare Valley and Margaret River GIs. These wines are worth the extra outlay, but they are being outshouted for the time being by the lowest-common-denominator stuff, all those boring branded wines with which your local supermarket shelves will reliably be groaning.

Most of Australia's regions experience reliably hot, dry growing conditions year on year. Within the overall pattern, however, there are cooler pockets where more temperate summers have a consequent effect on wine styles. They include the Margaret River GI of Western Australia, inland regions such as the Clare and Eden Valleys in South Australia, and much of Tasmania. By contrast, the vineyards of New South Wales and Queensland, being that much nearer the Equator, have a correspondingly fiercer climate to contend with, in which the spring can bring virtual drought while the harvest season suffers torrential rains.

The vineyards are strung throughout a swathe of southeast Australia, from north of Adelaide in the state of South Australia, through Victoria and up to the Hunter Valley, north of Sydney. There is a small outpost on a high plateau called the Granite Belt just into Queensland, as well as small but important plantings in the state of Western Australia. The cool-climate island of Tasmania, in the Tasman Sea south of Victoria, has isolated vineyards, mainly on its northern edge.

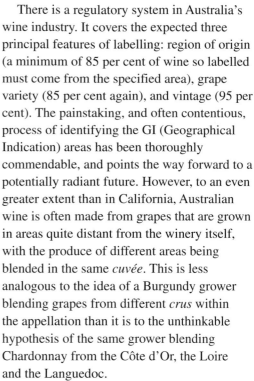

There is a regulatory system in Australia's wine industry. It covers the expected three principal features of labelling: region of origin (a minimum of 85 per cent of wine so labelled must come from the specified area), grape variety (85 per cent again), and vintage (95 per cent). The painstaking, and often contentious, process of identifying the GI (Geographical Indication) areas has been thoroughly commendable, and points the way forward to a potentially radiant future. However, to an even greater extent than in California, Australian wine is often made from grapes that are grown in areas quite distant from the winery itself, with the produce of different areas being blended in the same *cuvée*. This is less analogous to the idea of a Burgundy grower blending grapes from different *crus* within the appellation than it is to the unthinkable hypothesis of the same grower blending Chardonnay from the Côte d'Or, the Loire and the Languedoc.

THE GRAPES

Australia's premium white grape varieties are led by Chardonnay, planted more or less wherever vines are grown. At its ripest, it produces the broad-beamed, sunny, golden wines the world has come to adore, but experiments with producing a leaner, more delicately complex style are likely to be the best. Subtle variations of style are as much to do with the vinification regimes of individual winemakers as they are of sites chosen. Some Chardonnay is kept back for blending as a crowd-pleasing component with other grapes such as Semillon and Colombard.

After Chardonnay comes Semillon, which gives a fatter, riper wine here than in Europe. In its dry, unoaked and unblended guise, this is very much an Australian original. Always popular at home, it has had to be patient in awaiting international consumer recognition, but these are definitely wines worth getting to know. Sauvignon Blanc is occasionally blended with Semillon, as in Bordeaux, but is more often seen on its own. It is a grape that many winemakers are only just learning how to handle, earlier examples often suffering from a lack of clarity or inappropriate excessive oaking.

Riesling is many ways the backbone of fine white wine production, and is particularly important in South Australia. Its fruit may be more plangently citric even than in dry Alsace

Riesling, and its acidity much less of a shock to the tastebuds, but the wines are quite as capable of developing interestingly in the bottle.

Other classic white grapes planted in small quantities include Gewürztraminer, the Rhône grapes Viognier and Marsanne (both of which have done well), and Chenin Blanc.

Less illustriously, there are widespread plantings in the irrigated Murray River region of South Australia of an indifferent white variety called Sultana. As its name implies, much of it ends up being processed as dried grapes, but a lot is still used for wine, often the bulk output of bag-in-box wines that accounts for an important proportion of the domestic market. Muscat of Alexandria, which goes under the local name of Muscat Gordo Blanco, also plays a role in volume production, and is not an ingredient of the premium Liqueur Muscats. Colombard is grown too, but on nothing like the scale that it appears in South Africa.

Chief among reds is Shiraz (the Syrah of the northern Rhône), another grape that Australia fashioned in its own image. The reds of the northern Rhône are varietal Syrahs too of course, but the southern-hemisphere style is hugely rich, creamy and blackberryish, with little or none of the black-pepper rasp or sharp tannins of young Rhône wines. At its least sensitively vinified, Shiraz turns out roaringly alcoholic wines (14.5 per cent is nothing) with a blurred, stewed flavour like cheap jam, the sweetness of which is then made the more repellent with oak (or oak-chip) treatment. At its best, it produces wines of monumental, unforgettable intensity, inky concentration, and a whole range of fruit and exotic spice notes.

Shiraz is frequently blended with Cabernet Sauvignon, generally forming the greater element in the mix. The effect can be to stiffen the sinew of the otherwise soft-centred ripe Shiraz, or to mitigate some of young Cabernet's severity where Shiraz is the junior partner. Cabernet is also valued as a varietal in its own right, though, and can offer incontrovertible evidence to those sceptical of the wine-taster's vocabulary that Cabernet Sauvignon really can taste intensely of blackcurrants.

Increasingly, where Cabernet is blended, it is with its traditional claret bedfellows, Merlot and Cabernet Franc (with dashes of Petit Verdot here and there). Merlot is now the third most widely planted red grape, one consequence of which in the future may well be more varietal

Merlot, not hitherto – and unusually in the southern hemisphere – one of the Australian industry's specialities.

Grenache looked until recently as if it might be doomed to die out as a humdrum variety used to bulk everyday reds. A wave of wines made according to the southern Rhône recipe, from Grenache, Shiraz and Mourvèdre (the last often known as Mataro), and styled as GSM blends, has pinpointed the potential of the perennially underrated Grenache.

Pinot Noir is gradually getting better. Much of what's grown goes into premium bottle-fermented sparkling wines conceived in the champagne image, but there are doughty souls, as there are wherever quality red wine is made, determined to make world-class red varietal Pinot. The first signs of modest success are with us, as suitable sites are identified for the famously unforgiving grape.

Minority red grapes include Tarrango, a crossing of white Sultana with the port grape Touriga Nacional (vinified by some in the style of a slightly more muscular north Italian red), and Italy's Nebbiolo and Sangiovese. A grape called Cienna, crossed from a minor Spanish variety with Cabernet Sauvignon, might one day set the world alight.

The grounds of St Hallett's in the Barossa Valley (below), where 100-year-old Shiraz vines still yield fabulous wines.

Red gum trees in Western Australia (above) flower at grape-harvest time, distracting birds from eating the grapes.

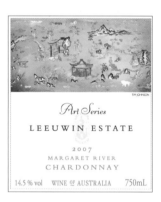

Western Australia's vineyards lie at the southwestern tip of the state (right), with the top producers clustered in the Margaret River region close to the Indian Ocean.

WESTERN AUSTRALIA

Swan District One of the very hottest regions in a hot country, this GI in the Swan Valley was once the main growing area of Western Australia. For a while, it went into decline as a result of the identification of cooler sites further south, but is now re-emerging as a producer of well-defined varietal wines. The Houghton winery makes a range of good generic wines here, together with improbable varietals bottled under the Moondah Brook label, such as Chenin Blanc and Verdelho (the latter one of the white grapes of Madeira).

OTHER PRODUCERS: Sandalford, Lamont, Faber.

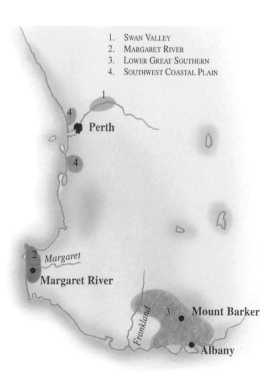

1. SWAN VALLEY
2. MARGARET RIVER
3. LOWER GREAT SOUTHERN
4. SOUTHWEST COASTAL PLAIN

Margaret River One of the great talking-points of Australian wine lately, the milder climate of the Margaret River GI has led to the production of some intriguing wines in a considerably less upfront style than is traditionally associated with Australia. Cooling breezes off the Indian Ocean exert a moderating influence here, in a country that doesn't generally receive the same maritime amelioration that, say, South Africa or the western US states do. Consequently, the Margaret River's Chardonnays have an almost Burgundian profile, and may require much less acid adjustment than those from South Australia, while the Cabernets are leaner and more closed in their youth. Sauvignons are briskly fresh and herbaceous, while the Semillons are crisp but healthily rounded.

Cullens is one of Margaret River's best estates, making nutty, savoury Chardonnay in a restrained style. Moss Wood makes a slightly richer version which, in some vintages, has the unmistakable waft of buttered leeks familiar to lovers of Puligny-Montrachet. Cullens also makes a benchmark toasty Semillon without oak as well as impressive Pinot Noir. Cape Mentelle, the winery that founded the much-lauded Cloudy Bay in New Zealand, has its Australian base in this district, where it produces an apple-and-melon blend of Semillon and Sauvignon, and even has some plantings of Zinfandel.

Leeuwin Estate is one of the most ambitious wineries in all of Australia. Its expensive but indisputably brilliant Chardonnay is an object-lesson to others. A varietally intense Cabernet and pin-sharp, citrus-soaked Riesling show its versatile abilities to the full. The long-established Vasse Felix winery's Shiraz is plump and rich, without slumping into jamminess.

OTHER PRODUCERS: Houghton, Pierro, Brookland Valley, Voyager, Devil's Lair, Woodlands.

Great Southern Western Australia's largest wine area is situated a little to the east of the Margaret River. In the GIs of **Mount Barker**, **Frankland River**, **Albany**, **Denmark** and **Porongurup**, it is beginning to fulfil its early promise quite emphatically. An entire range of grapes succeeds here, including the finicky Pinot and Sauvignon. The potential for Rieslings in particular is extremely exciting.

A Mount Barker winery, Plantagenet, does all sorts of things well, including a meaty Cabernet to age, tropically juicy Riesling and lemon-butter Chardonnay. Goundrey, also in Mount Barker, has raised some eyebrows with its good-

value bottlings of creamy Chardonnay and cassis-scented Cabernet. Another sharply focused, lime-zesty Riesling is made by the Howard Park winery.

OTHER PRODUCERS: Harewood, Houghton, West Cape Howe, Castle Rock.

SOUTH AUSTRALIA

The most copious wine-producing state of Australia is home to many internationally famous wineries. Its vineyard regions are fairly widely scattered throughout the southeast of the state, with the result that pronounced differences between them can actually be tasted in the glass. In the southern district of Coonawarra, South Australia boasts one of the most distinctive growing regions anywhere in the southern hemisphere. Almost every major variety performs well, and botrytized dessert wines – from Semillon and Riesling – have become a notable South Australia speciality.

Clare Valley One of the cooler growing regions, Clare consists of four interconnected valleys – the Clare, Skillogalee, Watervale and Polish River. The premium varietal here has to be Riesling, which achieves diamond-bright, intensely defined lime-juice and petrol characteristics from the best growers. Semillon is good too, in the austere, minerally, unwooded style, Viognier is elegantly aromatic, while Chardonnay can be a little on the shy and retiring side, unusual in Australia. Reds are lean as well, often with pronounced tannins and acidity, but for that reason do perform well if bottle-aged.

Tim Knappstein's Rieslings are indicative of the Clare style – smoky, full-bodied and zesty, and ageing to a delicious pungency. His Cabernet is good too. Skillogalee and Pikes are textbook Riesling specialists (the latter also makes a first-division Chardonnay). Another Tim, Tim Adams, makes spectacularly concentrated Semillon and deep, long-lived Shiraz. The Jim Barry winery attracts followers for its crisp Rieslings and Sauvignons, as well as a hauntingly aromatic Shiraz labelled Armagh. The Leasingham label, owned by the Constellation Wines conglomerate, is a good source of simple Clare varietals, including a ripely blackcurranty Shiraz.

OTHER PRODUCERS: Petaluma, Mount Horrocks, Wendouree, Grosset.

Riverland The backwash area of South Australia, making bulk wine for the bargain end of the market, is located on heavily irrigated vineyard land along the Murray River. Plantings of the more mundane varieties are concentrated here.

Among the better wines, Yalumba's Oxford Landing range is sourced from here, and includes a commendable GSM blend, a juicy Cabernet rosé, and an unexpectedly crisp Sauvignon. Angove is a decent volume producer, whose wines often appear under supermarket own-brands. Banrock Station is another widely seen Riverland wine brand. A substantial portion of Riverland production goes into wine-boxes, by no means of unacceptable quality, but best glugged back round the barbie.

A springtime scene (above) in the Polish Hill area of South Australia's Clare Valley, home to fine whites.

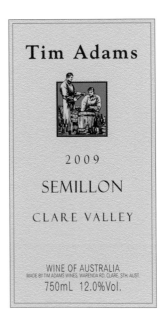

*Penfolds' space-age
Nuriootpa winery (right)
in the Barossa Valley,
South Australia.*

*The most prolific wine-
producer in Australia, South
Australia's vineyards extend
across the state (below),
offering distinctively
different styles of wine.*

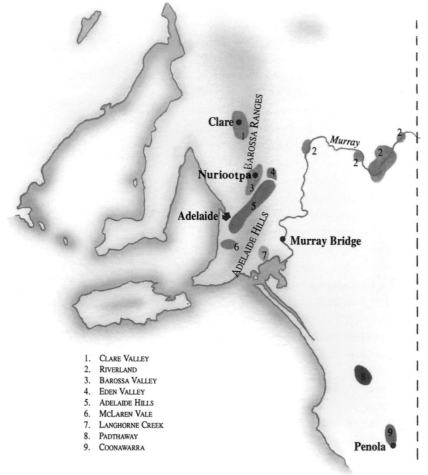

1. CLARE VALLEY
2. RIVERLAND
3. BAROSSA VALLEY
4. EDEN VALLEY
5. ADELAIDE HILLS
6. MCLAREN VALE
7. LANGHORNE CREEK
8. PADTHAWAY
9. COONAWARRA

Barossa Valley One of the first regional names
in Australian wine that overseas customers
came to recognize, the hot Barossa Valley
northeast of Adelaide is in many ways the
epicentre of the whole industry. It was settled
and planted by Germans and Poles in the 19th
century, and today is where much of the harvest
from neighbouring regions finds its way to
be crushed. A high proportion of Barossa's
wineries, therefore, are not necessarily making
exclusively Barossa wine.

The bottom of the valley has the hottest
microclimate, and is the source of some of
Australia's most intensely coloured and alcoholic
reds. Shiraz from this region attains incomparable
levels of concentration, the epitome of which is
Penfolds Grange, the Barossa's legendary *grand
cru*. Growers in search of cooler conditions for
the Rieslings and Chardonnays for which the
area is equally famed have planted higher up
on the valley hillsides.

Penfolds remains the pre-eminent Barossa
name for a comprehensive range of varietals
and blends to suit all pockets. From its simple,
zesty Riesling and oak-driven, full-on Chardonnay,
to its versatile and splendidly crafted reds,
quality exudes from every bottle. Among the
red highlights are the Bin 28 Kalimna Shiraz,

always a supple, brambly masterpiece, Bin 389 Cabernet-Shiraz, and the sensationally concentrated, ink-black Bin 707 Cabernet Sauvignon. The fabled Grange is nearly all Shiraz, a colossal yet immaculately graceful wine, full of the aromas of preserved purple fruits, soft leather and wild herbs, and capable of ageing in the bottle for decades. It isn't cheap, but it is still a fraction of the price of the Château Pétrus to which it has often been compared. Penfolds' bottlings of Coonawarra wines (see below), especially the Cabernet, are more purely indicative of the region than virtually any others.

Other large-scale operators include Orlando Wines, makers since 1976 of the best-selling Jacob's Creek range, and Seppelt, whose extraordinarily diverse portfolio takes in premium sparkling wines such as the bone-dry Salinger and trail-blazing sparkling Shiraz (think alcoholic fizzy blackcurrant cordial), together with authoritative fortifieds, among which the sherry styles stand out (see page 245).

A list of excellent smaller wineries would have to include Grant Burge (appetizingly nutty Zerk Vineyard Semillon-Viognier and a soft, plummy Hillcot Merlot), St Hallett (famous Old Block Shiraz from century-old vines), Peter Lehmann (minty, almost claret-like Stonewell Shiraz), Rockford (idiosyncratic, smooth-contoured Basket Press Shiraz) and Wolf Blass (a comprehensive range of generics, including good Gold Label Riesling).
OTHER PRODUCERS: Charles Melton, Turkey Flat, Duval, Barossa Valley Estate.

Eden Valley A group of high valleys in the Barossa Ranges, the Eden Valley GI is, properly speaking, a continuation of the Barossa region. It is considerably cooler than the Barossa Valley itself, though, and those gentler conditions show up in the wines, especially in the significant quantities of dry, citrically tangy Riesling the area produces.

One of the biggest names in Eden is Yalumba, which incorporates the Hill-Smith, Heggies and Pewsey Vale labels, as well as bottling under its own name. The Hill-Smith Sauvignon is an especially poignant wine, an eloquent riposte to those who claim that Australians don't understand the grape. Pewsey Vale and Heggies Rieslings both represent benchmark lemon-and-lime versions of that variety. Yalumba's own Octavius Shiraz is a triumph, a superbly complex red with a beguiling waft of coffee. The company's sparklers, such as the seriously complex Yalumba D Cuvée, and fortifieds like the chocolatey, caramelly Clocktower, are also to be reckoned with.

Henschke is another name to drop. It owns some of the oldest vineyard land for miles around, its shatteringly profound Hill of Grace Shiraz made from 100-year-old vines. Its Mount Edelstone is another top-drawer Shiraz, while Cyril Henschke is fine, concentrated Cabernet that demands ageing. The whites are good too, particularly the pungent, petrolly Julius Riesling, another one to age, and the nutty, lime-scented Louis Semillon.

The hot, dry Barossa Valley (above) is South Australia's premier wine region.

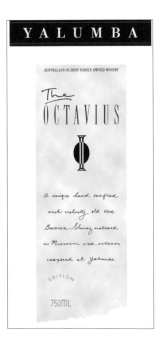

A camel sanctuary amid the vines (below) in the flat expanse of South Australia's McLaren Vale.

Adelaide Hills The hill ranges east of the city are fairly sparsely planted, but represent another favourable microclimate for growers looking for relief from South Australia's heat. Sparkling wines from here have been among the finest. Petaluma is the most widely-known name around here, although its more celebrated bottlings come from Coonawarra fruit (see below). Bridgewater Mill is its alternative label, and includes a good citrus-fresh Chardonnay. Pirramimma's Cabernet has an attractive eucalyptus note.

OTHER PRODUCERS: Nepenthe, Shaw & Smith, Geoff Weaver.

McLaren Vale South of Adelaide, this flat, expansive GI has carved out a regional identity for itself with wines that are increasingly being made in much subtler style than was once the case. Exquisite, richly constituted reds, including ground-breaking Shiraz-Viognier blends, are pouring forth. The climate remains a bit too baking for fully focused whites, though there are exceptions.

Chapel Hill has some superbly honed reds from Cabernet and Shiraz. Chateau Reynella makes powerhouse Basket Press Shiraz here too, under the auspices of the Constellation conglomerate. Among Cabernets, Wirra Wirra's Dead Ringer bottling exhibits all the cassis intensity looked for in South Australia, while Primo Estate's unctuous Joseph La Magia, a botrytized Riesling with a dollop of raisined Gewürztraminer, is a curvaceous charmer. Wandering winemaker Geoff Merrill is here too, making a range of good-value varietals, including a raspberryish rosé from Grenache, and some peachy Reserve Chardonnay.

OTHER PRODUCERS: Tatachilla, Clarendon Hills, SC Pannell, Fox Creek, Hardys.

Langhorne Creek The Langhorne Creek district is east of McLaren Vale, but shares much the same characteristics. Good reds from Cabernet and Shiraz, exotically perfumed Shiraz-Viognier blends after the northern Rhône idiom, and small but increasing quantities of dry Verdelho (one of the madeira grapes), are worth investigating.

Padthaway The Padthaway GI is a sort of northern outpost of the more famous Coonawarra region. Lying in the southeast corner of the state of South Australia, it is nearly as cool as its neighbour, and has a little of the prized *terra rossa* soil of Coonawarra. Whereas the latter has developed a reputation for red wines, Padthaway has become something of a white-wine enclave – specifically Chardonnay, Riesling and Sauvignon. Most of the vineyard land is owned by companies based in other areas, but who make special *cuvées* that carry the GI name on the label.

Orlando, Seppelt and Penfolds all have interests in Padthaway. Penfolds Chardonnay from the region is one of the most richly buttery, and the Lindemans Padthaway bottling is almost as powerful. Henry's Drive is an excellent producer with some sublimely aromatic Cabernet and Shiraz, and Constellation's Stonehaven is a reliable label.

Coonawarra Just south of Padthaway is the region that got everybody so excited about Australia in the first place. Declared a GI in 2001, Coonawarra's unique blend of cool climate and *terra rossa* soil – the paprika-coloured red loam that lends the vineyards such a striking appearance – is without doubt responsible for the obvious class of its wines.

Coonawarra's finest bottles provide the answer to that interminable rhetorical question that still fuels debates between the Old and New Worlds: does vineyard siting, or *terroir*, make a difference? Not all of Coonawarra's vines are planted on the red soil, and those that aren't do seem to lack that extra dimension of perfume and complexity boasted by those that are.

It is the reds, Shiraz and most notably Cabernet Sauvignon, that best demonstrate the regional identity, although there are some good Chardonnays and even Rieslings as well. The Cabernets are made in a positively French idiom, in that their youthful tannins can be decidedly severe, and the aromatic components stubbornly refuse at first to show themselves. When they do open out, however, there is nothing remotely French about them. They have

a pronounced savoury quality, often resembling mocha coffee beans, sometimes a deliberate slight volatility like Worcestershire sauce, but underlying them is that dry, subtly spiced dark fruit, with the odd date or prune thrown in among the teeming blackcurrants.

There are more wineries actually based here than in Padthaway, but the headline-hitting wines have tended to be made by outsiders owning priceless Coonawarra land. Penfolds makes some of its most extravagantly beautiful Cabernet from grapes grown here; its range offers an obvious starting-point. Petaluma has long had a reputation for a hugely intense Cabernet-Merlot blend, simply called Petaluma Coonawarra. The high-volume Rosemount company from New South Wales has a well-made Coonawarra Show Reserve Cabernet too.

Among wineries located in the region, Hollick makes a glorious, challenging Ravenswood Cabernet, as well as a more immediately accessible Cabernet-Merlot blend and fresh, limey Riesling. Katnook Estate makes tobaccoey Cabernet and a big, fleshy Chardonnay, while Penley, a relative newcomer, produces densely textured Cabernet and a brambly, gamey Shiraz. Wynn's is a well-known name, and an ultra-reliable producer of ripe-fruited, unoaked Shiraz, smoky Chardonnay, a sweetly limey Riesling and a pitch-black, massively structured, top-of-the-range Cabernet called John Riddoch (it needs about ten years to come round). OTHER PRODUCERS: Majella, Balnaves, Brand's, Zema, Parker.

The name that everyone recognizes as uniquely Australian (above), Coonawarra is the most southerly of South Australia's wine regions.

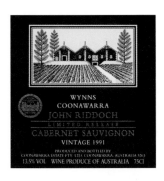

VICTORIA

Victoria's vineyards suffered badly in the worldwide phylloxera plague (which South Australia managed to escape), but the cooler southern reaches of the state are now producing fine varietals and sparklers to compete with the best, and there are more than 500 wineries. In the northeast, Australia's celebrated fortified wines reach their apogee.

Drumborg Very cool western region, its main player being Seppelt, which uses grapes from here to make some attractive varietals, such as Pinot Gris and Riesling.

Grampians/Pyrenees These contiguous areas are further inland than Drumborg, and consequently somewhat warmer. They have a strong tradition in sparkling wines. Increasingly, though, it is becoming clear that the potential for Australia's two premier red grapes, Cabernet and Shiraz, is most exciting of all. Chardonnays tend to be fashioned in the rounded and richly oaked style.

Mount Langi Ghiran is one of the high fliers of this region, with a Shiraz in an intriguingly restrained style, and Cabernet with plenty of extract. Its Riesling has long been one of the best, and is structured for ageing. Cathcart Ridge makes a particularly lush, chocolatey Shiraz, while the Best's winery has a portfolio of cheap and cheerful varietals, including good, lemon-meringue Chardonnay.

OTHER PRODUCERS: Dalwhinnie, Summerfield, Redbank, The Story, Seppelt.

High-altitude cool vineyards of Victoria's Great Dividing Range (above), source of delicate Riesling and subtle Chardonnay.

1. DRUMBORG
2. GREAT WESTERN
3. GEELONG
4. YARRA VALLEY
5. MORNINGTON PENINSULA
6. GOULBURN VALLEY
7. GLENROWAN-MILAWA
8. RUTHERGLEN
9. MURRAY RIVER
10. LAUNCESTON
11. BICHENO
12. HOBART

From the cooler coastal areas to the hot inland regions, the smaller state of Victoria (right) produces a wide range of wine styles, including the famous liqueur Muscats made in the northeast.

Geelong First of a ring of small regions surrounding Melbourne (Geelong is just west of the city), which are home to some of the more far-sighted and ambitious of Australia's current generation of winemakers. Bannockburn has a brilliant range of authentically Burgundian Chardonnays and Pinot Noirs, and nor does the Cabernet lack for anything in varietal richness. By Farr is a punning label for the Farr family's breathtaking Pinot Noirs and Shirazes.

Yarra Valley The temperate Yarra is Victoria's answer to South Australia's Coonawarra, a prime site for highly individual winemaking and superlative cool-climate varietals. This is one of the most promising areas in Australia for Pinot Noir, with fine examples from Green Point, Coldstream Hills, Tarrawarra and Mount Mary. There was a tendency in the past to overoak the wines, which is now thankfully being resisted. Green Point (the export name for Moët's Domaine Chandon) also makes a very classy, lightly buttery, nutmeggy Chardonnay – not a million miles from the style of California's Sonoma – as well as its much-praised fizz. The Cabernets and Shirazes of Yarra Yering are idiosyncratic creations fully worth the high asking price. St Huberts makes a deep, satisfying Cabernet to last.
OTHER PRODUCERS: Diamond Valley, Yering Station, Oakridge, Carlei.

Mornington Peninsula This little peninsula southeast of Melbourne has seen intensive new plantings in recent years, and is now crowded with boutique wineries. Like the Yarra, it is a region of stylistic pioneers making innovative waves. Kooyong has fabulous single-vineyard Pinot Noirs and Chardonnays, as does Moorooduc, fermented with wild yeasts. Stonier's Merricks has textbook Chardonnay in the full-blown opulent style, and some finely crafted sparklers.
OTHER PRODUCERS: Paringa, Hurley, Ten Minutes by Tractor.

Goulburn Valley North of the Yarra, Goulburn is an expansive valley region that contains some of the oldest wineries and vineyards in Australia, whose vines miraculously escaped the worst of the phylloxera wave. Tahbilk has some century-old vines; its Reserve bottlings of Shiraz and Cabernet are bursting with venerable class. This is one of the properties that pioneered varietal Marsanne in Australia. It certainly has a style all its own, but its clinging, top-heavy, buttery banana quality is too much

for some. The Mitchelton winery produces a Rhône-style blend of Marsanne, Roussanne and Viognier called Airstrip. Delatite offers a broadly based range from its high-altitude vineyards. Snappy Riesling, delicately scented Gewürztraminer, rose-petally Pinot Noir and an expressive, spicy Tempranillo called Donald supplement the excellent Shiraz and Cabernet.

Glenrowan/Milawa As you head into the northeastern sector of Victoria, you are heading towards fortified country (see page 245). At Milawa, though, table wines are made in quantity, the most important producer being Brown Brothers, one of the vanguard companies that blazed the trail for Australian wines in the UK and US. Its range is wide, and more stimulating than it used to be. Look out for finely etched Limited Release Chardonnay, the cherry-fruited Barbera lookalike Tarrango, earthy Patricia Cabernet Sauvignon, deliciously peachy late-picked Muscat, and some fine fizz from all three champagne grapes.

Rutherglen Pre-eminent for Liqueur Muscats (see page 245).

New vineyards planted by Brown Brothers (below), one of hotter, inland Glenrowan-Milawa's top producers of table wines.

Vineyards of the Lower Hunter (above) suffer more from tropical rain storms than those in its more northerly partner, the Upper Hunter.

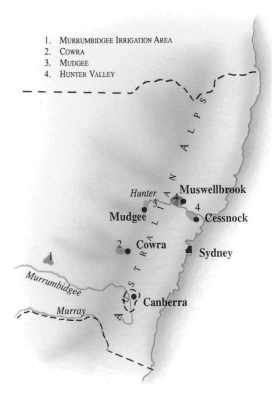

1. MURRUMBIDGEE IRRIGATION AREA
2. COWRA
3. MUDGEE
4. HUNTER VALLEY

The hot Hunter Valley, north of Sydney (right), is New South Wales' finest wine region.

NEW SOUTH WALES

Although it contains the Hunter Valley region of worldwide repute, New South Wales only accounts for a relatively tiny fraction of Australia's annual wine production. Its climate is as hot and hard for growers to contend with as parts of South Australia.

Riverina The lion's share of the output here is of wines destined for boxes and own-brand bottlings, grown on land irrigated by the Murrumbidgee River. Botrytized Semillon is an unlikely exception to the humdrum rule, and comes in especially distinguished form from the De Bortoli winery.

Cowra Small region supplying much of the Hunter Valley's raw material. Hunter winery Rothbury makes an impressive Cowra Chardonnay, though.

Mudgee The Mudgee district was sufficiently proud of its regional pedigree to have awarded itself an appellation even before the GI system was put into practice. A pity then that much of the produce of this hot dry region goes to beef up Hunter's wines when their harvests are hit by rain. Firm Cabernet and stout Shiraz are the baseline (Botobolar's opulent Shiraz is a stunner), but Chardonnays are improving too.

Hunter Valley Divided into Upper and Lower Hunter, this hot, extensive valley is the premium wine region of New South Wales. The Upper section is quite a way to the north of the Lower, and manages to escape the tropical rains that can disrupt the Lower Hunter vintage. Dry Semillon, practically an indigenous Hunter style of great lineage, is the proudest boast. It's often fairly low in alcohol, austerely hard and minerally, and famously takes on a burnt-toast quality as it matures in the bottle. This has fooled many a taster into thinking it has been aged in charred oak. Red wines can be a bit muddy – a lot of that sweet plum-jam style of Shiraz comes from the Hunter – but they are improving.

Good dry Semillons include McWilliams Elizabeth amd Lovedale wines, Tyrrell's Vat 1 and Brokenwood. Rothbury makes a slim but beguiling Shiraz, Rosemount a show-stopping, vegetally Burgundian Roxburgh Chardonnay, Tyrrell's an exciting, offbeat range sold under Vat numbers (such as the famed Vat 6 Pinot and the butterscotchy Vat 47 Chardonnay), and Brokenwood a reverberating Shiraz sombrely called Graveyard Vineyard.

OTHER PRODUCERS: Lake's Folly, Tower, Keith Tulloch, Thomas.

QUEENSLAND

Right on the border with New South Wales is a GI area unromantically known as the **Granite Belt**. Its altitude always looked like making it a promising place to grow grapes, and there are now over 60 wineries established here. For the time being, not a lot of what they produce makes it much further than Sydney, but names to look out for in time will include Boireann, Robert Channon and Preston Peak.

TASMANIA

Led by the visionary and multi-talented Andrew Pirie, a small band of Tasmania producers set out in the 1970s to show the world that the island can make sharply defined varietals, especially Pinot Noir and Chardonnay, in a distinctively European idiom. Although the whole island constitutes a single GI, it has two main centres of production at Launceston in the northeast and Hobart in the south.

Pipers Brook winery, in the northern region of the same name, makes exemplary Pinot Noir, hard in youth and needing time, a subtly steely Chardonnay and some crisp, zesty Riesling. Moorilla Estate produces good beefy Pinot, and improving Gewürztraminer. Heemskerk has some big Cabernets and has diversified into fizz, in association with the champagne house Louis Roederer, under the Jansz label. Tasmanian fizz has been superb across the board.
OTHER PRODUCERS: Bay of Fires, Freycinet, Frogmore Creek.

FORTIFIED WINES

There are two basic categories of Australian fortified wine. One derives from the days when the hot southern-hemisphere countries all had a shot at imitating the traditional methods and flavours of port and sherry. Indeed, those terms were in widespread use in Australia itself, though they are now on the wane. Among the port-styles are extremely sweet, strawberry jam-like wines made from fortified Shiraz, of which some are vintage-dated. Extended wood-ageing washes out the colour of some, which are then referred to – as in the Douro – as Tawny. The sherry styles are even rarer, but can be much better. Seppelt makes a comprehensive range of tangy, salty fino (labelled DP117), hazelnutty amontillado (DP116) and toffeeish oloroso (DP38).

The second category is unique to Australia. Liqueur Muscat and Liqueur Tokay are breathtakingly rich fortified wines made from,

respectively, Muscat Blanc à Petits Grains (here known as Brown Muscat for the dun-skinned variant locally grown) or Muscadelle, the minority grape of Sauternes. The production area is mainly in northeast Victoria around the town of **Rutherglen**, although some are also made in **Glenrowan**, a little to the south.

Their production seems to combine a little of every traditional method for making liquorous dessert wines. Firstly, the grapes are left to shrivel on the vine. They are then pressed and the viscous juice partially fermented, but fortified with grape spirit long before the piercing sweetness has even begun to fade. After that, they are aged and blended from a barrel system something like the *soleras* of Jerez.

The Muscats, especially, are shockingly intense. Pure orange marmalade when you stick your nose in, they dissolve in the mouth into a glutinous amalgam of milk chocolate, sticky dates and candied orange rind, with a finish that persists on the back of the palate for minutes on end.
PRODUCERS: Stanton & Killeen, Chambers, Morris, Yalumba, Campbell's.

Heemskerk Vineyards in the Pipers Brook region of Tasmania (above), makers of notably well-built Cabernet and elegant sparkling wines.

NEW ZEALAND

In just 20 years, New Zealand's winemakers have taken the world by storm to become the fastest growing wine country in the world. Undaunted by geographical isolation, they have established a strong regional identity.

THIS IS WHERE the global wine tour makes its final stop, at the world's most southerly vineyards on the North and South Islands of New Zealand. Any further, and we would be trying to make icewine in the Antarctic.

In terms of its age, the New Zealand wine industry really is the junior partner among the southern-hemisphere countries. Viticulture only really started being taken for a serious proposition here in the 1970s. Undoubtedly spurred by the prodigious worldwide success of Australia, New Zealand carved out its own niche. It could hardly have been otherwise. Not only are the volumes produced much smaller than Australia's, but the climate is entirely different.

The start was about as unpromising as it was almost everywhere else. Experimental plantings in the 19th century were quickly laid waste by phylloxera, and what they were replaced with was hybrid grapes of mixed *vinifera* and native American parentage. On top of that, national licensing laws were among the most restrictive in the English-speaking world, with supermarkets only being permitted to sell the country's own wines since the beginning of the 1990s.

What eventually put New Zealand on the map in the closing years of the 20th century was a single grape variety, and not exactly an unfamiliar one at that. If you had started planning a marketing push in the 1980s for a brand-new wine-producing country, and said that its vineyards looked like they were capable of excelling at one varietal wine in particular, you might have got people's attention. When you then, with the appropriate drum-roll and cymbal-clash, announced that that varietal was going to be Sauvignon Blanc, you might have been treated to a wall of uncomfortable silence.

It wasn't that Sauvignon wasn't a familiar and useful variety. Look at Sancerre, after all, and Pouilly-Fumé. It's just that it wasn't ever seen as being exactly on the A-list. Could a fledgling wine industry really establish itself on a grape that, at best, made simple, fruity quaffing wine, the sort of thing that was nice enough as a summer aperitif perhaps, but was hardly the stuff of legend?

The difference was that nobody had tasted Sauvignon Blanc that was anything like this before. If the grape had traditionally been viewed outside the Upper Loire as brash and unmalleable, or as just plain deadly dull when overcropped, Sauvignons from the Marlborough district of the South Island, New Zealand wine's Garden of Eden, rewrote the rulebook.

There is more uplifting, happy fruit flavour in Marlborough Sauvignon than there is in any other dry white wine on earth. It's a great wine to start off novice tasters with, because even when they struggle to sniff out the cherries in Pinot Noir or the honey in Semillon, the fruit

The world's most southerly vineyards operate in a damp, cool climate. Except for South Island's Central Otago, New Zealand's wine regions (below) lie on or close to the coast.

1. AUCKLAND
2. GISBORNE
3. HAWKES BAY
4. WAIRARAPA
5. NELSON
6. MARLBOROUGH
7. CANTERBURY
8. CENTRAL OTAGO

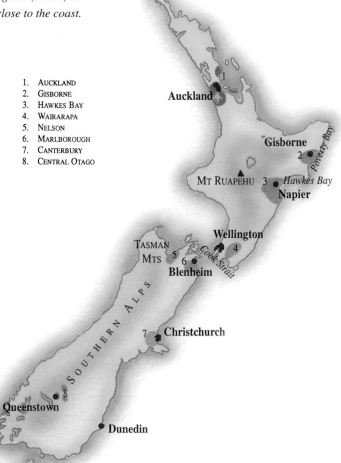

aromas that Marlborough Sauvignon throws out at you come almost too thick and fast to name. The Sauvignon was soon followed by almost equally fruit-fuelled Chardonnay and Riesling.

Reds lagged behind for a while, as one might have expected in a generally cool, damp climate. Much Cabernet Sauvignon was excessively light and herbaceous, its whiff of raw green pepper skin too often complaining of climatic indignities in the vineyard. With better selection of planting areas, and judicious blending with Merlot, that picture has now improved beyond recognition. Even better has been Pinot Noir, always a likelier bet in a cool climate, with wines that are now challenging the best of California for sheer opulence of fruit, and bright balancing acidity.

And what should the other cool-climate success be? Think northern France, think southern England. Sparkling wines made by the traditional method have also played a heroic part here, the results given the vote of confidence by the appearance of a Champagne delegation looking to invest. There is even a clutch of superb botrytized dessert wines.

It hasn't all been plain sailing commercially. The New Zealand wine industry has targeted the greater part of its export effort at the UK, which admittedly has paid off rather well. The path-breaking Cloudy Bay winery became the country's *grand cru* producer for Sauvignon and Chardonnay, some rich, concentrated red blends, and in time one of the more deeply flavoured fizzes. At the happy-go-lucky end of the market, Montana Sauvignon Blanc was one of the red-hot wines on the British market from the late 1980s on. But elsewhere?

While the British were knocking back New Zealand Sauvignon, the influential American wine constituency remained for a long time completely in the dark about the country's potential, while all the while Australia had stolen a march on it. That is slowly but surely changing, but when all is said and drunk, there basically just isn't that much New Zealand wine to go around each year, especially when growing and harvesting conditions can be so severe. In a good year, it produces about a tenth of what Australia does, and *they* haven't got enough to supply the demand.

Not only does New Zealand have a cool climate, it also has a damp one. Annual rainfall is plentifully distributed throughout the year, with the result that vines often yielded too

vigorously, giving low-quality fruit, or else the grapes were diluted by water penetration during the all-important ripening phase. New techniques in vineyard management, introduced towards the turn of the century, widely rectified those particular problems, but the fact remains that vintages are still subject to far wider variation than they are in sunny Australia, a thousand miles off in the distance. 2002 wasn't great for Sauvignon, for example, 2003 fairly awful for red varieties.

The love-affair with Marlborough Sauvignon Blanc began with the wines of Montana. Machine-harvesters at work (above) picking Sauvignon grapes at Montana's Brancott Estate, Marlborough, South Island.

Stunning landscape of inland South Island (left), on the shore of Lake Wanaka in Central Otago.

Ngatarawa Winery and vineyards (above) in the well-established Hawkes Bay region of North Island.

The growing regions are scattered throughout an extensive stretch of both islands, North and South, for all that the total acreage is still very modest. With the exception of southerly Otago, they are all situated on or near the coasts, mostly on the Pacific side.

The classification system, it's fair to say, is still in its infancy. The two principal designations, North and South Island, are subdivided into the ten regions listed below, but a lot of New Zealand wine is still blended from grapes grown by contract growers in different regions. In time, something like a true geographical appellation system will emerge. No other southern-hemisphere country is more obviously suited to one, after all.

THE GRAPES

That old failsafe Müller-Thurgau once occupied pole position in the vineyards, but has now been put in its place rather decisively by Sauvignon and Chardonnay spreading like wildfire. Chardonnay achieves more overt fruit character in New Zealand than it does seemingly anywhere else. Aromas of peach, banana and pear are quite common, and not especially disguisable by oak treatments. Some wineries have attempted to capture a more Burgundian ethos, with buttery richness as opposed to fruit-salad freshness, but they are by no means the norm.

Sauvignon Blanc has been the great white hope of New Zealand wine – better here than in the Loire, many think, for sheer fruit-powered dynamism. There are quite dramatic stylistic differences among the wineries, some emphasizing the green, herbaceous flavours of gooseberries, asparagus and freshly washed watercress, others plunging headlong into tropicality with mango, passion-fruit, pineapple and musky Charentais melon. I have tasted Marlborough Sauvignons with scents of red peppers, grated carrot, the purest blackcurrant juice, even candied cherries. It is one exciting wine when it wants to be. On the other hand, there are too many wines now that don't have the requisite acid balance, offering a mouthful of juicy fruit but without the structure to pull it all into focus. I hope we see the back of those before too long.

Riesling can achieve classical steeliness, without quite the petrolly pungency of Australian versions, the weakest tasting rather limp and confected. Then there's a dash of Chenin Blanc, which should enjoy the climate, some delicate but recognizable Gewürztraminer, and limited plantings of so far rather unremarkable Semillon, better blended than made as a varietal.

Pinot Noir is now the most widely planted red grape, and is flexing its muscles on the world stage with wines of scintillating complexity, diamond-bright fruit and plenty of ageing potential, as thrilling and distinguished as the best of Carneros or Oregon. As well as being built on good, solid, raspberry fruit foundations, they also display a distinctly Burgundian reluctance to charm in their first flush, and nothing quite succeeds like a classy Pinot Noir that makes you do all the work. A fair amount of the Pinot goes into quality sparklers, white and rosé.

Merlot is striking out on its own in some parts, while playing its historically sanctioned role of chaperoning Cabernet Sauvignon in others. Cabernet itself has improved enormously. Those vegetal flavours that once dogged its image are occasionally still in evidence, but many are exhibiting much deeper, plummier concentration than before.

NORTH ISLAND

Northland The whole show began in the far north of the North Island in what is just about the warmest part of the country. It nearly died out as a wine region, but its potential as a site for warm-climate varietals has been recognized, and there are now around 15 wineries here growing mostly Cabernet and Merlot.

Auckland The area in the immediate vicinity of Auckland was also at one time in decline as a wine region, as attention was resolutely turned to more fashionable districts further south, but it's now gaining in status as an auspicious locale for well-built Bordeaux-blend reds. It is warm, but prone to harvest rains, which means fruit from elsewhere often has to be brought in to beef up the blends, but in the kinder years, it's looking good. The region includes a good sub-zone called **Matakana**, north of the city, as well as **Waiheke Island**, situated in the harbour. Kumeu River makes a profoundly Burgundian and quite atypical Chardonnay, while opulent reds from all five Bordeaux grapes come from Waiheke's Stonyridge.

OTHER PRODUCERS: Te Motu, Goldwater, Matua Valley, Coopers Creek, Te Whau.

Waikato/Bay of Plenty A small but expanding region just south of Auckland. It's fairly warm and might be good for reds, but Chardonnay is the strongest suit so far.

Gisborne On the east coast of the North Island, Gisborne has now found its feet as a quality region. So good at premium white varietals has it become that it now styles itself Chardonnay Capital of New Zealand. As well as that hardy perennial, Gewürztraminer has performed creditably, as have Pinot Gris and Chenin Blanc, and there are some excellent traditional-method sparkling wines.

Two of the the country's biggest companies, Montana and Corbans, both have footholds in Gisborne. Millton Vineyards is an organic producer, making some of its wines according to biodynamic principles. Its Clos de Ste Anne Chardonnay is a thunderously rich, complex wine. Auckland producer Nobilo makes a more restrained, gently oaked Poverty Bay Chardonnay.

OTHER PRODUCERS: Vinoptima, Lake Road.

Hawkes Bay Further down the coast, in the environs of Napier, Hawkes Bay is one of New Zealand's longer-established wine regions. Like Gisborne, it has a reputation for Chardonnay, as well as some subtler, gentler Sauvignon than is commonly met with further south. Red Bordeaux blends are improving significantly from the sunnier vineyards, especially from the **Gimblett Gravels** district.

Hawkes Bay winery Te Mata makes one of the most authoritative ranges of wines in the region, taking in soft, gooseberryish Sauvignon (Castle Hill), discreetly buttery Chardonnay

(Elston) and full-frontal, muscular Cabernet-Merlot (Coleraine), as well as some impressive, peppery Syrah (Bullnose). The Villa Maria conglomerate, which owns both the Vidal and Esk Valley labels, makes some tasty Sauvignon and good, savoury Pinot Noir. Ngatarawa makes ripely expressive Cabernet-Merlot, and fine noble-rotted Riesling.

OTHER PRODUCERS: Craggy Range, Trinity Hill, Unison, CJ Pask.

The damp climate encourages vines to grow too vigorously. Pruning and leaf-trimming help control their growth here at Esk Valley vineyards in Hawkes Bay (above).

Vines were only planted in Marlborough (below) as recently as the 1970s, by big producer Montana. The region is now synonymous with fruit-rich Sauvignon.

Wairarapa At the very southern tip of the North Island, near the national capital, Wellington, Wairarapa is home to some of the country's best small growers. Reds are the declared speciality, whether from Pinot Noir or Cabernet, and many of the recent generation of wines are hugely impressive. A sub-region, **Martinborough**, has emerged as particularly superb for clean, raspberry-fruited, deeply complex Pinots with Burgundian levels of acidity and concentration. Brittle and nervy in their youth, they demand several years' bottle-age to show what they are capable of.

Martinborough Vineyards produces outstanding Pinot, and finely crafted Chardonnay and Riesling. Ata Rangi's Pinot is resonant, subtly spiced and meaty, its Célèbre Cabernet-Merlot blend rich, ripe and plumped up with a little Syrah. Paddy Borthwick has superbly defined, memorable Riesling and a vivid, appley Sauvignon Blanc.
OTHER PRODUCERS: Dry River, Palliser Estate, Escarpment.

SOUTH ISLAND
Nelson A hilly region on the fringes of the Tasman mountains, Nelson is Chardonnay country par excellence. Only a handful of wineries have made their home here, in a damp but otherwise promising cool-climate district, but the wine quality is very persuasive. Neudorf makes a finely honed Chardonnay, while Seifried has crisp Riesling in dry and lightly sweet versions, positively flavoured Pinot, rich Chardonnay and tangy Sauvignon.
Marlborough Centred on the town of Blenheim at the northern end of the South Island, Marlborough has been the greatest of all New Zealand wine regions. Little matter that it still doesn't have a particularly elevated reputation for red wines, it is the source of many of the country's most sharply definitive whites, with Sauvignon Blanc at the head of the pack. The region is cool but relatively dry, and its misty autumns mean that botrytized Rieslings are possible in most vintages. Chardonnay plays an important role too. The two most important districts are the **Wairau** and **Awatere Valleys**.

Montana, the New Zealand wine colossus, basically invented Marlborough as a wine region in the 1970s when it planted the first vines here, and its top-value benchmark Sauvignon became a contemporary classic wine. It also makes some good dessert Riesling, and quietly impressive single-estate Pinot Noir.

Cloudy Bay was the second winery to startle the world with its much-sought limited quantities of Marlborough Sauvignon, an expensive, but profoundly eloquent wine. It was joined by a deep, complex Chardonnay, a damson-rich Cabernet-Merlot blend, and a range of massively intense, richly toasty sparklers under the Pelorus label.

Hunter's Estate is another great name for opulent Sauvignon and Chardonnay, Jackson Estate makes soft biscuity Chardonnay and an emphatic, explosive Sauvignon, Vavasour has high-octane versions of both, Seresin offers gooseberry-crammed Sauvignon, Wairau River has a taut, orchard-fruited Sauvignon and melt-in-the-mouth Chardonnay. And so forth.

Marlborough is also where most of New Zealand's traditional-method sparklers are made, often with expertise and investment from champagne houses such as Veuve Clicquot and Deutz. Pinot Noir and Chardonnay are the grapes used, and many show just how

New Zealand's cool climate is showing itself adept as a source of méthode traditionnelle sparklers, especially in the Marlborough area (left).

distinguished sparkling wines can be from a cool climate. Acidity levels are sometimes a little eye-watering, but the overall balance and finesse of the best are beyond question.

Apart from Cloudy Bay's Pelorus, Deutz Marlborough Cuvée, released by Montana, is crisp, dry and elegant. Cellier Le Brun, a sparkling specialist, has some beautifully refined fizz of convincing complexity. OTHER PRODUCERS: Fromm, Forrest, Nautilus, Wither Hills, Dog Point, Framingham, Oyster Bay, Astrolabe, Saint Clair.

Canterbury/Waipara Valley Centred on the city of Christchurch, Canterbury's vineyards are cooler still than those of Marlborough, with the most elegant wines to date. Chardonnay and Pinot are the varietals of choice, but there is

good Riesling too. Pegasus Bay offers ample-fleshed Chardonnays and Pinots, as does Giesen, which also makes noble-rotted Riesling when it can. Daniel Schuster has ostentatiously good Pinot, while St Helena has soft, creamy Pinot Gris and Pinot Blanc.

Central Otago East of the town of Queensland, Central Otago is the most dynamic region of all, and the world's most southerly. It's also the only inland region, with a rapidly growing number of innovative producers. Pinot Noirs (especially from Mt Difficulty and Peregrine) have been astonishing; there is scented Gewürztraminer, fine Riesling and some gently aromatic Pinot Gris. OTHER PRODUCERS: Felton Road, Quartz Reef, Carrick, Rippon.

CONCLUSION

The world of wine can be a baffling place to the uninitiated. It once seemed fraught with snobbery, a world in which novices could only fall flat on their faces as they tripped themselves up by ordering the wrong wine in the restaurant. You had to have serious money to indulge in a passion for wine – that, and somewhere to lay down your bottles of Château Mouton-Rothschild and *grand cru* Corton-Charlemagne while you waited for them to mature.

That world thankfully disappeared some time after the second world war. Most of us don't spend two days' wages on a single bottle of wine, and not many of us, as far as I know, live in houses with wine-cellars. Wine democratized as the industry itself became more broadly based. Once the wines of the so-called New World (that part of the world that, as far as Europeans are concerned, covers everywhere that isn't Europe) gained a significant foothold in the wine marketplace, from the 1980s on, the old hierarchies began to dissolve.

Which isn't to say that there isn't still good wine and bad wine. Bad wines, like poverty, will always be with us. One of the by-products of the quality revolution in wine, though, has been to make those discriminations relative. The good wine remains as exciting and revelatory as it always was, but the bad has mostly now graduated up to mediocre. The chances of finding something utterly undrinkable, short of actually faulty, are much smaller than they were 30 years ago. So that's a good thing, isn't it?

In terms of basic drinkability, it is. But what it has brought in its wake is a suffocating homogenization of wine styles. Just as a successful movie spawns a whole series of sequels, or other films in the same essential idiom, so successful wine styles are equally susceptible of imitation.

During the 1980s and 90s, all anybody seemed to want was oaky Chardonnay. In the past decade, Sauvignon and – to a lesser extent – Viognier have become the mood of the moment, as people looked for aromatic, tangy flavours without the encumbrance of oak. Tastes in red wine develop more slowly, but the thirst for sweetly ripe, often jammy reds with sprawling, obvious fruit flavours has influenced the making of red wines up to the highest levels.

So what are the antidotes to these trends? A wholesale rediscovery of the best wines of southern Europe, from the Rhône, the Languedoc and Gascony in France, via the Iberian peninsula (especially southern Portugal), to the patchwork of vinous potential that is Italy is long overdue. There are grape varieties all over these areas that you may never have heard of, just waiting to be discovered, always supposing you can find them in the shops.

A more discerning approach to the North American and southern-hemisphere winemaking countries is needed. We ought, as consumers, to work out which grape varieties work best from which regions (and, of course, from which wine-producers), instead of seeing non-European wine as a great, shapeless, unregulated marketplace in which anything goes.

That latter tendency brings us to the question of classification systems. The development of regional definitions, and their legal codification, in the newer wine countries are essential tools of the drive for quality, even if the regulations about what you might grow, and how much of it, are less constricting than they tend to be in the old European heartlands. The reason for this development is simple and irresistible.

It is that, one fine day in one fine vintage, you find that the Pinot Noir you have made from that little sheltered patch of vines halfway up Crooked Hill is the best damn wine you ever made in your life. So in future, you will avoid blending those grapes with grapes from your other Pinot plots, and you will send it out into the world proudly labelled Crooked Hill Pinot Noir. And, stripped of all the mystification, that's all that is meant by the concept of *terroir* and the appellation system.

The debate about *terroir* has, I agree, reached an unhelpfully totemic level in some quarters. It is now being used by some wine commentators as though it referred to nothing more precise than tradition or custom. In its original French usage, though, it denotes geographical specificity, the idea that the produce of this particular patch of earth tastes so distinctive and so good, time after time, that it's worth protecting it legally, against both external imitators and internal corner-cutting.

That has to be better than mass-producing identikit wines in a one-size-fits-all mentality. Apart from making life more interesting for the wine-drinker, it also spurs the best producers themselves on to their greatest efforts. It may sound paradoxical to put it in this way, but if we truly want to preserve diversity, the appellation systems are the only game in town.

As I hope you will have gathered from browsing through this book, I have a lot of criticisms to make about developments in virtually all of the world's major wine regions, to a greater extent than I had when I first got interested in wine in the 1980s. But of all the categories of alcoholic drink available to us, wine is far and away the one that most spurs these contentious and, to many of us, wholly absorbing debates. We wouldn't have strong opinions if we didn't care about it. And the other thing I hope to have shown is that wine remains for me a very precious part of our heritage.

INDEX